SHANDY HALL, COXWOLD, after the restoration of the roof and external fabric, August 1969.

The Winged Skull

PAPERS FROM THE LAURENCE STERNE BICENTENARY CONFERENCE

AT THE UNIVERSITY OF YORK

and sponsored by

McMASTER UNIVERSITY

THE UNIVERSITY OF YORK

THE NEW PALTZ COLLEGE OF
THE STATE UNIVERSITY
OF NEW YORK

Edited by Arthur H. Cash
and John M. Stedmond

THE KENT STATE UNIVERSITY PRESS

Published simultaneously in Great Britain
by Methuen & Co. Ltd.
11 New Fetter Lane London EC4

Designed by Ruari McLean
Printed in England by Westerham Press
Westerham Kent

To
LEWIS PERRY CURTIS

Preface

When word spread about London in 1760 that the gay and naughty book which had just appeared, *The Life and Opinions of Tristram Shandy, Gentleman*, was written by a clergyman, many people were shocked. The wit and urbanity of the man himself, when he came to town, did not upset them, for they were used to worldly clerics. The two volumes of his sermons, printed a few weeks later, were orthodox enough. They were offended only because this Anglican priest dared to print the sort of humor which clergymen were expected to express in private. Sterne, never an easy hypocrite, refused to reform. Discretion, that "prudent old gentlewoman," would enervate his books and rob them of their joy. "True *Shandeism*, think what you will against it, opens the heart and lungs . . . it forces the blood and other vital fluids of the body to run freely thro' its channels, and makes the wheel of life run long and chearfully round."

In point of fact, the author of this expansive Shandyism was a very sick man, subject to recurrent hemorrhages of his consumptive lungs, always aware that his delight in life was mocked by Death. Nowhere is the irony of the Shandian world more evident than in Sterne's play upon the theme of time, explored in the present volume by Jean-Jacques Mayoux. "Time wastes too fast," cries Tristram:

> every letter I trace tells me with what rapidity Life follows my pen; the days and hours of it, more precious, my dear *Jenny!* than the rubies about thy neck, are flying over our heads like light clouds of a windy day, never to return more——every thing presses on——whilst thou art twisting that lock,——see! it grows grey.

Yet death evokes no defiance in Sterne. The days and hours may be all too swift, but they are beautiful and precious. The intrepid cheerfulness of this clergyman-turned-author we can hardly doubt was rooted in his Christianity. Though he retired from parochial duties, he continued to perform his priestly functions willingly when called upon. He preached upon occasion and remained inordinately fond of his own sermons. He denied himself few pleasures during his final sickly years, which were also years of fame and brilliant writing, but the last trembling letters from his pen traced out a Christian benediction upon his friends, Commodore and Mrs James. Sterne knew that death would not relent, but he believed it would be transcended by the certain immortality given by God, and perhaps by a less certain immortality of creative genius. The two are symbolized together by the prayers of the Bourbonnais peasants in *A Sentimental Journey* which are not spoken or sung, but danced. Sterne wrote on the verge of tragedy, but he wrote comedy.

Two hundred years and six months after Sterne's death, a group of his admirers, mostly university lecturers, professors, and students, convened at the University of York for the Laurence Sterne Bicentenary Conference, which met 2–5 September 1968. Through seminars, lectures, discussions, visits to the Minster, the archives of York, and Sterne's parishes, they celebrated in a myriad ways the immortality of Sterne's artistry. They had also come hoping to rebury him, for the obsolete London graveyard where Sterne had been buried in 1768 was to give way before a new apartment complex. Although certain Shandian knots in the ecclesiastical law prevented the search for his remains at this time, it still seemed appropriate that these Sternians, albeit from many nations and representing many faiths, should acknowledge the eternality of spirit promised by Sterne's religion. On a memorable day, the entire Conference visited Sutton-on-the-Forest, where Sterne was Vicar for thirty years, glanced at Stillington, his second parish, were received at Newburgh Priory, the estate of his patron, Lord Fauconberg, and finally arrived at Coxwold, the third of Sterne's parishes, where he lived during the period of his great writing. They entered the Church of St Michael for a memorial service, and with the present Vicar, the Rev. Canon Harry Broughton, they prayed in their individual ways for the soul of Laurence Sterne and gave thanks for the blessing of his genius and "those insights into human nature and divine values which put him (as indeed they put all prophets) ahead of his time." Canon Broughton gave thanks for Sterne's hatred of slavery, his large-hearted sympathy with the poor, his generosity of nature, and that "for him, the false demarcation wall between sacred and secular was broken down, and that he had the courage to throw off and to disown the false values of puritanism." In the sermon which followed—published in this volume—the Rev. Canon Reginald Cant, Chancellor of York Minster, spoke of the qualities in Sterne which he admired, "perhaps most of all his dislike of that deadly virtue of discretion, 'which encompasses the heart with adamant.'" The service was moving and gratifying, especially to this congregation, aware that for two centuries the church has been silent upon the subject of Laurence Sterne.

Sterne died at his lodgings in Old Bond Street, London, on 18 March 1768. His wife and daughter being at York, only three mourners attended the interment, Commodore William James, Sterne's printer Thomas Becket, and his lawyer Samuel Salt. The graveyard had already been disturbed by body snatchers, and Sterne himself may have read—and laughed over—an account which appeared four months before in the St James's Chronicle of 26 November:

> The Burying-Ground in Oxford-Road, belonging to the Parish of St. George's Hanover-Square, having been lately robbed of several dead Bodies, a Watch was placed there attended by a large Mastiff Dog, notwithstanding which, on Sunday Night last some Villains found Means to steal out another dead Body, and carried off the very Dog.

It now seems quite certain that Sterne's body was also stolen, taken to Cambridge, and used for an anatomy lecture, as the scholarly Edmund Malone recorded upon the testimony of an eye witness. Permission for the exhumation was finally granted in the spring of 1969, and early in June the workmen commenced digging. They found, not one skull, but several. That development was not entirely Shandian, for it is a common experience of archaeologists. The identification of Sterne's skull turned out to be surprisingly simple. Mr Harvey Ross, a Harley Street surgeon, measured the skulls and compared them with the famous Nollekens bust of Sterne. The measurements of one matched the bust very closely. The crown of this skull had been sawn off. Evidence of autopsy is exceedingly rare in eighteenth-century graves; so this discovery strongly corroborates Malone's bizarre report while at the same time it makes the identification more certain. The anatomist, it would seem, after the body was recognized, discreetly had it returned to the graveyard. When the story got out, the newspapers naturally quoted from the grave-digger's scene of Hamlet, as indeed they did two centuries later after the second exhumation. Sterne had always encouraged the public to identify him with the Yorkshire parson of his novels named Yorick.

Now Sterne's bones lie in Coxwold churchyard, where they were reburied with all due rites on 8 June 1969.

The peregrinations of his clay, could Sterne have known about them, would hardly have distressed him. He would have appreciated the spirit of inquiry of Dr Charles Collignon, the Professor of Anatomy at Cambridge, who, if not much of an anatomist, was something of a philosopher. If he ever read Collignon's *Enquiry into the Structure of the Human Body, Relative to Its Supposed Influence on the Morals of Mankind,* 1764, Sterne would have applauded the doctor's argument that the physical body, while influencing the temperament, does not affect the freedom of the will. How complimented Sterne would have felt that two hundred and one years later his bones were rescued through the combined efforts of Coxwold Parish and an organization called the Laurence Sterne Trust. He would have been highly pleased with his second funeral, conducted by members of his own cathedral chapter, and having no false modesty ("I wrote not to be *fed*, but to be *famous*"), the crowd of reporters and the popping camera bulbs would have delighted him.

We trust that he would have liked also the Laurence Sterne Bi-centenary Conference and would not have found in its meetings material for a satire on pedantry. The papers and discussions were designed to balance the historical approach to Sterne with the critical, on the one hand to place his work more precisely into the broad history of his era or into the English literary traditions, and on the other to look critically at the timeless characteristics of his fiction or—as was often said—at its modernity, though the two approaches inevitably shade into one another. The rising popularity of *Tristram Shandy* and *A Sentimental Journey*, evidenced in the amazing number of recent studies and editions, shows that Sterne indeed strikes home to many of our present concerns. The critical essays published here, roughly half the collection, explore the reasons why it has become so easy and natural to think of Sterne as "our contemporary." The historical approach is represented in part by the papers grouped under "Sterne and His Time," but also in part of those labeled "Sterne and the World," which tell portions of the remarkable history of Sterne's influence upon the literatures of other languages and societies. Would it not have astonished Sterne's first critics, "Messrs, the monthly Reviewers," that *Tristram Shandy* translated into Japanese should sell more than 20,000 copies! Under the appendix "Of Books" are materials which will be used in a great variety of ways by future scholars and editors of Sterne. Kenneth Monkman and J. C. T. Oates are too accomplished in the skills of descriptive bibliography to permit us to call their contributions "bibliography"; nevertheless, their catalogue of a portion of the display they collected at the York Minster Library during the Conference is the first step toward a Sterne bibliography since Wilbur Cross's appendix to the 1929 edition of his *Life*. They describe any number of editions, translations, and imitations of Sterne of which other scholars have not been aware. The curious reader will find in their catalogue a number of surprises, including three minor writings of Sterne heretofore unknown. All three are connected with Sterne's controversy with "J. S." during the by-election of 1741/2, and one is in verse.

These several contributions are offered as a memorial to Laurence Sterne, who has been paid too few honors for one who wrote so brilliantly and affected the world so profoundly. His contemporaries, puzzled by his artistic integrity or embarrassed by his candor, made little effort to honor him. A year or so after Sterne died, David Garrick, hearing that no stone had been raised to Sterne's memory, wrote an epitaph:

> Shall Pride a heap of Sculptur'd marble raise,
> Some unmourn'd, worthless, titled Fool to praise?
> And shall we not by one poor Grave-stone learn
> Where Humor, Wit and Genius sleep with Sterne?

Soon thereafter, two Masons set up a stone at the grave, though Sterne had not been a member of their order. It did not bear Garrick's epitaph.

The Laurence Sterne Trust was organized in 1966 to establish a memorial suitable to our historically minded age—Sterne's house at Coxwold, the house close to the church which Sterne and his friends jokingly named Shandy Hall. It stood a melancholy ruin when the Conference visited it. By now the Trust has raised two thirds of the needed funds, purchased the freehold, and restored the structural frame and roof. If support can be found for the restoration of the interior, which is yet a havoc, Shandy Hall will be opened as a museum.

Originally a medieval farm house, Shandy Hall once consisted of a single, high, barn-like room; the fire was built on the floor and the smoke escaped through a hole in the roof. In Tudor times a floor was inserted and both levels were cut into rooms. From this era date the egregiously large kitchen chimney and the curious primitive wall paintings discovered underneath the panels. Sterne himself was responsible for the final interior features, the handsome paneling, corner cupboard, and fireplaces; and he seems to have added the facade on the end which faces the garden. The result is a pleasing mixture of Georgian formality with the coziness of low ceilings, twisting stairways, and small rooms—a delightfully odd, charming house, which Sterne found hospitable to his muse. Here he wrote most of *Tristram Shandy* and all of *A Sentimental Journey*.

The contributors to the present collection have dedicated the royalties to the Laurence Sterne Trust for use in the restoration of Shandy Hall.

A. H. C., New Paltz, New York
J. M. S., Kingston, Ontario

Acknowledgments

The editors' greatest debt is to a hundred or more people who strongly influenced this volume although they could not be represented in it: those who participated in the seminars and lively discussions of the Laurence Sterne Bicentenary Conference, who made it an occasion not only for the sharing of ideas but also of wit, good humor, and sentiment.

A large individual debt of gratitude is due to Dr Ian Jack of Pembroke College, Cambridge, who, after working with the editors on the Selection Committee, was prevented from attending the Conference.

The title "The Winged Skull" is the creation of Katherine Anne Porter, who used it for her review of Lodwick Hartley's *This is Lorence* in *The Nation* of 17 July 1943. We wish to thank James J. Storrow, Jr, publisher of *The Nation*, for permission to borrow it.

We are grateful for help in preparing the typescript given by the late Mrs Nona Stedmond.

In the name of all participants in the Conference, we thank the three institutions which sponsored it: McMaster University, the University of York, and the New Paltz College of the State University of New York.

More particularly we want to thank our genial host and President, Professor Philip Brockbank; our long-suffering Secretary and business manager, Dr James W. Harper, both of the University of York; our diligent and diplomatic Vice-President, Professor Roy M. Wiles of McMaster University; and our hard-working seminar chairmen, Mr J. C. T. Oates, Professors John Traugott, Gardner D. Stout, Jr, A. Owen Aldridge and John M. Stedmond.

We are grateful to Mrs Marion Egerton of the Laurence Sterne Trust, Mrs Julia Monkman, and Mrs Dorothy Cash, who helped to plan and execute the tours and social gatherings; to Dr E. A. Gee for the tours of York Minster and Byland Abbey and for his delightful spontaneous lectures as we passed through the Yorkshire countryside; to the Rev. and Mrs Francis Wilson and Mr Philip Ward, our hosts for the visit to Sutton-on-the-Forest; to Capt. and Mrs V. M. Wombwell, for receiving us at Newburgh Priory; the Rev. Canon and Mrs Harry Broughton for the memorial service at Coxwold and the Rev. Canon Reginald Cant for his sermon; the Dean and Chapter of York for the tea at Gray's Court, the erstwhile home of Dr Jaques Sterne, and to Miss Wythe and other ladies who so graciously served it.

Our thanks too for a variety of helps given by Miss Elizabeth Brunskill, the former Librarian of the Minster Library; Mr David Blake of the University of York; Professor Angelina Rosalia Pietrangeli of the University of Illinois; Mr and Mrs F. Amies of Gilling; Mr and Mrs Goodall and Mrs Radcliffe, the Fauconberg Arms, Coxwold; Ben Johnson Printers, Ltd; the secretaries of the English departments at the three sponsoring universities and at Queen's University; the staff of the King's Manor, now part of the University of York, where the Conference Banquet was served; the staff of Langwith College, where we resided and held most of the meetings, most especially the cheerful porters of Langwith.

The participants much appreciated the remarkable display of clerical documents relating to Sterne collected at the Borthwick Institute for Historical Research by Mrs Norah K. Gurney, Mr Neville Webb, and Mrs Ann Rycraft. They are grateful for the hospitality and many services of C. B. L. Barr and the staff of the York Minster Library.

A special thanks is due to Mr Francis Monkman, who directed the program of Sternian music at the Banquet, to Miss Clare Wright (cello), Miss Pauline Chadwick (soprano), and Mr David Ward (baritone), who with Mr Monkman performed it so delightfully. Mrs Brockbank was a gracious hostess at the Banquet, and Dr E. M. Sigsworth gave a stimulating address. The port generously sent for the occasion by Messrs Croft, Ltd, the company established by the family of Sterne's good friend Stephen Croft, did not arrive in time. It was used for the recruitment of those who attended Sterne's latest funeral.

Documentation

In the following papers, the works and letters of Laurence Sterne are cited in parentheses. The following texts have been used:

THE LIFE AND OPINIONS OF TRISTRAM SHANDY, GENTLEMAN. Edited by James Aiken Work. New York: *Odyssey Press*, 1940.

A SENTIMENTAL JOURNEY THROUGH FRANCE AND ITALY BY MR. YORICK. Edited by Gardner D. Stout, Jr, Berkeley and Los Angeles: *University of California Press*, 1967.

COMPLETE WORKS AND LIFE OF LAURENCE STERNE. [Edited by] Wilbur L. Cross. New York: *J. F. Taylor*, 1904. 12 vols. Reissued by the Clonmel Society, 12 vols. bound as 6, with the same pagination throughout.

LETTERS OF LAURENCE STERNE. Edited by Lewis Perry Curtis. Oxford: *Clarendon Press*, 1935.

ONE

Of Time

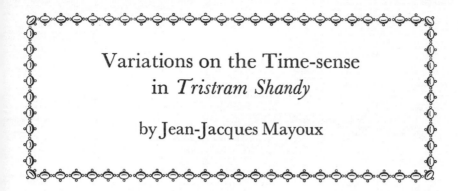

Variations on the Time-sense in *Tristram Shandy*

by Jean-Jacques Mayoux

The Novelist, so Forster says, must tell a story. A story can do, in theory and perhaps even in practice, without space. It cannot do without time. Time belongs, ineluctably, to the story telling as much as it would to the structure of a piece of music, and more than it would, for instance, to a philosophical essay, or even to a poem. The essay has taken time to write, takes time to read, but does not incorporate, *need* not at any rate, a time-structure. If all writing belongs to the arts of time, narrative writing differs radically from the rest: in it the time which literally it takes, say if we read it aloud, or the time which was taken in the writing, in both cases objective clock-time, is hopelessly tangled, inexorably overwhelmed and superseded, by the evocation of the factitious, fictitious time supposedly taken by the series of events in the story. In the creative imagination, I mean that of the ideal reader as well as the writer's, there is little awareness of this dual time-structure. Spontaneously, the imagination tends to ignore the props and the scaffoldings of the story telling so that it may concentrate on the effect of the story told. Willing suspension of disbelief is at that price. It was Sterne's invention, the product of his genius, helped I suppose by his total indifference to the creation of belief, to reverse this habit of fiction-writing and fiction-reading. It has been the characteristic effort of his admirable willfulness to blend and confuse the time-structure of the story with the time-infrastructure of the writing, for the delight of extricating them again, of analyzing their relations, of arranging them into telling patterns.

Moreover it has been his historic choice to concentrate on the subjectivity, on the workings of the mind where the primary integration of the several time-structures had occurred. Of all of Sterne's erratic or obsessive book-reading, nothing perhaps should be retained

Professor of English Literature, University of Paris at the Sorbonne as essential, not even Rabelais or Cervantes, except Locke, whose importance concerning the genesis and conduct of this book Professor Traugott was the first to stress and analyze. Fielding was interested in Hume's ethics. Sterne was concerned by the problem of existence, of, let us be more precise, intellectual existence in relation to literary creation; and the key to it was provided by Locke's *Essay*, which he terms, so aptly to his purpose, "a history-book . . . of what passes in a man's own mind" (II, 2, p. 85). How does Sterne see the Lockian succession of ideas and its equation to subjective time? We might say *where*, instead of *how*, for the context and situation are very relevant. While Walter and Toby are waiting anxiously for news of Tristram's birth, Walter discovers that in terms of clock-time they have remained thus for only two hours and ten minutes. "But," he remarks, "it seems an age" (III, 18, p. 189). It is then that my uncle Toby stumbles on the Lockian definition by remarking that their impression is due to the succession of their ideas; and Walter, much piqued because he meant to be the one to give the formula, proceeds to ascertain that Toby does not know what he is talking about, and to secure compensation for his injured vanity by bringing out a lengthy near-quotation from Locke. The episode is helpful, if less than illuminating. Clock-time and mental time, it might be said, follow after all parallel roads, the one with necessarily even pace, the other at a more erratic and fanciful gait according to the rhythms, currents, wanderings generated (to retain our instance) in and between those two heads. Each consciousness is double; it carries the sense of one's own existence, with all its concerns butting in, and a vague, discontinuous awareness of the external world implying external time. The resulting impression is a cross-product of the two systems, creating a particular tempo. The tempo here was sluggish, as slowed down by anxiety and absence of mind.

The main revelation or confirmation, due to Locke or upheld by Locke, was that life was lived in the mind. The old vision of the microcosm was as important again to Sterne as it could have been to Donne; and Sterne may well be termed a metaphysical novelist. We hear his frequent echoes in those metaphysical writers of our own times, Virginia Woolf and James Joyce.

In this vision, each living person, even the humblest, down to Susannah or Obadiah, is such a microcosm, whose stream of consciousness reacts to the death of Bobby in its own way: green satin nightgown to be had from the mourning, or pasture land not to be

4

Contents

SIX IN MEMORY

APPENDIX OF BOOKS

Illustrations

sold but to be put into shape. And each microcosm has its own time-dimension, enclosed and separate, with its own structure, rhythm, and flow. Life, Sterne has discovered, as it is lived mostly inside, is carried on in solitude. He is less dramatic about it than his modern successors and does not emphasize or sentimentalize the point. What he gives us is a comedy of absurdities which can be equated with the effects of the singular, individual, time-dimension being brought up against the plurality of individuals. It takes place when, from his own private path, the individual emerges into the common way, clad in his oddity, having pursued his own trend up to the precise instant of his emerging, and meeting on the one hand what we term objective reality, on the other hand, other microcosms. Then bridge meets bridge, Dr Slop's bridge for a crushed nose is mistaken for my uncle Toby's bridge for military transit, and *quid pro quos* soon build up. Not all microcosms, of course, are equally fruitful; not all are equal to showing this dominant seclusion in such a manner as to remain interesting. Joyce has only granted interior monologues to three characters. Similarly, of his own obsessive tendencies subdued by humorous self-awareness, Sterne has made up his two humorists, of whom one, my uncle Toby, must be our special concern, for his very special and revealing time dimension.

* * *

After receiving his wound, which owing to its obvious although uncertain sexual character we may term a trauma, the existence of this active and unimaginative spirit seems to have fallen into a sluggish flow, as of a slowly moving backwater, its proper current having stopped on that fatal day. Another of those modern writers that I find myself so frequently quoting, William Faulkner, has, in *Light in August*, created a near-tragic yet grotesque character, the Reverend Hightower, whose personal time-flow has been stopped, it would seem, before it could have started in his proper person with his individual life, by fantastic inherited memories of the civil war which also amount to a decisive, inhibiting trauma, so that he can only rehearse and repeat indefinitely that ghostly scene, that heroic vision, perhaps of a merely grotesque reality—the ride of his ancestor through the town.

My uncle Toby, in the long monotonous days of his sick bed, has been put suddenly on to the plan of recalling in infinite detail the military events of his own campaigns and service that led to his disablement. The normal life movement which carries a thick past

5

towards the open future to which it is connected by some active project has become altered to a closed world of memories.

That is the first stage of my uncle Toby's diseased time. It becomes a subsidiary element of a second stage characterized by what we may term parodic time. For now Toby has left his own past behind without returning to a present of his own. The succession of his ideas is in abeyance, and has been replaced by the succession of the news brought by the *Gazette*. Inspired by Trim's invention, he follows and repeats, on the absurd mirror of his bowling green, the campaigns, sieges, and conquests of the Allies. Yet, however insignificantly, he goes on living in his own right, I mean in his own body, going through the day's physiological quota of sensations and actions, and his assuming also the large burden of collective history in his own single person makes up a comically double time-dimension. We read that the siege of Dendermond by the Allies went so fast "that they scarce allowed him time to get his dinner" (VI, 8, p. 423), or again, we see him, "after passing the French lines, *as he eat his egg at supper*, from *thence* [i.e. both from supper and the French lines] break into the heart of France" (35, p. 466). In these two significantly similar instances, time in the head is willfully brought up against what we may term time in the body, or may prefer to term objective reality.

And then suddenly, the widow Wadman appears, and compels my uncle Toby to notice her and finally to fall in love with her; and he rediscovers living time; his time-sense is again activated; the world of memories is again subjected to present awareness and, existentially speaking, to a project looking towards the future. The life rhythm is shown by Sterne as quickened almost to the point of impatience and fretfulness. My uncle Toby can thus be taken as a case-study of the time-sense.

He has been held to be a mask for Sterne's sentiment. Is he not also a light caricature of the artist's way, of Sterne's way, as an artist, of finding substitutes for the reality of life? What I have termed his parodic time could then be seen as clumsy and home-made, but of a type with the artist's re-creation of time. My uncle Toby is a bad or at least an inferior artist, being, if I may risk this anachronism, a photographic imitator or illustrator of time. Sterne's reflecting memory, rearranged in ingenious patterns, takes its own time-substitutes on an altogether higher level.

*　　*　　*

6

There is among these various microcosms a master-mind at work, that of the author, self-built and projected into one of them, that of the narrator. Tristram's head includes all that is to be found in a book truly presented in the title, whatever obtuse or cavilling critics may have said to the contrary, as giving his "life and opinions." He, Tristram, it is, whether we take him as author or narrator, who has the ordering of everything. He is a genial conjurer calling forth whom or what he wants when he wants, and showing a vivid consciousness of his power, a firm intent to make full use of it, to disturb the film of appearances or the dull routine of pseudo-objectivity. He will arrange instead a complicated system, or interstructuration, of significant relations which will be found to be, almost entirely, time-relations. He does it most successfully—triumphantly—but rather in the manner of a skillful clown, pretending to be perplexed, tangled even, by the difficulties that he himself has created. He it is who directs the game, and very carefully engineers its turns and hesitations, all hanging round the absurd encounters that we have described above. But if he gives us in full the comedy of broken solitudes, he is no less fascinated by the way in which, in the prevailing separateness, these private worlds have been shaped, organized, developed, each according to its special pattern or system, building up a human memory, which receives a constant influx of "ideas" stored in readiness for future recombination and re-appearance.

Again, at work and prevailing on those several memories, Sterne, or Tristram, is a master-memory. Sterne the artist is aware that there, in this complexus of memories, under this pleasant guise or disguise of plurality, rests his inspiration. His consciousness of this is the source of a new vision, one which is revealed when Sterne writes: "*I have got* entirely out of Auxerre in this journey *which I am writing now*, and I am got half way out of Auxerre in that *which I shall write hereafter*." And further down, "*I am this moment* walking across the market place of Auxerre with my father and my uncle Toby" (VII, 28, pp. 515–516).

Let us pay all due attention to this grammar, which we might call the living grammar of literary creation—to these challenging present tenses referring us to the non-present of memory; and to the more challenging blend of past and future in one sentence: the past of the remembered, the future of the unwritten intention, already sketchily present before the creative mind. How clearly this lucid description shifts the burden of reality from the event to the recalling, from the recalling to the telling. The second half of the first sentence—"I am got half way out of Auxerre in that which I shall write hereafter"—invites special analysis because at first sight it appears a meaningless paradox. It means in fact that a memory (or what the writer asks us to take as a memory) related to this further journey has crossed his mind, and temporarily interfered with the other journey. It could have been pushed aside. But it is Sterne's way to welcome mental interference and to make of it all he can.

*　　*　　*

We may add that in willful confusion he frequently pretends to believe that the future of the yet untold, that is, the future in his mind, is the objective future of the not yet occurred in reality, which allows him to say in Chapter 39 of Volume VI that owing to the servants' premature passing on of the news he will be able to enter upon my uncle Toby's amours a fortnight before their existence.

With perhaps a little overmuch eighteenth-century showmanship, a little over-stressing and yet a little summariness, Sterne or his Tristram opens up in the end the world of private time where Lockian ideas have become part of a thick, obscurely organized co-existence, any fragment of which is ready, at the beck and call of very capricious chains of associations, to emerge as memory manifest in the stream of consciousness as we know it. With Sterne we enter at one leap yet somehow decisively the world of memory which was only to become ours by general consent in Romantic times.

Memory is ambiguous: it originates in the past but it is only known in the present. There is no conscious reality that is not present, that is not part of this thick present which the creative imagination may organize and display. Again, this was one of Sterne's new interests: the mind, caught and held in a unit of its living processes, with all its intricate relations and the constant interchange between the inner and the outer world—precisely what Virginia Woolf will define as the moment. The substance of her essay under that title is, potentially, to be found in Sterne.

In this vision, what is real, what counts, is the activity, the movement of the living mind between points, the drama, the vividness of its jumps, the strange states in which we can perceive the fascinating Janus-like alternation of its workings. The inner, subjective world is enclosed, but it is a vast universe, the possession of which, with freedom

to range through it, far from inducing claustrophobia, as it will in Samuel Beckett, is exhilarating. There is a joy in the freedom of this inner world, and Sterne's very grammar proclaims it. It puts us in the mood to understand and to accept what is the key to the narrative method in *Tristram Shandy*: that the writer may go backward and forward along the line of his story. These dips, then these returns, from points of memory to the present, are no accident: they give, within the uncertain dimensions of the consciousness, the time-depth and relief required also by Sterne's vision.

*   *   *

From his vantage points—the present and a human head—Sterne orders and constructs all times and their relations to ensure the utmost intellectual interest. Not until our own day was so much interest to be taken in those relations. Let us take as an instance the invention of ways to suggest simultaneousness. Time must be left at a standstill and then be found again precisely as it was, where it was. So we read: "I think, replied my uncle Toby, taking his pipe from his mouth . . ." (I, 21, p. 63). Two pages further on, we read of my uncle Toby, "whom *all this while* we have left knocking the ashes out of his tobacco pipe"; and lastly, *thirty-three pages later*, we have, "I think, replied my uncle Toby,——taking, *as I told you*, his pipe from his mouth . . ." (II, 6, p. 99). There has been, and he wants us conscious of it, a considerable time lapse in *the telling* of the story, in the writing, and it was marked in the middle-reference by "*all this while*." But there has been no corresponding time, no time at all, in the story told. So certain films, like Buñuel's *Angel of Death*, come suddenly to a standstill because time has stopped; we may then hear a comment or shift scene until it starts again.

Thus there has been created by Sterne's ingenuity what we may term a comic suspense. Not until De Quincey's compositions of time in *Murder Considered as One of the Fine Arts*, or *The English Mail Coach*, shall we find anything so precisely and finely engineered.

Moreover, while my uncle Toby's advance in time has thus been stopped, it is obvious that the writer is free to take us anywhere else, to bring before us any other character. The principle of simultaneousness has been established as soon as means have been found to make it manifest: while story-time is not moving on, the people in the story remain available in suspended activity. Sterne has made full and mani-

9

fold use of the distinction that he has been so careful to establish between his own or his narrator's time and that of the story. It does more than give him this extraordinary freedom to digress, which he rather stresses and exaggerates than conceals. It gives the characters a corresponding freedom to live on while the author chooses to forget about them. The effects can be of something more important in *Tristram Shandy* than simultaneousness, and that is continuity. It is one of the great and fascinating paradoxes of the book that out of a willful discontinuity this continuity is born. The mother-cat gaily lives her own life: the kittens seem forgotten; but she knows that when she comes back to them she will find that they are still there, or in serial terms, are there again, having quietly lived on. Sterne is absolutely conscious of his method, and duly stresses this point, that his story with the characters living in it goes on without him while he is indulging in digression: "I constantly take care to order affairs so, that my main business does not stand still in my absence" (p. 72). For playful safety's sake, he can wait till they are steadily employed or asleep before he turns to his Preface. But the point is, once you, the creative writer, that is, the creator of time, have set time going—the separate time of a story—the separate time-dimension of its characters—you cannot stop it, except by your own obtuseness. Existence, if you have believed in it enough, if you trust it, shows in your creatures its well-known tendency to persevere in existing. This is possible, even natural, precisely because what interests Sterne is not the singularity of any action but just such a daily continuity, almost indifferent or undifferentiated, of existence.

In the narrative, continuity through the discontinuous can be seen, for instance, in a passage which looks at first sight strikingly similar to the one about my uncle Toby and his pipe. It again relates to Toby's slow-witted efforts to communicate. "I wish, quoth my uncle Toby, you had seen what prodigious armies we had in Flanders" (II, 18, p. 144). After eleven pages of quite other matter, "'I wish, Dr Slop,' quoth my uncle Toby (*repeating his wish* for Dr Slop *a second time*, and with a degree of more zeal and earnestness in his manner of wishing, than he had wished it at first)——'I wish, Dr Slop,' quoth my uncle Toby..." (III, 1, p. 157).

And in the next page, Walter takes up the topic: "What prodigious armies...." Here we see that between the broaching and the resumption of the topic, there has been, however small, a real lapse of story-time, of living time: the characters have lived *on*, be it a few minutes. In such a way, by such means, a continuity has been established. In a remarkable manner, Sterne's world is a world of bodies alive; and they are in touch with objects which also have their strong inanimate continuity. Prostrate on the bed in despair, Walter lets his hand rest on the handle of the chamber-pot, of which he remains vaguely conscious until he begins to rally and shift his position. Meanwhile my uncle Toby remains seated "in his old fringed chair, valanced around with party-coloured worsted bobs" (p. 278, cf. pp. 216, 274). Thus carefully defined, thus present before us, the chair remains, to be called up again, later in the same passage: it is an element of the dimension of the moment, which is yet another novelty of the Sternian time-vision.

* * *

Thus the time-sense has appeared dispersed between the creation and the creator. Knowing Sterne, we must be aware, and I stressed it from the first, that the creator is the more, the essentially important. Time as construction, time as play of the mind belongs to the writer. True, time is time and a story is a story. But all of the story-time is his to play with *from the start*; or rather it can be seen as all past from the first—if it is the usual type of a story and relates to a now closed cycle of events. But conversely, in this creator's vision, what of it has not yet been written about partakes of a double aspect: it is both past and future. Hence the challenging phrase, "a cow *broke* in (*to-morrow morning*) to my uncle Toby's fortifications" (III, 38, p. 235), wherein at any rate we keep to one definition of time—to external time, if anything can be termed external that has been produced by the writer's imagination. In Volume III, Chapter 11, we had an even bolder statement of the turning of matter into mind, of a length of time into a spread of words: "when the door hastily opening *in the next chapter but one*" (p. 179). Once again the fantastic language and jarring grammar reveal the true seat, the purely mental reality of time.

Yet I suppose that this freedom, not so much of reality as of unreality, palls. For in the passage of challenging paradox about Auxerre, an end is put to it. I may be invited to mix in my mental cocktail-shaker three Auxerres and one Lyons, but finally a compelling awareness gets hold of me and substitutes for the phantoms and fantasms of memory the truth, the only absolute truth, of the present instant in which the inky pen touches paper—not the remembered or the imagined, but the writer at the writing of it in the Toulouse pavilion, not in a thick present any more, but in an absolute present. "Time: the Present"—the *pressant*, as Joyce might say—such could be Sterne's prevailing stage-direction.

In the end, time as a thick present is the overall dominant, burdened with all the remembered past and pregnant with all the intended future in the writer's imagination; a present in which, in contrast with the ordinary novelist, Sterne dwells complacently, and which eventually narrows down to the sharp bodily present of the moving hand and the beating heart. His writing, he states early on, is a sort of conversation, not so much between the characters as between the author and the reader in yet another present, the time of their imaginary meeting. Before that there is something touching in his frequent insistence on his physical presence on the day, hour, instant, at which the pen, ink-laden, scratches the paper. His humanity, open and defenseless, is entrusted to ours, now, beyond the absurd grave. We read, "this very day, in which I am now writing this book . . . which is March 9, 1759" (p. 44). Then, "this very rainy day, March 26, 1759, and betwixt the hours of nine and ten in the morning" (p. 64). Is it by chance that the last reference of this sort insists so much more on the living person? In Volume IX, Chapter 1, we read, "here am I sitting, this 12th day of August, 1766, in a purple jerkin and yellow pair of slippers, without either wig or cap on" (p. 600). There is a strange and disturbing magic in his sitting thus, so clear, for two centuries. Even the past that he writes about is referred to this absolute present: "the door . . . somewhat a-jar——*as it stands just now*" (V, 6, p. 358). The determination to maintain in a future present his living dialogue with the reader is everywhere. We need not be surprised if it includes a little philandering, if the ideal reader is a fair lady whom he scolds amicably for not being aware of theological implications: "How could you, Madam, be so inattentive . . . ?" (I, 20, p. 56).

*   *   *

On the outer side the book is a conversation; but on the inner, it is difficult to ignore Sterne's own musical images, which go so well with the musical aspects of his genius. As he says "to write a book is for all the world like humming a song——be but in tune with yourself . . . 'tis no matter how high or how low you take it" (IV, 25, p. 315). Thus, from time used up and, as it were, wasted in chronological sequences of

events, we see, separating itself by nature and quality, what we may term pure time, or what Gertrude Stein would have termed time as composition: not external any more but a representation, or, in Stein language again, an arrangement. The finest expression of this is where Sterne begins with the reader's time—"It is about an hour and a half's tolerable good reading since my uncle Toby rung the bell"—then takes in the time of the event under consideration (Obadiah's expedition to fetch Dr Slop), finally the time that the writer's imagination has meanwhile expounded and organized round the figure of my uncle Toby, brought "from Namur, quite across all Flanders, into England," to be *"ill upon my hands near four years,"* then to be set down in Yorkshire, "all which," Sterne ends, bringing together at last in the game of representation the writer's and the reader's time, "all which put together, must have prepared the reader's imagination for the entrance of Dr Slop upon the stage,——as much, at least . . . as a dance, a song, or a concerto *between the acts*" (II, 8, pp. 103–104)—an admirable sentence which I have always conjectured must have given Virginia Woolf the title (and more) of her last novel, and which insists on the musical character, the musical rhythms, and tempos, and movements, of literary creation.

*   *   *

Thus the writer feels himself to be free and master of time—until he sets himself the impossible aim, which was to be pursued by Proust in other ways, of regaining lost time, or, in Sterne's view, of equating and synchronizing primary reality and its representation, life and recollection, living time and writing time. Never was hare more perplexed by the tortoise-race of life, or more willful in his musings by the way, but never was willfulness better grounded on the consciousness that the musings made no difference. While we still hear from chapter to chapter many a triumphant assertion of the writer's freedom, the first hint of concern about the problem of getting the writing abreast of the living is heard as early as Volume I, Chapter 14: "I have been at it these six weeks, making all the speed I possibly could,——and am not yet born" (p. 37). It is heard again, very similarly, in Chapter 38 of Volume III: "I have left my father lying across his bed, and my uncle Toby in his old fringed chair . . . and promised I would go back to them in half an hour, and five and thirty minutes are laps'd already" (p. 235). Playing his usual game, of pretending that imaginary time and his relation to it are real, he professes himself sadly perplexed, having so many things to tell, including the cow's future conduct, all "in five minutes less, than no time at all." The problem, if it were less palpably fanciful, would be merely technical. Sterne, at his happy gambols between his two worlds, does not yet take himself seriously. In Volume IV, Chapter 13, is to be found the first passage in which the problem is more firmly and simply faced, in which the flippancy seems barely to cover with the appearance of comic despair, his anxiety at the impossibility of bringing finally together in chronological coincidence life as it has been lived and the story of it—because life goes too fast.

> I am this month one whole year older than I was this time twelve-month; and having got . . . almost into the middle of my fourth volume——and no farther than to my first day's life—— 'tis demonstrative that I have three hundred and sixty-four days more life to write just now, than when I first set out; so that instead of advancing, as a common writer, in my work with what I have been doing at it——on the contrary, I am just thrown so many volumes back. . . .
> ——I shall never overtake myself . . . (pp. 285–286).

The game is hopeless, and increasingly so, in a monstrously growing ratio. It is the writer's duty, the mark of his honesty, not to abridge or omit anything that is significant; and nothing is more significant than the insignificant. It may take two chapters to do justice to the talk of Walter and Toby going down the stairs, but justice must be done, and the consequences faced.

Yes, of course, all this is said in a flippant and jesting tone. Can we fail, however, to perceive that the theme is becoming obsessive, and to detect under the surface what I have termed anxiety and might perhaps term anguish? Do we not perceive a change of tempo, almost imperceptible perhaps until we reach Volume VII, and then suddenly overwhelming? Can we ignore the urgency in that first chapter, the all-too-real panting for breath, the frightened heartbeat, and the fascinating adaptation of the language to the condition, the ending of the amused rococo twists and flourishes, the short sentences and the frequent staccato rhythms? "For I have forty volumes to write, and forty thousand things to say and do, which no body in the world will say and do for me. . . ." ("except thyself," he adds for his friend

Eugenius, but we need not take *that* seriously) (p. 480). Here again what we have heard is the voice of the passionate individualism that we connect with our own century, the voice of André Gide about "l'individu irremplaçable." So that this unchristian pastor can feel honest despair about the brevity of his life: as "I who must be cut short in the midst of my days..." (p. 495).

Synchronizing is hopeless, but as much truth of oneself as possible should be given "*whilst* these few scatter'd spirits *remain*" (p. 480). The *whilst* and the *remain* show the awareness of time the destroyer to the full. Until Sterne turns again to my uncle Toby, it will not cease. There is a little self-pity in this fourteenth chapter, in this "I who must be cut short in the midst of my days," in the wistful evocation of the times fifty years hence that he will not see; but there is much more human tenderness, much more pity for the general human plight, for the horrible equation in it of time and change, ceaseless, ruthless change and decay. "Aimez ce que jamais on ne verra deux fois," Vigny the Romantic will say, turning away from nature to woman. And here we have, peeping below the jests, a Romantic Sterne, in the choice at Montreuil of Janatone before the church of St Austreberte, which will be there and the same these fifty years to come to be admired or measured—"but he who measures thee, Janatone, but do it now—thou carriest the principles of change within thy frame" (p. 490).

Now this cruel awareness of time as change gets such a hold of his imagination that in a remarkable manner he adapts himself to its rhythms so as once more to master it: he turns inevitable change into the free creation of change by speed. It may be that as long as the horror of change as a premise of dissolution has been with mankind, mankind has also known, within its technical means, this passion for speed, this urge to outrun its own predetermined, ruthless movement onwards and downwards. We forget about the panting and the heartbeat. Death may pursue, but we can race faster; and again in speed joy is with us. "So much of motion," we read in Chapter 13, "is so much of life, and so much of joy ... to stand still, or get on *but slowly*, is death and the devil——" (p. 493).

Yet in the midst of this proclaimed elation we may hear the reality of the flight in the breathless rhythms, in the very system of dashes: "——No;——I cannot stop a moment to give you the character of the people——their genius——their manners——their customs——their laws——their religion——their government——their manufactures

——their commerce——their finances..." (Chapter 19, p. 502).

And in Chapter 17 we had "Crack, crack——crack, crack——crack, crack——so this is Paris" (p. 498). That much repeated noise is merely the postilion's whip's; yet somehow in this atmosphere of Volume VII, we hear something like the rattle of bones in Bürger's *Lenore*, we feel that this was asking at least for Rowlandson's illustrations to the *English Dance of Death* and its grim merriment. We must remember Sterne's own life and condition, and as we commemorate both his genius and the date of his death, recall his awareness, at the time that he was writing this book, that it was impending. His correspondence tells the tale, as in the letter of 1765, written after three hemorrhages: "I find I must once more fly from death whilst I have strength . . . (*Letters*, p. 257). Regain lost time when life is lost—it cannot be done. He knows, and with that newly gained purity of style, he addresses his "dear Jenny" in unforgettable terms: "Time wastes too fast: every letter I trace tells me with what rapidity Life follows my pen; the days and hours of it . . . are flying over our heads like light clouds of a windy day, never to return more——every thing presses on——whilst thou art twisting that lock,——see! it grows grey" (IX, 8, pp. 610–611).

Sterne was aware before Beckett of the fantastic nullity of time, of its compressibility, so total that as Pozzo reminds us in *Waiting for Godot*, a life can be said to begin and to end on the same day, the same instant.

* * *

This, then, is my construction of time and the time-sense in *Tristram Shandy*. It may be said against it that it is highly subjective. It would be the less Sternian if it were not. Yes, admittedly, my ideas got up with me and were clad in my clothes. I have, however, attempted to transcend subjectivity by seeking coherence. My system, that is, was meant to take in and to bring together in unified or at least cohesive meaning most if not all relevant facts and points in the book. The resulting view could be said to present the dialectics of freedom and necessity. The first proposition, which could be put almost better in Leibnitzian than in Lockian terms (bating pre-established harmony), is that the human world is made up of microcosmic, enclosed units, of windowless monads, which, forming as they proceed and pursuing a private time-dimension, bump clumsily again and again against each other or the world of objects and circumstances in the process of what is fondly termed communication. This is all haphazard, but Sterne the artist sees his chance in this mischance, instead of ignoring it, as was the custom of his fellow-novelists. Out of the comic absurdities he makes a pattern, he produces a design.

The second essential point is that his perhaps crowning inspiration has been to fling himself into his own stew in the guise of the narrator, Tristram, the like of whom had never been seen, and was not to be seen again until Proust's Marcel. He orders and directs the patterns and his own place in them; he inserts into their already considerable intricacy his own double time-dimension, that of Tristram the man and that of Tristram the artist. While the other microcosmic units were bound by necessity, the artist recaptures freedom through composition: all times, as he finds several occasions to say, belong to him. He takes his stand in the present, wherefrom he juggles triumphantly with all past. The present is his strong anchorage in reality.

The third point is, as it seems to me, that his constant stressing and over-stressing of his freedom covers an anxiety. At any rate, if all time belongs to him, he belongs to time, and he knows it. Volume VII is perhaps a break and perhaps merely a belated admission into the consciousness of the fear that had been there obscurely from the beginning, the fear that time was prevailing against him, irresistibly, and that the recovery of lost time was doomed. All that the artist can do is, like the musician, to *compose* time from this piling waste. If Sterne so frequently brings in musical references, it is because he was knowingly musical; it is also because music is the most perfect, freest triumph over time. But both his imagination and his technique, so modern when not hopelessly rococo, suggest to us striking affinities with that art of our time, perhaps the best endowed with means to manipulate time in all manners and directions, I mean the cinema. Ellipse and montage are here everywhere. We have seen simultaneousness putting in an appearance, continuity asserted. Volume VII, at the end of its anxious tussle with time, has one more, the most vivid, cinematic device. As my tentative fabric is about to dissolve, I cannot do better than recall the most graceful and tenderly wistful "dissolve," or "fade-out-fade-in," of all time. It is found in Tristram's encounter with Nannette:

> Capriciously did she bend her head on one side, and dance up
> insiduous——Then 'tis time to dance off, quoth I; so changing

only partners and tunes, I danced it away from Lunel to Montpellier——from thence to Pescnas, Beziers——I danced it along through Narbonne, Carcasson, and Castle Naudairy, till at last I danced myself into Perdrillo's pavillion ... (p. 538).

Where we shall leave him to escape from time in the composition of my uncle Toby's amours.

TWO

Sterne and Our Time

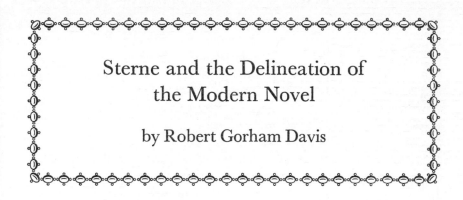

Sterne and the Delineation of the Modern Novel

by Robert Gorham Davis

"I might easily have written this story in the traditional manner," James Joyce told Eugene Jolas, in explaining to him the structure of *Finnegans Wake*. "It is not very difficult to follow a simple chronological scheme which the critics will understand. But I after all am trying to tell the story of this Chapelizod family in a new way.

"Time and the river and the mountain are the real heroes of my book. Yet the elements are exactly what every novelist might use: man and woman, birth, childhood, night, sleep, marriage, prayer, death. There is nothing paradoxical about this. Only I am trying to build many planes of narrative with a single esthetic purpose. Did you ever read Laurence Sterne"?[1]

By invoking Sterne, when he rejected the traditional manner for a "new way," Joyce was following what was itself an old and well established tradition. For a century and a half, not only in England, but in Germany, Russia and France, those writing appreciatively of experiments in the form of the novel almost invariably cited *Tristram Shandy*.

In 1917, reviewing *A Portrait of the Artist* by the then unknown Dubliner, H. G. Wells said it was to be ranked with the works of Sterne and Swift, that "Sterne himself could not have done the Christmas dinner better."[2] The names of the two witty word-playing Anglo-Irishmen stuck together in Joyce's mind ever after, and turn up in multifarious guises in the puns and portmanteau conglomerates of *Finnegans Wake*. In *The Books at the Wake* James Atherton quotes a number of these many linkages; among them, "swift to mate errthors, stern to checkself," "O, sey but swift," followed by "sign it sternly." Motion is "swiftly sterneward." There is "a stern poise for a swift pounce." "Have you ever thought of hitching your stern and being ourdeaned."[3]

Professor of English, Columbia University

The very conclusion of *Finnegans Wake*, the broken sentence at the ending, was suggested, Joyce hints, by the similar ending, or non-ending, of Sterne's *Sentimental Journey*. The *Wake* as a whole is a "joornee saintomichael . . . up the jiminy Tristopher and into the shandy westerness," where on a "shandymound" or Sandymount, Finn's body lies. [4]

Wells reviewed *A Portrait* over fifty years ago. The kind of young litterateurs who would have been reading its successor, *Ulysses*, in the early twenties, were reading the work of Samuel Beckett in the early sixties—himself both a Sternian and a Joycian—whose *Watt*, as Frederick Hoffman says, is "full of Shandian gimmicks," and whose dying Malone and the Unnamable are as absorbedly writing in the prospect of death as Tristram, though in so different a spirit.

Between the early twenties and the late sixties, experimentation in the form and character of the novel moved from England to the United States and then to France. Faulkner was influenced by Joyce; Sartre, by Faulkner. In their preoccupation with time or with simultaneities of consciousness, or in the relationship between the true author and the pretended author, any number of novels of the last half century have resembled *Tristram Shandy*. But because it is so traditional to cite Sterne when confronted with striking formal experimentation of almost any kind, the comparison is often made very casually and loosely.

Though Proust and Faulkner are time-obsessed, their times are very different from each other's time and from Tristram Shandy's time even more. The differences, indeed, are more important than the similarities, and require perceptive and careful articulation. Other-wise, as often happens, we shall be attributing to the age of Locke or Bergson and Einstein discoveries about time, about the relation of past, present and future in the human consciousness, that had already been fully explored by Augustine in that famous passage at the end of Chapter XV of the *Confessions*.

Instead, then, of treating the principal modern novelists in such a fashion, trying in each case to determine in what respects they do or do not resemble Sterne, I shall do what is more in accord with my own critical interests and the central concern of this conference, and talk about Sterne's delineation of the formal structure of the modern novel, the ontology of the novel, the idea or "rhetoric" of the novel, as it appears to us in the sixties. This has been as brilliant a period in the theoretic discussion of the novel as in the writing of novels, with all the contributions made to that discussion by depth psychology, phenomenology, linguistics, semantics and communication theory generally.

It was a revealing experience to study *Tristram Shandy* very carefully once again in the light of all that we have learned from French structuralists and existentialists, from Sartre and Lévi-Strauss, from the practitioners and theorists of the new French novel, Sarraute and Butor and Robbe-Grillet, or from American and Canadian students of communication like Walter Ong and Marshall McLuhan. These last are men fascinated by the way media dominate what they mediate, by the way in which, in modern action-art, the process of making or destructively unmaking becomes the form and even the substance of what is made. When we add all this to what we have been saying to our students for the last twenty years about the mode of existence of the literary work of art, reading with them Wellek and Warren or Joseph Frank on spatial form or L. C. Knights on "How many Children had Lady Macbeth?", it seems to me that we still must say that *Tristram Shandy* demonstrates more fully and translucently the basic ontology of the novel, the sense of what the novel really is and does, as we have come to understand it in recent decades, than any single modern novel you can mention, no matter in what particular respects that other novel may have gone beyond *Tristram Shandy*.

There is nothing anti-historical about saying this, and no reading into *Tristram Shandy* of anything not put there consciously by Sterne himself. The same thing cannot be done with Fielding, Richardson, Smollett or Defoe, though it can to a degree with Swift. Sterne simply saw with great clarity what is ontologically and experientially implied by the form he was employing, and expressed this clear vision with equal art and wit. What requires historical explanation is the fact that his discoveries vanished from the consciousness of his successors in the British novel for the next hundred and fifty years.

From the beginning, the novel has been self-conscious, self-conscious about its relation to the other genres, self-conscious about the relation within itself of documented history to fiction, of illusion to reality. It has consistently made fun of its novelistic predecessors in the name of its own superior truth to experience, yet, since it delights in supporting that claim with plainly spurious documentation, it equally readily makes fun of itself. This is all in *Don Quixote*, in the spoofing intrusion of the Moorish historian Cid Hamet Benengali, whose scrupulous accuracy requires him to know whether Don Quixote spent the night under a cork tree or an oak, and in the beginning of the continuation of the novel, where Samson Carrisco and others question the authenticity of the story from which they derive their very existence.

Since fiction is lying, since the events it describes occurred nowhere, its very being is non-being. It is big with negation, and the author has to know when to avow what he is doing, when to deny it, when to support lies with other kinds of lies, when with truths, or the appearance of truth, when with probabilities or improbabilities, possibilities or impossibilities, and when to make of all these a structure that has its own independently satisfying mode of being. To ask just where this structure *has* its being, whether in human minds, or on paper, or in a fixed sequence of verbal significations, is—as we shall see—like asking where thoughts exist in space. But it is a question which *Tristram Shandy* properly asks over and over again in an ingenious variety of ways.

To the multiply ambiguous self-consciousness of the novel, as Cervantes played with it, we need only add the self-consciousness about consciousness itself, which Sterne learned from John Locke, and we have most of the ingredients that we need to take the not very long step to, say, the ambiguities of *Last Year at Marienbad*.

It is a question of consciousness, but only indirectly and incidentally the consciousness that might be attributed to characters. We know that Sterne was not a stream-of-consciousness writer in the twentieth-century sense at all, as Fluchère and others have convincingly shown. We never go into the minds of Walter Shandy and Uncle Toby; we know their thoughts only from what they say and do. And even the consciousness of the narrator is primarily that of a writer who is in turn conscious of the consciousness of his reader, which is the end toward which all his efforts are directed. Tristram says, "when a man is telling a story in the strange way I do mine, he is obliged continually to be going backwards and forwards to keep all tight together in the reader's fancy" (VI, 33, p. 462). Robbe-Grillet says of the film *Last Year at Marienbad*, "The only important character is the spectator, in his mind unfolds the whole story which is precisely imagined by him." The last part of Robbe-Grillet's statement is itself a fiction, of course. The film does the imagining, or imaging, and the spectator sits passively in the darkened theatre receiving physically on the retina of his eye what has been arranged for him by others.

It is the same with *Tristram Shandy*. Tristram says that he is "halving" the matter of imagining, with the reader, keeping "his imagination as busy as my own," and follows this with a series of injunctions to imagine, like those that Shakespeare gives his audience in *Henry V*. "Let the reader imagine then, that Dr. *Slop* has told his tale. . . . Let him suppose, that *Obadiah* has told his tale. . . . Let him imagine, that my father has stepp'd up stairs to see my mother:——And, to conclude this work of imagination,——let him imagine the doctor wash'd,——rubb'd down,——condoled with,——felicitated,——got into a pair of *Obadiah*'s pumps, stepping forwards towards the door . . ." (II, 11, p. 109).

This is playful pretense, of course. The reader imagines what he is told to imagine. The pair of pumps are supplied not by the reader but by the author. They were in the author's imagination before they were in the reader's. But what quite explicitly fascinates Sterne is the way that the pumps get from the one mind to the other. The author does not supply the physical pumps themselves or even a mental image of them. Sterne's image of the pumps was different from ours (who knows what pumps were like then?) and neither image is directly examinable, even by the one who holds it. Mental images are illusory references to what they are images or ideas of. Directly introspected, they transform themselves or vanish, become black figures on a black background. The columns of our apparently clear image of the Parthenon, in Alain's famous illustration, turn out to be uncountable unless we already know in advance what their number is.

Sterne did not supply shoes or the image of them, but simply words, the phrase "a pair of Obadiah's pumps." What comes between mind and mind are words, words slippery, ambiguous, open to each man's interpretation, yet intelligible, conveying ideas by the very fact of being words. Sterne, a writer, pretends to despair of them, as Eliot did in the *Four Quartets*. "I hate set dissertations," Tristram cries, "and above all things in the world, 'tis one of the silliest things in one of them, to darken your hypothesis by placing a number of tall, opake words, one before another, in a right line, betwixt your own and your reader's conception——when in all likelihood, if you had looked about, you might have seen something standing, or hanging up, which would have cleared the point at once" (III, 20, p. 200). The opaque words one before another in a right line represent, of course, the Gutenberg linearity against which Marshall McLuhan and Father Ong have reacted so strongly!

Gestures, objects, Trim's stick or forefinger, and silence itself are often more expressive than speech. "In this interest in silence rather than in speech," Virginia Woolf said, "Sterne is the forerunner of the moderns."[5] And, we may add, the more modern moderns. Sterne is as aware of the problems of incommunicability as Ionesco or Pinter or Carson McCullers, who have gone further in this direction than Mrs Woolf could have imagined. *Tristram Shandy* is full of failures in communication. Tristram gets his name because of one of them. The sounds of Maria's pipe awaken sentiments as no speech could do, but it is from words and words alone that we know Maria, or rather not Maria, but Tristram's feelings about her, or his idea of her, mixed with the joke about her goat and the quality of the inn at Moulins.

In the marvelous chapter about Maria, with its invocation to the muse of his beloved Cervantes, Tristram begins by saying that though he is now coming to the choicest morsel in his story, anyone is "welcome to take my pen . . . I see the difficulties of the descriptions I'm going to give——and feel my want of powers." Through France and Italy Uncle Toby's amours had been "running all the way in my head, they had the same effect upon me as if they had been my own." They run in his head as his chaise runs through the countryside, a consciousness that has to be put into words, not by way of record, of fact, but in such a way as to create a comparable consciousness in the reader. "I was in the most perfect state of bounty and good will; and felt the kindliest harmony vibrating within me, with every oscillation of the chaise alike; so that whether the roads were rough or smooth, it made no difference; every thing I saw, or had to do with, touch'd upon some secret spring either of sentiment or rapture" (IX, 24, pp. 627, 629).

Tristram's rapture in thinking of Uncle Toby is the rapture that the book is designed to cause in the reader. The first rapture, insofar as it is Tristram's, is imaginary; the second is real. Both depend on thoughts. What is the nature of these thoughts and where do they occur? In his preface to *The Interior Distance*, Georges Poulet says that although thoughts are always thoughts of something, turned invincibly toward the outside, leaping over voids, meeting certain obstacles, enveloping or invading certain objects, at the same time thoughts are simply thoughts, existing in themselves, isolated, mentally, in an interior depth which images from the outside come to populate, an interior vacancy in which the world is redisposed.

"Objectively literature is made up of formal works, the contours of which stand out with a greater or lesser clarity. They are poems, maxims, novels, plays. Subjectively, literature is not at all formal. It is the reality of a thought that is always particular, always anterior and posterior to any object; one which, across and beyond all objects, ceaselessly reveals the strange and natural impossibility in which it finds itself, of ever having an objective existence."[6]

Where, then, did this delight in thinking of the amours of Uncle Toby have its being as an objective reality? Not in the mind of Tristram Shandy, who never existed, just as, Robbe-Grillet tells us, there was really no last year at Marienbad, any more than there was a pleasant or unpleasant childhood for Lady Macbeth. Such emotions as Sterne himself felt were not caused by memories of Uncle Toby's courting of the Widow Wadman, because that never existed either, but by anticipation of the pleasure that he was going to take in telling the story that conveyed and created such a romance, a pleasure in the fulfillment of which every digression, interruption, double entendre, dash and comma has its important place. Though anterior to and productive of them, Sterne's delight is caused by exactly the same narrative and verbal play that causes the reader's delight. Sterne moves toward it—it is his goal—and then the reader moves on from it; it is his starting line, as in a relay race. Sterne's mind and the reader's meet precisely in the book itself, in the book as an arrangement of words, as a physical object that can be held in the hand, and where thought, however paradoxically and ambiguously, finds an objective existence.

These paradoxes, of course, reside in the ambiguities of words, in the ambiguity of the very word "book" itself. You can read a book or use it to prop open a window. The phrase "Tristram Shandy" out of context can mean the fictional character or the reading experience the novel as a whole offers or a particular title which the bookseller—and even here I make a metonymic leap—has or has not in stock and which he can wrap in paper and pass over a counter. Sterne's constant play with words is a way of making us recognize a whole group of irreconcilable dualities that are implicit in the novel as a literary form and as a form of experience.

In relation to what I am going to say about the preoccupations of modern critics of the novel, I want to summarize briefly the nature of three interrelated dualities, and show how Sterne manipulates them through the ambiguity of words. These dualities involve the difference between experiencing an event and telling about it, between an idea and what it is an idea of, and between a sign and its signification.

By the very use of verbs in the past tense, epic seems to separate an event in time from the telling of it. When epic tells of a telling, as with Odysseus' narrative at the banquet of the Phaeacians, or Trim's narrative of his brother's wooing, the separation is doubled. Homer uses a past tense about Odysseus, and Odysseus uses a past tense about his adventures, and one can proceed to any multiple of tellings about tellings about tellings. Epic tellings traditionally begin *in medias res*, and the order in which events are described need not correspond at all to the order in which they occurred. The telling is governed not by the event but by its own narrative conventions, by the purpose of the telling, the occasion and the audience. Groups of narratives without regard to the time and place of their occurrence can be brought together to illustrate a theme, as in the *Anatomy of Melancholy*. In the odes of Pindar sections of different stories, associated in very different ways with the subject, and widely separated in time, space and degree of probability, are intricately and allusively woven together. In real life when friends are reminiscing together, constant interruptions, digressions, movements back and forth in time are taken for granted, and these in turn are nothing to what goes on with incredible rapidity within the mind itself. Far from causing amazement, Sterne's narrative method should seem the most natural thing in the world. It is thoroughly consistent with the nature of literature and of thought, is fully and explicitly aware of what it is and what it is doing, and it presents, with perfect art, an appearance of complete spontaneity that actually is completely controlled.

The reason it seems so strange—or used to—is that it conflicts with the dominant tradition in the novel, especially in the nineteenth century, which denies or conceals one half of its own nature, which assimilates fiction to history, and makes the event and its morality or meaning dominate or even seem to cause the telling of the story. It puts all its emphasis on a presentation so full, so detailed and so sustained of what is often an extremely artificial plot, because it wants to create the illusion of something directly experienced, as if we were ourselves observing the incident itself or participating in it or being inside the minds and bodies of the participants.

This illusory, impossible merging of event and telling is contained in the ambiguity of the word "history" itself, which eighteenth-century novelists appropriated for their fictions. The word *history* can mean the events that occurred in a country's history or a historian's telling of them, and often, even when the word is used in context, it is uncertain which of the two is meant. But there is also an ambiguity about history as a telling of which most people are not aware, and which further confuses the relationship between history and fiction.

Readers often unthinkingly suppose that what the historian gives them are not ideas of events but the events themselves, that the events are somehow to be found in the pages of his book, whereas what the novelist offers is an unreality out of his own head. It is assumed that whereas the names "Uncle Toby" and "Corporal Trim" refer to fictional characters made up by Sterne, the word "Napoleon" used by historians refers to Napoleon himself, to a man. But the Napoleon of one historian is as different from the Napoleon of another as the Odysseus of the *Odyssey* is different from the Odysseus of the *Ajax* or the *Philoctetes*. Histories of Napoleon may contain incidents that never happened at all, just as there was no last year at Marienbad. But I myself fell into a verbal trap by saying that histories "contain incidents." Written histories do not contain incidents, they contain groups of words having significations, but these significations are not the events themselves.[7] Except where wild improbabilities are introduced, there is no way of distinguishing a fictional account of what never occurred from an historical account of what did. The reason is that they are the same thing—verbal structures. The happenings they present are not happenings in history, but happenings in the reader's mind, stimulated by the string of words which resulted from and express happenings in the writer's mind. There are, of course, real differences between history and fiction in their ways of relating words and ideas to the complex orderings of perceptual experience from which those ideas ultimately derive. But everything from problems of admissible courtroom evidence to the historicity of the Old and New Testaments shows how difficult it is to define and establish these differences.

Cervantes understood this perfectly, which is why he had such fun with his Arab historian. Sterne understood it perfectly too. He gave the Shandy family as complete and consistent a history as Faulkner did the Compsons in *The Sound and the Fury*. Theodore Baird, years ago, worked out all the dates. Though he is writing about events which

occurred long before his birth, Tristram describes them with a speci-
ficity which never could have been reported to him. But unlike the
traditional illusionist novelists who, imitating a false conception of
written history, pretend to take us back in time to the events themselves, Sterne makes perfectly clear what he is doing. It is not a
pretense—or any violation of calendar time—that we are present at
the actions recounted in the book or that they go on while they are
being written about or read about, and stop when the writing or reading stops. The actions are imaginative actions caused by the words,
and naturally they go on while the words are going on and stop when
they stop. "But I forget my uncle *Toby*, whom all this while we have
left knocking the ashes out of his tobacco pipe" (I, 21, p. 65). Necessarily we are present at the actions, because we are reading the words
which create them. All this Sterne makes playfully but consistently
explicit. "So then, friend! you have got my father and my uncle *Toby*
off the stairs, and seen them to bed?——And how did you manage
it?——You dropp'd a curtain at the stairs foot——I thought you had
no other way for it——Here's a crown for your trouble" (IV, 14,
pp. 286–287). Obviously this is not a return to the past, to 1703 or
1713. There is no conflict over times. As Robbe-Grillet insists of the
film *Last Year at Marienbad*, the time is the time of the artistic experience. For Tristram Shandy, who does not exist, the time is the
time of writing, of which he frequently gives the dates; for Sterne and
the reader, who do exist, though two hundred years apart, the time is
the time the words are written or read. A character can be left immobilized for a couple of chapters, just because this is a book and he is
a character in one, and not a creature of flesh and blood living in real
time. Modern film directors frequently freeze a character in a still
position. One purpose is to remind us that we are watching images on a
screen and not life itself.

The second ambiguity with which Sterne plays—stimulated by
reading Locke—is the ambiguity between thoughts and what they are
thoughts of. Here, too, the ambiguity is embodied in the polysemantic,
metaphoric or metonymic character of words themselves. It is a
crucial matter because, as we have seen, both histories and fictions
consist not of events themselves but ideas and imaginings of events put
into words. Words as such do not distinguish between (1) an abstract
idea, or (2) a mental image of something, or (3) the thing itself. The
same word can name one or two or all together.

A thought occurs in time, but does it occur in space? It occurs among other thoughts in a train or succession. Its space is the interior space that Poulet speaks of, not space in an extended, physical sense. If we think of France, or a fortified city in France such as Dunkirk, is Dunkirk in our head or interior space, or have we moved imaginatively to France, or are there two Dunkirks, one in our head and one in France, or perhaps three or more, since Dunkirk itself has changed in ways that we do not know, and the word as word has all sorts of historic reverberations. The imagining or memory of a place can be very different from the place itself, as directly perceived.

After the treaty of Utrecht, uncle Toby destroys the fortifications at Dunkirk. Or rather he destroys the model of them made on the bowling green with such precision of measurement by Corporal Trim. There is an obvious similarity between the serious play on the bowling green and the serious play of writing a novel. Just as Tristram can leave his characters immobilized for a couple of chapters while he discourses on other matters, Toby and Trim can leave the war in France to go home to supper and bed, and then resume the next day where they left off. Trim's exactitude in measuring out the fortifications is playfully matched by Tristram when he describes his father's position on the bed or Trim's inclination when he read the sermon—eighty-five degrees and a half on the plain of the horizon. This is a playful, not a deceptive, exactitude in history-making, less like Joyce's exactitude in the Ithaca section of *Ulysses* than like Beckett's structural manipulations in *Watt*, when he tells exactly what Messrs O'Meldon, Magershon, MacStern, de Baker and Fitzwein could each see when they looked at each other in more than twenty ways of looking. "When five men look at one another, though in theory only twenty looks are necessary, every man looking four times, yet in practice this number is seldom sufficient, on account of the multitude of looks that go astray."[8]

Uncle Toby gives final instructions to Corporal Trim for destroying the fortifications at Utrecht: "next fill up the harbour,——then retire into the citadel, and blow it up into the air; and having done that, corporal, we'll embark for *England*.——We are there, quoth the corporal, recollecting himself——Very true, said my uncle *Toby*—— looking at the church" (VI, 34, p. 465). The individual words may have as referents the actual places in France, their play replicas on the bowling green, or the ideas of either or both in the mind of uncle Toby.

After the peace of Utrecht, "No more could my uncle *Toby*, after passing the *French* lines, as he eat his egg at supper, from thence break into the heart of *France*,——cross over the *Oyes*, and with all *Picardie* open behind him, march up to the gates of *Paris*, and fall asleep with nothing but ideas of glory" (VI, 35, p. 466). There is the same ambiguity when Walter Shandy, planning Bobby's grand tour, is described as if he were actually taking it.

> But the waters are out, said *Obadiah*,——opening the door again.
> Till that moment, my father, who had a map of *Sanson's*, and a book of the post roads before him, had kept his hand upon the head of his compasses, with one foot of them fixed upon *Nevers*, the last stage he had paid for——purposing to go on from that point with his journey and calculation, as soon as *Obadiah* quitted the room; but this second attack of *Obadiah's*, in opening the door and laying the whole country under water, was too much.——He let go his compasses——or rather with a mixed motion betwixt accident and anger, he threw them upon the table; and then there was nothing for him to do, but to return back to *Calais* (like many others) as wise as he had set out (V, 2, p. 349).

With these travel preoccupations, it is natural, when Toby, reading the letter announcing Bobby's death, says "he's gone" that Walter should exclaim, "What——without leave——without money. . . . No:——he is dead, my dear brother, quoth my uncle *Toby*" (p. 350).

Notice also in the passage above, the statement that Obadiah had laid the whole country under water. He laid it under water by saying it was under water. This is not word magic, but simply what fiction does. The words make the fact, and this is true experientially, as we have seen, of the novel as a whole.

In discussions of time and simultaneity in *Tristram Shandy* one inevitably quotes the famous passage in which Tristram says, "I have brought myself into such a situation, as no traveller ever stood before me; for I am this moment walking across the market-place of *Auxerre* with my father and my uncle *Toby*, in our way back to dinner——and I am this moment also entering *Lyons* with my post-chaise broke into a thousand pieces——and I am moreover this moment in a handsome pavillion built by *Pringello*, upon the banks of the *Garonne*, which Mons. *Sligniac* has lent me, and where I now sit rhapsodizing all these affairs" (VII, 28, pp. 515–516).

If we consider what the consciousness would be at that moment of a Tristram who actually existed, we can see that we are dealing with two quite different kinds of situations, both non-verbal. Tristram is physically present in the pavilion on the Garonne, responding perceptively with eye and ear to what is around him. The two other experiences, at Auxerre and Lyons, are merely remembered, and however vivid a memory may be, it is very different indeed from present perceptional experience of what one can touch and see. This important difference seems to be obviated by using exactly the same words for all three, as if they were of the same quality and kind.

But from the point of view of the reader for whom these experiences have become words, they are the same, since he is not any more in the pavilion than he is at Lyons or Auxerre. He experiences directly neither perception of—or from—the first, nor memories of the second and third, all largely non-verbal. These three experiences are somebody else's—an imaginary somebody else—put into words, and they all occurred—insofar as they occurred at all—in the past, and therefore they all actually have the same availability. Real time for the reader is the present time of reading and imagining, and in relation to that real time, all past events have the same status, in that their imaginative availability is not affected by their relative distance in a suppositious chronological time past. That is why the treatment of time in *Tristram Shandy* or *The Sound and the Fury* is not as difficult or paradoxical as it is sometimes made to be.

I spoke earlier of the telling about a telling in epic as separating us by two removes from the event told, but this is really not true. Imaginatively speaking, the great hall of the Phaeacians is no nearer to us than Calypso's isle or the cave of Polyphemus. In the movies a flashback is just as immediate and vivid as the supposedly present scene it flashes back from, and in news reports on television some artificial device has to be used to distinguish what has previously been recorded from what is transmitted live. *Tristram Shandy* is in perfect accord with the operation of memory in leaping back and forth in time and reporting events of various degrees of remoteness with equal vividness and immediacy. The relationship of actual events to each other in historic time is very important, of course. This is what history as discipline is about, but disciplined history, governed by consistency and strict rules of evidence, represents a difficult and to some extent an artificial reconstruction, with which, as Lord Raglan reminded us, the folk mind—quite ready to make Charlemagne contemporary with Pontius Pilate or St George—has little patience. And for any of us, where the artistic imagination is concerned, Antony and Cleopatra are if anything less remote than the Duke of Marlborough and William the First.

All this Sterne clearly understood. The only "now" for him was the "now" of the reader as he sat with a book in his hand, turning pages, skipping ahead, or rereading a chapter at the author's direction. Writing on the book as object, with Sterne particularly in mind, the French novelist Butor speaks of the fruitful ambiguity of the very word "volume," itself. A book is three-dimensional, Butor says, the eye runs along the line, down the page, and as the pages are turned, the volume on the left increases, the volume on the right decreases. But left and right pages, verso and recto, are not equal, the recto is a "good" page. With juxtalinear translation, as in the Latin of the curse adapted for Obadiah, or the story by Slawkenbergius, the eye moves back and forth from verso to recto. Sterne handles this counterpoint deliciously, Butor says; Sterne "is, moreover, up to the present the greatest artist that I know in the organization of the volume."[9] *Tristram Shandy* is a prime example of everything Butor mentions, use of footnotes, diagrams, inserted texts (some in foreign languages), and all sorts of typographical ingenuity. Some of these devices had already appeared, of course, in the *Tale of a Tub*, and in Rabelais.

Butor is especially struck by Sterne's invitation to the reader to go back and forth in the text, something which cannot be done with tapes or records or moving pictures, and not easily with microfilms. As a physical thing, in a sense outside time, a book permits us to move freely within it, to repeat the reading, to return to the text and leave it as we will. So Tristram leaves and returns to his characters, who sometimes stop moving when they are left, just as a book while it sits on the shelves becomes almost, but not completely, a physical object. It is a static object holding within itself the potentiality of an artistic experience which for each individual will occur in time and take time. An author can resist such movement back and forth through the pages, can write so as to make it difficult, or he can facilitate it and try to control it, as Sterne does. The ability to move freely back and forth in the pages is like the ability to move freely back and forth in time. Here Sterne is obviously different from Proust and Freud, for whom the recovery in memory of a past event, often very difficult to achieve, is itself a consequential, transforming event, part of a deterministic sequence.[10]

Sterne's sense of the book as object, event, and work of art shows the true symbolist's ability to respond fully and realistically to the vehicle of his symbolism in its own natural immediacy, quite independently of the meaning it conveys, in a way that later enriches signification. This is also expressed in Sterne's sense of the human body, with all its failings, as vehicle of mind and psyche. Such awareness of the independence of the vehicle makes him as sharply aware as any twentieth-century theorist of semantics of the mysteries contained in the leap from sign to signification.

I have said that Sterne is not a Freudian in his treatment of the unconscious, nor do his works lend themselves readily to a Freudian analysis which assumes the determining presence in them of psychological elements of whose significance the author himself is unaware. Like Sartre, Sterne's whole emphasis is on knowing what goes on in the conscience, and in distinguishing between the authentic and inauthentic in human thought and feeling.

Sterne, however, is as insistent as the most orthodox Freudian on the fact that for some imaginations at some times every straight object, every stick, candle wick, nose can stand for the male genital, and every hole, slit, crevice and curve, for the female. This was not peculiar to him in the eighteenth century. John Stedmond has called attention to Pope's Scriblerian definition of the prurient style in the *Art of Sinking*, "a stile," Pope says, "every where known by the *same Marks*, the Images of the Genital Parts of Men and Women. It consists wholly of Metaphors drawn from two most fruitful Sources or Springs, the very *Bathos* of the human Body, that is to say . . ." and this last promising phrase Pope follows, as teasingly as Sterne, with three asterisks and then thirteen.[11]

Sterne was also Freudian in making repressions and chastity a generating force in the multiplication of such metaphors. Setting forth "the dangers of accessory ideas," the curate of d'Estella recalled that noses had suffered some centuries ago in Europe the ruinous associations that he now sees besetting whiskers, and "have not beds and bolsters, and night-caps and chamber-pots stood upon the brink of destruction ever since? Are not trouse, and placket-holes, and pump-handles——and spigots and faucets, in danger still, from the same association?——chastity, by nature the gentlest of all affections——

35

give it but its head——'tis like a ramping and a roaring lion" (V, 1, pp. 347–348). Such associations do not need to be taught, and they pervade more than the mind. "There are some trains of certain ideas," Tristram writes, "which leave prints of themselves about our eyes and eye-brows; and there is a consciousness of it, somewhere about the heart, which serves but to make these etchings the stronger ——we see, spell, and put them together without a dictionary" (pp. 346–347).

What is especially of interest today is Sterne's clear technical sense of the semantics of this situation. In the last decade or so, Freud has enjoyed a return of reputation in France among psychologists, like Lacan, and among linguists and structural anthropologists, not so much for his therapy or sexual theories, but for the pioneering brilliance of his structuralist interpretation of wit, and of verbal play and of meaning in dreams.

When Toby mutters the words "right end" of a woman, which Walter had just used rather scornfully to him, he fixes "his two eyes insensibly as he muttered them, upon a small crevice, form'd by a bad joint in the chimney-piece" (II, 7, p. 102). Despite the word "insensibly" and the mention of the crevice, it would seem inappropriate to make a twentieth-century analysis of this unconscious association if Sterne did not himself require it—or, rather, supply it—over a hundred pages later. "Here are two senses, cried *Eugenius*, as we walk'd along, pointing with the fore finger of his right hand to the word *Crevice*, in the fifty-second page of the second volume of this books of books——here are two senses,——quoth he.——And here are two roads, replied I, turning short upon him,——a dirty and a clean one" (III, 31, p. 218).

Tristram—thinking, of course, of Locke's *Essay*—hates to have to define a word, to define is to distrust, he says, but to prevent misinterpretation, he declares that by "the word *Nose*, throughout all this long chapter of noses, and in every other part of my work, where the word *Nose* occurs,——I declare, by that word I mean a Nose, and nothing more, or less" (p. 218). This is teasing play, based on a precise knowledge of what a Freudian symbol is. Of course the word "nose" means nose, and "spigot," spigot. If the noses and key-holes and fur hats which appear imagistically in dreams and fairytales as symbols were not first of all actually or literally noses and key-holes and fur hats, they could not be symbols of something else. In dreams and the plastic arts there need be no words. When a word is used in this kind of symbol-situation, we have three elements: the word and what the word literally stands for, and then what that objective referent, by associations of similarity or contiguity, unconsciously symbolizes. When Uncle Toby looks insensibly at the crevice, a crevice is actually there physically, and the word "crevice" does not appear in his consciousness at all. When the author first uses the word crevice it is quite literally in reference to the crevice caused by the bad joint in the chimney piece. What it unconsciously suggests to Uncle Toby or is suggested by, is another matter. This implicit association is made explicit in the gloss by Eugenius.

The same clarity occurs with other Freudian elements in *Tristram Shandy*. The novel begins appropriately with the primal scene, the sexual congress of parents, as indeed, according to Walter Shandy, civil government began, "the foundation of which being laid in the first conjunction betwixt male and female, for procreation of the species" (V, 31, p. 390). According to Freudians, the so-called "family romance," featuring a mysteriously found child of what is later discovered to be royal origin, grows, among other things, out of the child's inability to face the literal facts of his own parents' engendering of him. Tristram does face it, and has such control over it imaginatively that he can interrupt it for the winding of the clock and then resume it again. So with fear of the engulfing or devouring woman and fear of castration and impotence, which for Jung and Freud give shape and psychic charge to the basic myths, again, Sterne presents these basic masculine anxieties in perfectly clear-sighted and undisguised fashion.

Though he starts *ab ovo* with the egg of Leda, and ends with his father's bull, which "might have done for *Europa* herself in purer times"—notice the "purer"—Sterne has none of the mythographic feeling which modern novelists have attempted to revive, and which dominated one branch of our criticism for twenty years. Yet he makes Tristram an anti-hero in the most correctly mythological way. Tristram returns several times to the question of whether the mother is kin to her son. This question underlies the *Oresteia* and the shift from matriarchy to patriarchy which Robert Graves uses to explain so many of the myths. It is dramatized in more mysterious ways when two men, Dr Slop and Uncle Toby, without the assistance of women, reenact the birth, and again in the incident in which the orator gives

37

birth to a bambino from under his cloak. These have a similar psychic basis as the birth of Athena and second birth of Dionysus.

In his book *The Hero*, Lord Raglan contends that the narrative incidents of myth develop out of magic and ritual, and that the particular magic acts and rites on which the stories of great heroes are based are those centering around conception, birth, naming or christening, circumcision, entrance into manhood (or "breeching"). These, of course, are precisely the important adventures—more often misadventures—in Tristram's life. Obadiah even ties knots, which we know from Frazer's *Golden Bough* is a magic way of making birth difficult. Important rites of passage significantly omitted are those of marriage and burial. A consummated marriage is impossible both for the hero and Uncle Toby, with whom the hero is closely identified. Death, from which he flies, is manifestly not impossible, but it cannot be included in the novel until it happens, and then the teller cannot tell it because he is not there to do so. It is *in*cluded by the novel's not being *con*cluded.

All this Tristram faces frankly, with no compensating fantasies or displacements. He dances toward the nutbrown maid, but dances away again when he finds himself focussing on the slit in her dress. Uncle Toby bears the mysterious wound of the Fisher King, the wound of Ahab, the wound in the groin of Adonis and the other annual gods of the vegetation myths, but neither this wound nor Tristram's physical failures in love are given the social, the "wasteland" significance of the war wound of Jake Barnes. Is it all a cock and bull story and nothing more? No, it is a book of tremendous courage, in which Sterne, with great openness of mind, as A. A. Mendilow has told us, willed his whole existence.

I began with Joyce; I shall end with Mann. From Goethe on, with Goethe's mockery in *Wilhelm Meister* of a hero who is his own persona, the German literary tradition drew quite explicitly on Sterne in the development of romantic irony. Kierkegaard carried this to its most brilliant extreme, in his dazzling interplay of fictitious authors and fictitious documents, which must be edited and contradicted. Romantic irony overlaps with Socratic irony in keeping the reader on his guard, making him work, making him aware of the ambiguities of language and the uncertainty of knowledge. It establishes with him an exchange that seems to go on both inside and outside the work, but that actually goes on only within it, since it is entirely presented and controlled by the work. It was because he recognized the autonomy of the work as a self-sufficient structure of words that Sterne gave us the character Tristram Shandy in place of the omniscient auctorial comment of a Fielding or a Thackeray.

Thomas Mann was not departing, then, from his native tradition in deliberately choosing to read each day in the United States a few pages of *Tristram* while writing his culminating work, the massive, mythological Joseph series. Oscar Seidlin shows Mann's kinship with Sterne in their sense both of language and of art as play. Characters in Mann are aware that they are living a story, with all the questions of identity that this raises. Toby's whole committed life in the novel is a double reenactment, on the bowling green and in the novel, of the campaigns of the Duke of Marlborough. In the works of Sterne and Mann, Seidlin says, language "enters as a character in its own right, leads a life of its own, and is allowed all the playfulness which is the privilege of an actor in a play. It has a double face, a double aspect; it *is* the story, but at the same time acts in the story. It is the poet's expression, but he keeps it at a distance as well, and this is . . . the true meaning of irony." The whole of the Joseph series is "a play, a festival, a festive repetition," and a jest, too, Jehova's jest, *Gottesscherz*.[12]

These passages came back to me when I heard the most Shandian slip that the Chancellor of York made in his graceful, just, and appreciative tribute in the church at Coxwold. Where he meant to speak of Laurence as "praying" before God, he said most appropriately "playing." But *Hamlet* is a play, and so is *Lear*. Playing can be praying, especially in a man fleeing so swiftly before that "whoreson Death." In the affecting service at Coxwold, Sterne was apostrophized in the second person as "Laurence," just as Tristram, in one of the most moving passages of the book, directly addresses Uncle Toby. A living presence, a "you," a "thou," was felt to be in the church, with whom it was possible to have such dialogue as Tristram has with his readers. And it was also even more appropriate that to that service no bones or earth could be brought from Sterne's actual grave, that they were tied up in London by legal knots as tight as the leather ones tied by Obadiah.

To invoke the living Sterne, a book is better than bones. It is not primarily Uncle Toby and Walter Shandy who live in the novel. Considered as living persons they are extraordinarily limited. For all the remembering that goes on, Walter says nothing of what must have been an adventurous life in Turkey. Though Walter and Toby mean so much to the childhood of Tristram, they, in turn, seem to have had no childhood together. Sterne is their father and mother both. And where he lives is in every sentence and paragraph and chapter, in such marvelous passages as the one in the Invocation chapter which takes us by rapid shifts from Maria to her goats to the Inn at Moulins. Nothing is more ephemeral than psychic states, and yet the swiftly passing psychic states of a man two hundred years dead brought us all from Australia and America and Japan. Tristram is in Auxerre, Sterne is in Coxwold and London, and playing before God, but we are all together in the same place, for where we really are is in Sterne's mind, and where he really is, is in ours.

NOTES

1. Eugene Jolas, "My Friend James Joyce," in S. Givens, ed., *James Joyce: Two Decades of Criticism* (New York, 1948), pp. 11–12.

2. Richard Ellmann, *James Joyce* (New York, 1959), p. 427.

3. James S. Atherton, *The Books at the Wake* (London, 1959), p. 123.

4. James Joyce, *Finnegans Wake* (London, 1950), pp. 621, 21, 323.

5. Virginia Woolf, *Collected Essays* (London, 1966), p. 98.

6. Georges Poulet, *The Interior Distance* (Baltimore, 1959), pp. vii–viii.

7. "In linguistics, the nature of the signified has given rise to discussions which have centered chiefly on its degree of 'reality'; all agree, however, on emphasizing the fact that the signified is not 'a thing' but a mental representation of the 'thing.' . . . Saussure himself has clearly marked the mental nature of signified by calling it a *concept*: the signified of the word *ox* is not the animal *ox*, but its mental image. . . . " Roland Barthes, *Elements of Semiology* (London, 1967), pp. 42–43.

8. Samuel Beckett, *Watt* (Paris, 1958), pp. 191–192.

9. Michel Butor, *Inventory Essay* (New York, 1968). p. 56.

10. Proust contended, as a matter of fact, that it is impossible to recapture the past by an act of will. "And so it is with our own past. It is a labour in vain to attempt to recapture it: all the efforts of our intellect must prove futile. The past is hidden somewhere outside the realm, beyond the reach of intellect, in some material object (in the sensation which that material object will give us) which we do not suspect. And as for that object, it depends on chance whether we come upon it or not before we ourselves must die." *Swann's Way*, Part One (London, 1964), pp. 57–58.

11. *Miscellanies*, ed. Pope and Swift, Vol. IV (London, 1727), p. 67.

12. Oskar Seidlin, "Thomas Mann's *Joseph the Provider* and Laurence Sterne's *Tristram Shandy*," *Essays in German and Comparative Literature* (Chapel Hill, 1961), pp. 186, 190.

Sterne, Our Contemporary

by Denis Donoghue

In Volume IX, Chapter 4 of *Tristram Shandy* Toby and Trim arrive
within twenty paces of Mrs Wadman's door. If plot means anything,
the attack should now begin. Military preparations have been ample.
But Toby hesitates. Perhaps the Widow will take it amiss. Trim encourages him. The Widow will take it, he says "just as the *Jew's*
widow at *Lisbon* took it of my brother *Tom*" (p. 603). As soon as Tom is
mentioned, however indecorously, his tragic fate is recalled, Trim
cannot leave the case. If Tom had not married the Jew's widow, he
would not have been dragged off to the Inquisition. "'Tis a cursed
place," Trim says: "when once a poor creature is in, he is in, an'
please your honour, for ever." So the Corporal moralizes the occasion.
Nothing can be so sad as confinement for life, nothing so sweet as
liberty. Toby agrees. Then Trim, rising to the new note, begins a
sentence: "Whilst a man is free," he says; but he ends the sentence
with a flourish of his stick (p. 604). The flourish is not described; but
by the magical resources of the printing press it is represented in a fine
gesture, a brave flourish of print halfway down the page. We are reminded of Locke's chapter "Of the Imperfection of Words" in the
Essay, where he suggests that "words standing for things which are
known and distinguished by their outward shapes should be expressed
by little draughts and prints made of them." Sterne's bold flourish of
print stands for Trim's feeling, his impression, his idea, far more
accurately than mere words. Of course it is possible to describe the joy
of freedom, using nothing but words. Sterne makes a fair shot at this
mark in the *Sentimental Journey*, a set-piece in the chapter "The Pass-
port: The Hotel at Paris." "'Tis thou, thrice sweet and gracious
goddess," he says, "whom all in public or in private worship, whose

Professor and Chairman, Modern English and American Literature, University
College, Dublin

taste is grateful, and ever wil be so, till NATURE herself shall change"
(p. 199). These words are useful enough if freedom is to be invoked; or
even for the more delicate purpose of indicating Yorick's general sense
of freedom. But they are imperfect, in Locke's sense. We are led to
think that they do not fully render the idea, the impression in Yorick's
mind; or they render it as a general sentiment, a commonplace of
feeling. The requirement in this respect is severe. The sign on the page
should mark the feeling with preternatural intimacy. The ideal sign is
the painting of Socrates, already praised in *Tristram Shandy*. Raphael's
painting is so faithful to its occasion that, when you see it, you know
precisely what Socrates was saying at that moment. The words are
embodied in the gesture. Given the gesture, we require no remarkable
imagination to set out the Socratic argument, as indeed Sterne sets it
out in Volume IV, Chapter 7. The sinuous line on the page in Volume
IX mimes the movement of Trim's stick, which in turn mimes the
movement of his feeling. Sterne is not describing freedom; he is giving
the exact figure in which Trim's sense of freedom is enacted.

I have gone into this episode in some detail because it is an exemplary moment in *Tristram Shandy*. Ostensibly, the topic is freedom, but
what the words serve is Trim's feeling. Freedom provides the raw
material, subject to the qualification that many other abstractions
would have answered as well. If we refer to Trim's sense of freedom, we
write sense in italics, freedom in romans. The sense is the thing. The
proof is that nothing in this episode tells us anything about freedom, if
we separate the common ideal from Trim's particular possession of it.
But everything, including the printing press, conspires to reveal Trim
in this gesture. The direction of our interest is from object to subject,
from form to feeling. We are not allowed to rest until that sequence is
fulfilled.

It is usual to say that this is according to Locke. Sterne has said it
already. The *Essay*, he says, "is a history-book, Sir . . . of what passes in
a man's own mind" (II, 2, p. 85). We postpone consideration of the
silent question, whether any other history matters. It is according to
Locke that we remark the propriety of Trim's flourish. We suppose
that many ideas or impressions of freedom came into the sensorium of
an old soldier, a corporal. We know that his powers of reflection are
consistent with his vocation. So it is proper that the scale of those
reflections is represented in a splendid gesture. Nothing less would be
enough. If the gesture has more of Trim than of freedom in it, that too

is proper, and some philosophers argue that it is inevitable. In the second Book of the *Essay* Locke says that the first source of our mental life is our senses, which "conversant about particular sensible objects, do convey into the mind several distinct perceptions of things, according to those various ways wherein those objects do affect them." And then, "the other fountain from which experience furnisheth the understanding with ideas is,—the perception of the operations of our own mind within us, as it is employed about the ideas it has got." But Locke does not say how much of our mental life is sensation and how much reflection. There are men in whom the proportion of reflection to sensation is inordinate; inordinately small or inordinately large. In fiction, Walter Shandy is one of these; his sensory experience is limited, but his reflective activities are comically exorbitant. We may say of Toby's sensory experience that it is enough to fill a book of adventure, and would require a larger book if his reflections upon that experience were not so sparing. Sterne says that "REASON is, half of it, SENSE," but he disturbs the symmetry at once by saying that "the measure of heaven itself is but the measure of our present appetites and concoctions" (VII, 13, p. 494). This is the idiom of sense, in Sterne's representation here the better half. But if we define reflection in generous terms, we find the rhetoric of the book proposing that what enters our minds by sense is casual; we are really defined by our reflection, it is our very own. The philosophic bearing is idealist. In the first volume of *The Philosophy of Symbolic Forms*, Cassirer says that "the spirit is purely passive in relation to its simple impressions, and need merely receive them in the form given from outside, but when it comes to combining these simple ideas, it represents its own nature far more than that of the objects outside it." It follows, then, that language "is not so much a reflection of material *reality*, as a reflection of mental operations." This is congenial to the language spoken at Shandy Hall, which is not entirely according to Locke. In Shandy Hall words are more intimately related to their speaker than to the official objects of their reference. Material reality is the spur to mental operations, but the reflective effect is greater than its cause. Trim may talk of freedom, but the words are primarily interested in revealing Trim. In Volume III, Chapter 9, Dr Slop looks at his obstetrical bag, and then he has a modest thought. "But here, you must distinguish," we are told; "the thought floated only in Dr. *Slop's* mind, without sail or ballast to it, as a simple proposition; millions of which, as your worship knows, are

44

every day swimming quietly in the middle of the thin juice of a man's understanding, without being carried backwards or forwards, till some little gusts of passion or interest drive them to one side "(p. 167). The justification of passion, as of interest, is the part it plays in the mechanical operation of the spirit; it is a form of energy, propelling a man's reflection, so that he may the better reveal himself. Words declare their speaker, in the first instance, and their ostensible object only insofar as that is compatible with their first inclination.

It is tempting to say, for the moment, that what enters a man's mind through his senses is of no account in its nature and quality; it is essential that it come, since otherwise the reflective faculty is idle, but its character is perhaps indifferent. Sensations are needed as material, but we are defined by the nature of our reflection, which includes association, combination, relation, not to speak yet of Walter Shandy's hypotheses. No event, no sensation is sufficiently powerful in its own right to impose itself upon man's reflective capacity. The character of the sensation is one thing, the nature of its reception another. This is one of the sources of comedy. Some of Sterne's richest effects come from this disparity. An event may appear to be irrefutable in its character, and perhaps we cannot think of receiving it on any terms other than its own, but we are deceived. In Volume V, Chapter 2, of *Tristram Shandy* the news of Bobby's death is brought to his father, to Toby, Trim, and the rest. Walter is at that moment riding his hobby-horse somewhere between Calais and Lyons; his reflection takes the form of an elaborate speech, the soothing commonplaces of oratory on the slight differences between good and evil. Trim makes a speech from a different tradition of rhetoric, richer in gesture and therefore more successfully pathetic. To Susannah, the death means mourning clothes, and her reflection is a mental tour of the wardrobe. To the scullion, Bobby's death is a striking reminder that she herself is alive. Trim ends his speech, and as talk of one death leads to talk of another, he gives the full history, the life and death of the Lieutenant. One impression incriminates another; thus life is lived. We live by passing time which, as Samuel Beckett says, would have passed anyway. The mind lives by instantaneous translation of its experience into esoteric and mutually incompatible languages.

The point to emphasize is that every object of experience is translated into the diverse terms of its perceiving subject; of the object itself, independent of the perceiving consciousness, nothing remains, except an ambiguous report. When Sterne calls *Tristram Shandy* "this rhapsodical work," he means that the governing terminology is the idiom of subject and process. The novelist is the contriver of process. In March, 1762, Sterne wrote to Garrick: "I cannot write—I do a thousand things which cut no figure, *but in the doing*" (*Letters*, p. 157). It is almost a motto for the entire work, where everything is known in the doing, not in the thing seen as done. Considering the relation between subject and object, we acknowledge that there are, indeed, objects; we read of noses, knots, whiskers, deaths, clocks, fortifications, and widows. We take these things at Sterne's word. But they are entertained rather than acknowledged: a novelist in this tradition of fiction condescends to his ostensible materials, they are his minions. They are received and allowed on the understanding that, after that service, they will make no other demand. The objects are treated as happenings; they have everything except rights. Like the Siege of Namur and the Treaty of Utrecht, they are so colored by subjectivity that their objective status cannot hope to be recovered. We say of this, somewhat rudely, that the objects are invited only to be insulted, thrown aside when the spirit has done with them. But in this tradition of literature and philosophy the spirit has always denied the seeming solidity of objects, their claim to remain impervious. Sterne is as extreme in this inclination as Borges in our own time, who likes nothing better than to be seen using the language of impervious objects, subject to the consideration that the impervious quality is merely ostensible. In Sterne's comedy things are dissolved, then made into hobbyhorses; concepts in Walter Shandy, battles in Toby. The book itself is Sterne's hobby-horse, as he acknowledged in a letter of 1760. Writers have always known that to use language in one way is to celebrate, as the greatest thing, a world outside the book; to use it in another way is to dissolve the world for the book's sake. In the age of print it became still easier to give the book this degree of precedence, as in *Tristram Shandy*, where the development of characters is far less compelling than the progression of chapters. Time may have more subtle divisions, but the divisions that count are the end of one chapter and the beginning of the next. A dangling participle may keep the whole world dangling.

The first law of subjectivity is that we move from one moment to another by responding to the chances of association. Words jump from one hobby-horse to another. Any sentence with the word "siege" in it sets Toby translating it into his own terms. Trim can recite the fifth Commandment, if he is allowed to start at the first. Walter Shandy's recourse to speculation and hypothesis is like a nervous tic, reducing all associations to one, the association of the mind with itself. Walter's mind is reflexive in the sense that it defines itself in one gesture, it reduces everything to itself. Tristram says at one point in Volume II: "It is the nature of an hypothesis . . . that it assimilates every thing to itself as proper nourishment; and, from the first moment of your begetting it, it generally grows the stronger by every thing you see, hear, read, or understand. This is of great use" (p. 151). It is of great use because it saves energy; so long as the mind is moving in that way, it is not tempted from the track of its business. So Walter is right, meaning logical, when he asks, "What is the character of a family to an hypothesis?". "Nay," he goes on, "what is the life of a family"?—a question as interesting as it is unanswerable (p. 69). Tristram called this rhetoric the *Argumentum ad Verecundiam, ex Absurdo, ex Fortiori* (p. 71).

We think of this as a hobby-horse, but it would be enough to call it a habit. Samuel Beckett says in his essay on Proust that habit is "the generic term for the countless treaties concluded between the countless subjects that constitute the individual and their countless correlative objects." "If habit is a second nature, Proust says, it keeps us in ignorance of our first." Habit, then, is a generic term, an abstraction. Locke says in Book II, Chapter 11 of his *Essay* that in abstraction "ideas taken from particular beings become general representatives of all of the same kind." Habit saves us the labor of dealing with every impression as if it were new. Our second nature saves us the labor of living by our first. It is assumed, of course, that there is a difference between the two. If there is no difference, the single nature is a comic humor. The first thing we feel about a comic humor is the logical nature of his activities; there are no contradictions. Sterne's art delights in the possession of comic humors. We come round to Walter Shandy, logician of hypotheses.

Walter is entirely logical, for instance, in calling upon language to aid him in the manufacture of hypotheses. The auxiliary verbs which he praises in Volume V, Chapter 43, are self-engendering devices. "Now, by the right use and application of these," he says, "there is no one idea can enter [the] brain how barren soever, but a magazine of conceptions and conclusions may be drawn forth from it" (p. 406). He offers proof in the fruitful activity of white bears, incited by these verbs. Trim has never seen a white bear, but he can discourse upon them, because his inventive powers are sustained by corresponding powers in language itself. So language, whatever we hope to say of the relation between word and thing, is incorrigibly idealist and subjectivist, when invention is in question. There is the case of the Parisian barber in the *Sentimental Journey*, though this time Yorick is somewhat insular in his response to the French way of speaking. The Frenchman, praising his buckle, asserted that it would stand being immersed in the ocean. Yorick knows that an English barber would be content to say that the buckle would stand being immersed in a pail of water. He then argues in favor of his countryman that at least it would be possible to test the English assertion, but a Parisian, living in an inland city, would be hard pressed to find an ocean. Yorick's conclusion is that the grandeur of the French Sublime is magnificent, but "is *more* in the *word*; and *less* in the *thing*" (p. 159).

If the subjective law obtains, with the connivance of a subjective language, the necessity of plot is doubtful. "In *Freeze-land, Fog-land*, and some other lands I wot of" (p. 539) plot is considered essential in a novel, and cabbages are planted in straight lines and stoical distances, but in this climate of fantasy and perspiration, where every idea, sensible and insensible, gets vent, the case for adventure is weak. The place of real adventure is within the mind, where the strongest auxiliaries live.

It was usual to say, before we became accustomed to such things, that *Tristram Shandy* has no plot. But we are slow to make this a settled point of dispute. *Tristram Shandy* has enough plot, and enough adventure, to keep itself going, so long as the principle of its motion is maintained. Defoe's art would not survive upon that measure. The action of *Tristram Shandy* is to exhibit the comic freedom of the mind; the only requirement of plot is that it sustain that cause. A little plot goes a long way when it reaches a suitably inventive mind. Besides, a commitment to adventure would imply a certain independent power in the world at large, as if facts, things, and objects were indeed obdurate—an implication alien to Sterne, if it is severely enforced. But it is not severely enforced. Indeed, some of the most remarkable effects in *Tristram Shandy* are achieved by setting the ostensible mechanism of adventure against the irrefutable force of word or feeling. In Volume I, Chapter 22, Sterne gives a hint: "By this contrivance," he says, "the machinery of my work is of a species by itself;

two contrary motions are introduced into it, and reconciled, which were thought to be at variance with each other. In a word, my work is digressive, and it is progressive too,——and at the same time" (p. 73). We say that the book is digressive in its first intention, and progressive in its second, but with an implication that both intentions are eventually fulfilled. The great advantage of a digressive manner is that any departures from it in the progressive way are likely to be momentous. In Volume V, Chapter 13, after Bobby's death, Walter Shandy makes a Socratic speech of desolation to Uncle Toby. Mrs Shandy is outside the door, eavesdropping. At one point Mr Shandy recites, " 'I have friends——I have relations,——I have three desolate children,' ——says *Socrates*" : but Mrs Shandy bursts in. "Then," she says, "you have one more, Mr. *Shandy*, than I know of." "By heaven! I have one less,——said my father, getting up and walking out of the room" (p. 370). Is not this one of those "familiar strokes and faint designations" (p. 73) which Sterne mentioned, far back in the book, designed to let the digression proceed while at the same time keeping the speaker's picture touched up, developed, modified? If it is, it is achieved not merely by having Mrs Shandy interrupt her husband's rhetoric in the interests of truth, but by having Mr Shandy break in upon rhetoric itself in the interests of a more poignant truth. The irony is that both are right.

In a later episode Mr Shandy is wrong. At the end of Volume V, Chapter 32, Trim has been going through the Ten Commandments. Shandy is not impressed: "SCIENCES MAY BE LEARNED BY ROTE, BUT WISDOM NOT." He declares that Trim has not a single "determinate idea annexed to any one word he has repeated" (p. 393). The phrase "determinate ideas" is the emendation which Locke inserted in the second, third, and fourth editions of the *Essay* instead of the "clear and distinct ideas" in the first edition. By determinate idea he means "some object in the mind, and consequently determined, i.e. such as it is there seen and perceived to be." "This, I think," Locke writes in the "Epistle to the Reader," "may fitly be called a determinate or determined idea, when such as it is at any time objectively in the mind and so determined there, it is annexed, and without variation determined, to a name or articulate sound, which is to be steadily the sign of that very same object of the mind, or determinate idea." Shandy is quizzing poor Trim as a strict son of Locke. Trim has emitted the names or articulate sounds. Now he must declare the corresponding idea. What dost thou mean, Trim, by *"honouring thy father and mother?"* It is a stern test, but Trim passes it triumphantly: "Allowing them, an' please your honour, three halfpence a day out of my pay, when they grew old." Words, forms, ideas, and charity are diversely great, but the greatest of these is charity. Even Locke would yield at this point. The relation between feeling and form is always indeterminate, but the moment when the force of one clashes with the force of the other is peculiarly moving. Interruption may come from either direction. A poem, it sometimes happens, seems unusually adequate to the feeling engaged; and when we count the lines, lo, they come to fourteen and rhyme in ways proper to the sonnet. Or a rhetorical structure seems willfully determined to exclude the world of telegrams and anger; and suddenly a telegram is delivered.

Sterne was peculiarly gifted in the apprehension of such moments, especially of moments in which a rhetorical structure is suddenly waved aside and we find ourselves, where we have an interest in being, on solid earth, surrounded by people, places, and things. F. R. Leavis accused Sterne of pretentious and nasty trifling, but I am not sure that the charge will hold. I would maintain that a fine moral awareness is revealed when the two worlds are allowed to collide. J. R. R. Tolkien distinguishes between the Primary World, the given world in which we eat, sleep, think, and work, and the Secondary World, different for each of us, the world of art or of any structure which we delight to make. We do not live in the secondary world; that world is fictive, the product of our need and our imagination. It is possible to keep the primary world and the secondary world apart, and there are strategic advantages in doing so, but it is wonderful when, for a moment, the two worlds touch. This happens when the primary world, perhaps in a "spot of time," seems wonderfully responsive to man's need and therefore an enchanted place. Or in the secondary world, when the fictive laws chime, for a moment, with the daily laws of earth. In Volume VI, Chapter 34 of *Tristram Shandy* we are told that when the Treaty of Utrecht was signed, Toby's fortifications were left idle for several pacific months, except that occasionally he would ride out to see that the Dunkirk machines were demolished, "according to stipulation." Toby and Trim discuss the best way of effecting the demolition, since that is in question. Toby offers an elaborate scenario, ending with the whole harbor blown into the air. "And having done that," he says, "we'll embark for *England*." "We are there, quoth the

corporal, recollecting himself." "Very true, said my uncle *Toby*——
looking at the church" (p. 465). This may be a trifle, but the art is not
trifling; nor is its feeling. There is no attempt, on Sterne's part, to
shame one world in the sight of the other. What is remarkable is the
flow of feeling between the two worlds, the subjective world of hobby-
horses and auxiliary verbs, and the historical world in which wars
are fought, treaties are signed, and an English queen is shy with
her allies.

Of course it is not necessary to maintain that in *Tristram Shandy* a
just regard is continuously held for the rival claims of subject and
object. The dominant procedure is subjectivist. But often, when we
least expect it, the objective world, the primary world, is suddenly
acknowledged, and the effect is momentous. For Sterne's comic purpose it is enough to allow that objects are not given to consciousness,
as Cassirer says, "in a rigid, finished state," but that "the relation of
representation to object presupposes an independent, spontaneous
act of consciousness." Sterne finds the act of consciousness fascinating
and, in many of its transactions, wonderfully comic. He does not
quarrel with realists or empiricists, but he finds it comic to proceed
upon a different assumption. If we think him "modern" in a sense in
which Pope, Swift, and Johnson are not, the reason is that his axioms
are psychological rather than moral. He is modern in the assumption
that the important events take place within the individual sensibility.
Pope, Swift, and Johnson assume that the important events take place
in the public world, the given world of time and place.

Subject to these qualifications, we ascribe to Sterne a position in the
first instance subjective and idealist. But he is a peaceful man by
nature, and a comedian by vocation; in both characters hospitable to
rival claims. Ascribing to him a double acknowledgment, we look for
a suitably peaceful terminology. There is a strange letter, dated 15
November 1767, in which Sterne writes of the *Sentimental Journey*,
"which shall make you cry as much as ever it made me laugh——or
I'll give up the Business of sentimental writing——& write to the
Body" (*Letters*, p. 401). It is an odd phrase. Sterne's idea of sentimental
writing is explained in a letter of 12 November: writing is sentimental
when it runs most "upon those gentler passions and affections" which
teach us to love the world and our fellow-creatures. But what is
writing to the body? Pornography, perhaps. But then it also means,
presumably, *Tristram Shandy*, where the language of wit is certified by

51

the sprightliness of the body. The soul may be a Christian, but the body is a pagan; a dualistic fact crucial to comedy. True, *Tristram Shandy* also invokes the heart. In Volume IV, Chapter 26, Yorick has some thoughts on preaching; he favors the direct approach, despises ostentation. "For my own part," he says, "I had rather direct five words point blank to the heart" (p. 317). Sterne endorses this preference when he compares Walter Shandy's rhetoric unfavorably with Trim's, though to modern taste Trim's performance is scarcely more winning than Walter's. Trim is supposed to go "strait forwards as nature could lead him, to the heart" (p. 359), but Nature's rhetoric is pretentious on this occasion. Presumably the heart is the force in domestic things which, in sublime things, is called genius—an original gift, like instinct in animals. There is a passage in Garat's *Mémoires Historiques sur la Vie de M. Suard* (Paris, 1820, Vol. II, pp. 148–49) which reports Sterne on this matter. Suard asked him to describe the natural and the acquired characteristics of genius. Sterne's answer is couched in subjective terms. He speaks of "le principe sacré qui forme l'âme, cette flamme immortelle qui nourrit la vie et la dévore, qui exalte et varie subitement toutes les sensations, et qu'on appelle *imagination, sensibilité*, suivant qu'elle represente sous les pinceaux d'un écrivain ou des tableaux ou des passions." The idealist tradition urges that the constitutive factor is the imagination, the power within. It follows that the idealist develops an elaborate idiom, different names for this inner power in its several manifestations. Cassirer has pointed out that in the seventeenth and eighteenth centuries this tradition was focused in a single center. "Both in thought and language," he says, "the new motion of a spiritual life far surpassing mere empirical-psychological reflection was epitomized in the concept of genius." The classic text is Diderot's *Lettre sur les sourds et muets*, where the concept of genius is "the point of ideal unity," as Cassirer calls it, toward which the spirit strives; in that center, all dichotomies of subject and object are resolved. The aim of such thought is to transform "the passive world of mere *impressions*, in which the spirit seems at first imprisoned, into a world that is pure *expression* of human spirit." Poetry has always aspired to this transformation, as if it resented the evidence of an impervious world. This desire is found even in more empirical traditions. Bacon's famous account of poesy in the *De Augmentis* reflects this inspiration: "Whence," he says, "it may be fairly thought to partake somewhat of a divine nature; because it raises the mind and carries it aloft, accommodating the shows of things to the desires of the mind, not (like reason and history) buckling and bowing down the mind to the nature of things." There is no desire of the mind more fundamental than that of transforming the world, making the impressions which we receive from Nature appear as expressions of our own spirit. In descriptions of sensibility, the transforming power is often called the heart.

In Sterne, the first result of this idiom is that Nature becomes amenable to the inclinations of the mind. In Volume IV, Chapter 17, Tristram throws his wig in the air. Exasperated, he is then relieved. "Nor," he says, "do I think any thing else in *Nature*, would have given such immediate ease: She, dear Goddess, by an instantaneous impulse, in all *provoking cases*, determines us to a sally of this or that member——or else she thrusts us into this or that place, or posture of body, we know not why" (p. 293). The impulse is right, because Nature endorses the heart. The corresponding metaphors are familial and maternal. The *Sentimental Journey* itself, as Sterne says in one of the Versailles chapters, is "a quiet journey of the heart in pursuit of NATURE, and those affections which rise out of her, which make us love each other——and the world, better than we do" (p. 219). So the subjective terms begin to accrue: heart, genius, sensibility, affection, and (in a necessarily limited sense) Nature.

But the crucial word is Feeling. If the world is to be transformed, impressions appearing as expressions; if Locke's resistant world is to become the more susceptible world of Shaftesbury, Hume, and Diderot; feeling is the essential force. Feeling is the heart in motion, process personified; life itself, when life is understood in moving terms. "So much of motion, is so much of life, and so much of joy," Tristram says in Volume VII, Chapter 13, p. 493, surrounding life with two of the most powerful subjective terms. First among Sterne's values is the endless mobility of feeling, a delight in the self-creative plenitude of feeling. If the grace of mobility looks very like the dance of whim, Sterne is willing to bear that imputation, since whim, too, is subjective. Mobility of feeling is his way of circumventing the otherwise static relation between the mind and its materials. This is why Locke's account of the mind is not, to Sterne, enough. In Locke's world the relation between the mind and its materials is static because there is no allowance for the dynamic terminology of action. Impressions come unbidden to the sensorium, and there they are formed into

53

arrangements or relationships governed by reflection, association, abstraction, or chance. But these transactions do not permit anything more dynamic than arithmetical progression; one thing, then another, then another. If Sterne is a transitional figure, the reason is that he is moving toward a terminology of feeling, so that the mind's imprisonment in Locke's world, once recognized, may be broken. Feeling does in one way what genius or imagination do in their own ways; it transcends the limitations of historical experience, creating far other worlds and other seas of feeling. If life is determined by chance impressions, in the first instance, this restriction may be conceived as a kind of inner Fate, but the human spirit may still elude that determinism by its own resources. Sartre has said that the final aim of art is to reclaim the world by revealing it as it is, but as if it had its source in human liberty. In Sterne, the only liberty he takes is the liberty of endless feeling. The aim is to confound the historical determinism of experience by engaging the multiplicity of one's own powers. This makes a virtue of necessity; in this tradition a necessity transformed by feeling becomes the virtue of freedom. In his sermon on time and chance Sterne again makes a virtue of necessity by representing the offerings of chance as hidden decisions of a providential God. Those things "which to us seem merely *casual*" are "to him, certain and determined" (*Works*, V, p. 133). So God, too, is subject, Nature is subject, man is subject; and feeling is the proof.

The result is that many things are justified in this tradition which, in a rival tradition, are suspect. Passion is justified because as a vital force it operates within. After the "Maria" chapters of the *Sentimental Journey* Sterne has a famous aspostrophe to sensibility.

> Dear sensibility! source inexhausted of all that's precious in our joys, or costly in our sorrows! thou chainest thy martyr down upon his bed of straw——and 'tis thou who lifts him up to HEAVEN ——eternal fountain of our feelings!——'tis here I trace thee, ——and this is thy divinity which stirs within me————not, that in some sad and sickening moments, '*my soul shrinks back upon herself, and startles at destruction*'——mere pomp of words!——but that I feel some generous joys and generous cares beyond myself ——all comes from thee, great——great SENSORIUM of the world! which vibrates, if a hair of our heads but fall upon the ground, in the remotest desert of thy creation (pp. 277–278).

54

The idiom of subjectivity could hardly be more extreme. The difference between joys and cares is not important; the crucial point is the continuity of feeling, whatever the feeling is. If life is identified with feeling, the place of action in other traditions is taken by the flow of feeling in this one. We admit this when we say that the *Sentimental Journey* is a book of impressions rather than a travel book. We make the point more accurately if we say that it is a book of expressions. What it expresses is the world as feeling.

We approve of this tradition, or we disapprove. Generally, the English moralists have found Sterne in some measure offensive; he is either trivial or subversive. Certainly, he is alien to the English spirit, if that spirit is embodied in a literature which is largely social, political, and historical. We may assume that this is what Johnson meant when he told Boswell, "Nothing odd will do long. *Tristram Shandy* did not last." The English moral tradition does not approve of works which seem, even at a glance, odd. Coleridge's attack upon the cult of sensibility is only a more elaborate version of this distaste. Sensibility, "a constitutional quickness of sympathy with pain and pleasure," is based upon certain "parts and fragments of our nature" rather than upon the whole. It is therefore false. "All the evil achieved by Hobbes and the whole school of materialists will appear inconsiderable," Coleridge writes in *Aids to Reflection*, "if it be compared with the mischief effected and occasioned by the sentimental philosophy of Sterne, and his numerous imitators." "The vilest appetites," he continues, "and the most remorseless inconstancy towards their objects, acquired the titles of the *heart, the irresistible feelings, the too tender sensibility:* and if the frosts of prudence, the icy chains of human law thawed and vanished at the genial warmth of human nature, who could help it? It was an amiable weakness!" Virginia Woolf thought Sterne wonderful, except that he kept the joke of *Tristram Shandy* running too long. The *Sentimental Journey* was somewhat soft: Sterne was too much concerned with "our good opinion of his heart." "The mood," she maintains, "is subdued to one that is too uniformly kind, tender and compassionate to be quite natural." Perhaps it would be more accurate to say that in the *Sentimental Journey* Sterne is too readily delighted with a subjective idiom and its mobility. It is common to argue that the book is ironic, but the argument is weak. If we find the book soft, we must put up with it in that character and reflect that softness is inevitable in a work dedicated to the values of sensibility.

But perhaps the tradition is not, after all, as vulnerable as this account suggests. I have already proposed that Sterne's world need not be regarded as subjectively closed. But another defence is possible: that subjectivity is one of the perennial demands of the mind. I note that Susanne Langer in her recent book, *Mind*, proposes to treat the entire psychological field, "including human conception, responsible action, rationality, knowledge" as "a vast and branching development of feeling." True, she speaks of feeling, not of sensibility, but the difference is hard to establish. One idiom shades into the other. The argument is that the organism, "in toto and in every one of its parts, has to 'keep going'"; and in the subjective or idealist tradition it goes by feeling. So we should not underestimate the natural potentialities of a subjective idiom. The Man of Feeling is too often regarded as a mere historical phenomenon, a moment in the history of literature and psychology. In fact, he is perennial; irrefutable because always possible. He is always possible because he represents certain desires of the mind upon which the mind insists. The Man of Feeling is perennial because of the continuity of his sensations and the self-delighting power of his reflections. His only limitation is that he can never know whether feeling is enough, or whether its sole merit is that it keeps the organism employed. Psychological answers tend to be tautological. The Man of Feeling can never know when his feeling is adequate, because he cannot know what an adequate feeling would be: adequate to what? There are no criteria in feeling; there is only the satisfaction of its presence, or the despair of its end.

We are moving toward comedy, in the modern manner exemplified by Joyce and Beckett. Sterne employs the images of fact, time, and place; and he acknowledges them to the extent of that employment. He often uses them as a relief from the importunities of his feeling; as the most resolute idealist is pleased to be refuted, perhaps, by a Johnsonian stone. To Sterne, things are real, and their reality is comic: there is no contradiction. The relation between the mind and the things outside the mind is a relation of need and relief, a comic need, and a comic relief. Beckett says in the essay on Proust that "exemption from intrinsic flux in a given object does not change the fact that it is the correlative of a subject that does not enjoy such immunity." By heart and sensibility Sterne makes up for the frustrations of the flux, bridging the gap between subject and object by subjective energy, by the continuity of feeling. If feeling is continuous, the fluidity of subject does not matter. Sterne defeats frustration by taking it as it comes, making virtues of necessities. If you say with Beckett that the observer infects the observed with his own mobility, you may say it ruefully or you may say it as a comic gesture. *Tristram Shandy* and the *Sentimental Journey* make the same assumptions about human nature, the mind, the body, the sensorium; but the tone of one differs from the tone of the other. Suppose a man were to write a novel, treating every characteristic mode of the mind as an amiable and necessary foible; might it not turn out like *Tristram Shandy*, given Sterne's genius? And suppose he were to write another book to suggest that all men share in the possession of amiable foibles and could not live without them; might it not turn out like *A Sentimental Journey*, given the same genius? Kenneth Burke has remarked that "the progress of humane enlightenment can go no further than in picturing people not as *vicious*, but as *mistaken*." "When you add," he continues, "that people are *necessarily* mistaken, that *all* people are exposed to situations in which they must act as fools, that *every* insight contains its own special kind of blindness, you complete the comic circle, returning again to the lesson of humility that underlies great tragedy."

We speak of Sterne our contemporary, but the word is ambiguous. We say that Sterne is modern and that Swift, Pope, and Johnson are not. Boswell recalls an occasion on which Johnson teased his friend "the lively Miss Monckton." The lady had insisted that some of Sterne's writings were very pathetic. Johnson denied it. "I am sure," Miss Monckton maintained, "they have affected *me*." "Why," said Johnson, smiling and rolling himself about, "that is because, dearest, you're a dunce." Johnson is not denying that some readers find Sterne's writings affecting. Still, he insists that by common or public standards Sterne's writings fail. They fail, we may assume, because in their oddity they devote themselves to the exception rather than to the rule. Johnson represents that general sense of life in which reality is deemed to be tangible, verifiable, and public. He knows that there are obstacles to this view, but he refuses to give them more allowance than is appropriate to local difficulties. Sterne is fascinated by the obstacles, he prefers them to the truth they impede. As a comedian he loves to rebuke the axioms of common sense. We think of this as a modern stance, critical, comic, and subversive. But we should not push the difference too far. There is no reason to speak of Sterne as if he were

Kafka, Musil, or Beckett. He is a man of his time, though he complicates our sense of that time. Indeed, it may be maintained that the differences between Sterne and Johnson allow for a body of feeling, since that is the crucial term, common to both. There is no reason to think that Sterne merely denied, or that Johnson merely asserted; their differences are not incorrigible. Sterne's comic intransigence is not, after all, prohibitive. He does not undermine the common assumptions of his age, though it is the nature of his comedy to ensure that those assumptions are not too glibly held. Perhaps what is exemplary in Sterne is the urbane tone which suffuses his intransigence, as if in that urbanity the acerbities of true and false, subject and object, might still be appeased.

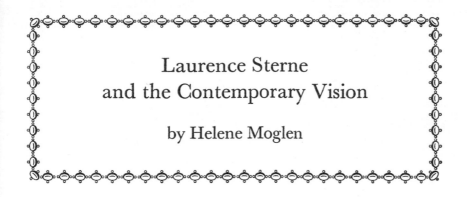

Laurence Sterne
and the Contemporary Vision

by Helene Moglen

What is the twentieth-century reader to make of *Tristram Shandy*—this strange rambling work that hides its purpose and unity beneath a cloak of chaos and confusion, telling a story not of men's lives but of their minds? And how indeed is the reader to explain its surprising contemporaneity? It must seem likely that Sterne consciously set out to write a different kind of novel, but its specific sources remain difficult to analyze. Responding to the tradition of learned wit and deriving the basic viewpoint and technique from his creative reading of John Locke, Sterne seemed to use only that which could be most easily assimilated from the novel that was being written in his own time. Much of that which remained he ignored—but some, he parodied. The result was a work of astonishing creativity and originality that stands apart throughout the eighteenth and nineteenth centuries. Ultimately, one concludes, it is the philosophical perspective that determines the modernity of the vision.

Sterne's own habit of mind made him easily receptive to the paradoxes of Locke's optimistic scepticism and the framework and implications of the *Essay* were a creative spring for Sterne's development of a superb system of ironies. At the center of Sterne's vision was his two-fold image of Locke—the sensitive man of intuition and the rigorous philosopher. The conflict of these two roles, as it is expressed in the radical contradictions of Locke's approach, seemed to represent for Sterne a universal dilemma that involved a disparity between the endless striving toward the illusion and the fact of an inescapable reality: the fruitless search for an incontrovertible truth hidden beneath relativity.

According to Locke's epistemology, man is dependent for his knowledge upon his senses and the information which he can generalize

Assistant Professor of English, New York University

from his observations and reflections. It follows that he can never be sure of the correspondence of his concepts to the real world. Insisting that substance and primary qualities are real and reality only partially knowable, Locke is forced to appeal to a "deus ex machina" to insure the valid interraction of mind and matter.

> The first are simple ideas, which since the mind, as has been showed, can by no means make to itself, must necessarily be the product of things operating on the mind, in a natural way, and producing therein those perceptions which by the Wisdom and Will of our Maker they are ordained and adapted to. From whence it follows, that simple ideas are not fictions of our fancies, but the natural and regular productions of things without us, really operating upon us; and so carry with them all the conformity which is intended; or which our state requires. . . .[1]

This was an evasion rather than a solution. Sterne accepted the paradox but rejected the compromise. Instead, in *Tristram Shandy*, he commits himself to the epistemological subjectivism which Locke only partially accepts. The Shandys all live in private worlds of their own eccentric perceptual creation. That which Tristram finds to be characteristic of Walter, he finds to be characteristic—in effect—of all:

> The truth was, his road lay so very far on one side, from that wherein most men travelled,——that every object before him presented a face and section of itself to his eye, altogether different from the plan and elevation of it seen by the rest of mankind.——In other words, 'twas a different object,——and in course was differently considered:
>
> This is the true reason, that my dear *Jenny* and I, as well as all the world besides us, have such eternal squabbles about nothing (V, 24, p. 382).

The associational determinism which Locke describes in the fourth edition of his essay is found by Sterne to permeate virtually every aspect of the individual's intellectual life.

In the Third Book of the *Essay* Locke discusses the formation of abstract ideas which do not have their source in the perceptual world. He suggests here that the idea is actually an arbitrarily fixed collection of ideas and that objective validity can be insured only through the precise definition of general terms. With this concept we are given the beginning of a theory of meaning which does, in fact, seem to be a cornerstone of the philosophy.

> For, the connexion between the loose parts of these complex ideas being made by the mind, this union, which has no particular foundation in nature, would cease again, were there not something that did, as it were, hold it together, and keep the parts from scattering. Though therefore it be the mind that makes the collection, it is the name which is as it were the knot that ties them fast together (III, v, 10, 49–50).

This universal is fixed by the precise definition that calls it into being and the agreement that maintains it. Again, however, Locke is unwilling to accept the implications of his reasoning. He does not want to center his epistemology on a theory of meaning that emphasizes the peculiarities of the individual experience. Instead, he begs the question by insisting that language, while essential to thought, is not to be identified with it. The concept is, to some extent, independent of the word, and depends for its existence upon the real essences from which sense perceptions are derived.

Throughout this section of the *Essay* Locke demonstrates an ultimate faith in the efficacy of language and sets out to lay open and correct the misuses of language which he considered to be of primary importance in philosophical and scientific discourse (III, v, 16, 53–55). To remedy the imperfection of language he urges perfect and exact definition when dealing with substances and mixed modes (III, xi, 15, 156; III, xi, 19, 158), so that clear and determinate ideas will always be affixed to words. He seems to presuppose, fallaciously, that general agreement with regard to a definition is really an indication of the validity of a proposition. His apparent aim is to purify language—all language that is not used simply for civil discourse—so that it will no longer have a subjective reference.

For Sterne this is, of course, impossible. He sees the personal fallacy as responsible for the use and interpretation of every word. Accepting Locke's premises concerning the necessity of definition, Sterne indicates again and again the way in which confusion can result from one's use of the most straightforward names. Puns, innuendoes and double entendres, transform the simple object, whose identity and characteristics would be similarly defined by all, into causes of painful and inarticulate confusion. Noses, whiskers, placket-holes, spigots, bridges, trenches: all are traps for the unwary, snares for the repressed and deluded. Emotions, predispositions and personal conditioning make definition impossible. Ambiguities abound and, while they may appear in the imprecision of language itself, they are primarily the result of individual eccentricites.

Sterne's relation to the epistemological and linguistic theories of Locke provides us with the link necessary to our understanding of the relation of Sterne to the contemporary vision. It is in his commitment to Locke's subjective relativism, in his willingness to extend it into every area of man's intellectual, emotional and aesthetic life, that Sterne the philosopher looks ahead to some aspects of the thought of Bergson, James and Freud, the three major philosophical influences on the modern novel. In this way, Sterne the novelist anticipates contemporary literary themes and narrative techniques.

Of the three modern figures it is Bergson who has the closest connection to Locke. It is between them that we find the greatest number of crucial similarities—in their concepts of identity, language and time. There are more fragmentary echoes in James' concept of the "stream of consciousness" and in Freud's definition of the self. Of course, this is not to suggest that the systems of the three men can be equated. It is only an indication of the fact that, in the consideration of the impact of a systematic philosophy upon a literary movement, it is the general orientation in psychological and aesthetic areas which is important. These attitudes are translated by the novelist into concrete experiential terms. To the extent that Bergson, James and Freud shared a general romantic orientation their influence was shared. To the extent that Bergson articulated this point of view most extensively in aesthetic terms, his influence can be seen as dominant.

Those aspects of Bergson's philosophy that were most relevant to the development of the modern novel were his concept of the self and its external reality, and his attitude toward language. In the *Introduction to Metaphysics* Bergson tells us that philosophers distinguish two ways in which an object of the external world can be known. The first method is a relative one, for it suggests that we perceive the object from different points of view and describe it in symbolic and conceptual terms. The second technique provides for entrance into the object itself by means of an effort of the imagination or intuitive faculty. It is thus that one is able to attain the absolute which offers an immediate experience of that which is both unique and ineffable. To analyze the object according to the former method is to reduce it to elements which are known to be common to it and to other objects, and is therefore to express the thing as a function of something else. To enter the object by empathizing with it is to possess it completely and unquestioningly.

The ultimate purpose of knowledge and the goal of metaphysics is to grasp the "élan vital"—the creative force driving life to ever higher levels of organization, the unique nature of all animate life and the ultimate principle of existence.[2] This can be accomplished only through an act of intuition rather than by the activity of the intellect, through the intuition of the one object which gives us a sense of the creative evolution which is life itself. This object is our own personality. Through introspection we discover a ceaselessly changing process which is the constant, moving, varying, colorful flow of personality. The process is called by Bergson "durée" and it is the pure time which is absolute reality revealed in the inner flow of self. Knowledge gained by means of self-analysis can, in turn, be followed by a process of abstraction and conceptualization. It is therefore possible to move from intuition to concept, while the reverse procedure, according to Bergson, is not feasible.[3] Metaphysics therefore establishes the conclusion that mobility is reality.

Closely bound up with Bergson's "durée" is his concept of memory: that memories of past things interpenetrate the present experience. Past and present are joined in a unity of consciousness which is an irreversible flowing to the future. Bertrand Russell, in *A History of Western Philosophy*, points out the extent to which Bergson here maintains an idealist position. Russell explains that "his theory of time is seen to be simply a theory which omits time altogether." Bergson is not recognizing a "real" past, but is speaking only of "the present idea of the past." Russell goes on to suggest that this is an instance of a more general confusion "between an act of knowing and that which is known." Since Bergson maintains that all knowledge consists of images, matter and the perception of matter are the same thing.[4]

It is possible to see some of the ways in which Bergson's view of the self—and its relation to an external reality—was anticipated by Locke. As empiricists, both men shared a basic suspicion of the powers of reason. While Bergson was, at times, willing to admit the possibility that reason and scientific method could aid the efforts of intuition and metaphysics, he always insisted upon the superiority of intuition in achieving an insight into "truth." Locke viewed the possibilities for knowledge with some scepticism but maintained his faith in reasonableness—in the mind's potential power to master abstraction and order experience, given the benefit of education and self-discipline. Locke was unable to embrace the idealist resolution of the mind-matter controversy and his acceptance of a Newtonian universe prevented him from following the implications of his epistemological scepticism. Instead of recognizing the creative functioning of the mind in accordance with its own laws, he persisted in defining learning as discovery or apprehension. His unwillingness to adhere to a total subjectivism involved him in constant contradiction. Of course, to the extent that Bergson attempted to compromise his idealism in his treatment of mind, matter and expression—he too becomes involved in contradiction.

In Bergson's insistence upon the turning inward of the individual as the beginning of knowledge, in his view of the constantly changing self which contains its past in its present, in his consequent recognition of the importance of memory, we find some of Locke's fundamental but inadequately developed principles. Locke's theory of association does, after all, give to the memory a specifically originative and synthesizing function. The reflective consciousness determines the irrational, subjective and unique nature of the self (II, xxvii, 17, 458–459). Identity is the extension of consciousness into the past (II, xxvii, 16, 458). Furthermore, although Locke does seem to define the contents of consciousness as discrete but interrelated units, his formulation of the "train of ideas," with its emphasis upon a personally defined, inner sense of time, corresponds in its general feeling to Bergson's "durée." It is upon this correspondence that Mendilow bases his suggestion that Locke's associationist psychology with its corollary of the time-shift technique had a meaning for Sterne similar to that of Bergson's theory of duration for the modern writer:

> They aim at conveying the effect of an all-pervading present of which past and future are part, in preference to an orderly progression in time of separated discontinuous events.[5]

The empiricist view of reality shared by both men determined the nature of their observations about language. W. M. Urban, in his book *Language and Reality*, explains that the high valuation of language is the underlying assumption of all periods of rationalism and is accompanied by a belief in universals. The low valuation of language, which is discovered in all critical periods of culture, is the underlying assumption of the empiricists and is accompanied by some form of nominalism.[6]

It is not surprising, then, that the optimistic scepticism which characterized Locke's appraisal of the powers of reason characterized his judgments concerning the potentialities of language as well, while Bergson's linguistic philosophy reflect a more acute scepticism. In Bergson's thought, language—both the natural language of everyday speech and the artificial language of the sciences—is the tool of the intellect and the means of conceptualization. It is because of language that we have developed the habit of setting out time in space. It is language which "gives a fixed form to fleeting sensation."[7] It is language which encourages us to see sensation as part of the object itself, to perceive the effect through its cause and through the words which translate it. Language makes us believe in the unchangeableness of our sensations and often deceives us as to their very nature.

In this way language will, for example, denote the deeper, subtly differentiated states of the self by the same words. And by associating state with state and object with object, by setting them side by side, it will fail to translate completely that which our souls experience. Indeed, for Bergson there is no common measure for mind and language.[8] The idea of multiplicity, without its relation to number or space, although clear for pure reflective thought, cannot be translated into the language of common sense. Although it is useful for the purpose of science and essential for common communication,[9] the natural and artificial languages can neither grasp the true reality nor understand the essence of being. Intuition alone is capable of this.

Bergson is indecisive in establishing the relation of intuition and expression. In *An Introduction to Metaphysics*, Bergson implies that intuition does not permit of expression.

> If there exists any means of possessing a reality absolutely instead of knowing it relatively, of placing oneself within it instead of looking at it from outside points of view, of having the intuition instead of making the analysis: in short, of seizing it without any expression, translation, or symbolic representation—metaphysics is that means. Metaphysics, then, is the science which claims to dispense with symbols.[10]

Language is created by the intellect and is insufficient for the attainment of the realization of truth. The essence may be grasped—but it cannot be expressed.

However, Bergson does not consistently take this negative position. He also suggests that a new language must be sought which will be derived from the natural language and will consist of a more artistic means of expression that will employ metaphor and image in its descriptions. Since one is always conscious of the illusory nature of the image—never mistaking it for an actual representation—the integrity of the intuition can be maintained while communication of the absolute is made possible.[11] Clearly, Bergson is here equating metaphysics and poetry. He advocates the use of a poetic form of statement, comparing the metaphysician's goal with the poet's desire to catch a fleeting glimpse of a mobile reality. The implications for art are obviously positive since Bergson gives to the poetic insight a new validity and technique, as surely as he has given to it, with his emphasis upon the self, a new subject.

If we now consider Sterne's attitude toward language as it develops from his reading of Locke and is related to Bergson, we again find strong similarities to Bergson's more extreme philosophy. Sterne's scepticism extends to all knowledge. He reveals the fallacy underlying all usage, all interpretation, all definition. Speech, like perception, is incapable of offering any but the individual, relative truth. All language is as susceptible to interpretation as the emptiest sound, as the most ambiguous exclamation—as susceptible to interpretation as Phutatorius's cry of "zounds" in response to the surprising presence of a hot chestnut inside his breeches. The nominalism, which is only suggested by Locke, is extended by Sterne until language is revealed to be at the root of the chaos, the confusion, the misunderstandings of everyday life and intellectual discourse.

Furthermore, the tragedy of the Shandys—which is derived from Sterne's image of Locke—is not unlike the plight of Bergson's misdirected intellectual. It lies, for example, in Walter's search for absolute truths formulated by reason, in his faith in concepts which are imposed upon the faulty, misleading, and subjective data of experience. It lies in the belief of each of the Shandy males in his own subjective vision as an objectively valid version of reality. However, although Sterne does not suggest the possibilities of intuition in forwarding the cause of formal knowledge or metaphysical understanding, he does, with his theory of empathy, make possible meaningful and ethical human relationships that transcend the limitations of language. Further, the uneasy dualism of Bergson's view has its counterpart in Sterne's alternative to mute sympathy—his celebration in Tristram of wit which, by employing the imagination to perceive and using metaphor and symbol to express, is alone capable of capturing and retaining the rich, elusive meaning of multiplicity and ambiguity.

In those areas in which Locke and Sterne's thought seems to be prophetic of Bergson's philosophy, it seems also to be prophetic of some limited aspects of the writings of William James and Freud. This can, of course, be traced to the fact that James and Freud developed independently, along specifically psychological lines, those relevant elements of Bergson's metaphysics.

Although the thought of Bergson and James seems to converge in the sphere of literary influence, James' theory of consciousness preceded Bergson's which, while later, was apparently developed independently.[12] In the ninth chapter of his *Principles of Psychology*, James denies the subject-object dualism which is a source of contradiction in the epistemologies of both Locke and Bergson. His "radical empiricism" insists that everything is composed of "pure experience" which cannot be atomistically described. Here James introduces his famous metaphor for the functioning of consciousness—a metaphor that has been used to describe the narrative method of such writers as Proust, Gide, Joyce, and Virginia Woolf.

> Consciousness, then, does not appear to itself chopped up in bits. Such words as "chain" or "train" do not describe it fitly as it presents itself in the first instance. It is jointed; it flows. A "river" or a "stream" is the metaphor by which it is most naturally described. *In talking of it hereafter, let us call it the stream of thought, of consciousness, or of subjective life.*[13]

James emphasizes the importance of the experience of the interior rhythm which exists apart from language and, as sensibility, plays an important role in creative functions.

> The difference in the rate of change lies at the basis of a difference of subjective states of which we ought immediately to speak. When the rate is slow we are aware of the object of our thought in

a comparatively restful and stable way. When rapid, we are aware of a passage, a relation, a transition *from* it, or *between* it and something else. As we take, in fact, a general view of the wonderful stream of our consciousness, what strikes us first is this different pace of its parts.[14]

His conception is of the fluidity of consciousness, of the sensible perception of the flux, and the equation of memory and identity:

Experience is remoulding us every moment, and our mental reaction on every given thing is really a resultant of our experience of the whole world up to that date.[15]

All are important in providing the novel of subjectivity, that dedicates itself to the painstaking study and recreation of consciousness, with its motivating impulse and theoretical framework.

It is, of course, impossible to separate the later influence of James from that of Bergson. Both make themselves felt in the same areas, and both elaborate further the growing romanticism that ruled all spheres of intellectual investigation. Still another related elaboration of this same tradition can be found in the work of Freud and the psychoanalytic movement, as Lionel Trilling suggests when he traces the tradition back to 1762 and Diderot's *Rameau's Nephew*:

... psychoanalysis is one of the culminations of the Romanticist literature of the nineteenth century ... this literature, despite its avowals, was itself scientific in at least the sense of being passionately devoted to a research into the self.[16]

In fact, the Freudian view of character and the unconscious is not, in some respects, different from that suggested by Locke. There are, throughout *An Essay Concerning Human Understanding*, frequent if vague allusions to irrational elements of the mind that exert an influence which, while not totally explicable, are in some way connected with an individual's experience. In fact, as Ernest Tuveson points out, Locke goes beyond this and suggests, in his edition of 1690 (II, i, 22), that children acquire simple ideas early, perhaps in the womb, which persist even though the mind cannot be aware of them. There is, in these unremembered ideas which influence a mind that is ignorant of their presence, some implication of the unconscious.[17] There is the same implication in Locke's discussion of the irrational nature of association which can, in its most extreme forms, become a kind of madness.

Further, Locke's concept of identity as a function of memory is prophetic of Freud's view just as it is an earlier, simplified form of the definitions of self offered by James and Bergson. All of these men give us a theory of consciousness in which the past is contained in the present, affecting behavior and determining emotional and intellectual response. It is in this way that the psychoanalytic emphasis upon the reconstruction of the self is made aesthetically meaningful. It is only through the analysis of the totality of the individual's life that we are able to achieve a valid understanding of his personality. The method of analysis demands in art, as it had in psychology, the creation of a new form. It is therefore fascinating, although not really surprising, that the form which Sterne developed as a result of his interpretation of Locke, should be in many ways similar to those adopted by the novelists who were influenced by Bergson, James and Freud.

Germaine Brée gives us the key to the nature of the parallel development when she writes of Gide:

> In search of the novel, Gide found that the only novel worth writing is always one and the same—the novel that reveals the inadequacy of all fiction when it is confronted with life. Gide is not a creator but a destroyer of fictional worlds.[18]

For Sterne and the stream-of-consciousness writers of this century the public symbols and social values of the conventional novel proved inadequate to the task of conveying the complexity of psychological truth. In order to describe a world which could have no existence apart from the agents who internalized it, the artist established a new relationship with his work—a relationship that involved him as a man and as a writer as well as a philosopher concerned with basic metaphysical, epistemological and aesthetic problems. It is in his own image that Sterne creates Tristram, as Joyce creates Stephen, Proust Marcel, and Gide Edouard. It is in relation to the surrogate artist that all of the characters are defined. Although they develop identities of their own, it is to the central figure that they are always referred, to their place in the continual flux and reflexivity of his consciousness. It is with profit that we compare Sterne's use of Tristram with Gide's use of Edouard in *The Counterfeiters*, here described by Miss Brée.

69

The problem Gide raises is the problem of maintaining an inner integrity by "composing" honestly out of a double reality one's individual self and the independent workings of the world around one, a self-evaluation that is never final and that is essentially a search for a true form of living.[19]

And the similarities are as great and as interesting between Sterne and Proust, for Marcel looks, with Tristram, into himself in order to find a principle of unity that will give order to the constantly changing self and meaning to the external world that cannot be objectively known. Despite the sophistication of Proust's concept of memory and the mastery with which he communicates and brings together the elements of Marcel's search for identity, the underlying assumptions of his work ally him with Locke.

In the stream-of-consciousness novel the rhythms of the mind replace the movement of a conventional plot sequence. A. A. Mendilow describes the action of this psychological novel as

> . . . the replacing of causality on the plane of action by pure sequence on the plane of thought-feeling—a kind of picaresque novel of the day-dreaming mind.

Sterne, with his associationist-impressionism, prefigured the time-shift technique that came in the wake of Bergson and James.[20] The confused chronology, the complicated system of cross-references, the erratic syntax and the eccentric development of language are all part of the method that Virginia Woolf, for one, consciously adopted. Further, Sterne's treatment of time was, as we have seen, a natural extension of his concepts of the nature of the self and the role of the artist, and it was no less prophetic than these.

Indeed, Hans Castorp in *The Magic Mountain* could well be speaking for Tristram-Sterne as well as for Bergson or James when he says:

> But after all, time isn't actual! When it seems long to you, then it *is* long; when it seems short, why, then it is short. But how long, or how short, it actually is, that nobody knows. . . .
> We say of time that it passes. Very good, let it pass. But to be able to measure it—wait a minute: to be susceptible of being measured, time must flow evenly, but who ever said it did that? As far as our consciousness is concerned it doesn't, we only assume that it does

for the sake of convenience; and our units of measurement are purely arbitrary, sheer conventions.[21]

Similarly, Proust's attempts to overcome Time, to reach self-definition through the analysis of memory and to grasp the images of memory through a process of association are not, on the surface, unlike Sterne's attempts—although the articulations of Proust's concept are clearly more complex. Virginia Woolf's emphasis on psychological time, marked by the mind's reception of and response to impressions, is but an extension of Sterne's associational technique and testifies to the truth of her claims of indebtedness. All of the writer surrogates share with Tristram the painful dilemma in which he finds himself at *Auxerre*. Here all the dimensions of time, which he attempts to maintain distinctly, threaten to converge, burying him in confusion and defeating his attempts at self-definition:

> . . . I am this moment walking across the market-place of *Auxerre* with my father and my uncle *Toby*, in our way back to dinner—— and I am this moment also entering *Lyons* with my post-chaise broke into a thousand pieces——and I am moreover this moment in a handsome pavillion built by *Pringello*, upon the banks of the *Garonne*, which Mons. *Sligniac* has lent me, and where I now sit rhapsodizing all these affairs (VII, 28, p. 516).

It follows as well, that Locke and Bergson's suspicion of language, their sense of the difficulties of expressing that which is intuitive or unique in experience, should be reflected in the writing of both Sterne and his modern counterparts. Because the simultaneity and ambiguity of experience had now to be communicated, the emphasis came to be placed on the connotative and impressionistic aspects of language. It is in *Ulysses* and *Finnegans Wake* that we find the most extreme and exciting development of Sterne's linguistic experimentation.[22] Again a greater sophistication gives rise to a complexity that is quantitatively different from Sterne's technique, but grows from common roots and has a common goal. While Joyce's distortions of language develop from a careful differentiation and description of the conscious, subconscious and unconscious levels of mind, while they are woven together to form an incredibly patterned tapestry of meaning, the effects that they achieve are in many ways similar to those that result from Sterne's more random and limited method.

The germs of parallel development are found also in the concept of character which Sterne shares, in a general way, with the modern psychological novelist. Martin Turnell describes the nature of Proust's "prisoner-hero":

> ... he is the passive victim who is exposed to almost every conceivable kind of pressure and obsession known to human society. For he is the prisoner ... of emotions, habits, of his own sensibility and, ultimately, of time.

The applicability of this definition to Sterne's characters as well as to those of Proust, Joyce, Gide and Virginia Woolf is clear. Similarly, Turnell's definition of Marcel as "the artist-prisoner whose only salvation is in his vocation"[23] is applicable to Tristram as it is to all of the artist-hero figures that dominate and unify the stream-of-consciousness novel.

Because isolation is the result of man's attempt to communicate with other men and because futility and frustration result from his attempts to order and control his external reality, the themes of the modern psychological novel, as those of *Tristram Shandy*, are given a subjective reference. The concern is always with attitude rather than event. Language, death and sexuality are functions of the self, modes of apprehension, expressions of personality. The characters do not act. They are acted upon and must only learn how best to deal with their illusions of freedom. The dilemma is not one which permits of resolution. For Virginia Woolf self-discovery is generally accepted as a prelude to death. For Joyce, as for Sterne, there can be no self-discovery. There is only the endless repetition of the quest.

Sterne, having interpreted Locke freely and prophetically, simultaneously created the stream-of-consciousness novel and brought it to the farthest thematic and structural limits possible for the eighteenth century. It remained for Joyce to explore definitively the formal possibilities of this genre. In *Ulysses* and, more particularly, in *Finnegans Wake*, he produced novels that paralleled *Tristram Shandy* in their eccentricity and originality.

That which makes Sterne so astonishingly contemporary, then, is the sense of relativity, the wise acceptance of absurdity, that is a natural outgrowth of radical empiricism. His sense of absurdity extended to include the futility of human reason, the uselessness of language, the hopelessness of aspiration. Tristram seeks with the anti-hero of the contemporary world an answer to the unanswerable question, "Who am I?"; an escape from the inescapable fact that was himself.

> Inconsistent soul that man is!——languishing under wounds, which he has the power to heal!——his whole life a contradiction to his knowledge (III, 21, p. 203).

This is the paradox of Walter's life, of Toby's life, of Yorick's life. For Sterne it was the paradox of Locke as well. Thus his irony was not limited to petty concerns and small men. Its implications were cosmic. Ultimately it is Sterne's awareness of the aspiration and the eternal frustration that gives his novel its sense of tragedy. It is his insistence upon the common-place, incongruous roots of the aspiration that makes his work comic. With this peculiarly modern, tragi-comic quality, *Tristram Shandy* demands its place as a profoundly serious comment on the human condition. As Sigurd Burckhardt points out:

> Sterne had learned from Swift. As the last irony of *A Modest Proposal* is that it is *not* ironic, that—society being what it is—Swift's ghastly humanitarianism is genuine and an ironic reading merely an evasion of his cruelly literal point, so Sterne's final joke is again and again that he is not joking.[24]

It is in his role of satirist that Sterne identifies himself as a writer of the eighteenth century. In his relation to the reader, in his critical analysis of modes of thought, in his insistence upon participation, he is allied with the Augustans: deeply critical, sharply ironic and, in his view of wit and imagination, ultimately optimistic. Sterne does, in the fascinating complexity of *Tristram Shandy*, demand a large price of his reader, and he does at times verge on complete disaster. But just as Tristram triumphs because he must persist, creating through the fertility of his imagination a sense of the impenetrable multiplicity, so does *Tristram Shandy* itself emerge as a monument to the creative power of art. In this sense the novel does become at last a dialogue between Sterne and the reader, a dialogue from which the reader after much difficulty has profited greatly. Therefore, we can ask of *Tristram Shandy*, as Northrop Frye asks of *Finnegans Wake*:

> Who then is the hero who achieves the permanent quest . . . No character in the book itself seems a likely candidate; yet one feels

that this book gives us something more than the merely irresponsible irony of a turning cycle. Eventually it dawns on us that it is the *reader* who achieves the quest; the reader who, to the extent that he masters the book of Doublends Jined, is able to look down on its rotation, and see its form as something more than rotation.[25]

There is, of course, always the danger that the contemporary reader will find more in this ambiguous and paradoxical work than its author could himself have conceived. The greater danger is that we should, in our pride of complexity, forget the joy and the love of Sterne's work, for Sterne was, above all, an apostle of these. The final irony which we should consider, therefore, is this: he who wrote a work that seems to us so prophetic in its awareness of multiplicity, so incisive in its ironic vision, so brilliant in its complexity of execution, was a confirmed believer in the simplest of truths.

NOTES

1. John Locke, *An Essay Concerning Human Understanding*, ed. A. C. Fraser (Oxford, 1894), Vol. II, IV, iv, 4, 229. All succeeding references will be to this edition.

2. Henri Bergson, *An Introduction to Metaphysics*, trans. T. E. Hulme (New York, 1955), pp. 21–22.

3. Ibid., pp. 24–29.

4. *A History of Western Philosophy* (New York, 1964), pp. 807–808.

5. *Time and the Novel* (New York, 1952), p. 169.

6. New York, 1939, pp. 10–12.

7. *Time and Free Will*, trans. F. L. Pogson (London, 1912), p. 77.

8. Ibid., pp. 165–166.

9. See *Creative Evolution*, trans. Arthur Mitcher (London, 1919), pp. 166–168. Here Bergson expressed a full awareness of some characteristic values of language.

10. Trans. T. E. Hulme (New York, 1955), p. 24.

11. Ibid., pp. 27–28.

12. In 1884 in *Mind*, IX, 1–26, 188–205, James published two articles which put forth two distinctive doctrines. The first, which was later elaborated upon in the ninth chapter of his *Principles of Psychology*, offered a conception of thought as a stream in which relations are the immediate data of perception, and the second described emotion as organic sensation. Bergson, in his first book, *Time and Free Will*, 1889, cites the second article. Later, in an essay in *Revue Philosophique*, LV, 229, he denies any knowledge of the first.

13. Chicago, 1952, p. 154.

14. Ibid., pp. 157–158.

15. James, p. 152.

16. "Freud and Literature," *Literary Opinion in America*, ed. Morton Zabel (New York, 1951), p. 677.

17. "Locke and the Dissolution of the Ego," *Modern Philology* (February 1955), 170.

18. Germaine Brée and Margaret Guiton, *An Age of Fiction: The French Novel from Gide to Camus* (Rutgers, 1957), p. 39.

19. Ibid., p. 38.

20. Mendilow, p. 160.

21. Thomas Mann, *The Magic Mountain* (New York, 1924), p. 66.

22. It is interesting to note that Joyce makes specific mention of Tristram in the second paragraph of *Finnegans Wake*.

23. *The Novel in France* (New York, 1951), p. 375.

24. "Tristram Shandy's Law of Gravity," *ELH* (March 1961), p. 70–71.

25. Northrop Frye, *Anatomy of Criticism* (Princeton, 1957), pp. 323–324.

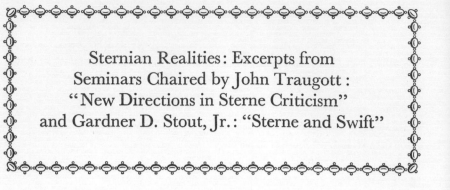

Sternian Realities: Excerpts from
Seminars Chaired by John Traugott:
"New Directions in Sterne Criticism"
and Gardner D. Stout, Jr.: "Sterne and Swift"

Professor John Traugott: Sterne no longer suffers from neo-classical critical principles. The terrible blight that fell upon English criticism when the maxim of Horace that art was to be delight with instruction was rather pompously perverted, I think by Addison, to art as instruction, with delight being the disguise for the instruction, certainly afflicted Sterne's reputation disastrously in the eighteenth and nineteenth centuries. And after all why should not the neo-classical critics have had their revenge upon him? He is a parodist of neo-classical genres, more especially of the techniques of narrative that the eighteenth century and the nineteenth century valued. He was a subversive and often prurient jester obsessed with his duty to demonstrate to the polite world the chaos of its morality, or, as he put it, the proof that the delicacy and concupiscence of the polite world were in fact the same thing. He was as well a jester who brought a radical scepticism to neo-classical notions of rationality and of the integrity of personality. When Johnson, then, said with real animosity, concerning Sterne, that nothing odd will last, I think he was probably defending himself from his fear that existence itself might be odd and might be as indeterminate as Sterne's works suggest.

So the two neo-classical charges against Sterne—that he was immoral and that he was a subversive jester, now are dead letters. As for his immorality, what his contemporaries called his scabbiness, we like that. It might even pass for a virtue today. His subversion of notions of neo-classical reason and personality we find in tune with our own relentless and I am afraid sometimes pompous exposé of absurdity in existence. Not for nothing did Sterne trace his ancestry to Yorick. The Yorkshire parson, Sterne, like Hamlet, certainly

Professors Traugott and Stout are both in the Department of English, University of California at Berkeley imagined that the world's absolute meanings were to be found only in Yorick's empty eyes. But in some miraculous way Sterne finds such a reality a reassuring joke. His sentimentalism is found and nourished in this terrible jest of solipsism. And before we begin I want to quote a brilliant remark by Coleridge (who says the best things about everyone) on Sterne's technique in discovering reality, pointing to the strangeness of existence: "I would remark," says Coleridge, "that there is a sort of knowingness, the wit of which depends—1st, on the modesty it gives pain to; or 2dly, on the innocence and innocent ignorance over which it triumphs; or, 3dly, on a certain oscillation in the individual's own mind between the remaining good and the encroaching evil of his nature—a sort of dallying with the devil . . . so that the mind has in its own white and black angel the same or similar amusement, as may be supposed to take place between an old debauchee and a prude,—she feeling resentment, on the one hand, from a prudential anxiety to preserve appearances and have a character, and, on the other, an inward sympathy with the enemy. . . ."

I think that, with very different moral evaluations from those that Coleridge put upon this technique of Sterne's, these are fundamentally twentieth-century views of the subversive jester in Sterne, and they suggest an aspect of his art that may very well come up in our discussions today—his tinkering with reality, his confusing of fiction and actuality, his destroying of illusion, his making us conscious of convention, and his abolishing of cause and effect in time. The question we ask ourselves very often nowadays is, by what form is this non-classical view of life to be represented? Sterne today makes us ask where the boundaries are between the thing represented and the form and style of its representation. No wonder that the twentieth century has rehabilitated the man, Sterne, and battened on his work as though it were a lifeline to humanity. For here, miraculously, in an eighteenth-century artist, who ignores nature's simple plan, with its springs and cogs, to discover fragmentary and solipsistic life, *we* discover a kind of fellow spirit. We tend, then, to think of Sterne as having, first of all, perhaps because of his connection with Locke, a philosophical apprehension of reality. And then we try to make clear to ourselves the peculiar mode of representation by which Sterne seizes this reality. And finally we are concerned with the technical resources of his style.

Professor Jean-Jacques Mayoux: One might start by drawing attention to Professor Traugott's suggestion that Sterne's world was an

77

anticipation of our world of the absurd. I don't know what the general feeling will be about that. For me Sterne's world was not absurd—although his characters were. I think that it is important to make the distinction that Sterne was very much of his century, inasmuch as there was still in him a kind of confidence, strangely enough, that the world was there. As the philosophers of the empiricist school, whether Locke or Hume or Berkeley, suggested one after the other, it might be out of our reach, we might be living in an enclosed world, but the world was *there*, with some solidity. And after all I'm not sure that Sterne did not even feel that if we were aware and vigilant enough we might have some real contact with it. He had at any rate a strong sense of existence, and even within its bounds and limits, of *being*—a sense of the conditions of existence (quite apart from that fanciful dancing gait of his) which comes out almost from the beginning.

I have in mind passages like this one in Volume I, Chapter 13, about the midwife whose "fame had spread itself to the very out-edge and circumference of that circle of importance, of which kind every soul living, whether he has a shirt to his back or no,——has one surrounding him. . . . In the present case, if I remember, I fixed it at about four or five miles . . ." (p. 35). This seems to me to give an astonishingly vivid sense of what human life really is—this remark about the midwife and her circle of existence, about what radiated from her, what came back to her. And I find myself coming to our own time, and to Virginia Woolf—for here is the genesis of Jacob's room. Jacob's "room"—the word itself, being symbolical—means the concentric circles around Jacob's personality, and the other circles that intersect with it at various points. Possibly, because of modern techniques of communication, Jacob's room might be a hundred miles in circumference rather than five—but it is exactly the same.

Again, there is a kind of hardness to the world itself, of which Sterne is very much aware despite his subjectivity. In this connection, a phrase strikes me: "the country thereabouts being nothing but a deep clay" (p. 12). Here you have something that you would not find in Fielding, or even in Smollett, who also has some sense of this hardness of the world, of the universe we might say,—this strong awareness, I will not say of objective reality, but of the reality of objects. Take the description of the saddle: "he was master of a very handsome demi-peak'd saddle, quilted on the seat with green plush, garnished with a double row of silver-headed studs, and a noble pair of shining brass stirrups, with a housing altogether suitable, of grey superfine cloth, with an edging of black lace, terminating in a deep, black, silk fringe, *poudré d'or*,——all which he had purchased . . ." and so on (pp. 18–19).

This delight in the precision of description is extremely important because it transcends any sort of parodic impulse in Sterne. It seems to me we should examine the way in which Sterne is a parodist—the way in which his use of parody differs from that of the Scriblerians. His delight in the reality of an object like the saddle, an almost sensual delight, suggests that he probably needed that sort of happiness, that joy in coming into contact with the object itself, in absorbing it into himself with such wondrous description. I might remind you again of the chair in which Uncle Toby sat, the chair that was *there* in such a fascinating degree that we felt that it was part of a continuity, that somehow there was a security in the presence of my uncle Toby because of the presence of that chair. The description of the chair shows a sensitive delight in the detail of reality—a strong part of Sterne's imagination of which we must be aware. There is almost a genius for description in him that can easily be neglected in favor of what I have called his gambols.

This delight in objects and objective reality touches, I suppose, on his strong awareness of bodies. But here we come against one aspect of parody. Curiously enough, physical presence, of which he is so much aware, becomes both a mystery and an amusement and a joke in contrast with the subjective life. It is difficult to reconcile subjective life, the inner existence, with the physical aspects of it. You will surely remember what I might call the Lillabullero passage at the end of Chapter 6 of Volume III: "My uncle *Toby* instantly withdrew his hand from off my father's knee, reclined his body gently back in his chair, raised his head till he could just see the cornish of the room,"—here is that same astonishing precision of presence: Sterne's characters are present to him because they are himself, in a way— " . . . and then directing the buccinatory muscles along his cheeks, and the orbicular muscles around his lips to do their duty——he whistled *Lillabullero*" (p. 164). Here again is that fascinating passing from the outside to the inside and then outside again, but in a different manner, which ends in a kind of parody, and yet the parody is meaningful of the awareness of this curious mechanism of our life, our existence.

And so from the body's life we pass to the fascinating aspect of attitude—because here again we have the double aspect. It is too easy to say that when Sterne describes Trim's attitude as he is going to read the sermon it is mere parody of the pompous technicalities of geometry applied to human beings, and also of the pompous aspect of, let us say, Hogarth's *Analysis of Beauty*. Sterne was profoundly seduced by the *Analysis of Beauty*, and we see traces of that aesthetic seduction everywhere in his book. In Trim's attitude there is something that is parody, and yet transcends parody in the delight of representation. Yes, of course, it is comic if you like, but it is also a way in which I can account exactly for physical presence. And this double aspect, this special class of parody, is like Beckett. Remember for instance the beginning of Watt—the presence of Watt as we first see him. Remember, oh, I should say, a hundred passages in every one of Beckett's novels in which you have this reduction of the human being to the mere geometry of his aspect or his movement. Again, there is Watt's way of walking, which is one of Beckett's fantastic gaits, but is described in terms of perfect and strict geometry. It is comic, it is amusing, but it *is*, as I said, a mode of representation.

Let us then take Trim and his attitude: "He stood before them with his body swayed, and bent forwards just so far, as to make an angle of 85 degrees and a half upon the plain of the horizon;——which sound orators, to whom I address this, know very well, to be the true persuasive angle of incidence;——in any other angle you may talk and preach;——'tis certain,——and it is done every day;——but with what effect,——I leave the world to judge! The necessity of this precise angle of 85 degrees and a half to a mathematical exactness,—— does it not shew us, by the way,——how the arts and sciences mutually befriend each other?" This, of course, is the amusement. And again, "How the duce Corporal *Trim*, who knew not so much as an acute angle from an obtuse one, came to hit it so exactly;——or whether it was chance or nature, or good sense or imitation, *&c.* shall be commented upon in that part of this cyclopaedia of arts and sciences, where the instrumental parts of the eloquence of the senate, the pulpit, the bar, the coffee-house, the bed-chamber, and fire-side, fall under consideration. He stood,——for I repeat it, to take the picture of him in at one view, with his body sway'd, and somewhat bent forwards, ——his right-leg firm under him, sustaining seven-eighths of his whole weight,——the foot of his left-leg, the defect of which was no disadvantage to his attitude, advanced a little,——not laterally, nor forwards, but in a line betwixt them;——his knee bent, but that not violently,——but so as to fall within the limits of the line of beauty; ——and I add, of the line of science too . . ." and so on, and so on (p. 122).

This passage it seems to me is wonderful because of that difficult double view—I'm amused and I am amusing, and at the same time. Here I am accounting for something in a way that could not be replaced by any other way—typical of the eighteenth century, per-haps, in its exploration of new ways, including the ways of science. You see the difference from Swift's savage, snarling attacks whenever he comes across anything like science. This is very different, this gentle way of absorbing what a sort of scientific technique of description could give him, while at the same time laughing at it. Still this passage reminds me of what Diderot, who was such a Sternian, as you know, did so seriously: examining the ways in which architects, for instance Michelangelo in the dome of St Peter's and so on, reached their awareness of the perfect dome—whether it was some kind of intuition of such a dome, or whether it was accumulated experience which we then called intuition, and so on. This is a sort of transition to that subject which connects Sterne and Diderot—what I should call the hieroglyph (and here again Professor Davis* has said some meaningful things on this subject). The hieroglyph is the true phrasing, the true expression that would connect us with reality, with the hard object that is *there*. Now we must first of all take into account the inadequacy of spoken or written language—or words, for it is not only the Guten-berg galaxy, but it is simply the fact that we use words, and that they do not normally put us in touch with reality. Not that Sterne is not fascinated with language itself and its possibilities. Remember the passage of the auxiliary verbs, a passage which is again almost Beckettian, since what does it mean except that when I tell a story I am dealing only with contingency and virtualities, and that I am therefore really putting phrases together, putting sentences together, organizing them round their verbs, using auxiliary verbs to modify the negative, the positive, the interrogative sense, and so on. I'm playing with contingencies. It seems to me quite important that my father should have had that matter so clearly in mind.

And another point which is also extremely significant is the story of the white bear, because here is Hamm in *Endgame* telling his story, his final story I think it is, and telling it in a sort of challenging manner,

*Professor Robert Gorham Davis, who participated in the seminars.

making it as grotesque as he can: "It was fine weather. It was horribly windy. It was . . ." and so on—you see the style of it. Well, the white bear story you probably remember: "A WHITE BEAR! Very well. Have I ever seen one? Might I ever have seen one? Am I ever to see one? Ought I ever to have seen one? Or can I ever see one? Would I had seen a white bear! (for how can I imagine it?) If I should see a white bear, what should I say? If I should never see a white bear, what then? If I never have, can, must or shall see a white bear alive; have I ever seen the skin of one? Did I ever see one painted?—described? Have I never dreamed of one?" (pp. 406–407). The whole passage is marvelous, of course, and nothing I think in the whole book is more curiously modern—Ionesco or Beckett, or whoever you like. And this, as you remember, is echoed by my uncle Toby listening to Trim trying to tell his story of the king of Bohemia and his seven castles. Trim succeeds at last in bringing out the king of Bohemia, *happening* to walk out, and then at once he is interrupted by my uncle Toby, who says "*happening* [to walk out] is right." Here is for once a curiously technical awareness of my uncle Toby: "'Twas a matter of contingency, which might happen, or not, just as chance ordered it" (p. 567). This matter of the contingency of all story-telling was to fascinate Diderot first and Beckett last—for Beckett has this kind of horror of contingency, which emerges whenever he pretends to be telling a story.

And so we come back to our point of attitudes, and you see with Trim how we could find silent language—the language of gesture. This touches upon the absolute. Diderot in his *Paradoxe sur le comédien* shows the kind of absolute which can occur in perfect silence. Lady Macbeth washing her hands is to Diderot the most complete bit of reality in the whole play. That is real—nothing else, nothing that she says has that degree of reality. Well, Sterne gives us that with his character who can be so exasperating, and yet is so useful—Corporal Trim. You remember the passage connected with Bobby's death, and how Trim expresses his feelings about that death in two hieroglyphic gestures. First of all, he strikes his stick into the ground, and this, Sterne says, showed how we were *there*, and strongly there—one day— part of this world of reality. And then he dropped his hat, like that, and that showed what death was, better than any long discourse could have done it. Curiously enough, this gesture-speech of Trim's is repeated in the episode of the amours, triumphantly, with the flourish of Trim's stick, and you remember the comment on those thousand syllogisms of my father which would not have been so eloquent about the delights of freedom as that twirl and flourish of Trim's stick. There is therefore in Sterne, and beyond all parody, yet as you see connected with what I have said about attitudes and so on, this search for the speech absolute, because it is a speech which tries to be nearly an awareness of some sort of absolutely physical reality.

* * *

Professor A. A. Mendilow: I should like to bring up the problem of the deep-lying major strategies behind the more local tactics of specific forms or patterns that have been considered hitherto, and I would like to take as my cue a phrase of Professor Davis's that the Sternian world is one governed by irrational chance, a reference by Professor Mayoux to the problems of freedom and necessity, and his reference today to a world that is not the world of the absurd, although the characters are. From that I would like to suggest one of the more deep-lying and fundamental—well, let's use the phrase that Wordsworth used— structures such as the mind builds for itself: that is to say, the grids we place upon actuality to form our own private realities, those ways by which we select, organize and arrange and inform with value and invest with form and meaning the multitudinous, multifarious pheno- mena that impinge on our senses.

Now, I think that I can discern in Sterne (and I think it goes far deeper than Sterne, through an entire theory of genre) two different kinds of entities: one might call them the scheme of things—an open or a closed scheme of things—and the conception of character—an open or a closed conception of character. Let me define my terms very briefly in a sort of oral shorthand. By a closed universe or closed scheme of things I mean the retributive, predestined world governed by Nemesis, Gods, fate, destiny, will, cosmic forces, whatever you will; something calculable, determined, as I say—a mighty maze perhaps, but not without a plan. On a lower social level—the way of the world as some kind of fixed scheme. By an open universe, on the other hand—I mean the incalculable universe, where anything may happen, where the best laid plans of mice and men gang aft agley, the principle of inadvertence; and here chance collocations, the world of chance, may operate. Now I have two schemes of the world, and if you now take characters, you have the open mind, he who regards himself free to challenge as an individual the principles of the universe; and the closed mind—determined, conditioned by codes and conventions.

Now it seems to me that there are in *Tristram Shandy* both types of collocations—well there are four possibilities shall I say?—the closed mind confronting the closed world, perhaps that might be the medieval; the open mind confronting the open world might be the world of the absurd, the modernist, futurist kind of world. What I am concerned with is the confrontation of the opposites. Now if you have the closed world, determined by chance Nemesis, challenged by the individual who wants to assert his own individuality and his freedom of choice, then you might have tragedy—the classical kind of tragedy. On the other hand, if you have the incalculable universe confronted by a person behaving according to the codes as though everything were fixed, you have comedy. As a type example, one might give that of the old film of Charlie Chaplin who is reduced in the wilds of the Arctic north to boiling his boots, and he presents himself with a dish of boiled sole (a lovely pun). The soles of his boots are carefully flavored, presented tastefully on a plate; he eats them delicately, after peppering and salting them, with a knife and fork, and then takes each nail and sucks it. He is behaving according to the code. You have, then, I think, the world of chance confronted by people who conform to a code, irrespective of the incalculable inadvertence of the universe where names, and blinds, and bridges, and noses, and all kinds of things interfere with what one expects, where the historiographer cannot "drive on his history . . . straight forward," where each one has his hobby-horse, his humor, and behaves as though things were fixed. There is one instance of a closed world of what Sterne calls "fatality," namely the "tragedy" of the "mercurial" Yorick who lacked "exact regularity of sense and humours" and outraged the "grand confederacy" of society by his idiosyncratic and unconventional behavior. Eugenius foretold his "destiny" correctly, and he died "quite broken hearted." I think that that kind of pattern might suggest an interesting way of examining the whole structure in the light of some more deep-lying pattern of perception—those patterns that every culture, every age, and every individual has, and which underlie specific codes.

Traugott: It is particularly interesting that Mr Mayoux talks about the way in which Sterne represents the object and the way in which the characters get a hold on reality through the object, and Mr Mendilow talks in larger terms about genre and really comes back to the same thing that everyone does come back to who talks about Sterne, and that is this problem of reality in Sterne. There is very great consciousness in the reader, and in the writer as well, of this problem of reality— what it is. And this is something that does not appear, it seems to me, in other eighteenth-century writers. One never thinks of the problem of the nature of reality in *Clarissa* or in Smollett, and this seems to me an important difference.

Mendilow: That is the point I wanted to return to and that I hoped Professor Mayoux would develop more when he was talking about reality and parody at the beginning, because I was thinking once again of Swift's *Gulliver's Travels,* which is to some extent a parody of stories like *Robinson Crusoe* with their preoccupation with material reality, and to some extent, of course, a parody of the methods of the Royal Society. Now how do you tell, when someone like Swift is describing the Brobdingnagian women as he does with his grotesque particularity, how do you tell when this is primarily a reaction against the literary convention or attitude of mind and when it is primarily an assertion of reality of will? Was Swift really asserting reality in your sense when he was producing those sections of *Gulliver's Travels*?

Mayoux: I suppose, yes—in spite of himself, I would say. This is the difference between Swift and Sterne, who did not do it in spite of himself.

Professor Gardner Stout: I want to ask why you say, "in spite of himself" —in relation to Swift? What current or temperamental bent does it run against in Swift?

Mayoux: Because Swift was, I don't know what the apt neurological analysis would be, but certainly he was schizoidic if not schizophrenic, and by instinct and by impulse he would carry on within something like solipsism almost, and contact with reality had not for him the element that I associated with Sterne, the element of what I call delight. There is no delight in Swift, that is the point it seems to me.

Stout: He is then disgusted by contact with reality?

Mayoux: He is disgusted—or separate. When he is not disgusted, he still is separate, it seems to me.

Professor Claude Rawson: I wonder if I could raise this question of the absurd again, and very largely in support of what Professor Mayoux has said, that there does seem to me to be this very radical difference between the situations in Sterne where gesture takes over from language, and the kind of situation that one gets in books of our own time, as in the famous passage where Camus, describing absurdity in the *Myth of Sisyphus*, gives the image of the man in the telephone box—we see him speaking through the glass but we don't hear him—there is a sense of total dissociation because his words are prevented from reaching out to us. Now in Sterne's situations, for example in the grisette episode in the first volume of *Sentimental Journey* ("The Gloves. Paris") where there is a subtle communication of looks between Sterne and the girl, and Sterne says that all the languages of Babel put together could never really express this communication—there seems to me a very positive faith of an essentially romantic kind in the power of the unspoken to achieve communication. What has been dropped is the rationalist supposition that reason and rational discourse can be a means, or is the only means, to communication; but I think that what has been substituted is a kind of Wordsworthian world—as when Wordsworth feels a bond with the solitary Highland lass precisely because he doesn't understand her language—and where, moreover, unheard melodies are celebrated above heard ones. We have in Sterne a similar kind of comforting closed world where contingency provides the comforts of epiphany and insight and pleasure, as distinct from the organized closed world of the Augustans which is systematic. But it does seem to me that this kind of image suggests how relatively little of a break Romanticism was and what a very dreadful break "cruelty" and "absurdism" with all their suggestion of open-ended, inexplicable alienation, are. And really, all the talk about absurdism being a continuation of Romanticism clearly is true, but has spent itself a bit, and in a sense it is more interesting now to see Romanticism as partly an end product of Augustanism.

Traugott: I think that is a very good point. It brings us to a paradox in Sterne that someone may want to comment on, a paradox that criticism ought to treat: that *Tristram Shandy* is a very gay, reassuring, and in a crazy way optimistic work, in spite of the horrible solipsism, in spite of the black humor, grim things, really terribly grim things, like Walter's speaking to Mrs Shandy about a Caesarian operation and her turning suddenly as pale as ashes as he describes the knife and the way it will go through her (there are really scary things all the way through Sterne when you look beneath the surface). This is a fact that criticism must take account of, that if Sterne is adumbrating the world of absurdity, nevertheless it is quite different from ours, as you say. And there is another quality to account for in Sterne—*how* it comes about that through this terror and absurdity and solipsism Sterne discovers something joyful.

Stout: I would like to suggest one aspect of this problem. Mr Traugott talked earlier about the pompous insistence on absurdity in our time, and I share his feelings. It has become so fashionable, that if we don't see things that way we are a bit out of it. It seems to me that one of the things that Sterne is willing to acknowledge, in a way which I think some modern writers are not, is that he sees perfectly clearly that *Tristram Shandy* itself is a triumph of communication, so that however brilliantly and fully it represents solipsism, it is also the greatest imaginable triumph over the solipsism that it represents. I am not sure how you go about accounting for this, but I think that it is something that Sterne is willing to acknowledge. He is willing to see this aspect of reality—that we are really caught up in these small closed worlds—and to represent this fact fully, and at the same time, with perfect inconsistency, to insist on his ability to break out of solipsistic isolation. And he is not concerned about being inconsistent. It seems to me a good deal of modern writing which insists upon absurdity is so busy maintaining its own decorums and conventions of absurdity that it begins to lose contact with some of its own realities.

Mayoux: It must be stressed, I think, that Walter is a solipsist and Toby is a solipsist, but Tristram is no solipsist.

Traugott: That Tristram is not solipsistic is very important, isn't it, when we talk about freedom and necessity—for somehow Tristram is the freest spirit going in the eighteenth century.

Professor Helene Moglen: I think that might be accounted for by Sterne's celebration of wit and imagination—through the use of metaphor and his whole concept of character, he really does proclaim the ascendancy of imagination over reason. The shortcoming of reason leads to a solipsistic situation, but the way in which you can overcome it is through the delightful use of the imaginative mind, which is what Tristram stands for, after all, I would think.

Traugott: So we come back then to the discussion of wit as a kind of way of apprehending reality—the joy of wit.

Stout: I wonder whether here Sterne's play with Locke isn't very important—and the two knobs on the back of the chair—since his wit, if you consider it in terms of this problem of solipsism, becomes the bridge between two essentially dissimilar objects—the knower and the thing known. And it would become an extension of Sterne's faith in wit to make these assemblages—the thing that Locke didn't want—the assembling with one another of two things which are essentially incompatible, such as Tristram's mind and the world it knows.

Mrs Moglen: Also I think that Tristram stands between Walter as reason and Toby as feeling, both of whom provide this kind of gulf, and it is really Tristram, again with wit, who is able to bridge that.

Mayoux: The two knobs remind me of one aspect which we haven't so far referred to, and that is, of course, symbolism. I mentioned objects as objects, but objects as symbols are extremely important, and I wonder whether, from page to page, we could not trace that curious awareness of the symbol value of objects. Probably the most delightful use of that in the whole book is the chaise-vamper's wife's papillottes in Lyon and how Tristram rescues his remarks from the charming woman's head, but twisted this way and that. It's an admirable symbol, it seems to me, with its sensuous, erotic aspects, but also with this very significant, perpetual tendency to transmute an idea into something plastic, material and significant. It seems to me that this plastic, material embodiment is something that he seeks constantly, and that probably we could find a hundred instances of it.

Stout: The visual effect of the words on the page laid out in order becomes a kind of plastic symbol of time itself.

Mayoux: Well, of the typography generally you might say that there is a musical aspect to Sterne. The structure of dashes and asterisks and all that has certainly a time meaning.

Professor Robert Gorham Davis: Yes, it has been pointed out that you don't have simple linearity of words following each other, but you have lines and you have pages, and you have opposite pages; you can go back and forth between the Latin and the English; you can go back to the book itself, because the book is a volume, is a space in which you can move very freely.

Traugott: All this talk about technique adds up to freedom doesn't it—the freedom of the art and the freedom of the artist? Perhaps someone would like to say something about the role of sentimentalism in this? How does sentimentalism contribute to the sense of freedom that the character Tristram gives us? I think that we tend to suppress, if we like Sterne, the notion that he was a sentimentalist, because the word has such a bad meaning today. But I don't think you can suppress the notion. His sentimentalism may be very intimately connected with this sense of freedom, the sense of being able to bridge the void, to find out who is out there and what it feels like to contact that other being out there. This may be very important in Sterne's whole conception of the freedom of the artist.

Rawson: I think Sterne is able to be coy about wit and to use wit as, in fact, a mode of solipsism. And though I think I agree with you that Tristram isn't a solipsist, I feel fairly persuaded that Sterne, using Tristram, is; and that the kind of freedom Sterne has is precisely the kind of freedom that, in a completely unconscious way, Swift's whole temperament reached for and denied itself in the *Tale of a Tub*, where you have something of Sterne's intimate play of coy self-expression and self-enjoyment, but radically alienated by a sort of parodic opposite—by Swift's so firmly dissociating himself from the author of the *Tale*. In a sense, Swift gets away with being coyly witty and self-indulgent while repudiating coyness and self-indulgence, whereas what has happened in Sterne is that he accepts these qualities with laughter and without any real element of repudiation.

Traugott: That is very good, because there is an obvious connection between Sterne and Swift, and yet they are so very different. And it may be that what Swift had a tendency towards, the unfolding of fantastic metaphors and so forth, which he then parodied or suppressed in some way, Sterne simply took as his method and let it go.

Rawson: He seems the first of a very long line, actually, to use parody as a mode of self-exhibition. After him came Byron, Laforgue, Wallace Stevens, etc.

Another participant: I would like to say a word about sentimentalism. The sentiment throughout *Tristram Shandy*, which is characteristic of humanity above all, isn't sentimentality, which I take to be something cheaply overdone. In the few passages that we take exception to and say, this is patently ridiculous, we are just having our emotions played with. These always seem to me to be just Sterne having a joke with us. In some of the passages that have been regarded as indecent, I think he is just trying to shock us—the Abbess of Andoüillets is one example of course of the sheer willful wish to shock us—and I think he is doing the same thing, for example, with Le Fever, where he brings the thing to a sort of tragical conclusion, but when you get to the end, it isn't tragic at all—as you take out your handkerchief he knocks you on the head: "shall I go on?——No" (p. 426).

Traugott: He certainly makes fun of himself, doesn't he? But you can't escape the fact that sentimentalism, in a good sense that is, is the apprehension by sentiment of other human beings.

Rawson: Aren't we talking at cross purposes, if I may say so? I mean there is a certain sense of *sentimentalism*, which I thought Mr Traugott was using, the historical sense, in relation to a certain kind of attitude towards the life of feeling. Then there is a pejorative sense, which you are assuming.

Mayoux: But it is difficult to escape the fact that in the most pejorative sense Sterne is a sentimentalist also. If you read the *Journal to Eliza* you cannot escape it.

Another participant: It seems to me that in *Tristram Shandy* he gets the better of it by puncturing the sentiment with a joke and that all the most sentimental episodes end either in a kind of joke or anti-climax.

Rawson: But the puncturing itself is sentimental in a bad sense, I would say. There's a kind of self-exhibition through the puncturing of one's own sentiment which becomes a kind of playing with oneself.

*　　*　　*

Traugott: To compare Swift and Sterne: it seems to me that a problem we have consistently recurred to is, how does Sterne perceive reality? What is reality in Sterne? Swift, on the other hand, takes his stand with the tradition of natural law. That is, he hopes that the world is much as, say, Aquinas or Hooker described it: that there is a rational scheme to the universe. He hopes there is, but in the end he doesn't believe it. And so *Gulliver's Travels* is in the end a very despairing and I think bleak book by a man who has taken his stand with a certain view of existence and cannot find enough support for it. Now Tristram's sceptical book asks, what is beyond me, how can I find it, how can I apprehend it, how can I feel it? So there are quite different kinds of irony in *Tristram Shandy* and *Gulliver's Travels*.

I think you have only to look at the King of Brobdingnag's, or the Houyhnhnm's, remarks on England to see that they are saying simply that men ought to act according to natural law but that in fact they don't. This disparity is a horrible thing for Swift. It's not just that he is outraged because they don't, but that, underneath it all, he knows they can't.

Stout: I wonder if this bears on the way in which Swift, I think, tends to accuse people of being human beings?—on the curious state of mind in which he goes at you because he has discovered you are human?

Professor Denis Donoghue: Doesn't Swift attack you also not just because he discovers you are human, but he discovers that you are aspiring to be God. It seems to me that he is constantly attacking what he deems to be the most arrant pretensions of all kinds, because we may say he has a fairly restricted notion of what it means to be human, and the boundaries of the human are destroyed by pretensions of this kind—and that way danger and madness lie. It seems to me that when he is inveighing against pride it is on the basis of an essentially restricted notion of what being human means. This is why I think that his satire is powerfully directed against attempts to evade the limitations of humanity and it's also why, certainly by twentieth-century standards, we must say that his notion of the psychological possibilities of being human is restrictive. This is one of the reasons why we are in some senses more attuned to Sterne, who allows us to be twentieth-century in certain respects—in respects which Swift would really forbid us to be, or ridicule us for being.

Traugott: No. I just don't agree with you at all. It seems to me that Swift is *not* attacking mankind for aspiring too high; surely it isn't aspiring too high to wish not to blow people up, or not to produce wars which destroy cultures and humanity; this is not aspiring too high, this is only what human beings ought to aspire to, in Swift's scheme of things. It isn't to being divine or anything like that; it's just to being decent—whatever they are, I can't use the term human beings, because that's destroyed—but to being rational beings.

Rawson: But in a sense, doesn't Swift's style carry us a great deal further than this—to all kinds of subversions that are not the official theme? While a work like *Gulliver*, or the *Tale*, sets up ideals of restraint and good sense, the feeling of the work as Swift produces it is full of lack of restraint, full of emotional violence—the way ideals of decorum are set up or implied and the way Swift performs all kinds of indecencies within the work. There seems to be here a kind of Swiftian relationship with his own standards which is profoundly subversive of these standards in a way in which *Tristram Shandy* is not in the least subversive. *Tristram Shandy* creates a kind of total permissiveness for itself, so that nothing that Tristram ever does has any real air of revolt against any standards that are at all alive in the book. In that kind of sense I would like to suggest, outrageous as it may sound, that what the *Tale of a Tub* is really parodying is Sterne, in advance—that it is subversive precisely because Swift has this Shandian potential in sight here, and is also attacking it.

Stout: I think there are some respects in which you could say that, though not in a conscious, programmatic way. *Tristram Shandy* comprises many of the same facts that are exhibited in the world of *A Tale of a Tub* and *Gulliver's Travels*; and that, through many of the same devices, it redeems those worlds, domesticates them. It seems to me that if you put Uncle Toby and the Yahoo together, it is hard to avoid the feeling that Sterne was aware of and exploited the contrast between them. After all Swift describes a soldier as a Yahoo hired to kill other Yahoos in cold blood; and in *Tristram Shandy* we get Uncle Toby.

* * *

Mayoux: I would like to make a very simple suggestion about Sterne's and Swift's uses of irony. It seems to me that *irony* is almost a worn word that we have largely replaced in modern idiom with the word *distance*. Distance always tends to be ironic distance, so to speak. In this way I think we can easily distinguish what happens first to the Sternian characters and then to the Swiftian. Obviously there is a difference between Yorick and Tristram as characters. In *Tristram Shandy*, Yorick is from the first seen sentimentally—remember the three chapters of the first volume which are so sentimental and in which you wonder whether he can be so sentimental about a self-image without at the same time laughing at it. In the same way, in the *Sentimental Journey* surely Sterne is being sentimental, about Yorick, about his travels and so on. And being sentimental to such an extent, he cannot help being amused at his own sentimentality. Even in the title, I think, you see that distance projected, so to speak. On the other hand, it seems to me that there is practically no distance between Sterne and Tristram, and this is the important thing. There is no distance between Sterne and Tristram, but all the distance comes within Tristram's own personality, and it is that distance through which he plays with all that he encounters—which is the superb and gay irony of the book. On the other hand, we could say that there is

SONG WRITTEN BY STERNE, possibly Sterne and
Garrick, for Catherine Fourmantel. In *A Collection
of New Songs Sung by Mr. Beard, Miss Stevenson and
Miss Fromantel* [sic] *at Ranelagh*, 1765, at the
Library of King's College, Cambridge.

STERNE'S REPUTED BIRTHPLACE in Mary Street, Clonmel, Co. Tipperary, Ireland. Standing before the house, Dr Philip O'Connell, Clonmel antiquarian. See No. 2, p. 280.

obviously a great distance between Swift and Gulliver, but no distance at all within Gulliver's perception; and that is why, in spite of my reservations concerning the subconscious psyche, which seems to me so important, I would grant you easily that Gulliver is no character in the sense that Tristram is, precisely because there is no distance at all within Gulliver himself.

THREE

Sterne and his Time

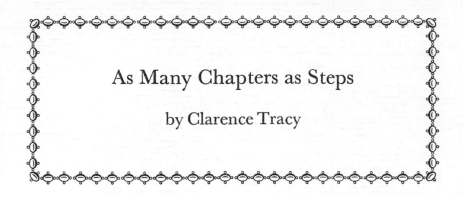

As Many Chapters as Steps

by Clarence Tracy

"Nothing odd will do long," Johnson once said to Boswell when the latter had been ridiculing a publication by their friend Baretti that he described as "some ludicrous fantastick dialogues between two coach-horses, and other such stuff." Then, to back up his observation with an illustration, he added: " 'Tristram Shandy' did not last."[1] Whether or not his association of ideas—*Tristram Shandy* with Baretti's ludicrous fantastic stuff—would have amused Sterne is a question that must be left to those more expert in the Sternian sensibility; but *Tristram Shandy* did last, and Johnson's pronouncement has gone down to posterity as an example of the obtuseness that is typical of critics when confronted with works of original genius. Nevertheless critics are still agreeing with him about its oddness, calling it a work *sui generis* and thinking of it as a sport in the generations of the eighteenth-century novel. But are they, and was Johnson, right? Was *Tristram Shandy* really so very odd?

Johnson's judgment does not concern us here, but those of the moderns do. The trouble is today that readers and critics are apt to have preconceived notions of what an eighteenth-century work of literature should be like and of what characteristics would make it odd. There is a myth that the eighteenth century was unoriginal, overmuch concerned with form and the classical genres, and hence incapable of a *Tristram Shandy* except as a vagary of genius. It is strange that an age that discovered and developed the realist novel and the intimate biography should be called unoriginal. But the charge respecting the genres is easier to understand; writers in that period did think a lot about them, if only out of respect for what they had meant to writers in the past. What is often overlooked is that in the eighteenth century the genres were malleable and that the great writers of that age seldom

Professor of English, Acadia University

stuck to any of them with pedantic fidelity. In fact, few ages have had a stronger sense of contemporary values than the eighteenth century or less respect for literary antiquarianism. The genres, even while being deferred to, were bent to new, contemporary uses, a process in which they were combined with one another and revamped with a free hand. Three of them—the elegy, the panegyric, and the satire—permuted and transformed explain, according to Rachel Trickett, most of the poetry of the School of Wit.[2] Addison, wishing to gain critical acceptance for that disreputable genre the ballad, held over it the critical umbrella of the epic and won his case, though nobody thought him silly enough to mistake *Chevy Chase* for an epic. Everybody, however, was prepared to accept a basic similarity between things very much unlike in appearance. In Pope, that great master of modernization, all the genres became as fluid as the bodies of his sylphs:

> Transparent Forms, too fine for mortal Sight,
> Their fluid Bodies half dissolv'd in Light.

Now the novelists were working in a new genre and felt a little insecure. There were no rules and few precedents for them except what had been provided by the romances, a kind of fiction for which there was at the time little critical respect. Though the novelists were not afraid of novelty and were prepared to erect a Palladian mansion on the foundations of the old Gothic manor house, they liked the feeling that there were foundations to build upon. Fielding, the most classically minded of them all, invoked the authority of Homer and conceived his theory of the comic epic in prose to win critical acceptance for a kind of writing that was essentially new. Richardson, in *Clarissa*, straddled precedents so diverse as Greek tragedy and the commercial letter writer's manual. Consequently Sterne, when he began to write, found the genres in a plastic condition and the public prepared for a high-handed treatment of them. He went to work more jauntily than the others, parading novelty and eccentricity where they had paraded conformity to tradition. His most striking innovations, however, were in technique and manner: such as his cheeky punctuation, for example, which concealed basic qualities that place him in the very heart of the eighteenth century. His reliance on the epistemology of Locke aligns him with the central tradition of the thought of his age, and his latitudinarian theology was far from eccentric. Many precedents, moreover, existed for a satire on pedantry, and comedy was a dominant mode of writing in the time. The ties that bind *Tristram Shandy* to its age are numerous.

One of those ties that critics have failed to notice is the striking similarity between developments in the eighteenth-century novel, especially Sterne's, and those in eighteenth-century biography, though Professor Pottle has recently remarked on Boswell's debt to Richardson.[3] This failure is the more surprising because biography, next to the novel, is the most important new literary mode in which the eighteenth century chose to express itself, and because the two obviously have much in common. Fielding often referred to his novels as biographies, when he was not calling them epics, and most of the novelists of the period gave titles to their works that suggest biographies: "The Life and Strange Surprising Adventures of . . . ," "The Life of . . . ," "The Life and Opinions of. . . ." This association came about naturally. As a branch of history, biography commended itself in an age devoted to the empirical investigation of truth and it had respectable antecedents in the sixteenth and seventeenth centuries, to say nothing of Plutarch. The novel, on the other hand, had at first to contend with a deep-seated prejudice against fiction, and, before 1770, was ashamed of its only direct literary ancestor, the romance. Consequently both Defoe and Richardson pretended that they were not the authors of fictions but the editors of documents containing true histories—a pretence that reappeared in many a novel through the century and that was parodied by Richard Graves in *The Spiritual Quixote* (1773) and Jane Austen in *Northanger Abbey* (1818). Consequently it would be easy for what Sterne called the naive reader to confuse an epistolary novel of the period with one of the ever-popular collections of actual letters or with a biography in the life-and-letters tradition, such as Mason's *Gray*. Indeed, readers and writers then seldom drew the hard and fast line that we are accustomed to between creative or imaginative literature on the one hand and scientific or historical writing on the other, and would have been puzzled by the controversy that was such a bother to Harold Nicholson, Virginia Woolf, and others, over whether or not biography is an art or a science. The eighteenth-century reader, even if not deceived into mistaking a novel for a biography, nevertheless expected it to be a faithful imitation of nature and to give him an accurate account of the manners of an age and of human character and behavior in all ages. He had very much the same expectations from a biography.

In the eighteenth century, biography was rising rapidly in popularity and undergoing a transformation. Older biography had concerned itself mainly with kings, statesmen, generals, and saints, and its avowed purpose had been to hold up to the younger generation models of wisdom and virtue. Though intimate details were seldom entirely avoided, and in a domestic idyl like Roper's life of More one was even given a glimpse of the subject's hair shirt, the style on the whole was formal and the effect statuesque. Oddly enough, during the later seventeenth century the protocol grew even stiffer. Thomas Sprat, for example, writing the life of Cowley in 1668, explained that though he had in his hands a number of Cowley's private letters, full of "native tenderness and innocent gaiety," he had decided to omit them from his biography because Cowley's soul appeared in them "undressed" and in a "negligent habit, . . . fit to be seen by one or two in a chamber, but not to go abroad into the streets."[4] In biography, evidently, one should encounter only the public face. Accordingly Plutarch's edifying lives of Greek and Roman statesmen were retranslated as a textbook on morals, and Isaac Walton added five saints to the hagiography of his national church. But in the eighteenth century this starched-shirt kind of biography soon began to be out of place and before long gave way to something more relaxed and informal, more in keeping with the temper of the new age.

The campaign against the grand style in biography was led by Roger North in a general preface to his *Life of the Lord Keeper North* that must have been written before 1734 but that remained in manuscript until it was partially rescued from oblivion in 1962 by Professor James Clifford. In it North expressed himself trenchantly on the theory of biography. He was an out and out advocate of plain truth and the private face. "What signifies it to us," he asked, "how many battles Alexander fought. It were more to the purpose to say how often he was drunk. . . ." But North was not a muck-raker; he merely believed that more useful lessons could be learned from a narrative that told the unvarnished truth about human behavior than from the most carefully composed exemplum. "I should gladly meet with an author," he went on to say, "that in the course of a written life delineates to us in lively examples the precipitous steps, and dangerous meanders of youth, the difficulties of riper years, and the fondness of old age, and where one may see distinctly the early application of some persons to proper employments, with the eventual prosperities attending them.

As by what small beginnings they advanced to great estates, with the methods, and true causes of it stated. And on the other side the devious courses, and errours of persons vicious and idle, who from plentiful fortunes, and fair reputations, fell to want, and more than balanced the account of their luxury and folly, by substantial misery and infamy." The clue to men's successes and failures in life, he felt, was to be found not in their public actions, which are only the visible portion of the iceberg of character, but in the minutiae of their daily lives, in how they behave at dinner, how they treat their families, friends, servants, and dogs, in how they go up and down stairs. Nor, according to North, are such facts necessarily dull; it all depends on the skill of the writer. In a passage strongly suggestive of Sterne, he wrote: "After all a dullness is never to be charged on a subject but on the author. . . . An Italian found means to raise up an heroic poem upon a village quarrel about a water bucket, and a Frenchman upon the lazy friar's contest about the reading desk, not forgetting Rabelais' bloody war about a plum cake."[5] Had he been writing a third of a century later, he might have added Sterne's amusing tale about a cock and a bull.

Why North's preface was not published in the eighteenth century is not known, but his opinions did percolate out through incidental statements and concrete examples in his published biographies. Samuel Johnson, who held similar ones on biography, was not so reticent. His *Account of the Life of Mr. Richard Savage* (1744), his best biography, is a splendid realization of his theories, which so far he had not given to the public. But essays by him on the subject appeared fairly soon in the *Rambler* (1750) and the *Idler* (1759). More pointed comments were made in his conversations, the record of which does not antedate his first meeting with Boswell in 1762 and mostly did not get into print until Boswell brought out his *Tour* in 1785 and his *Life of Johnson* in 1791. But, unlike North, Johnson was a celebrated personage whose opinions on literary as well as other matters were widely reported by word of mouth. They may be briefly summarized by saying that he believed strongly in the value to biographical writing of what he called at some times *anecdotes* and at others *diminutive observations*.[6] He used the word *anecdote* in the French sense and defined it in his *Dictionary* (fourth edition) as "a biographical incident; a minute passage of private life." He urged Boswell to fill his journal with them, and in his *Journey to the Western Islands* (1775) he defended them:

These diminutive observations seem to take away something from the dignity of writing, and therefore are never communicated but with hesitation, and a little fear of abasement and contempt. But it must be remembered, that life consists not of a series of illustrious actions, or elegant enjoyments; the greater part of our time passes in compliance with necessities, in the performance of daily duties, in the removal of small inconveniences, in the procurement of petty pleasures; and we are well or ill at ease, as the main stream of life glides on smoothly, or is ruffled by small obstacles and frequent interruption.[7]

His fear of abasement and contempt was not without cause. The author of an anonymous *Art of Criticism* published in 1789 remarked that Johnson shared with Plutarch "a considerable spice of the old woman," and as late as 1809, when the art of biography had been almost taken over by gossips, a Yankee by the name of Royall Tyler emerged from his backwoods to observe in a volume of essays called *The Yankee in London* that Johnson had "set the fashion of this gossiping biography." He went on to castigate him soundly for collecting "those little ana which make weak readers laugh and wise men grieve. From him we learn that Addison tippled, and his wife was a termagant; that Prior affected sordid converse in base company, and that his Chloe was a despicable drab; that Pope was a glutton, and fell sacrifice to a silver sauce-pan, in which it was his delight to heat potted lampries; and that Rag Smith was a sloven." But the protest came too late and would have been in vain even if it had come earlier. Nearly everyone in the late eighteenth century was liberally spiced with the old woman and was scribbling anecdotes like mad.

That Johnson and other eighteenth-century biographers used anecdotes freely has long been well known, but critics have not discriminated clearly enough the motives for their use and so have failed to appreciate the full significance of the changes that were being made in the art. One may distinguish three motives: the scientific, the aesthetic, and the ethical.

As to the first of these, it was recognized that truthfulness is the most valuable quality that a biography may possess, and eighteenth-century biographers turned their backs on the deductive methods used by writers like Walton. Antiquarianism flourished, biographical reference books proliferated, biographies began to be documented and footnoted, and facts came to be considered valuable in themselves even when the biographer could not draw conclusions from them. Indeed, the besetting sin of biographies in this period is to be lumpy with facts, a sin that sometimes inspired satirists but that really was the shadow cast by a virtue. For to the eighteenth-century empiricist—and all the best eighteenth-century biographers were empiricists—truth is first apprehended through its smallest units of fact, units small enough to be clearly seen and rigorously verified. General concepts, such as interpretations of character, may be legitimately formed only after all the data are in. Accordingly the eighteenth-century biographer was first of all a collector of facts whose use of anecdotes or diminutive observations grew out of his scientific scepticism and his inductive methods.

The second use of anecdotes was aesthetic. Biography is an art as well as a science. The biographer has not only to investigate the truth but also to present it in a manner that will arrest the attention of the reader and make a lasting impression. The value of the visual image to the poet was clear in the eighteenth century: Johnson's Imlac served his apprenticeship as a poet not only in playing the sedulous ape to all the great poets of the past but also in ransacking the world for images for later use in his own poems. The biographer, too, needed images, or anecdotes, or details—they are not all the same thing but are like enough to show the parallel lines on which poetry, the biography, and the novel were developing. Roger North, in a passage already quoted, expressed his conviction that such details need not be dull so long as the writer has the skill to make them interesting. He might have gone farther and pointed out that it is such details, when rightly handled, that make a biography lively. Johnson never discussed the aesthetics of biography—only its ethics—and in his own biographies used anecdotes less frequently than might have been expected. But when he tells us about Swift's washing his hands with oriental scrupulosity, or Thomson's following with his lip the words spoken by the actors performing one of his own plays, or Cowley's first coming upon the *Faerie Queene* in the window-seat of his mother's cottage, or of Cromwell's riding abroad in a tie-wig, he may have been letting us into the secret places in those men's souls, but, as he must have been well aware, he was also painting indelible pictures on our memories.

In the third place the anecdote was used as an instrument for carrying out the ethical purpose of biography. Earlier biographies had normally been written about the public lives of exalted personages, who were held up for either approval or detestation depending on whether or not their actions accorded with accepted moral standards. But the eighteenth-century biographer discovered that the lives of ordinary men are as full of ethical import as those of the great and are rather more worth study because the issues raised by them are ones with which we ourselves may be confronted. "I have often thought," remarked Johnson, "that there has rarely passed a life of which a judicious and faithful narrative would not be useful."[8] That is a characteristically strong, Johnsonian statement, not perhaps to be taken literally, but to be read as an indication of the way his mind was going. His final word should be noted. When he wrote "useful," he did not mean that such biographies might be used as simple parables of right and wrong, like Bishop Hall's *Characters of Virtues and Vices*. Johnson's moral world was more complex than that. The general principles of the moral life, no doubt, to his mind, had been laid down in revelation, but the application of them to particular cases is not always clear; much may be learned from the study of the circumstances in which actual lives are lived. In his own biography of Savage, for example, he presented his subject as neither a good man nor a bad one, but as an unhappy one whose unhappiness was due partly to his own folly and partly to his fate. Accordingly Johnson wound up by writing: "This Relation will not be wholly without its Use, if. . . ." And he completed the sentence by enumerating the moral conclusions that a thoughtful person might draw from the life of even such a dubious character as Richard Savage. Johnson may have picked up this approach from one of his most revered intellectual heroes, Francis Bacon, who had suggested in his *Advancement of Learning* that a new, scientifically based ethical system may be formulated only after a great many biographies have been written, biographies that will be case histories like that of Savage, which study the ways in which men have achieved happiness or failed to achieve it. To adapt a phrase used by a later practitioner, the biographer is a naturalist of souls, a collector of moral specimens for laboratory study. The biographer's concern is with the real world of imperfect, suffering humanity, seen in all its cross-purposes and moral confusions, and especially with average human experience for it provides him with the random samples that as a scientist he can deal with. He looks with particular interest not only at the common man, but at his daily life, which is made up of trivia.

For the eighteenth century had learned that the seat of the moral life is inward and that men's happiness often depends more on his small actions than on his great ones—on a gesture, an inflection of the voice, a turning to the left rather than to the right. It is on such steps as these that he climbs to happiness or descends into misery.

With modifications the same three motives for the use of anecdotes were as operative with the novelist as with the biographer. Setting out also to delineate character and to depict the manners of society, the novelist also found that the most effective way to do so was through atoms of apparently verifiable fact. Of course, being a novelist, he was free to invent his facts. But at the same time, having to reckon with the natural tendency of his readers to dismiss his work as mere fiction, he was at pains to win confidence by making it look as much as he could like a biography. Various mythical devices were resorted to: the old manuscript found in a chest of drawers, the epistolary correspondence of which the novelist was merely the editor, the pseudo-autobiography. And he introduced masses of facts and pseudo-facts. Now, almost the best known fact about Sterne is his interest in detail, or what Johnson called diminutive observations or anecdotes and Roger North minutiae. This is commonly traced back to Locke and his emphasis on the percept, especially the visual one—in other words it is accounted for in terms of eighteenth-century empiricism. Though not dealing in real facts like the biographer's, facts that have to be won with the hard labor of research, Sterne nevertheless gave the impression that his story was a true one, a genuine family history that might be authenticated by documents just as a biography might. In the first volume of *Tristram Shandy* alone, for example, he referred his readers to such source materials as his "father's pocket-book, which now lies upon the table" (I, 4, p. 9), to the mid-wife's license to practise (7, p. 12), to "a most antient account of the [Yorick] family, wrote upon strong vellum, and now in perfect preservation" (11, p. 23), to "*Saxo-Grammaticus's Danish* history" (p. 24), to his mother's marriage settlement (14, p. 36 ff.), and to a memorial presented to the doctors of the Sorbonne (20, pp. 58–62). And so on through the remaining eight volumes. These citations were, of course, part of his satire on pedantry, but nevertheless they also help to establish the credibility of the narrative. This, Sterne seemed to be saying, is a true story about real people, and if you doubt any part of it Tristram will be happy to let you examine his documents. Sterne's pseudo-facts were mingled with such masses of real facts drawn from the common fund of human experience in the eighteenth century that the whole blended together in the reader's mind as a history of unimpeachable veracity.

Intimately blended with this scientific or pseudo-scientific use of anecdotes in the novel was their use for aesthetic reasons—to give vividness. In spite of the strange vagaries that Sterne gave way to, *Tristram Shandy* has many of the characteristics of Flemish realism in painting. Few novels of any period of time leave more brilliant pictures on one's memory than it does. The scenes that took place on the bowling green, for example, with its hedge and sentry-box, its drawbridge and its mortars made from old boots—to say nothing of the Widow Wadman—shine in retrospect like the illustrations in some childhood story book. The reason is mainly Sterne's use of detail, especially visual imagery. Examples may be found anywhere. Remember, for example, the poor ass, "who had just turned in with a couple of large panniers upon his back, to collect eleemosunary turnip tops and cabbage-leaves; and stood dubious, with his two forefeet on the inside of the threshold, and with his two hinder feet towards the street, as not knowing very well whether he was to go in, or no" (VII, 32, p. 522). That is merely one of numerous similar incidents, and it was chosen because it suggests another famous entrance, this one from Boswell's *Johnson*:

> When we entered Mr. Dilly's drawing room, he found himself in the midst of a company he did not know. I kept myself snug and silent, watching how he would conduct himself. I observed him whispering to Mr. Dilly, "Who is that gentleman, Sir?"—"Mr. Arthur Lee."—JOHNSON. "Too, too, too," (under his breath), which was one of his habitual mutterings. . . . "And who is the gentleman in lace?"—"Mr. Wilkes, Sir." This information confounded him still more; he had some difficulty to restrain himself, and taking up a book, sat down upon a window-seat and read, or at least kept his eye upon it intently for some time, till he composed himself. [9]

In both these extracts surely what gives them liveliness is detail.

Finally the third use of anecdotes in Sterne, the moral one, scarcely needs to be enlarged upon. They anchor the narrative firmly in common life, the life led by people like ourselves. My uncle Toby's saving the life of a fly, Susannah's dreaming of a green silk night-gown,

Corporal Trim's dropping his hat, or My Father's coming down stairs with leaden footsteps—a chapter at a time—are the stuff of our own lives and lead us to reflect on our common destinies, on our relations with our friends, and our duties to our neighbors, and on the means whereby we may seek joys and share our sorrows. They take us into the recesses of the human heart. Though it is not the business of the novelist to construct a system of teaching out of these data of moral experience, like Bacon's ideal biographer, nevertheless they are charged with moral meanings that must have been deliberate and that the sensitive reader will not misunderstand. Moreover, as Roger North saw, they are more meaningful than the exempla of Plutarch drawn from the ranks of the exceptional. The novel like the biography had become a school of common life and in so doing both had become prime instruments of moral comprehension.

The extensive use of anecdotes in eighteenth-century biography also necessarily affected its structure. Earlier biographies had what might be called closed form; they consisted of a series of selected facts arranged in chronological order sandwiched between a formal intro-duction and a carefully composed character-sketch that served as a conclusion. The latter is most significant; it was the *pièce de resistance* of the whole performance, and it owed much to character-writers such as Overbury, Webster, Hall, and Earle. The assumption behind it is that individual human character is unchanging, and that every aspect of it that reveals itself from time to time on one's journey from birth to death may be schematized. Even the child was only the man in miniature to an age unaware of child psychology. Character in these posed portraits, moreover, was seen as a generalization and not in-duced point by point from the subject's actions; indeed, there was often little or no explicit tie-in between the facts and the character-sketch, and what little there was is the wrong way on: the character determined the facts, rather than the facts the character. Remnants of this way of writing, to be sure, survived into the eighteenth century. Johnson's *Savage* ended with a character-sketch, and each of his *Lives of the Poets* had one to serve as a connecting link between its bio-graphical and its critical portions. Even Boswell's *Johnson* ended with a character-sketch. But though these biographies retained something of the old form, a new spirit is felt. Johnson did not confine his comments on Savage's character to the final sketch, but allowed him to reveal himself to us through his words and actions as he lived. Boswell's character-sketch of Johnson, though long, is so unmemorable that few readers remember it. Before we come to it we have lived through a couple of thousand pages consisting mostly of anecdotes that have made Johnson talk and act before our eyes, establishing his character in a dynamic way that makes the sketch otiose. Moreover, though he undoubtedly had preconceptions about Johnson's character and consciously or unconsciously distorted the image to some extent in order to satisfy his own psychological needs, Boswell did not present *his* Johnson as the final, definitive one. He gave us all the facts he had, but he admitted that he did not know everything there was to know. He never penetrated the secret of the orange peels, for example, and he wished that all of Johnson's friends had also kept journals from which even more facts might have been retrieved. "Had his other friends been as diligent and ardent as I was," he wrote, "he might have been almost entirely preserved."[10] Boswell's words remind one of those of Saint John in the closing chapter of his gospel, to the effect that the whole world would not contain all the books that might be written on his subject. This is why Boswell's form is open. Long as his book is, it is only the beginning of an ideal one that might have gone on forever, there being no logical limits in the form itself.

Resemblances in form between the biography and the novel are not hard to find. The novelists, like the biographers, retained an interest in the formal character-sketch and often used it for the purpose of introducing a new member of their dramatis personae. But in the novel, as in the biography, it declined steadily in importance during the century, falling from its position as a posed full-length portrait to become little more than a stage direction. Sterne more than once drew attention to this change in technique: once, for example, in the blank leaf on which the reader was invited to draw his own sketch of the Widow Wadman, and again in the sketch of Uncle Toby that apparently never got written—that is, formally—but that was actually being written dynamically in the words and actions of Uncle Toby himself all the time that work on it was being postponed. This change from statics to dynamics involved a new type of structure. Since both novels and biographies had come to consist mainly of anecdotes, each of which was trivial in itself—like Johnson's orange peels and the squeaky door-hinge in the Sterne house—and since selectivity was minimized, obviously length became important. If truth was to be inferred from a mass of small facts, room had to be made for that mass. Just as Bos-

A **Paragraph** taken from the *York-Courant*,
June 9th **1741**.

YORK *June* 9th **1741**.

YESTERDAY in the Afternoon before a very numerous Body of
Citizens collected for that Purpose, was launch'd a new Keel belonging to the Famous *John Garbut*, well known in this City by the Name
of *General Garbut*, and named the Kaye and Wentworth. It is to go
upon the Coal Trade chiefly; And it is to be hoped that all the *Honest*
Citizens will ever remember both the Name of the Vessel and the *great
Services done to the Publick by the Master of it*, at the last Election.

From the *York Gazetteer*, *June* 16th **1741**.

YORK, *June* 16th 1741.

THE great Sense of Gratitude express'd in the last Week's *Courant*,
for the Services which *Garbut* had done the Public at the late
Election for the City, has given Rise, to the following Querys, which are
seriously address'd to the unprejudiced.

1st *Query*. Whether, in *Foro Conscientiæ*, there are not many kinds of
Bribery besides That, of giving Money? If so, Whether Those who Caress
and pay public Court to such a Fellow as *Garbut*, for the Services he
has done them, are not guilty of one of the lowest and most infamous
Species of it?

2d. *Query*. Whether Elections ought not by our Laws to be Free,
unawed and undisturbed? If so, Whether a Person who raised and headed
Tumults to perplex and prolong them, and was distinguished for Nothing
but a riotous, insulting Behaviour, deserves either Thanks or Recompence,
from any but *Those*, who are Enemies to the Constitution, and consequently to their King and Country.

3d. *Query*. Whether Those who can stoop to work with so low a Tool
as *Garbut*, and when the Work is over can still stoop lower to Thank
and Flatter him, have not let fall'n the Mask of Patriotism and discovered
under it, more of the Spirit of Slavery than Liberty?
If these Querys should be answer'd to the disadvantage of the Author
of the Paragraph in the *Courant* (as they must be, by every cool and im-
partial Man)

4th *Query*. Whether the Author of the said Paragraph from his many
clumsy Attempts at Wit, and this last Instance of his surprizing Genius
both for History and Politicks, has not left it a disputable Point in which
of the Three he deserves most Contempt?

YORK, *August* 31st **1741**.

ON *Saturday* last the famous *John Garbut*, well known in this City
by the Name of *General Garbut*, Master of a New Keel called
the *Kaye* and *Wentworth*, who was lately so much extolled in the *York
Courant* for the Services he had done the Public, was apprehended at *Selby*,
and committed to *York-Castle* for returning from Transportation, which
is Felony without Benefit of the Clergy.

EARLIEST KNOWN SURVIVING PIECE OF STERNE'S POLITICAL JOURNALISM, reprinted
from a lost issue of the *York Gazetteer*. At the Leeds Central Library. Hitherto
unpublished. See No. 6, p. 282.

To the Rev. Mr. *James Scott* at *Leeds.*

SIR,

I Have read over your Letter publish'd in the last York Courant,
wherein you complain of the Injury done you in being pointed out
as the Author of the Letters upon
the Election sign'd J. S. for which
in the Close of your Letter you
expect the Satisfaction of being
ask'd Pardon.

Be pleased, Sir, for a Moment to
suspend your Pretensions to this Act
of Submission, whilst I condole with
you upon the Hurt your Reputation must have felt from so heavy
an Imputation; an Imputation which
must have given you many an uneasy Moment, before it could have
reduced you to the vexatious Necessity of denying yourself concern'd
as the Author of any one Line laid
to your Charge.——I am heartily glad of it. —— Had your Hands,
Sir, or any Gentleman's been employed in collecting such a dirty
Heap of Calumny and Falshood, I
know of no Specific Water subtle
enough to have wash'd them clean
again.

But I might have spar'd You and
Myself the Trouble of this Reflection; The Pains and Method you
have taken to vindicate and clear
your Character from such a Stain
necessarily anticipates what is, and
indeed what can be said of this Nature upon the Occasion.

You must now, Reverend Sir,
prepare yourself to be inform'd by
what Fatality this Load of Infamy
was dropt at *your* Door.

When J. S's first Letter came
out in Vindication of Mr. Fox's
OWN good Sense and FAMILY
Pedigree, a Critical Review of jt
was offer'd to the Printer of the
York Courant, but could not gain
admittance :——All had been well, if
the Printer had contented Himself
with the true Excuse, " That his
natural Tenderness for Nonsense and

Abuse would not suffer him to see
it ridiculed or detected. But this
would have been trying the Cause
at his own Proper Cost, instead of
Yours, and therefore in his Courant
of *Sept.* 29, to which I refer you,
He pleads the Benefit of the Clergy,
and justifys his Refusal of the Paper
with saying it reflected upon a *Worthy Clergyman.* As this was near a
Month before the *Query* upon
Query appear'd, you see, Sir, a Chronological Argument (which is the
strongest kind of Proof) That you
are not indebted to *that* Paper for
the Imputation. Your Expectations
of being ask'd Pardon are now va-
nishing, and I might take the Opportunity of insulting you in my Turn,
and with your own Weapons. I
might ask you *whether your own
Guesses, without previous Inquiry or
due Information* whether L. S. was
really the Author of this Report,
are to be allowed sufficient Grounds
for demanding public Satisfaction ;
I might Triumph over the *Vanity*
as well as the Disappointment of
the HOMAGE you expected ;——But
I leave you, Sir, to the Severity of
your own Reflections; and, to shew
you I have some Charity, I assure
you, That ever since you have dis-
claim'd all Right of Parentage to
J. S's Letters, I have heartily pit-
ty'd the poor fatherless Offspring,
left to perish in the wide, unhospi-
table World, without Friend or Patron to own or nourish them. Whoever begot them, his Picture has
been taken both in its true Light
and Attitude, and if the Colouring
is harsh, or the Out-Lines dispro-
portion'd, They are to be charged
upon the natural Strength or defect
of Features in the Brats from whence
the Piece was copied.

I am, Tours,

York, *Nov.* 27. 1741.

HITHERTO UNPUBLISHED BROADSIDE at the York Minster Library. Sterne reveals the
identity of his antagonist, "J. S." He later decided he was mistaken. See Nos. 11, 12,
p. 283.

well's *Johnson* went on for two thousand pages and ought to have gone on longer, so *Tristram Shandy* might have gone on appearing at the rate of two volumes a year indefinitely. Whether or not it was actually finished according to plan does not matter; the point is that it looks as if it might have gone on forever in order to tell the whole story of Tristram. For to Sterne and Boswell time is an unending continuum, and the *whole* story of any man's life is coterminous only with it. Only in an open form may that truth be conveyed.

Implicit in this new notion of structure was a new notion of the biographer himself. He had become no longer the self-effacing artist in full control of his technique but a medium through whom truth itself speaks. The qualities to be valued in him were less sense, industry, judgment, and skill, than mere garrulity. The less brains he had the better, because if he had had brains he might have used them to select his materials and impress his own evaluations on them. Maria Edgeworth, in her preface to *Castle Rackrent*, put it clearly:

> Some may perhaps imagine, that the value of biography depends upon the judgment and taste of the biographer; but on the contrary it may be maintained, that the merits of a biographer are inversely as the extent of his intellectual powers and of his literary talents.

On the basis of that strange theory Macaulay and other writers of his period promoted Boswell to the front rank of English biographers. He was the prince of biographers because he was an idiot! It is not hard to see the resemblance between that view of Boswell and Tristram the Zany. But one must go farther. Since the idiot-biographer eructates his anecdotes from the depths of his own self-consciousness, he was necessarily an autobiographer as well as a biographer, his recollections of what other people did and said being all related in his mind to himself, the center of his world. Boswell, as everybody knows, began his *Life of Johnson* with leaves torn out of his own journals, and he himself remained very much in the finished narrative as one of its star performers. Indeed, both Boswell and Tristram were show-men, writing about themselves primarily and never ceasing to be self-conscious, while succeeding best in giving a vivid picture of one or more of their friends. The fact that Tristram was ostensibly an auto-biographer and Boswell a biographer makes little difference, for the former told us little about himself and a great deal about his father, his uncle, Corporal Tim, and the rest of his cast, and the latter almost as much about himself as Johnson. So Tristram and Boswell must be enrolled together in the ranks of the self-conscious narrators of long, rambling, revealing tales.

In this paper no particular hypothesis has been advanced about Sterne's indebtedness to anybody or anybody's indebtedness to him. Whether he read much biography is not known, though Walter Shandy did write a life of Socrates. All that has been attempted is to suggest that developments in the novel and the biography were running in the same direction and that people were thinking similarly about them both. One must not assert that *Tristram Shandy* was exactly like Boswell's *Johnson* in form, but surely both are examples of open form, which is perhaps only another way of putting Northrop Frye's comment that the second half of the eighteenth century had come to look upon literature as a process rather than as a product. If that process called for a vast accumulation of anecdotes in the novel, it is only sensible to look for parallels in what was going on elsewhere in Sterne's own time. To refer the reader to Locke is not unreasonable, in view of Sterne's known interest in Locke, but to find an exclusive source for his techniques in Locke is going too far. To see Sterne as untypical of his age, as an oddity, and to think of him as a prophet crying out in the sterile wilderness of the eighteenth century about the stream of consciousness or existentialism is absurd. It is only another form of that heresy called pre-romanticism embraced by critics who pick out of the eighteenth century all that they find admirable in it and label it a foretaste of great things to come. Let us instead give thanks that the eighteenth century was rich and fertile enough to produce, among other great works of literature, *Tristram Shandy*.

NOTES

1. *Boswell's Life of Johnson*, ed. Hill-Powell (Oxford, 1934),2, 449.
2. Rachel Trickett, *The Honest Muse* (Oxford, 1967).
3. Frederick A. Pottle, *James Boswell: The Earlier Years, 1740–69* (London, 1966), pp. 63 and 92.
4. Reprinted in J. L. Clifford's *Biography as an Art* (New York, 1962), p. 12.
5. Clifford, pp. 29 and 31–32.
6. Cf: Clarence Tracy, "Johnson and the Art of Anecdote," *University of Toronto Quarterly*, 15 (1945-46), 86–93.
7. *Johnson's Journey to the Western Islands of Scotland . . .* , ed. R. W. Chapman (London, 1930), pp. 19–20.
8. *Rambler*, No. 60 (1750).
9. Boswell, 3, 68.
10. Boswell, 1, 30.

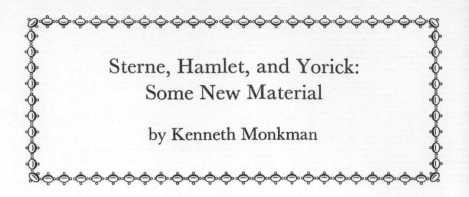

Sterne, Hamlet, and Yorick: Some New Material

by Kenneth Monkman

When I read, in modern studies of Sterne, lists of the writers who have influenced him and helped to form his style, I am surprised to find that one name is seldom mentioned. I mean that of Shakespeare. Possibly he is overlooked because his influence is taken for granted upon all English writers of any stature who came after him, always excepting George Bernard Shaw. But I suggest that there are closer links between Sterne and Shakespeare than can be simply taken for granted, and that a detailed study of the way Shakespeare's words and thinking are woven into the texture of *Tristram Shandy* and *A Sentimental Journey*, and indeed into everything Sterne wrote, might well prove rewarding.

I don't propose to make that study here. But I hope to show briefly that Sterne did have a special relationship with Shakespeare, and one moreover which he was well aware of long before Tristram was begotten and born.

Most of all, and most clearly, that relationship seems to me to have been with *Hamlet*. I don't refer simply to the obvious matter of Sterne's adoption of the name of Yorick, deep though that might be said to go. Time and again in his writings there are echoes, and more than echoes, of Shakespeare's most devious, most heteroclitical, most variously-discussed play. When Dr Slop enters the back-parlour after his fall in the mud, he appears, we are told, *"unwiped, unappointed, unanealed"* (II, 10, p. 107), an echo, this, which Sterne instantly picks up and amplifies: "He stood like *Hamlet*'s ghost, motionless and speechless, for a full minute and a half...." Again, Walter Shandy and Uncle Toby's discourse on Time and Eternity "was a discourse devoutly to be wished for" (III, 19, p. 191); and Walter, amid his researches into the mechanical disadvantages of childbirth, breaks out

Honorary Secretary of the Laurence Sterne Trust

"Angels and Ministers of grace defend us! . . .——can any soul with-
stand this shock?" (II, 19, p. 151), an apostrophe which springs to
Tristram's lips a few chapters later as he writes his Author's Preface:
"Angels and ministers of grace defend us! What a dismal thing would
it have been to have governed a kingdom, to have fought a battle, . . .
or got a child, . . . with so *plentiful a lack* of wit and judgment about us!"
(III, 20, p. 196)—Hamlet, incidentally, here dragging in Falstaff.

In *The Journal to Eliza*, on 13 May 1767, Sterne writes that he has
invitations to dine with "7 or 8 of our Grandees . . . before I leave
Town," adding, "[I] shall go like a Lamb to the Slaughter——'*Man
delights not me*——*nor Woman*'" (*Letters*, p. 339). Later that month he
scribbles from his sick-bed at Coxwold that he is "so emaciated, and
unlike what I was, I could scarse be angry with thee Eliza, if thou
Coulds not remember me, did heaven send me across thy way."
Again he picks up the echo and amplifies it: "Alas! poor Yorick!——
'*remember thee! Pale Ghost*——*remember thee*——*whilst Memory holds a
seat in this* distracted World——Remember thee,——Yes, from the
Table of her Memory, shall just Eliza wipe away all trivial men——
& leave a throne for Yorick——" (p. 346).

Three years earlier, on the point of beginning volumes seven and
eight of *Tristram*, he writes to Mrs Montagu: "I am going to write a
world of Nonsense—if possible like a man of *Sense*—but there is the
Rub" (p. 216).

In *A Sentimental Journey*, it is Polonius who pops into Yorick's head
as he approaches his interview with the Count, and that leads, of
course, to the long scene where the Count takes him to be Shakespeare's Yorick in person.

Nor, I think, should we forget how both Hamlet and Sterne play
with the idea of the hobby-horse.

I am sure that other parallels and examples could be cited of direct
quotation and misquotation (for Sterne, as he admits in Volume IV of
Tristram, is in the habit of quoting from memory) to demonstrate that
Sterne knew his *Hamlet* intimately, and that this perhaps greatest
tragi-comedy ever written was never far from his mind. I would go
further and suggest that it may even have colored his view of life, and
that its ever-tormentingly mysterious mixture of wit, humor, emotion,
death, its jesting beside an open grave, its essential gaiety, in Yeats's
fine phrase, "transcending the dread," may have had a special
fascination for Sterne who, all his adult life, loved laughter but knew

that death was at his heels; and that it may have helped to make *Tristram Shandy* the deeply compelling and magical mixture it also is.

Let me quote the words of one English critic: "It has a taste of its own, an all-pervading relish which we recognize even in its smallest fragments, and which, once tasted, we recur to. When we want that taste, no other book will do instead. It may turn out in the end that the thing is not a complete success. This compelling quality in it may exist with some radical defect. But I doubt if we shall ever be able to say . . . that it is 'most certainly' a failure." That critic is C. S. Lewis and he was writing not about *Tristram Shandy* but about *Hamlet*. It is perhaps not altogether a coincidence that no play, and today very few books, have been so much argued about, and held up in so many conflicting lights, by so many critics, as these two. It was Oscar Wilde, I think, who once said: "the central problem in *Hamlet*"—dare I mention in this company that he might almost have added, "and in *Tristram Shandy* too"—"is whether or not the critics are mad."

I want now to put back the clock more than a dozen years from the first appearance of *Tristram*, to 1746 and 1747, years of some self-doubt and depression among Englishmen following the shock of the '45 rebellion. I am going to read you two letters printed in those years in a York newspaper of which I most fortunately and somewhat frighteningly possess the only known complete file for that period. And I am going to suggest that those pieces were written by Laurence Sterne.

But at this point I ought to make a small digression. The newspaper is the *York Journal*, or, as it soon renamed itself, *The Protestant York Courant*, set up in November 1745 to support the Whig cause in York and district against the pro-Tory *York Courant* published by Caesar Ward. In the sale-catalogue of books issued by Messrs. Todd & Sotheran soon after Sterne's death, and containing his library, is listed a file of this newspaper which Professor L. P. Curtis, in his *The Politicks of Laurence Sterne*, took to be Sterne's own copy. I can now reveal, alas, that it was not his copy, for what is clearly the same file, covering exactly the same dates, is the one now in my collection, and it is clear from contemporary manuscript markings that the papers were originally delivered to the Rev. George Goundrill, Vicar of Sproatley, a parish in the East Riding of Yorkshire, who died within a few weeks of Sterne in 1768. So his library must have been lumped with Sterne's in the catalogue. I give this warning to those who may feel tempted, as indeed one or two writers already have been, to conclude that because a book is listed in what has come to be called Sterne's sale-catalogue it necessarily was in his library.

Back now to the summer of 1746 when one of the things the citizens of York were worried about was that, although the rebellion had been crushed, far too many papists, non-jurors, and Jacobites, they felt, still lived within the walls, where they were an irritating reminder of the very narrow escape the city had just had from occupation, if not worse, by Prince Charles Edward's forces. A reminder, too, that if it should all happen again, there was an active fifth column in their midst. In that situation, on 1 July, a long letter appeared on the front page of the *Protestant York Courant* purporting to be written by a local shopkeeper who signed himself "A Commoner."

This remarkably articulate shopkeeper begins by reminding his fellow citizens that in the recent rebellion "it was the Hand of Popery which labour'd to destroy us"; therefore it "puzzles me much; that whilst We rejoice so much at the Victory which has been determin'd in our Favour . . . we should, at the same Time, within our own City, argue in the Favour, should caress, should take within our Bosoms some of those very People, whose Principles, whose Religion and Riches, have been the Means of forming this unnatural Rebellion. . . ." "Of this Truth," he goes on,

> there is certain and undoubted Proof, and this *WE* have had daily Opportunities of observing from their Behaviour amongst us. How did every Misfortune we met with convey Life and Chearfulness into their Hearts and Looks? This they were so far from endeavouring to conceal, that they triumph'd in it. How did every Success obtained by our Arms cast a Damp and Sullenness upon them? This, perhaps, they might *endeavour*, but they could *not* conceal. At *Cope*'s unfortunate Defeat they *exulted*; at the Affair of *Falkirk* they almost ventur'd to *triumph*.
>
> But *Culloden* was a Stroke they could never recover; the News of it made them shrink and tremble; the Run-away Highlanders could hardly be seized with a greater Panick; and now, like *Yorick*'s Skull, they are quite Chop-fallen. Where be their Gibes? their Gambols? their Songs? their Flashes of Merriment? Not one now to mock their own Grinning.—These are the People that triumphed in our Misfortunes, that repine and languish at

our Happiness; these are they whom many of my Fellow Citizens are imprudent enough to defend and caress, whose Residence amongst us they wish, and endeavour to promote.—*O! they are civil, good-natured Folks, they are quiet and harmless Subjects—they are People of Quality and Condition, they come on Purpose to live at Ease, and spend their Money amongst us, to make us a rich and flourishing City.* 'Tis well if they who argue thus speak from Experience; if I was a Papist or Jacobite, perhaps I might talk in the same Stile; but as I have the *Misfortune* to be a Protestant, and a loyal Subject to the King, I can say, with much Truth, that for the twenty Years in which I have been in Business, I have not, during all that Space of Time, taken the Value of five Shillings of their Money....

After a good deal more in the same vein, he adds,

Where then is the Reasonableness of caressing such People, of inviting them to stay amongst us? We cannot wish them to be here without expecting to starve ourselves, whilst our Rivals in Trade prosper: For as long as they do remain amongst us, so long as we are crowded with *Rapparees* and *Priests*, we can never expect to see our own Trades flourish, or our own neighbouring Gentry (from whom is our natural Support) live amongst us as they formerly did, and would again, if we were free from such *destructive Inmates*. For who, that could avoid it, would chuse to come into bad and dangerous Company? Who, that has any where else to live, would suffer himself to be coop'd up in the same Town with Papists and——————Their late behaviour will explain my Meaning.

Therefore, my Fellow Citizens, instead of wishing them to live amongst us, let us earnestly wish them to retire from us; like their Friend Cardinal *Wolsey*, let us wish a long Farewel to all their Greatness, if they please, for ever. For this I will venture to say, that as our City has never flourished since they abounded in it, so will it never flourish while they do abound.

There is not space here to dissect the style of this militant Whig "shopkeeper" who quotes readily from *Hamlet* (from the Yorick scene moreover) and *King Henry VIII* and who rides his Grub-street hack with much more pace and assurance than any local tradesman ever could. Even less is there time to set him against the vast and, for the most part, dull canvas of mid-eighteenth-century provincial journalism when few editors reached further than for a pot of paste, scissors, and a pile of the latest London papers.

All I can do here is to draw attention, in what is clearly no more than a hurriedly-written piece of *ad hoc* Protestant propaganda, to the devices whereby a rigid style is in process of being loosened: the non-essential italics (even capital italics) for rhetorical emphasis, the non-syntactical dash (in one case an exaggeratedly long one), and the sudden jump of "voices" as the writer switches from attacker to apologist without a word of warning: "*O! they are civil, good-natured Folks....,*" etc. To one who has spent countless hours in the past thirty years exploring the back streets of eighteenth-century literature, these things stand out perhaps the more, especially in a provincial context.

One small piece of external evidence pointing to Sterne I might also mention. The writer of the letter was seemingly anxious, as we know Sterne was, to cut a figure in the wider world; for soon after it appeared in the *Protestant York Courant* he sent a cutting of it to the *Gentleman's Magazine* in London. The *Magazine* did not reprint it. Whereupon the letter-writer, seizing upon a small peg that happened to present itself in the news at the end of the year, sent a second cutting, with a covering note; and this time the *Magazine* did print it, in the Supplement for 1746. One is reminded of the persistence and ingenuity which Sterne later employed to push the first two volumes of *Tristram Shandy* southwards to London.

We now jump to 1747, a year in which, it might be mentioned, *Hamlet* was performed at the Theatre in the Mint Yard, York, in April, and made some local stir, the part of the Prince being performed "by a Gentleman from London who never appeared here before." During the summer that followed, there was a sharp and humiliating setback for the Protestant allied forces in the Low Countries, when the Dutch defenders of the besieged key town of Bergen-op-Zoom suddenly pulled out and the place fell to the French. Some time later, on the third of November, another unusual letter led the front page of the *Protestant York Courant*. A very unusual letter indeed. "Sir," it begins:

> As I may possibly become a Correspondent of yours, it will not be amiss to give you some Account of Myself, and let you know what I am, and what you may expect from me.

Know then, I am what the World calls an *Old Batchelor*, and I have call'd myself *One* these many Years, and am now the less out of Countenance, when I come to receive that Appellation from others, or find myself treated with those little Marks of Disdain, or rather Vengeance, which rapacious Widows or disappointed Maids often throw in our Way.

In Religion I am a hearty Protestant; and, I can honestly say, I hate no Man upon Earth, for differing from me in Points merely religious; nay, I pity even the Papist when I consider him as nurs'd up in Bigotry and Nonsense, and from his Cradle made the Dupe of a few artful Hypocrites.———But when I see his avowed Enmity to both our Civil and Religious Constitution, when I consider that savage Zeal, which makes him hate and exterminate all without the Pales of his Church, all who do not measure their Faith by his Standard;—I think him a dangerous Creature, and heartily blame and condemn him.

As for Protestants, of every Denomination, I look on them with the Benevolence of a Brother, as embarked in the same glorious Cause, and asserting the sacred Rights of Conscience, in Opposition to the Roguery of Priests and Tyranny of Princes.

As for my Political Principles, I have the highest Opinion of the Constitution of my Country, and think it very safe in the Hands of our present Governors.

I do not know whether I should go on with my Picture, thus far I look tolerably well; however, I'll be so sincere as to confess to you, I have some Oddities, which I believe are common enough to those who have not known the Discipline of a married State. ———However, my Friends allow them to be very pardonable, as in my most violent Moods I never go beyond the Snapping of a Pipe, or the skimming my Hat and Wig across the Room.

As I have a warm Affection for my Country, I never hear any ill News from Abroad, but it costs me a Pipe or two, and the storming *Bergen-op-Zoom*, cost me no less than three Glasses and a China Cup, which were unluckily overturn'd by my Hat which I had tossed from me in my Wrath.

I imagine I make a queer Figure enough, as I march and countermarch hastily across my Room, make a sudden Halt, and perhaps stand in a musing Posture for some Time, and at last begin of exclaiming against the mighty Disturbers of this World, like *Virgil*'s Sybil,

> *Non vultus non color unus,*
> > *Sed pectus anhelum*
> *Et rabie fera corda tument.*

I here send you my *Reverie* upon the storming of *Bergen*.

Well! ambitious Tyrant,——Well dost thou inherit the Vices of thy Ancestors, who for a Succession of Ages were the common Disturbers of the Peace of *Europe*; whose Glory was placed, in being Absolute at Home, and Terrible Abroad,——who were still forging Chains for the Nations around them, or riveting these [*sic*] on their own Slaves still closer.

To be Lord of All!——for this thou violatest the sacred Ties of Kings, and art now, contrary to the Laws of Nations, invading a free and happy People; and, without once declaring War, dost thou ravage their Country, sack their Cities, and give the Inhabitants to the Sword, or to Violation.

Hear O Heavens, give Ear O Earth! are these the Glories of the Lords of lower World, this their Honour to spoil the Creation?

But know, ambitious Mortal, thou who wastes the World, and defaces the Works of God, thou who troubles the Earth, and fills it with Complainings, know the Measure of thy Iniquity is full, and the Day of Vengeance is approaching, when thou shalt curse thy own Ambition, and those false Honours thou hast built on the Ruins of Millions of thy Kind.

——The Day is at Hand, when the injured, supported with the Nations of *Europe*, equally alarmed for their own Liberties, shall call thee to a severe Account.——Remember thy haughty Grandfather and tremble.——Dearly did he answer for his perjured Conquests.——He whom his Flatterers impiously called the *Immortal*, the *All-powerful*, was sufficiently convinced how vain it was for Man to arrogate such Titles.——The same Providence still governs the World, and the supreme God, when thou art ripe for Destruction, shall send forth his Instruments to blast thy Pride, and teach such lawless Tyrants, that not Man, or his Imperious Will, but Justice, Truth and Liberty shall reign and prevail on the Earth.

Thus it is that I give Vent to an honest Passion for Liberty and my Country, and should be glad to raise the same just Abhorrence of Tyranny and Oppression in the Breast of my Countrymen.

I shall now and then send you half a Sheet of Thoughts, so long as I find you engaged in the true Interests of Liberty and your Country:—As I am in the Humour I shall fill it with Religion or Politicks, Love or Poetry, or any Thing I imagine may be either entertaining or useful to your Readers.

I think you will agree that neither the "reverie," as it is called, nor the persona of an "old batchelor" come off too well, and I suspect that the letter-writer thought so too, for despite the half-promise in his final paragraph, no further pieces in the same vein appeared in the succeeding months. Indeed, if the author was who I think he was, and if we remember our calendar of dates, this old bachelor was very soon deeply immersed in distractions of a distinctly unbachelor-like nature. The letter, you remember, appeared on November the 3rd. On December the 1st, Lydia Sterne was born. "We shall have a rare month of it," as Walter Shandy put it after Tristram's birth; "we shall have a devilish month of it, brother *Toby*, said my father, setting his arms a-kimbo, and shaking his head; fire, water, women, wind— brother *Toby*!" (IV, 16, pp. 291–292). To the family men in my audience I need say no more.

I don't myself think there can be any doubt that the author of this second letter was a recognizable Laurence Sterne. Again, there is no time here to go deeply into comparisons, but let me draw your attention to just a few brief parallels with known writings of his.

This self-confessedly odd, pipe-snapping, hat-tossing, wig-skimming letter-writer tells us: "I imagine I make a queer figure enough, as I march and countermarch hastily across my Room, make a sudden Halt, and perhaps stand in a musing Posture for some Time . . ." Now for *Tristram Shandy*: "Yorick, with his usual carelessness of heart, would . . . answer with a pshaw!——and if the subject was started in the fields,——with a hop, skip, and a jump, at the end of it . . ." (I, 12, p. 28).

Or take the moment when Tristram in his study throws a fair sheet of writing into the fire instead of the foul one: "Instantly I snatch'd off my wig, and threw it perpendicularly, with all imaginable violence, up to the top of the room——indeed I caught it as it fell——but there was an end of the matter; nor do I think any thing else in *Nature*, would have given such immediate ease: She, dear Goddess, by an instantaneous impulse, in all *provoking cases*, determines us to a sally of this or that member——or else she thrusts us into this or that place, or posture of body, we know not why——" (IV, 17, p. 293).

If, in form, the first half of the letter owes something to "the great Addison," to whom Sterne paid tribute more than once in *Tristram*, in content I suggest it looks forward to the Romantics, even to Rousseau. As for the curiously free "reverie,"* for all its strong Biblical echoes it seems to break new ground, though it is tempting to see in it a hint taken from Locke's definition of 1690: "When Ideas float in our mind, without any Reflection or regard of the Understanding, it is that which the French call *Resvery*; our language has scarse a name for it."

I quote again now from the "reverie," addressed to Louis the Fifteenth: "Know, ambitious Mortal, thou who wastes the World, and defaces the Works of God, thou who troubles the Earth, and fills it with Complainings, know the Measure of thy Iniquity is full, and the Day of Vengeance is approaching, when thou shalt curse thy own Ambition, and those false Honours thou hast built on the Ruin of Millions of thy Kind." Now a passage from one of Sterne's earlier sermons, *The Ways of Providence justified to Man*:

> Go then,——proud man!——and when thy head turns giddy with opinions of thy own wisdom, that thou wouldst correct the measures of the Almighty,—go then,—take a full view of thyself in this glass;—consider thy own faculties,—how narrow and imperfect;—how much they are checquered with truth and falsehood;—how little arrives at thy knowledge, and how darkly and confusedly thou discernest even that little. . . . (*Works*, V, ii, pp. 367–368)

And now, for further comparison, a passage from a letter written in the last year of Sterne's life:

> O Woman! to what purpose hast thou exercised this power over me? or, to answer what end in nature, was I led by so mysterious a path to know you,—to love You,—and fruitlessly to lament and sigh that I can only send my spirit after you, as I have done this

* It is worth recalling here that the *Fragment inédit* first published by Paul Stapfer in his *Laurence Sterne* (Paris, 1870) from a manuscript said to have been written by Sterne in his Sutton days twice describes itself as a "reverie."

night to my Cordelia—poor! spotless Shade! the world at least is
so merciful as not to be jealous of our Intercourse—I can paint
thee blessed Spirit all-generous and kind as hers I write to—I can
lie besides thy grave, and drop tears of tenderness upon the Turf
wch covers thee, and not one passenger turn his head aside to
remark or envy me— (*Letters*, p. 361)

The reference to Cordelia is, of course, to the imaginary nun with
whom in 1767, sick as he was and distraught by the absence of Eliza,
Sterne was wont to commune among the ruins of Byland Abbey, just
across the fields from Shandy Hall; and indeed I cannot but feel that
the reverie of 1747 contains foreshadowings of that final summer.

I believe, in these two letters made public here for the first time
since the 1740's—more vividly in the second one—we have evidence
that Sterne's pen was not altogether idle in the long preparatory years
at Sutton. Two of his many pens, I should say. For we must never
forget that *Tristram Shandy* was the successful fusion of a number of
Laurence Sternes who during it developed still further to become the
Yorick of *A Sentimental Journey*. That process of development began
many years before *Tristram*; and if it seems difficult, even distasteful,
to square the two letters with the later writings, I suggest that, instead,
they should be set beside the already acknowledged earlier ones. You
will find hack-journalism just as aggressively bigoted in the *York
Gazetteer* of 1741, and Protestant propaganda as rampantly anti-
Papistical in some of the earlier sermons.

In the mid-1740's, Sterne was still far from fusing his many styles—
and once again I stress *many*—into the one we instantly recognize
today. He was still far from achieving that intimate rapport with a
sympathetic reader in which, speaking as one of them, I think he
excels all other writers. But in the second letter at least, with its
moments of whim and impulse and its sudden confession, "I do not
know whether I should go on with my Picture," he was, within the
accepted contemporary form of a letter to a newspaper, already on the
way to establishing considerable rapport with an editor. Note also,
incidentally, that use of a painting metaphor. "Books, painting,
fiddling, and shooting were my amusements [at Sutton]," Sterne has
told us (*Letters*, p. 4).

When the brilliant, mischievous idea of combining the parson's
gown with cap-and-bells and putting on the mask of Yorick first came

to him, we do not know. The prompting for it was not far to seek—and not only in Shakespeare. A late uncle of mine, born and bred in York in the last century, once told me he could remember old people who pronounced the name of the place "Yorik." When *Tristram Shandy* came out, the name of one of its central characters must surely have rung a familiar bell in the ears of local readers.

I have only one word to add. I have not yet given you the name with which the second letter was signed. It was not "An Old Bachelor." Perhaps some of you have jumped to it already. It was of course— "Hamlet."

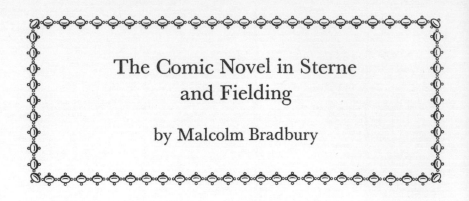

The Comic Novel in Sterne and Fielding

by Malcolm Bradbury

I wish either Professor Cash or Professor Stout, or indeed both of them, as they were in duty both equally bound to it, had minded what they were about when they begot this paper; had they duly considered how much depended upon what they were then doing; . . . I am verily persuaded I should have made a different figure in the world, from that in which the audience is likely to see me. Or to say the same thing differently (itself a good Sternian maneuver): when they conceived the idea of having a paper on irony in Sterne and Swift, they probably had in mind inviting a specialist in Sterne, and Swift, and irony, but, having to wind up the clock as well, they got me instead—not in the devout and specialized sense a Sternian or a Swiftian, but a hobby-horsist whose real interest lies broadly in the comic novel in its different species. But since the Sterne conference abounded in fictive occasions—the interment of non-bones; a visit to Byland Abbey undertaken from the wrong side of the wall, by description—it seems proper enough, finally, that a paper under the program title of "Irony in Swift and Sterne" should be really a paper on the comic novel in Sterne and Fielding.

There is an argument, one we all know, about the character of the English tradition in the novel which runs somewhat as follows: the typical species of the novel in England is the socio-moral novel, or the novel of manners and morals, the prime theme of which is the ethical conduct of man in a society relatively stable and secure. The novel, taking society as substance and not as an hypothesis, and life in time as a reality and not a deviance from the "real" life of consciousness or art or symbol, expresses a particular species of moral realism. It subjects social appearances to the tests of normal reality, and by dissolving hypocrisy and artifice and by burlesquing pride or vanity in the

Professor of American Studies, University of East Anglia

interests of a synthesis of greater ethical solidity, it witnesses to the fact that the social and moral world are contiguous: that the social world is properly conceived a moral world, in which manners can be redeemed from their apparent contingency by making them a species of morals. This kind of novel is realistic, by virtue of its empiricism and its concern with the particular stuff of life, particular experience affecting particular persons; but it is often also comic, since it explores dissonances between ethical absolutes or social virtues and the particular individual experience of these, and since it ends with a restoration, that replacement of the social norms, that giving back of sons to fathers, of lovers to lovers, which we associate with the resolution of a comic plot. Tom Jones becomes the good squire, and Emma Woodhouse—having completed the moral assault course Jane Austen sets for her—marries Mr Knightley, and the social order is somehow given back to us, having been experienced by a hero or heroine as an individual, a personal experience; it has been through the proofs of human reality, and it emerges, in its subdued way, as really real. On the way we have seen follies and deviances, hypocrisy disguised as goodness and goodness with the appearance of folly, comedy penetrating reality where it is a disguise and romping with reality where it is a farce. But if realism, empiricism, and historiography of the individual are a recognizable part of the novel's generic stuff, then repeatedly in England we have seen going along with it the comic spirit; so much so that a recognizable element of the generic type is the mode of comedy and then irony, parody, mock-heroic, burlesque, which are ways of saying the mode.

Or, to put this in E. M. Forster's terms, there is a basic species of the novel which regards the contingent world of life in time as reconcilable with that other element in which the novel must deal, the life by values; so contingency becomes plot, and life in time is finally teleological; the universe of chance becomes a universe of meaning, and the individual and history unite. This is a comic genre because the hero is characteristically one of us, deviating from sublime or heroic norms, but also because his capacity to draw misadventure and live through chance turns out to be a sustainable inquiry—the comic muse and fortune are really behind him, rejoicing in his follies and making them a genuine quest. So it is not surprising that when Henry Fielding wants to give a poetic description of the new form he is exploring, the novel novel, he speaks of that form as a comic epic in prose. Comic here prescribes several things: obviously a type of diction, which is anti-heroic, not at all concerned with high sentiments or elevating action, inducing a sense of the ludicrous rather than the sublime, enjoying burlesque; obviously an inclusiveness of social range, including many ranks and many manners, many incidents and more varied characters than romance, or tragedy or even stage-comedy; obviously an extended and comprehensive action or structure, large in social and ethical experience but also light. Indeed, judging from *Tom Jones*, Fielding seems to have taken a representative structure for the comic epic in prose as a reverse tragedy, in which the hero moves steadily downward toward a low point of fortune, and then rises again to success. But it also prescribes a fortunate universe, one in which special laws operate, so that the hero's misfortunes never seem finally severe; hence, Fielding can emphasize the unreality as well as the reality of the invented world of comic myth. So we are aware of unusual probabilities—we know that chance works in strange ways and that coincidence is a given—and we exist in a world of double expectations, for fortune, seemingly malign, is benign in a way appropriate to the generosity of comedy. Apparently a force for contingency, it is in fact the supreme plotter, twisting contingency about to show finally that it was all the time an order in the world. So Fielding at the end of *Tom Jones* reveals by remarkable sleight of hand that what we thought of as a pattern of episodes was really a plot, a causal sequence. Comedy by this view, then, is not only a diction or a tone of voice, not only an emphasis on the ridiculous or affected, but a special kind of action in a special kind of universe—one with genial laws which is controlled by the novelist who, holding fortune in his hand, can dispose it finally in an aesthetically and morally satisfying way. Clearly it is essential to Fielding's view (as to that of many subsequent comic novelists of his kind) that the universe is special, which is to say fictive, having its own orders and improbable probabilities; hence we recognize that comedy is not finally realism but a self-conscious fictive stylization. Social comedy, comedy of manners in this sense, may then engage us with duplicities and disguises, rogues and impostures, eccentricities and unearned punishments; it may create a sense of the falsities of the social fabric, or produce devastating exercises in irony, such distances between action and author as we find in Jane Austen; or it may involve us in mock-heroic and parody, and have a highly intensified fictiveness. Yet it may still be disposed toward the subject-matter of the social interaction of men, develop through their interaction and give social meaning to it, and restore the social order at the end (which is to say it may close its universe in a mood of social satisfaction). But clearly this kind of comic novel is not the only one there is; it hardly suggests the comic forces at work in Dickens or Melville or the modern ironists; and we make a mistake if we suppose that the eighteenth-century novel, in searching out its modes and its business, produced only that species. We sometimes take *Tristram Shandy*, which is a subversive novel, to be simply subversive of the generic type, a parody of it, the rules, the beginnings, middles and ends, the typographical presumptions, the conventional procedures of argument and discourse of the extant novel: "I shall confine myself neither to his [Horace's] rules, nor to any man's rules that ever lived," says Tristram/Sterne (I, 4, p. 8). But *Tristram Shandy* is more than an anti-novel; it is the working out of a different comic typology, and it is this aspect of the book I want to look at.

What kind of structure and procedure might a comic novel have if it is not of the species of social comedy? There are many such; but *Tristram Shandy* is an exemplary case. It is a comic novel; but it is not a novel in which fortune is finally benign or in which restitution of place is to be won—where unlucky Tom Jones or unlucky Jim becomes Lucky Jones or Lucky Jim—because it does not see comedy as a form but a condition. Tristram says of himself that "I have been the continual sport of what the world calls fortune; and though I will not wrong her by saying, She has ever made me feel the weight of any great or signal evil;——yet with all the good temper in the world, I affirm it of her, that in every stage of my life, and at every turn and corner where she could get fairly at me, the ungracious Duchess has pelted me with a set of as pitiful misadventures and cross accidents as ever small HERO sustained" (I, 5, p. 10). So comedy is rather the good temper with which we bear the ironical universe, and enables misfortune to take on a comic guise. *Tristram Shandy* is not a fiction in which the expectation of good fortune is established, and it hardly can be—since the misfortunes of the hero derive not from an uncertain place in the social order (a mystery, say, about his birth) nor from a moral incompleteness which would send him out on a moral quest, but from nature itself. Sterne must create both the misfortunes and that temper that will bear them like Beckett's Murphy: "And life in his mind gave him pleasure, such pleasure that pleasure was not the word." The narrator is a small hero established as a farcical victim within the novel, unable directly to dispose of the fortunes of his other "characters," for they are his "real" companions, nor indeed of his own fortunes, since these have already been determined from outside the action by the *true* novelist, Sterne himself, who has set this farcical world into motion and predetermined its society, logic and laws. Of course Sterne makes this fictional world penetrable in all sorts of ways; there is that curious and fascinating interaction back and forth of Tristram inside the story and Sterne outside it; the first-person narrative Tristram tells is one carefully made in order to be open to the novelist. So, for instance, experiences and ideas conceived subsequently to the initial creation of the novel can get in, while the book's peculiarly open-ended form is itself a solvent of that kind of fictional writing that sets up a world of expectations and tones which persuade us toward a view not only of the characters and events but also toward a sense of predetermined structural rhythm, a mental pattern of beginning, middle and end. The structure we are invited to accept is perpetually kept on a provisional basis, with constant permissions to reader and for that matter writer to leave the room at any point, so precluding a comic *action* as Fielding means it, a shape predetermined in the direction of an ending. Sterne leaves us precisely without that sense of an ending, that drift toward apocalyptic conclusiveness, that gives most novels their air of performing integrally as opposed to incidentally; and he does so in such a way as to create not only an accidental view of life but an accidental view of fiction, making his art open to superb serendipities. But as I have said the work allows for another kind of penetration, that of the coalescing and separating of narrator in the fictive world with narrator outside the fictive world, Shandy and Sterne, victim and maker. And so if one aspect of irony is distance between narrator and world, Sterne is free to play with it not only mimetically but at the core of his narrative situation: letting Tristram be ironic about the world he is in, but letting Sterne be ironic about Tristram.

So the freedom of telling the whole tale doesn't make Tristram entirely a free agent in the novel. The book makes him to begin with a victim of a preordained world ("this vile, dirty planet of ours") rather than the direct determinant of his own fate. His *life* is made for him— and not as a *history*, a life through event and society. It begins at the beginning, *ab ovo*, where lives usually do begin but not most plots; it begins not with a birth but a conception. A birth is usually a start into a system of adventures enacted through society and individual will. Tristram's fictive life starts prior to the existence of will; existence precedes essence in a very total sense; and fortune determines a fatality consonant not only with Tristram's subsequent career but with the total vision of the book. For Tristram's conception is the book's conception, the start of the telling. Tristram's is an incomplete conception—a botched performance mismanaged because progression and digression, physiology and chronology, intersect; not only must the character be created but the clock wound up. And the novel itself proceeds appropriately, by a principle of literary *coitus interruptus*, of questioned progression, half-negated fulfillment. The divergent world of personality and time then go on diverging and intersecting, here and there; not so as to suggest that the linear development of time holds the real meaning in life, and divergence is a comic episode of spectacular fictive freedom from the condition of time, but to suggest that the two worlds of life in time and life in mind are intersectional. As Tristram, speaking now as novelist, says: "I have constructed the main work and the adventitious parts of it with intersections, and have so complicated and involved the digressive and progressive movements, one wheel within another, that the whole machine, in general, has been kept a-going;——and, what's more, it shall be kept a-going these forty years, if it pleases the fountain of health to bless me so long with life and good spirits" (I, 22, pp. 73–74).

Digression is not divergence only, but provides an interlocking logic and indeed illuminates the life in time with the life by opinion, or wit, or ideas. It is indeed opinion that rescues life from its contingency: "It is the nature of an hypothesis, when once a man has conceived it, that it assimilates every thing to itself as proper nourishment; and, from the first moment of your begetting it, it generally grows the stronger by every thing you see, hear, read, or understand. This is of great use" (II, 19, p. 151). Opinions in *Tristram Shandy* are not of course truths but redemptive mechanisms; they are ideas as sensations and as personality. "But I say, *Toby*, when one runs over the catalogue of all the cross reckonings and sorrowful *items* with which the heart of man is overcharged, 'tis wonderful by what hidden resources the mind is enabled to stand it out, and bear itself up, as it does against the impositions laid upon our nature," says Mr Shandy (IV, 7, p. 277); and, resisting Toby's desire to identify these resources as religion, he attributes them to "that great and elastic power within us of counter-balancing evil, which like a secret spring in a well-ordered machine, though it can't prevent the shock——at least it imposes upon our sense of it" (IV, 8, p. 279). Mr Shandy's "transverse zig-zaggery" (III, 3, p. 160) is obviously such a survival-mechanism; thus the mind does stand it out. And this it does, not only because it is the focus of sensations, but also the active creator of opinions and ideas, which can themselves become objects of comedy, parody. The procedures of the mind, whether these are personal hobby-horses or traditional intel-lectual or rhetorical strategies, whether they are trains of association provoked by fictional events or by the comedy of the storytelling situa-tion, give us the method of *Tristram Shandy*.

On the one hand, then, the farce of a life; on the other hand, the comedy of ideas. The penetration of the two worlds gives us irony in another sense: a context of multiple presentation. *Tristram Shandy* as a telling has at least two beginnings before the one which sounds that linguistic register that has the feel of fiction: "I was begot in the night, betwixt the first *Sunday* and the first *Monday* in the month of *March* . . ." (I, 4, p. 8). And once we have that, we revert to the digressive question of how the date is arrived at in a world in which such information is not a given, but exists in a context of surmise and investigation. It is not ideas as such, but the way in which surmise and the determinism of opinion work, which gives *Tristram Shandy* its theme and progression; intellectual procedures substitute for narrative procedures, but in-tellectual procedures *encounter* narrative procedures and so can be violated, parodied, mocked. So these frames of ideas, these schemas of association and wit, these species of argument as rhetorical mode, create a context in which we can judge the narrative, but not find in it a single belief that is the author's belief, a permanent wisdom. The comedy of ideas becomes a comedy of ciphers; and that is how it is, I think, that we come to regard *Tristram Shandy* as doubly an ironical novel—a comedy of ideas which is also a comedy of misfortunes, a novel which ironically distances its world and then ironizes again about the procedures by which this is done. In this lies, surely, the beginnings of a new ironical mode in fiction. When we speak of irony in *Tristram Shandy* we therefore mean the word in a much more total sense than we do in speaking of the irony of Jane Austen or Henry Fielding, or even of Swift. It is not a species of presentation used toward the gaining of a comic resolution or the establishing of a vision, and it is not a moral instrument. It is rather a total vision, or itself a plot. It is that in *Tristram Shandy* which creates the world that might have been there if time and opinion were consonant, if the world was a meaning; and which then shows that meaning is in essence a fiction. It is that in *Tristram Shandy* which regards the real as an alien system of contingent things, having no consistent order to itself, but only that order which perceivers perceive in it, and then goes on to show that there are many perceivers. So the world is lapsed or lost in time; and it is discovered again and made gay by that art which matches the powers of the mind of perceivers, in short, by fictiveness—seen not as the possession of an author only, but as the active making of a world by its citizens, a world that is the context for myth but which cannot be given as one myth. This irony of fictiveness is in a sense pretty absolute to art. And it is in Sterne a species of *gaiety*, making the "wheel of life run long and chearfully round" (IV, 32, p. 338); the obverse gesture to Swift's irony, which deals with a universe equally ambiguous, but with a seriousness that is not ironic but satirical. Swift can never take the powers he has to annihilate his own opinion through irony as the end of the affair. But that is precisely, I think, what Sterne does. That is why he is finally an ironist and not a satirist, that kind of ironist whose vision is bleak but whose mode is benevolent. His enemy is not affectation or hypocrisy but finally gravity itself—which is why he can identify himself finally with the gay small hero, comically afflicted, who is able to forgive Dame Fortune because he is her joke, a human joke who like Yorick claims as his supreme gift the power of seeing himself in "the true point of Ridicule" (*Letters*, p. 74) where human affairs and destinies stand.

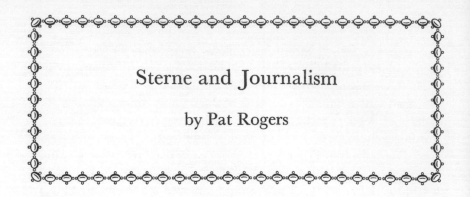

Sterne and Journalism

by Pat Rogers

My qualifications for writing on the subject of Laurence Sterne are very slight. Indeed, I am inclined to think that they consist largely in my birth and upbringing in close proximity to such barbarous sounding places as North Newbald, Pocklington, Rise, Long Riston and Givendale——names familiar to students of Sterne, but to very few others. I am neither an authority on Sterne nor an expert on the novel. It happens that for some years I have been a denizen of the minor courts and alleys off Grub Street. At best a harmless drudge, I have pursued such byways as popular historiography and political pamphleteering. However, it may be possible to achieve a fresh perspective by approaching Sterne from this slightly unusual angle.

A more honest title would have run: "The Relation of Sterne's Early Practice of, Concern with, and Awareness of Journalism to his Later Achievement in Fiction and in the Journal or Mock-Journal Form." That sounds more like an abstract of thesis than a title, and I hope it is not necessary to defend my relegation of this in favor of a less accurate but more manageable formula. If justification is required, let me impanel Tristram Shandy himself, who remarks in his delayed preface (III, 20, p. 200): "I hate set dissertations,——and above all things in the world, 'tis one of the silliest things in one of them, to darken your hypothesis by placing a number of tall, opake words, one before another, in a right line, betwixt your own and your reader's conception. . . ." My hypothesis, I trust, is not very dark. It is that we may be able to understand some of Sterne's fictional procedures a good deal better if we give more thought to his earliest phase as a writer than has generally been done. Thanks to Professor Cash and others, we are now accustomed to taking cognizance of the sermons when we come to assess the novelist. But Sterne's first published

Lecturer, King's College, University of London

writings were not sermons—indeed his journalistic productions made up the bulk of his public utterance right up till 1759.

It is a commonplace that an exceptionally high proportion of major writers in the Augustan era were widely active in the periodical press. And in most cases we have no difficulty in bringing this fact into consonance with their careers as a whole. We do not find it odd that Defoe—with his dogged concern for the here and now, his patience with the humdrum, his solid bourgeois predilection for the important things of life (such as the price of funds)—should have labored so many years on the *Review*. Here, it is the late incursion into the novel which seems accidental and even aberrant. Nor do we jib at including Fielding in this group: it is arguable that such papers as the *Covent Garden Journal*, nos. 2 and 10, belong to the precise literary genre which also contains the introductory chapters of *Tom Jones*. Indeed Fielding's preoccupation with what might be termed the problem of man versus society, the difficulties of everyday management, the state of the poor, the operation of the Riot Act, becomes increasingly apparent until in the end it bids fair to swamp the concerns of the creative artist altogether. Again, there is Swift's fierce involvement in public affairs, allied to his direct no-nonsense style of argumentation (real or assumed), which in combination makes his share in such undertakings as the *Examiner* seem almost a matter of course. Even Pope and the other Scriblerians fit with reasonable comfort into this bracket. Their fondness for the political squib derives immediately from the whole combative Scriblerian aesthetic, which might be described as converting the practical joke into a literary form. I leave out Addison and Steele because they did not achieve significant success in any imaginative form other than journalism. Among authors of the first rank this leaves Johnson, who is always a special case, Hume and very few others. It might be added in passing that even Locke had been transformed into a sort of periodical writer by the good offices of Jean LeClerc.

Sterne has always been embarrassingly hard to fit into this picture. He has been regarded as a literary buffoon, where the press is matter of fact. He exploits the heritage of learned wit: and English journalism has not displayed much trust for either of the qualities suggested in that phrase. He is unafraid of smut, whilst prudery (again, real or assumed) has been among the most engrained journalistic traits. He is capricious and copious, disorderly and opportunistic, self-indulgent and volatile:

133

all things remote from our image of the working journalist. That Sterne ever did write for the press has either been dismissed as a biographic irrelevancy or else been conveniently forgotten.

For present purposes we may adopt an arbitrary and summary definition of journalism—one which clearly wouldn't work in other contexts. It is, then, a mode of writing which deals in a short compass with topicalities, that is to say a changing or potentially changing situation. It may be occasional or regular in appearance, but the typical form I shall have chiefly in mind is the serial publication. In any case the conditions of its production are those of urgency. Its idiom, style and manner may cover a wide range, but characteristically its note is polemical even when the surface tone is objective. This definition obviously excludes such developments as the moral essay along the lines of the *Spectator*. That is deliberate, for as it is the function of a fence to mark off disputed territory which otherwise might be annexed, so it is one job of a definition to shut out as well as to shut in. In terms of lexical space a good definition must exclude the marginal; and for my purposes the *Spectator* lies outside the stockade.

We can now look at Sterne's actual practice in this light. Our knowledge of the subject has not materially advanced since Professor Curtis's outstandingly able and diligent researches forty years ago, though Mr Monkman has been steadily augmenting the factual detail. Basically, then, we know that Sterne wrote at his uncle's instigation for the *York Gazetteer* and *York Courant* in 1741–42. He *may* later have done a little more, for instance in connection with Dr John Burton's Jacobite activities around 1746. Elsewhere Mr Monkman gives evidence suggesting that Sterne may have been still in the periodical harness as late as 1747 or 1748. But we have little firm evidence to go on.

In the *Memoirs* which Laurence wrote long after for his daughter Lydia, he stated that he quarrelled with his uncle Jaques at some unspecified time, subsequent to 1742, "because I would not write paragraphs in the newspapers—though he was a party-man, I was not, and detested such dirty work: thinking it beneath me."[1] Croft has a similar passage. This has usually been taken at its face value, and seen to confirm the fact that here we have a straitjacket reluctantly donned and gladly cast off by one temperamentally unsuited to the role. But there are reservations to be made. In the first place Sterne's primary purpose is to account for the split with Jaques: and a man is not on his oath in explaining family quarrels. We have in addition two other good reasons to account for the rupture. Secondly, it should be recalled that after 1734 and 1741–42 there was only one contested election at York in Sterne's lifetime, that of 1758. It wasn't till 1774 that another contest was held, and thanks to Rockingham's manipulations this was fairly lukewarm as regards national political issues, though garnished with riots and orgies enough. We have it on the authority of Namier and Brooke that, although there was a large electorate at York, the feud between the corporation and the anti-corporation parties was "not strong" in relative terms. There was no fermenting agency such as a large dissenting population. "By 1768," writes John Brooke, "Whigs and Tories had become practically extinct at York"—and whilst something of the sort might have been true elsewhere, fiercely combated elections were none the less held,[2] leaving 1758 as a flashpoint. It might appear strange that Sterne did not enter the lists (his then ally Dean Fountaine was most active), for Sterne could not have been impressed by the effort of George Fox Lane (whose cause he had publicly opposed in 1742) to get his own son elected on a sort of double ticket. However, *The Political Romance* is, on one level, a response to the situation engendered by that election.[3] Thirdly, it is not clear how far Sterne was motivated by a personal loyalty to Robert Walpole. We have been taught to see the rise of the Pelhams as a gradual affair, with a mild encroachment by former Opposition members into the government but no sharp reversal of the status quo.[4] To contemporaries, I think, it was not so apparent that the old politics were to continue—not immediately apparent, anyway. The fall of Walpole was a more traumatic event than historians recently have tended to allow. And it is possible that Sterne, once he had decided he could do no more for Walpole, threw it all in. This would not mean disenchantment with politics as such, still less with journalism. It would be a realistic appraisal of one facet of the situation; an era was over and with it one kind of spur to polemical energy.

I am not trying to argue that Sterne hankered after a career in journalism in the days following the 1742 election. Nevertheless we ought not to imagine that his break with the political press was all that dramatic, all that clearcut, all that premeditated. When Sterne took up his pen in earnest around 1758, it would still be the *Courants* and the *Gazetteers* which gave him a measure of conviction and a sense of his own expressive powers. Through the long years of silence, with Archbishop Hutton as his enemy and his career apparently at a standstill, he would find inner sustenance in what he had done. How else can we account for the strange assurance with which he was to approach Dodsley in 1759 when the first installment of *Tristram* was ready? These are the accents of a man who has tasted public success, who has known what it is to cause a stir. And that, bearing in mind the kind of novelist Sterne was to become, was a significant memory to carry with him.

Understandably Curtis was a little overmodest about the importance of the material he presented; a natural caution not to make too much of his undertaking or of his detailed findings. He wrote that Sterne displayed "considerable aptitude" for political writing, and that the papers were prophetic of the fiction "in precision and dexterity" but not in style.[5] Today it is possible to test this judgment a little more fully because of the retrieval of further numbers of the *York Gazetteer* and additional broadside material which Mr Monkman has assembled. It is true that there is nothing very distinctive about the style of the leading articles, for which Sterne may have been responsible, in the *Gazetteer* during those early months of 1742.[6] But then after years of effort I cannot find evidence of any real principle of *Stiltrennung* operating with effect to eighteenth-century polemical literature. The language of politics, to be blunt, is broadly that of prose at large. There is a specialized vocabulary of individual words of contumely, and that the writer of the *Gazetteer* employs. A good sample number, with appropriate overtones, would be no. 45 (12 January 1742). This includes an attack on the mysterious "J. S.," now apparently not Scott but Stanhope. Phrases abound in this vein: "No quack so contemptible"; "I doubt not but a little Paper, intituled *Query upon Query*, has given you all a just Notion of this Scribbler's Integrity and Abilitys" (the mode of self-advertisement typical of the age, but also typical of the journalist at any time); "ridiculous Medly of Non-Sense and Scurrility"; "J. S. and such like infamous Emissaries of Division." These come from the usual thesaurus of invective. They are merely the "several ways of abusing one another" of which Swift had written. Besides, words do not in themselves constitute style. Here there is no "comic syntax," none of the urgency, the crosscurrents, the reversals and the fierce abridgment with which Sterne's mature style is attended. The sentences proceed in a declaratory, predicative way, well briefed from the start as to their ultimate direction. The prose never loses its route-map.

Yet this phase of writing (whose very conventionality and lack of Sternian quiddity is itself highly suggestive) may have meant something to the future novelist. I wish now to shift to a different perspective from that adopted thus far. Instead of combing the early prints and pamphlets for signs of what was to come, let us accept as fact that this is the only substantial body of writing Sterne is known to have given to the public before 1759. We can then look at his masterpiece and consider whether, *ex post facto*, we cannot discern traces of influence the other way around. All that is required for the moment is the concession that if such a link could be traced, it would be logical and plausible to assert it (whether or not the particular connections I offer are accepted) in the light of the fundamental fact established. The force of the conditional and the word "would" I shall return to at the end; it is to be hoped that the shade of Walter Shandy is appeased by such meticulous concern for an auxiliary verb.

What might Sterne have picked up that was novelistically available from his spell as a controversialist? I will suggest four headings, starting with the more straightforward, and perhaps superficial, and moving towards the more speculative and, I hope, interesting.

(1) Beginning with the slighter issues: Sterne must have developed whatever native gifts he possessed for observation of the scene around him. His ultimate vision, as Professor Mayoux suggests, may relate to the collisions of "windowless Leibnizian monads"; at a more basic level, however, he confronts the possibilities of those personal collisions, activated by the foibles and incongruities of character, which make up the human comedy. In the *Sentimental Journey* he refers to curiosity as "so low a principle of enquiry" ("The Riddle. Paris.", p. 244), but we need not attach too much weight to that. One specific point here is that contemporary journalism works very much through the frontal *ad hominem* attack: Sterne versus J.S., and so on. It's notable that there are many vestigial signs of such an approach in the earlier volumes especially of *Tristram Shandy*, for instance in the direct satire of Dr Burton. More widely, Sterne was given the chance to acquire the skills of fluent parody, the *reductio ad absurdum* of the opponent's case, and the like, which the contemporary press demanded of its writers. Equally the full transcript of Walter's marriage settlement (I, 15)

goes back not only to Renaissance and Scriblerian satire (Pope's *Stradling versus Stiles*, for example); it glances perhaps at the journalist's necessity always to quote his Exhibit A at length. The details of peace treaties, parliamentary addresses and charters are, of course, sprinkled regularly through Augustan polemic, in journals and pamphlets alike. This is the semblance of a veridical proof, given by a long itemized quasi-legal document. Today it is scholars who use documentation to document their own industry and to cover over rifts in an argument. In the eighteenth century it was the journalists who first caught the trick. Again there may be a parodic relation to journalism in Tristram's anxiety to quote his sources (often Uncle Toby), as if this guaranteed something or other. In addition, there is the frequent pretence of objectivity, often necessary in the polemical press but surely redundant in this context: "It is not my business to dip my pen in this controversy——much undoubtedly may be wrote on both sides of the question——all that concerns me as an historian, is to represent the matter of fact..." (IV, 27, p. 321). Again it is scholars who have taken to parading source material and ostentatiously proclaiming their disinterested stance.

(2) Consider what might be called the element of self-display on Sterne's part. Entire chapters (III, 28, for instance) are given over to the cult of literary personality. Advisedly I say "personality" and not "persona." One does not really like to abandon a ship which is sinking so fast—a few years ago everybody one met was talking about personae, and now one cannot cross the road without overhearing a recantation. But without insisting on the term it is perhaps safe to say this much: that Sterne did later write in the assumed guise of a certain Tristram Shandy (who may relate more or less to Laurence Sterne himself) and as a sentimental traveller and as Yorick who addresses his Eliza. Such a contrivance was first attempted in a letter ostensibly written by a merchant from Leeds late in 1741.

But, more widely, Sterne's entire rhetorical identity is pertinent. Now adopting the tone of an extension lecturer, now the garrulous raconteur, at one moment launching into thunderous apostrophe, at another slipping into formal invocation or obsequious dedication, his whole literary bearing is transformed at every juncture. Tristram relies on the "sweet pliability of men's spirit," as the *Journey* has it; his reader must likewise make himself into a sort of composite figure.

138

Never mind whether this is a true reflection of "our heteroclite Parson," of whom Warburton spoke to Garrick (*Letters*, p. 114). It is assuredly Tristram's character as a rhetorical agent. We have been taught, by Professor Traugott notably, to see Tristram as a rhetor figure. Now if the creative writer is the rhetor in his literary aspect, then the journalist is the mountebank in his literary aspect. Tristram's easy familiarity with his readers, for instance, derives from the mountebank's patter. His bewildering variety of forms of address—good folks, my dear Jenny, Madam, your worships, and so on—illustrates this facile confidence. The hack narrator of Swift's *Tale*, we recall, also claims intimacy with his readers, but not as Tristram does on the very first page, where we are already "good folks." By the end of a few pages (I, 6, p. 11) we are told that the "slight acquaintance which is now beginning betwixt us, will grow into familiarity; and that, unless one of us is in fault, will terminate in friendship." Such resolutely proffered friendship has almost the ring of a threat. It is a particular characteristic of the journalist, who has to establish a viable relationship with his audience quickly, to claim this sort of instant compatibility: a privilege now accorded only to television interviewers. The purposes Sterne makes the mannerism serve are, needless to say, much more serious; but the link is there. And, even more interesting, it is the characteristic of the journalist that he doesn't quite know from one day or week to the next the size and composition of his audience: it is a fluctuating population. Here we see something central, as I shall argue, to Sterne's effect—the trick of putting himself within self-imposed restrictions that belong to the world of the journalist and not to that of the novelist. At some level Sterne's multivocal technique may derive from a genuine uncertainty as to whom he really *was* addressing from his provincial parsonage.

(3) I shall say little about the importance of public events in the text of *Tristram Shandy*, although that is a point which could easily be developed. The book is threaded with allusions to men like Alberoni and to places such as Limerick, Bouchain and Utrecht. It could indeed be argued that before Scott no major English novelist gave significant historical events such fictional resonance—compare the mere noise off which is the Forty-Five in *Tom Jones*.[7] This is so whether or not we believe that the structure of the book was carefully charted by Sterne with a copy of that voluminous historian Rapin at his elbow. As a

matter of fact, Sterne does not seem to have been a particularly avid reader of historiography by the standards of his age, to judge from his personal library; his borrowings from the Minster Library only partially contradict this impression.[8]

But the importance of historicity, as it becomes chronology in a wider sense, is by no means confined to the mention of public events. The text of the novel is full of references to the date of Luther's birth and to the exact date of writing. This concern with the precise moment is found in the case of Swift's *Tale*, too, and Ronald Paulson has seen this as a kind of solipsism, an inability to get beyond the immediate and instantaneous. But it is the mark of every journalist, who has to believe that the present is the only fully real and interesting time. He cannot complain with Jules Laforgue, "Que la vie est donc quotidienne!" He has to rejoice in the diurnality of it all, to relish at once the sameness and routine of life along with the difference of each new day. (Of course there is sometimes not much difference, but it is the business of the newsman, now as in the time of George II, to convince us that there is.) The novelist can proceed on a Bergsonian assumption that time is continuous, with no real break or punctuation. The journalist must see the marking off of time as more than arbitrary; for him a new year is genuinely a new thing. Yesterday is divided from us by a sharp and unbreakable barrier; experience has its watersheds and we are always on the near side of one. Similarly we find Tristram saying things like this: "Fool that I was! nor can I recollect, (nor perhaps you) without turning back to the place, what it was that hindered me from letting the corporal tell it [the story of Le Fever] in his own words;——but the occasion is lost . . ." (VI, 5, pp. 415–416). The pretence is that what is remote is irrecoverable, and in any case totally forgotten. Actually the novelist, as opposed to the journalist, could go back and do it a different way. Sterne writes as though he were the prisoner of immediate circumstances, something which really is true of the periodical author.

In this light we may recall the ironic attempt by Tristram to chronicle his own progress, or lack of progress (IV, 13). Or the passage where Sterne satirizes the conventional travel writer—"Judge if I don't manage my plains better" (VII, 42, p. 535). The reporter is obliged to acknowledge the existence of plains; the novelist doesn't have to have plains at all. Sterne is allowing brute fact to dominate fiction as, inescapably, it dominates journalism. Time, in particular, is among the *disponibles* of the novelist's craft, a parameter within which a fair amount of elasticity is possible provided certain constants are preserved. Tristram behaves as if the passage of time *in* his narrative (as well as outside it) were ineluctable as the Law of Moses.

The composition of the last book is especially revealing in this context. At the start of Chapter 14 we read, "As I never had any intention of beginning the Digression, I am making all this preparation for, till I come to the 15th chapter——I have this chapter to put to whatever use I think proper" (p. 617). The suggestion is that Chapter 15 is a future juncture, an actual point of time ahead such as a journalist would be anticipating before he could write a given piece. Tristram could go right ahead with his digression, but his structural scheme has become a kind of calendar whose sequentiality must not be disturbed. Similarly, the start of Chapter 24 in the same book: ". . . I lost some fourscore ounces of blood this week in a most uncritical fever which attacked me at the beginning of this chapter . . ." (p. 627). The linear dimension of the book becomes a temporal scale. This is to internalize within the fictive structure the progress of external time—and this is the inevitable feature of journalism, as defined: that we read it aware of the lapse of days or hours since the last installment, before the next one. Journalism is that mode of writing where the passage of clock-time outside the text is a significant fact determining the internal fabric and literary shape. Sterne willfully devises his fiction as if the same conditions apply. But, ordinarily speaking, they do not.

One more example. At the start of Chapter 32, Tristram says, "There will be just time, whilst my uncle *Toby* and *Trim* are walking to my father's, to inform you . . ." (p. 643), and so on. Again Sterne imports the urgency and the charge that usually attaches to an event only in its immediate topical context, lending them to events in a sustained narrative where they should be lost. Once more he is writing as though his plot had to meet a perpetual deadline.

(4) But this is self-created; and equally so the arbitrary divisions of chapters and volumes. Sterne disposes the "essential and integrant parts" (Slawkenbergius's Tale) in a capricious manner. This is often interpreted as mere whimsicality, or at most an attempt to flout the traditional expectations of the novel. But it can be seen yet again as Sterne volunteering to deal in the opportunistic currency of the periodical writer. The space available to a journalist seems sometimes

to have been dictated by the amount of advertising which the printer had obtained; so that, in extreme cases, an author might have to handle a major public event in two or three short paragraphs and at another time stretch out trivial material to fill space.[9] In journalism the pressure of such other news as may be available counts as highly as the intrinsic importance of content. Now *Tristram Shandy* is written as though Sterne had some analogous pressure on him. He will hurry over some major plot development, and then spend pages on some trifling aside. Equally his habit of keeping two or three stories going, with the outcome of each unsure, is what the periodical writer is forced into by his ignorance of the future.

All these pointers could be summed up in a single formula. Sterne, I am contending, makes fiction aspire to the condition of journalism. Until recently nearly all novelists kept their dénouement a secret, though it is a pretty open secret in many Victorian novels, and worked gradually towards it. Nowadays this isn't always the case—to take one example, Muriel Spark has a fondness for letting us know the ultimate fate of a character at the outset, and then gradually "releasing" the whole story. Sterne seems unique in the degree to which he adopts the other extreme, and identifies himself with the reader's imperfect knowledge, so that Tristram himself hardly seems to know if a thing has or has not happened until he has got round to describing it. It only *is* in the full sense when it is down there in the book. Some of these elements might be explained by reference to an unplanned quality in the book, or to its publication in five batches spread over eight years. But mainly this is a novelistic and not a biographic feature. Sterne's novel is the way it is because, for whatever reason, he chose to impose on himself some of the pains and penalties—the uncertainty, the limited vision, the cramping effects, the imprisonment within the present, the loss of second chances—which are native to periodical journalism.

I promised earlier to revert to force of that conditional construction. It is true that the link between Sterne's early experience and the "journalistic" features I have been singling out remains a speculative one. It is possible that even if Sterne had *not* undergone this experience, he might still have produced a novel with many of the same attributes. But that is an unnecessary sophistication—because experience it he did—and the critic is not required to conjecture what might have been on any contrary assumption. At such moments he should melt as gracefully and unobtrusively as possible into his alter ego, the historian, and assert what was. In the light of the known facts concerning Sterne's earliest literary endeavors, it is bound to be a striking circumstance that we should find so many approximations to the technique of periodical writing in *Tristram Shandy*.

There is not space to extend these considerations, as they well could be extended, to Sterne's other work. In the case of the *Journal to Eliza*, it seems to me that there is an ulterior motive which takes the sequence right out of the conventional diary form. Sterne was not, I think, a natural diarist in the sense that Boswell might be said to be. Boswell, as Professor Hilles has well said, was driven by a conviction that he had not lived his own life fully till he had recorded it. Sterne uses the daily record to intensify his experience or to make it more intelligible than it would otherwise have been. There is a parallel in this respect with the *Journal to Stella*—a comparison which it is the foolish mode to reject as untenable. Swift uses his journal to achieve a mock intimacy, in an attempt to negotiate a difficult relationship; he attains a spurious ease of communication which was not possible in his ordinary dealings with Stella (on a fully adult level anyway). Sterne employs a similar device so as to concentrate all his emotional and psychic energy, which separation might otherwise have dispersed. "Mark!" he adjures Eliza, "you will dream of me this night——& if it is not recorded in your Journal——I'll say, you could not recollect it the day following" (*Letters*, p. 358). By this monstrous hyperbole he elevates the journal itself to an independent magnitude far beyond its real dimension. It is not very different from Tristram's game of erecting the time-scale under which the novel has been composed into an essential structural prop of that very novel.

I have tried to suggest some lines of inquiry which could be further pursued. If that were done, we might one day be able to discern, mixing in the festal dance of Sterne's art, a shadowy figure—that disreputable sister of Clio who has no name, but is the muse of journalism.

NOTES

1. *Letters*, p. 4. Cf. L. P. Curtis, *The Politicks of Laurence Sterne* (Oxford, 1929), p. 23; on the quarrel generally, see Cross, pp. 76, 93–110. Sidney Lee, in his article on Sterne in *DNB*, also implies that Sterne wrote for the press purely in order to humor his uncle.

2. *The House of Commons 1754–1790*, ed. Lewis Namier, John Brooke (London, 1964), I, 15, 79, 441–443.

3. The explicators of the "key" to the *Romance* have been seen as a satire on the Whig supporters gathered at the George Inn. Even if the allusion is less straightforward than that (as I myself would suppose) it is evident that the heightened political temperature of York in 1758 does add point to ecclesiastical burlesque. Another pointer can be found in the debt which the *Romance* owes to Arbuthnot's *John Bull*, a nakedly partisan contribution to Augustan satire.

4. See for instance J. B. Owen, *The Rise of the Pelhams* (London, 1957), *passim*, and especially p. 91. For slightly different emphases see A. S. Foord, *His Majesty's Opposition 1714–1830* (Oxford, 1964), p. 216, and Dorothy Marshall, *Eighteenth Century England* (London, 1962), pp. 187–190.

5. *Politicks*, pp. 132–133.

6. A file of the *Gazetteer* for 1742, virtually complete, came into the possession of my father and on his death in 1964 was presented to the Beverley Public Library by my mother, Mrs Irene Rogers. I am grateful to the Deputy Borough Librarian, Mr G. P. Brown, for allowing me to consult this file on several occasions.

   Early issues of this run (Sterne ceased to be involved with the journal by March of this year) contain few striking passages. Nos. 49 and 50 (9, 16 February 1742) incorporate what seems to be a word-by-word transcript of Fielding's *The Opposition: A Vision*, which had appeared in London two months previously. There is no indication of the source. It is expected that a fuller account of this material will be given by Kenneth Monkman in his study of Sterne's early years.

7. That the siege of Namur is as much an "event" in the plot of *Tristram Shandy* as is, say, Tristram's birth seems to me to need no argument. See Theodore Baird, "The Time-Scheme of *Tristram Shandy* and a Source," *PMLA*, LI (September 1936), 803–820, as well as the edition by Ian Watt (Boston, 1965), pp. 499–503.

8. We must, however, be cautious in using the printed catalogue, as Mr Monkman indicates elsewhere. The borrowings from the Minster Library were listed by the present Assistant Librarian in charge, Mr C. B. L. Barr, and circulated to those attending the Conference. The works Sterne took out from the Minster collection included three volumes of Bayle's *Dictionary*, various state papers of the seventeenth century, some ecclesiastical history, portions of Oldys's *Biographia Britannica* and five volumes of *An Universal History*. In fifteen years' borrowing this is not a hugely formidable list, and it includes little or no orthodox historiography of the Clarendon/Burnet order. Hume's *History* began to appear in the year the borrowing records end, and is naturally absent. A number of antiquarian works are listed as having been borrowed.

9. For some of the physical means by which text might be stretched out or contracted, see Stanley Morison, *The English Newspaper* (Cambridge, 1932), p. 86 and n. There were also literary means.

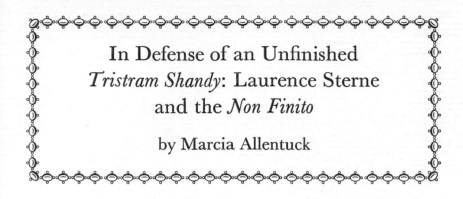

In Defense of an Unfinished
Tristram Shandy: Laurence Sterne
and the *Non Finito*

by Marcia Allentuck

I wish to approach Laurence Sterne's involvement with the fine arts from a new vantage point. It will not be my concern to cover again the territory so capably traversed by the modern explicators who have written about Sterne's familiarity with the theory and practice of drawing and painting. Rather, I intend to focus upon a single aspect of eighteenth-century aesthetic theory, to suggest how Sterne may have known and related to it, and finally to link this aspect to the problem of the ending of *Tristram Shandy*.[1]

If it may be said to end. For how does a writer limit by bounding with a finis a work which is already by definition as defiant of the limitations of traditional narrative, as circular and as open-ended, as replete with ongoing processes and reversible reactions as *Tristram Shandy*? To be sure, while there is no forced causality, the novel is not anti-teleological. Causes and effects form their discernible reticulations, leavened by the conviction that "we live amongst riddles and mysteries——the most obvious things, which come in our way, have dark sides, which the quickest sight cannot penetrate into; and even the clearest and most exalted understandings amongst us find ourselves puzzled and at a loss in almost every cranny of nature's works; so that this, like a thousand other things, falls out for us in a way, which tho' we cannot reason upon it,——yet we find the good of it . . ." (IV, 17, p. 293). This conviction in turn re-inforces the structural controls of continuation at the expense of determined finalities and neat meanderings towards closure. Sterne's development of his various themes never creates in his reader a sense of either immanent or imminent cessation; instead, the atmosphere is charged with a sense of

Associate Professor of English, City College of New York

virtually infinite and inscrutable extension, aborted only by the possibility of death.

No one has phrased the question of an ending better than did Henry James in his preface to *Roderick Hudson*,[2] when the tranquillity of recollection and the confidence bred by the mastery of his craft supported James's candid account. He speaks at first of his initial "ache of fear . . . of being unduly tempted and led on by 'development.'" The plenitude of materials available to the writer of long fiction overwhelmed James into believing that he, then a novice in the art of long fiction, could never stop the chain of composition: "They [the materials] are of the very essence of the novelist's process . . . but they impose on him, through the principle of continuity that rides them, a proportionate anxiety." James then proceeds to the crux:

> Up to what point is such and such a development *indispensable* to the interest? What is the point beyond which it ceases to be rigorously so? Where, for the complete expression of one's subject, does a particular relation stop—giving way to some other not concerned in that expression? Really, universally, relations stop nowhere, and the exquisite problem of the artist is eternally but to draw, by a geometry of his own, the circle within which they shall happily *appear* to do so. He is in the perpetual predicament that the continuity of things is the whole matter, for him, of comedy and tragedy; that this continuity is never, by the space of an instant or an inch, broken, and that, to do anything at all, he has at once intensely to consult and intensely to ignore it. [The artist works] . . . in terror, fairly, of the vast expanse of . . . surface . . . [of the] presumability *somewhere* of a convenient, of a visibly-appointed stopping-place.

Yet never once, in this eloquent yet enigmatic consideration of the complexities of closure, does James consider that *not* drawing the circle, *not* stopping the relations, in the sense of rounding them, out, is at times an even more expert way of solving the problems, and affirming the potencies of the continuity of which he speaks. (One wonders how he would have responded to D. H. Lawrence's prickly conclusion: "Bunk of beginnings and ends, and heads and tails. If he can't draw a ring round creation, and fasten the serpent's tail into his mouth with the padlock of one clinching idea, then creation can go to hell, as far as man is concerned.")

II

For several decades, Sterne scholars have addressed themselves to Sterne's response to the very challenge delineated by James, and specifically to the uncertainties of the form of closure, or "the sense of an ending," to use Frank Kermode's phrase without his eschatological resonances. After all, chiliasm was the very least of Sterne's concerns. Controversy has raged; those who have entered the lists have added substantially to the gaiety of Sterne studies by the energetic and ingenious inventiveness with which they have marshalled arguments either in support of a scrappy, disorganized, shakily rectilinear and arbitrarily concluded piece of work on the one hand, or, on the other, a subtly-structured, meticulously controlled, firmly circular or spiralling opus, one which would be complete wherever Sterne elected to stop it. My affinities rest with the latter group, but I am of their party as much for art-historical as for aesthetic reasons. My concern is with the novel as representative of the genre called by art historians *il non finito*, or, to use the more telling German phrase, *das Unvellendete als künstlerische Form.*[3]

By the *non finito* I do not mean a work in progress, in rough or unrealized form. I do not mean a work altered again and again by the artist, such as Washington Allston's painting, *Belshazzar's Feast*, over which he labored from 1817 to 1843, and on which he was still working on the day of his death, nor do I mean a work which was moving towards a declared end but was aborted by its creator's death, such as Alban Berg's second opera, *Lulu*. I am not concerned with a species of artistic defeat, an aesthetic failure in which desire outran performance, or a work interrupted, either by the ghost of the person from Porlock or by any other extraneous influences. I do not mean a mere fragment, but a work with its own complete expressive value. I refer to a work which the artist *intended* to leave unfinished, like a torso or a sketch, a work still whole within itself. Such a work bears the hallmark of a personal style, of a subjectivist conception of art. Such a work is the vital record of the artist's creative process and recognized to be a particular form of expression in its own right, challenging and motivating its audience to creative co-operation—to fill in and find out by empathy and association, and to cultivate a kind of negative capability which enables disinterested functioning, without easy satisfactions. Yet the master of the *non finito* is, like Sterne, never too obedient to the audience's presumed expectations. He seeks not conclusive closure but, as Sterne phrased it when speaking of Uncle Toby's "unsteady uses of words," a "fertile source of obscurity." But what is not easily apprehended is not necessarily imperfect or inadequate: an audience can exist with the work while exploring it without requiring final reconciliations or even consonances. For the artist composing a work of the *non finito* kind, what is finished is dead, or, as George Eliot rendered it in a letter to John Blackwood, "the fault lies in the very nature of a conclusion, which is at best a negation."[4]

There are no finer examples of the aesthetic validity and the self-sufficiency of the *non finito* than many such works by Michelangelo and Rodin. These works are in the *pars pro toto* mode. Michelangelo's were defended by Aldo Bertoni, who maintained that the sculptor stopped short of completion intentionally so that he might preserve the dynamic inner life of his figures.[5] Roger Fry defended Rodin's by asserting: "Every part of the figure is instinct with the central idea," and Rodin defended his own with the aphorism, "Beauty is like a god; a fragment of beauty is complete." Rodin's reply to Degas's protests about his armless and headless statue, *Walking Man*—"Have you ever seen a man walk on his head? As for the arms, I preferred to have him walk on his legs like ordinary mortals"[6]—is Shandian in substance and form. Indeed, the poet Rilke's defense of the additive and subtractive qualities of Rodin's *non finito* works, their self-sufficiency, is highly relevant here: "Rodin, knowing . . . that the entire body consists of scenes of life, of life that may become in every detail individual and great, has the power to give to any part of this vibrating surface the independence of a whole." If one were to press the analogy, one may see here a link with Sterne's metonymous handling of noses, defended by Coleridge when he spoke of the universality of Sterne's work, its self-sufficient expressiveness, wherein "each part is essentially a whole in itself." Such a work, then, may be likened to a modern action painting (in which each gesture of a brush that goes into its composition is a totality in itself), containing a succession of wholes uniting both form and spontaneity, and for which the question of an ending is beside the point.

III

Eighteenth-century theories about the aesthetic virtues of an unfinished work could not have been unknown to Sterne. The sale catalogue of his library[7] shows it to have contained several works presenting suggestive discussions of this matter, itself a paradox in a period thought but only a short time ago to be obsessed by closed forms and calculated regularities. For when aesthetic incompletion is defended, it is always against the background, tacit or explicit, of the perfectibility of art (as in the case, for example, of Winckelmann's admiration of the torso of Belvedere). In the period's early glances at the *non finito*, we can already discern a shift of sensibility to become more marked as the century went on. (I am not "periodizing" here, but merely remarking on an interesting and revealing tendency.) A Raphael, concerned with grace and beauty, must finish; a Michelangelo, involved with grandeur and sublimity, need not. Interest in the *non finito* was symptomatic of interest in the personal style, in a more subjectivist conception of art.

The specific term, *non finito*, does not occur in the criticism of the period, but the concept and its implications are treated in at least three representative works in Sterne's library, including Dryden's translation of Du Fresnoy's *Art of Painting*. In the preface, while making analogies, some admittedly tenuous, between poetry and painting, Dryden has this seminal section:

> We have the Proverb, *Manum de tabula*, from the Painters; which signifies, to know when to give over, and to lay by the Pencil . . . *Apelles* said of *Protogenes, That he knew not when to give over*. A Work may be over-wrought, as well as under-wrought: Too much Labour often takes away the Spirit, by adding to the polishing: so that there remains nothing but a dull Correctness, a Piece without any considerable Faults, but with few Beauties; for when the Spirits are drawn off, there is not but a *caput mortuum*.[8]

Some of these concepts, of course, stem from the Elder Pliny, in whose writings there is an awareness of the provocative stimulation which an unfinished work can afford to the imagination.

Roger de Piles's *Art of Painting* is parodied by Sterne in a memorable passage of *Tristram Shandy* when he plays with grading, as it were, a painting, or a literary work, for coloring, design, composition, and so on, as de Piles had done seriously when constructing his painter's scale in the original French version, the *Cours de peinture par principes* (1708).[9] Nevertheless, de Piles, despite the surface rigidities of his scale, reflected constantly on the problems of terminating and finishing.[10]

He wrote of Titian critically, for example, that "He finish'd his Pieces extreamly, and had no very particular Manner in the managing of his Pencil, because his Studies, and the care he took to temper one Colour by another, took away the appearance of a Free Hand . . ."[11] Of Sebastian Bourdon he asserted that "His Pieces are seldom finish'd, and those that are most so, are not always the most fine." De Piles's hostility to the academic notion of the *fine*, the dutifully completed, is apparent in his praise of Rubens: "His Labour was light, his Pencil Mellow, and his Pictures finish'd, but not like some Painter's *who with over-straining and earnestness of finishing their Pieces, do them more harm than good. . . .*"

Yet it was David Hume's essay, "Of Tragedy," which came closest, I believe, to the matter of the *non finito*, and to the peculiarly personal twist given it by Sterne's own situation. We recall that Hume considers—although he does not vigorously champion—DuBos's theory, embodied in his *Reflexions critiques sur la poesie et sur la peinture*, that, as Hume phrases it, the value of tragedy inheres in the "movements of the imagination" it arouses, however painful or difficult, for "no matter what the passion is . . . it is still better than that insipid languor which arises from perfect tranquillity and repose." But Hume casts about for other causes for the moving of the imagination, and summons the Elder Pliny. In his *Natural History* (Book 35), Pliny had defended the *non finito* as causing the increased pleasure of the spectator not only by challenging him mentally to posit a probable mode of completion on the basis of what had come before, but more importantly, in the case of the author who died before he could finish his work, by reminding him of the limits of mortality. In Hume's words,

> "It is very remarkable," says he [Pliny], "that the last works of celebrated artists, which they left imperfect, are always the most prized, much as . . . the MEDEA of TIMOMACHUS, and the VENUS of APELLES. These are valued even above their finished productions: The broken lineaments of the pieces and the half-formed idea of the painter are carefully studied; and our very grief for the curious hand, which had been stopped by death, is an additional increase to our pleasure."[12]

IV

Throughout *Tristram Shandy* the question of the end reverberates. Sterne plays with closual effects both as expressive and as formal devices. Even his caressings of the modes of beginning reflect his views of ending: "But now I am talking of beginning a book . . . of all the several ways of beginning a book which are now in practice throughout the known world, I am confident my own way of doing it is the best——I'm sure it is the most religious——for I begin with writing the first sentence——and trusting to Almighty God for the second. . . . Observe how one sentence of mine follows another, and how the plan follows the whole" (VIII, 2, p. 540). But to these views he has already taken characteristic exception in his first volume: "when a man sits down to write a history . . . he knows no more than his heels what lets and confounded hinderances he is to meet with in his way,——or what a dance he may be led, by one excursion or another, before all is over. Could a historiographer drive on his history, as a muleteer drives on his mule——straight forward;——for instance, from *Rome* all the way to *Loretto*, without ever once turning his head aside either to the right hand or to the left,——he might venture to foretell you to an hour when he should get to his journey's end;——but the thing is, morally speaking, impossible: For, if he is a man of the least spirit, he will have fifty deviations from a straight line to make with this or that party as he goes along, which he can no ways avoid. . . . In short, there is no end of it . . ." (I, 14, pp. 36–37). If Sterne trusted to Almighty God for the second sentence at least, what forces did he need to invoke for a conclusion? Significantly, he does not name them: "O ye POWERS! (for powers ye are, and great ones too)——which enable mortal man to tell a story worth the hearing,——that kindly shew him, where he is to begin it,——and where he is to end it,——what he is to put into it,——and what he is to leave out,——how much of it he is to cast into shade,——and whereabouts he is to throw his light! . . . I beg and beseech you . . . that at least you set up a guide-post . . . in mere charity to direct an uncertain devil . . ." (III, 23, p. 207).

I do not wish to denigrate Wayne Booth's article, "Did Sterne complete *Tristram Shandy*?" which appeared in 1951,[13] but the point is simply that Booth's thesis about the novel's ending does not hold up. Despite Booth's strenuous and impressive efforts to prove the contrary, there were possibilities for development other than the amours of Toby and the Widow Wadman; even if it can be argued that Sterne carried these as far as they could go, it certainly does not mean that the novel necessarily had to end with them. Sterne did not "complete the book as he had originally conceived it," as Booth would have it.

Indeed, he did not complete it at all. He stopped writing it—another matter altogether. It ceases without concluding.

Why cannot we accept Sterne at his word? We know that he had once planned to follow the Shandy family through a long and involved journey on the continent, and there are numerous references to an ongoing project: "a map, now in the hands of the engraver, which, with many other pieces and developments to this work, will be added to the end of the twentieth volume" (I, 13, pp. 35–36); "there are . . . endless genealogies. . . . In short, there is no end of it" (14, p. 37); "These unforeseen stoppages, which I own I had no conception of when I first set out;——but which, I am convinced now, will rather increase than diminish as I advance,——have struck out a hint which I am resolved to follow;——and that is,——not to be in a hurry;——but to go on leisurely, writing and publishing two volumes of my life every year;——which, if I am suffered to go on quietly, and can make a tolerable bargain with my bookseller, I shall continue to do as long as I live" (p. 37). Not a little of the antic chimera of perpetual motion is suggested by his apology for digressions: "Digressions, incontestably, are the sunshine;——they are the life, the soul of reading. . . . From the beginning of this . . . I have constructed the main work and the adventitious parts of it with such intersections, and have so complicated and involved the digressive and progressive movements, one wheel within another, that the whole machine, in general, has been kept a-going;——and, what's more, it shall be kept a-going these forty years, if it pleases the fountain of health to bless me so long with life and good spirits" (22, pp. 73–74).

Poignancy in the Plinian sense is added to the question of an ending in the passage just quoted; we also recall Sterne's virtual covenant with himself at the outset of the seventh volume, written during frequent lung hemorrhages: "I think, I said, I would write two volumes every year, provided the vile cough which then tormented me, and which to this hour I dread worse than the devil, would but give me leave. . . . I swore it should be kept a going at that rate these forty years if it pleased but the fountain of life to bless me so long with health and good spirits" (VII, 1, p. 479)—the earlier "life" now significantly changed to "health." What Dr Johnson, in his last *Idler* paper, has called the "horror of the last" permeates these statements; some of this anxiety had evaporated during a good period in July, 1766, when Sterne wrote to a friend: "at present I am in my peaceful retreat, writing the ninth volume of Tristram—I shall publish but one this year, and the next I shall begin a new work of four volumes, which when finish'd, I shall continue Tristram with fresh spirit" (*Letters*, p. 284). One month later, in August, Sterne announced his intention of publishing both the ninth and tenth volumes of the novel "next winter" (*Letters*, p. 288). But in January of 1767, he wrote baldly: "I miscarried of my tenth Volume by the violence of a fever, I just got thro'" (*Letters*, p. 294). In view of these statements and the entire tenor of the book, I cannot accept Booth's conjecture that "Sterne showed signs of growing tired of *Tristram*." The weariness and difficulty came from his state of health and normal fatigue after intense application, but not from the falling-off of interest in or commitment to the microcosm he had created and was intending to go on creating if he could.

To be sure, it would be an over-simplification to insist that Sterne stopped *Tristram Shandy* because the realities of his own personal situation forced him to do so, but these realities cannot be ignored. If they are coupled with his awareness of the tradition and the issues of the *non finito* (of course, he did not necessarily know it by this name), not only in the Medici tombs of Michelangelo, but also in the works from his own library, as well as in those of his favorites, Rabelais and Montaigne (the latter having predicted that his *Essays* would proceed "incessantly and without labour . . . so long as there shall be ink and paper in the world," another side of the *non finito*), the question of whether Sterne finished *Tristram Shandy* becomes unimportant.[14] What is important is Sterne's own position in the fourth volume: "In my opinion, to write a book is for all the world like humming a song——be but in tune with yourself . . . 'tis no matter how high or how low you take it" (IV, 25, p. 315). All of *Tristram Shandy*'s parts— from names to noses, and the vast territory in between—stand as wholes, stable, integral, complete, yet never final, never conclusive. Sterne was essentially in tune with the coherence and the open-endedness of the *non finito*: this can even be said to have been *his* hobby-horse. The glory of *Tristram Shandy* is that it *is* unfinished.

NOTES

1. I am grateful to the Director and the Trustees of the Henry E. Huntington Library for a research grant during the summer of 1968, when much of this essay was blocked out, and to the Librarian and his staff for many courtesies. I must also thank Professors Lorenz Eitner and Albert Elsen of the Department of Art History at Stanford University, Dr Frederick Cummings of the Detroit Institute of Art, and Professor Juergen Schulz of the Department of Art History at Brown University for helpful suggestions.

2. Henry James, *Roderick Hudson* (New York, 1935), pp. vi–viii.

3. Cf. J. A. Schmoll gen. Eisenwerth, *Der Torso als Symbol und Form* (Baden-Baden, 1954), *passim;* and *Das Unvollendete als künstlerische Form,* (Berne & Munich, 1959), *passim.* The latter collection of essays is indispensable for any adumbration of the concept, and Schmoll's concluding comment on the quest of the artist—"Er sucht den *Ursprung* der inneren Bilder, nicht ihre *Vollendung"*—an apposite epigraph for this essay.

4. Gordon S. Haight, ed., *The George Eliot Letters* (New Haven, 1954), II, p. 324.

5. Most of Michelangelo's contemporaries saw not vague intentions and unrealized objectives in his unfinished works, but rather deliberate elusiveness. Indeed, Michelangelo's own stated views suggest recognition of the expressive possibilities of the unfinished, as perusal of his sonnets and letters will support. His contemporaries were persuaded of the validity of the *non finito;* this is at least deducible from the numerous imitations that used to be attributed to Michelangelo himself chiefly because they were unfinished. His influence in this mode was as considerable as that in the finished one: his pupil Ascanio Condivi who in 1553 published a biography of his teacher, insisted that "unfinishedness" did not "obscure the perfection and beauty of the work" ("Lo sbozzo non impedisci la perfezione e la bellezza dell'opera.") Rodin, however, had a different view of Michelangelo and the *non finito:* "Art did not content him. He wanted infinity." This reflected Vasari's view that Michelangelo was perpetually dissatisfied with what he did.

6. Albert Elsen, *Rodin* (New York, 1963), pp. 173–174. His discussion of Rilke and Rodin follows.

7. *A Catalogue of a Curious and Valuable Collection of Books, among which are included the Entire Library of the late Reverend and Learned Laurence Sterne, A. M. . . . which will begin to be sold . . . on . . . August 23, 1768 . . . by J. Todd and H. Sotheran, Booksellers in York.* . . . I have used the facsimile reproduction of this sale catalogue, published in London in 1930. Not all of the books were Sterne's, but on the basis of the evidence of his references to other authors in his own writings, I believe that it is safe to assert that the books from this collection cited in this paper were indeed from Sterne's library.

8. *The Art of Painting: by C. A. Du Fresnoy: with Remarks Translated into English, with an Original Preface, Containing a Parallel between Painting and Poetry: by Mr. Dryden,* third edition, corrected and enlarged (London, 1716), pp. lviii–lix. This was the edition in Sterne's library.

9. Here Sterne abounds in analogical play, diminishing de Piles's dogmatism and his system-prone reasoning, his reductive pedantry: "My Lord, if you examine it over again, it is far from being a gross piece of daubing, as some dedications are. The design, your Lordship sees, is good, the colouring transparent,—— the drawing not amiss;——or to speak more like a man of science,——and measure my piece in the painter's scale, divided into 20,——I believe, my Lord, the out-lines will turn out as 12,——the composition as 9,——the colouring as 6,——the expression 13 and a half,——and the design,——if I may be

154

allowed, my Lord, to understand my own *design*, and supposing absolute perfection in designing, to be as 20,——I think it cannot well fall short of 19"
(I, 9, p. 16).

10. It should be pointed out that for the eighteenth-century theoretician, "finish"
meant the final surface texture, worked out only when all of the other components of the work were realized; thus, one did not "finish" the work until one
had virtually completed it; to neglect or underplay "finish" was less a fault than
a touchstone of fiery and fertile genius. The *non finito* was made to enhance the
sensation of the sublime in an extended sense in at least one instance in the
eighteenth century. When John Singleton Copley, in his painting *Watson and the
Shark*, left the shark unfinished, he was praised by at least one critic (*General
Advertiser*, 28 April 1778) for having enhanced the drama of the moment by
leaving to the viewer's imagination the defining of the limits of horror and terror.

11. *The Art of Painting, and the Lives of the Painters . . . Done from the French of Monsieur
de Piles* (London, 1706), pp. 192–193; p. 369. The 1743 English edition was in
Sterne's library.

12. David Hume, *Essays, Moral, Political, and Literary*, ed. T. H. Green and T. H.
Grose (London, 1882), I, pp. 258–265 passim. The 1758 edition of Hume's
Essays on Several Subjects, containing "Of Tragedy," was in Sterne's library. It is
tempting to conjecture that Sterne may have discussed aspects of this essay
with Hume when they met in Paris in the early 1760's. But no concrete evidence
exists, except that "*David* was disposed to make a little merry with the *Parson;*
and, in return, the Parson was equally disposed to make a little mirth with the
Infidel" (Letters, p. 218).

13. See *Modern Philology*, XLVIII, 3 (February, 1951), pp. 172–183, *passim*.

14. This problem of "finishing" is a perennial one among creative persons. Cf. the
statements of some modern artists of distinction, contained in *Modern Artists in
America, First Series*, a symposium edited by the artists Robert Motherwell and
Ad Reinhardt and published in New York in 1950 by Wittenborn Schultz. In the
discussion, Barnet Newman insisted: "I think the idea of a 'finished' picture is
a fiction. I think a man spends his whole life-time painting one picture or working
on one piece of sculpture. The question of stopping is really a decision of moral
consideration" (p. 12). Hans Hoffmann, on the other hand, confessed: "To me a
work is finished when all parts involved communicate themselves, so that they
don't need me." But the moderator, Robert Motherwell, very much on Sterne's
wave-length, asserted about the committed artist that he is "involved in
'process' and what is a 'finished' object is not so certain." Basically, however, the
panel agreed that what finishes a work of art is the artist's decision to let it alone.
The act of creation supersedes the mere product; the work is always finished or
never so, only controlled by the artist's imperative to turn to it again.

FOUR
Sterne and the World

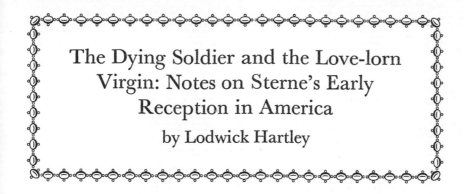

The Dying Soldier and the Love-lorn Virgin: Notes on Sterne's Early Reception in America

by Lodwick Hartley

On the bicentenary of the death of the eighteenth-century English novelist who seems most to belong to the twentieth, it is a matter both of curiosity and historical interest to examine the shifting moral and literary values that have made the reputation of the novelist in one century quite different from that in another. It is also important to examine how even his reception in his own century was influenced by the aesthetic and moral values of the geographical areas in which he found readers.

For our purposes, it is significant that it was a North Carolina admirer to whom in 1768 Sterne wrote one of his last and most interesting letters. Dr John Eustace of Wilmington had sent his favorite English author a walking stick with a curiously gnarled handle—a "piece of Shandean statuary" (as he called it) that he had received from the widow of Colonial Governor Dobbs. Sterne's reply is as full of gratitude for the appreciation of his American reader as it is of disappointment that his great fame in England had been neither constant nor universal. Like the walking stick, he remarked, his work had "more handles than one." However, he continued, "It is too much to write books and find heads to appreciate them" (*Letters*, p. 411).

Heads to appreciate he had assuredly found in eighteenth-century America, where he had highly-placed admirers and where in the period of great vogue after his death he was to have both admirers and imitators. These constituted interestingly different levels of intelligence. The admirers were, on the one hand, chiefly lawyers and statesmen of liberal democratic leanings, some of whom were very respectable indeed. The imitators, on the other hand, were likely to be

Professor and Head of English, North Carolina State University.

This essay has appeared in a somewhat different form in the *Southern Humanities Review*, III (1970), 69–80. Permission to reprint was granted fledgling novelists and literary amateurs, some of whom were quite bad.

Professor Richard Beale Davis has asserted that the wide-spread popularity of Sterne in eighteenth-century Virginia paved the way for the pervasive influence of the romanticism of Scott in that aristocratic society;[1] whereas John Dos Passos has made the somewhat broader and less defensible claim that "Sterne's frothy writings marked the skirmish line of whiggish philosophical thought in the same way as Shaw's writings a century later opened a path for the main body of socialist opinion."[2] Both these writers point out on safer grounds that the main characters of *Tristram Shandy* were familiar figures in the conversation of every literate Virginian. And it is clear that in sophisticated Virginia society of the period Sterne was valued not merely as a sentimentalist or humorist but also and more importantly as a practical philosopher and moralist. No matter how much his readers appreciated other aspects of his art, they were markedly impressed by his warm humanity and his insistence on fundamental goodness grounded in a philosophy of benevolence.

Virginia was, of course, only one area of intelligent interest. In towns like Philadelphia, Hartford, Boston, Baltimore, Charleston, and Wilmington, literary clubs discussed Sterne warmly and sympathetically along with Richardson, Smollett, and Dr Johnson.

Actually, the first great American to record a judgment of Sterne (if obliquely) was a Philadelphian, a cosmopolite, and a wit well acquainted with the best minds of Europe. In 1761 Franklin was quick to order Sterne's *Sermons* from his London publisher.[3]

Two years later Franklin wrote as a comment on the frontier life at Fort Pitt:

> The People have Balls for Dancing, and Assemblies for Religious Worship, but as they cannot yet afford to maintain both a clergyman and a Dancing-Master, the Dancing-master reads Prayers and one of Tristram Shandy's Sermons every Sunday.[4]

To Franklin, the witty and cultivated deist—one may infer—Sterne was more entertainer than theologian or moralist—in fact, a divine who, as Dr Johnson said, was likely to give only "the froth from the surface" of the cup of Salvation.

It is against this amused, common-sensical and gently skeptical view that we may measure the far more serious consideration accorded

Sterne by a great Virginian like Thomas Jefferson, who along with Franklin represented on the American side of the Atlantic the closest thing to the deists and atheists among the French *philosophes* who received Sterne so graciously even while he needled them on their irreligion. To Jefferson, Sterne became an immediate and natural interest. The statesman read the novels early and late in his career, giving such sober value to their morality as can be later found only in some critics of the mid-twentieth century.

Unlike Franklin who was a practical man of affairs and unlike such closer contemporaries as John Adams who had a jaundiced view of mankind and Hamilton who held the Hobbesian view that man was scoundrelly and required repression by authority, Jefferson was a democratic idealist. As Professor Adrienne Koch has observed, Jefferson's evolution from Epicureanism and Stoicism had eventuated in a Christian morality with emphasis on inward motive and intention, as well as on "the spirit of benevolence, charity, and the love of one's fellowmen . . . as the true expression of our natural, instinctive moral equipment."[5] This seemed to be the religion and the morality of Uncle Toby and of the Yorick of *A Sentimental Journey* and the *Sermons*, suggesting Locke and Shaftesbury filtered through Hartley and Hume —with all of whom Jefferson was well acquainted. Thus, writing to Robert Skipworth on 3 August 1771, on the general subject of the exercise of moral feelings through the reading of good fiction, Jefferson cites Yorick's account in *A Sentimental Journey* of his encounter with the "poor Franciscan" in Calais, whose begging he first rebuked and then yielded to. "We are equally sorrowful at the rebuke," Jefferson remarks, "and secretly resolve we will never do so: we are pleased with the subsequent atonement, and view with emulation a soul candidly acknowledging it's [*sic*] fault."[6]

Jefferson's best known and most extravagant statement was reserved for a letter that he wrote from Paris in 1787 to his nephew, Peter Carr—whose sexual morality, incidentally, along with his uncle's, has been impugned by some twentieth-century historians: "The writings of Sterne . . . form the best course of morality that ever was written."[7]

Yet however philosophically Jefferson may have thought that he was viewing Sterne, he could not—like many other people—resist giving in to him sentimentally. Observe him for example in April 1786, as he was returning to Paris, pausing long enough in Calais to give a small gratuity to a monk that his imagination allowed him to regard as a successor to Sterne's Franciscan and in this way dramatizing the belief earlier expressed to Skipworth.[8] The event and the gratuity were set down in the great man's account book. Moreover, during the last illness of his wife, Jefferson selected *Tristram Shandy*—especially the description of Uncle Toby's marching forth to lay siege to the Widow Wadman—for the two to read together; and together they copied the tender passage to "my dear Jenny" at the end of Volume IX, Chapter 8, pp. 610-611, beginning "Time wastes too fast" and ending ". . . every time I kiss thy hand to bid adieu, and every absence which follows it, are preludes to that eternal separation which we are shortly to make."[9]

Other prominent Virginians of the same period who read Sterne avidly and could quote him at will were John Taylor of Caroline and Francis Gilmer.[10] A little farther south there was a cultivated group of Sterne enthusiasts around Edenton, Brunswick, and Wilmington, like James Iredell, who became associate justice of the United States Supreme Court, and the Dr Eustace (already mentioned) who won a small but firm immortality as "the correspondent of Sterne."[11]

More important than these somewhat random examples is another public figure, who made some pretense to being a literary man as well. This was William Wirt, son of a Swiss father and native of Maryland, who came to Virginia at the age of twenty to set up a law practice, who formed close friendships with such important statesmen as Jefferson and Madison, and whose place in history was made by his serving as prosecutor at the trial of Aaron Burr and by his becoming attorney general under Monroe.[12]

No fact about Wirt has been more often cited than the description of his earliest law library which included "a copy of Blackstone, two volumes of Don Quixotte [*sic*], and a volume of *Tristram Shandy*."[13] His references to Sterne's works are numerous. Moreover, he attempted to imitate Sterne in *The British Spy*, a thin hodgepodge of quasi-essays that first came out in Richmond in 1803 and was later reprinted several times in England and America.[14]

Outside the South, another brilliant and tragic political figure of the era who found amusement and solace in Sterne was Aaron Burr. If we have no record of such frequent reading of Sterne as we have for his political rival, Jefferson, we do know that the novelist was a favorite of Burr. Van Wyck Brooks remarks that he brought up his beautiful and ill-fated daughter, Theodosia, on *Tristram Shandy*.[15] And Burr's early biographer, James Parton, is the source of a sentimental death-bed story involving the novelist. During his final illness—Parton's story runs—Burr had the comfort of having his friend, Mrs Joshua Webb, read Sterne to him. His favorite passages were, of course, those of Le Fever and Uncle Toby and the fly. One day Burr was apparently moved to remark with obvious relevance, "If I had read Sterne more, and Voltaire less, I should have known that the world was wide enough for Hamilton and me."[16]

Burr's father was the second president of Princeton. Another early president of the same university, Samuel Stanhope Smith, can be cited to demonstrate how Sterne's style could influence the correspondence of academic people of the time. Smith's charmingly Sternian correspondence is preserved in the Princeton University Library.[17] Moreover, William Ellery—Harvard graduate, lawyer, statesman, jurist, signer of the Declaration of Independence, and grandfather of Richard Henry Dana and William Ellery Channing—made numerous references to *Tristram Shandy* in his diaries and attempted the Shandian narrative form and point of view.[18] A New Yorker like young Daniel D. Tompkins, later to become vice-president under Monroe, recorded his enthusiasm for Sterne in his diary while he was a student at Columbia College, according him importance in the anti-slavery movement not often so positively recognized elsewhere. "It requires the pen of Sterne," he says, referring to a famous passage in *A Sentimental Journey* ("A Captive. Paris."), "to paint the horrors of Slavery and shew the miseries of slaves."[19] The list could be continued.[20]

Naturally, the admiring references to Sterne found in numerous diaries and letters do not tell the whole story. William Wirt gives what is more nearly the broader view when he refers to "the whimsical pages of *Tristram Shandy*, that book which everybody censures and admires alternately; and which will continue to be read, abused, and devoured, with ever fresh delight, as long as the world shall relish a joyous laugh, or a tear of delicious feeling."[21] Since he himself was one of the offenders, Wirt neglects to suggest that Sterne would not only be imitated widely but also, and most often, badly. In America as elsewhere the Sterne of the delicious tear vied with Sterne the philosopher and moralist; and at least quantitatively there can be no question as to which won out.

At this point a bibliographical note may be interesting.[22] The first American edition of a work by Sterne was apparently *A Sentimental Journey* published in Boston in 1786, followed two years later by another published in Philadelphia as "By the late celebrated Dr Sterne of Double Entendre Memory." The so-called *Works* appeared in Philadelphia three years later in two formats as a reprint of the London edition. Though there were no single reprints of *Tristram Shandy*, there were at least eight American editions or reprints of the *Journey* before 1800. The tenth English edition of *The Beauties of Sterne*—"Selected for the Heart of Sensibility," as the title page ran—was reprinted in Philadelphia in 1789; and other printings appeared in Philadelphia in 1791 and in Boston and Taunton, Massachusetts, in 1793. As in England, favorite episodes began to appear either in miscellanies, like that of the peasant mourning his dead ass in the *Literary Miscellany* published in Philadelphia in 1795; or in synthetic works, like *The Whole Story of the Sorrows of Maria* published in Boston and Salem in 1793; or in limited volumes of selections like *The Stories of Le Fever, of Poor Maria, and the Dead Ass*, published in New London, Connecticut, in 1806.[23]

Professor Tremaine McDowell observed as early as 1927 that it is Sterne's famous apostrophe to "Dear Sensibility . . . Eternal fountain of our feelings!" to which we must credit the establishment in American letters of "sensibility" in its new sense of the "delicate susceptibility of the heart"; and to it we must charge the numerous tears that dripped in more than thirty novels written in the closing decades of the century by William Hill Brown, Mrs Susanna H. Rowson, Mrs Hannah W. Foster, Gilbert Imlay, and Charles Brockden Brown[24]. In 1940 Professor Herbert Ross Brown provided further documentation for the contention that Sterne was "demonstrably the most powerful of the influences that produced sensibility in America."[25]

Though no attempt can be made here to discuss this influence in detail, we may document it at least to the extent of pointing out that it produced two landmarks in early American literary history: namely, the so-called first American novel and the first native American play published. And a few typical evidences of its manifestations in other novels and in periodical literature can be cited.

Though William Hill Brown cast the "first American novel," *The Power of Sympathy* of 1789, in a Richardsonian epistolary form, in tone the novel was Sternian all the way. If one wishes to demonstrate how

Sterne's imitators refused to let well enough alone, no better illustration could be found than Brown's own apostrophe to "Sensibility," drawing as it does both from the *Journey* and the *Sermons* and beginning:

> HAIL Sensibility! Sweetener of the joys of life! Heaven has implanted thee in the breasts of children—to soothe the sorrows of the afflicted—to mitigate the wounds of the stranger who falleth in our way.

Although Mrs Susanna Rowson's most obviously Sternian novel called *The Inquisitor; or Invisible Rambler* of 1794 happened to be written in England, her preface is a perfect illustration of the general pose assumed by American imitators. After admitting that she is like the artist "who copies a portrait painted by an eminent master" and that she has no illusions that her copy is "the least tinctured with the spirit and fire . . . of [the] bright original," she suggests that her books can be appreciated only when Sterne's works are not around:

> . . . but should Maria or LeFevre [*sic*] make their appearance, its weak rays will be extinguished by the tear of sensibility, which the love-lorn virgin and the dying soldier would excite.

The real center of the Sternian sentimental vogue in the closing decades of the century was the *Massachusetts Magazine* (1786–1796), a family journal designed to provide fare of "knowledge and rational entertainment" and imbued with a characteristic zeal for the improvement of manners and morals. Here may be found a wide array of Sternian imitations, parodies, and burlesques, extravagant praise, and even some expressions of moral alarm and censure. Reprints of letters and imitations from British magazines and other sources, the brief Eustace–Sterne correspondence, and the full-length farce based on *Tristram Shandy* (to be discussed forthwith) were included within its pages.

The *Massachusetts Magazine* was, of course, not alone in reflecting Sterne's influence or reaction to it. Almost as many evidences could be found in such periodicals as the *New York Magazine*, the *Weekly Magazine*, and *Port Folio*. So widespread, indeed, was the attempt to imitate Sterne that the "Sternian fragment" became almost a literary genre, producing an ultimately boring parade of little magazine pieces often "flanked," in Professor Brown's words, "by an elegant steel engraving with its inevitable representation of a marble urn and sensitive plant to help induce the particular variety of trance to enable the reader 'to frisk and curvet' through all the intricacies of sentiment."[26]

The fact that almost the complete spectrum of adulation and censure was present, at times detached from and at others related to those who most vied with Sterne in indulgence in sensibility, can be illustrated by the accusation made by Mrs Hannah Foster in her novel *The Boarding School* (1798) that there were "noxious insinuations of licentious wit" under Sterne's "artful blandishments of sympathetic sensibility." And, in spite of Jefferson's position to the contrary, there were always those who could charge, as a contributor to the *New England Quarterly* did in 1812, that in applying sensibility to illicit amorous attachments "few writers have done more injury to morals than Sterne."

When young William Dunlap was moved at the age of twenty-two to borrow *Tristram Shandy* for dramatic purposes, he elected to use Sterne for something other than his subtle artistry and delicacy of feeling. As the Irish dramatist Leonard McNally had found somewhat earlier, it was the farcical aspects of the work that impressed and inspired him. *The Father; or American Shandyism*, written in 1788, was presented in New York on 7 September 1789.

The play has an intricately complicated plot encompassing a morass of intrigues, disguises, and sentimental relationships typical of the comedy of its day and resolved by an equally typical recognition scene. Since the narrative line bears absolutely no resemblance to *Tristram Shandy*, a synopsis would be useless. The "Shandyism" so brashly "Americanized" involves a broad burlesque of Sterne's manner and style, as well as that of his principal characters and incidents.

For example, Colonel Duncan and his faithful Cartridge are Captain Shandy and Trim. Mrs Grenade, who is "so fond of everything military, that she makes the cook form every dish . . . into some kind of fortification," stands for the Widow Wadman. Susannah appears under her own name. And Dr Quiescent is Dr Slop. The story of Le Fever appears inevitably, as does the incident of Uncle Toby and the fly.

Within a few months of its production, the play had been presented seven times in New York—a good record for its day. Moreover, it appeared in book form and in the pages of the *Massachusetts Magazine* in the same year of its production. In addition, it was revived in 1807 in an altered version called *The Father of an Only Child*, with a curious omission of a reference to Shandyism.[27]

If the "dying soldier" appeared in his first stage success, Dunlap was later to give the "love-lorn virgin" an inning in a so-called opera named *Sterne's Maria; or the Vintage*, with music by a French emigré and a popular musician, M. Victor Pellissier. This work seems to have appeared on several occasions, but the manuscript has been lost. Only three songs from the opera survive.

In the new century, evidence of Sterne's influence began to appear in major writers. There was, for example, a significant influence on Washington Irving and a superficial one on Poe. Both Hawthorne and Oliver Wendell Holmes remembered Sterne in their travels, and so on. But these matters, as Sterne himself might say, will have to be dealt with in my next chapter.

When one looks at Sterne merely from the vantage point of his reception by his early readers, especially those in America (as I have attempted to show), it might well seem incredible that the novelists of our own time who have best prepared us to reread him in a new light are Joyce, Kafka, and Proust, and that the novelists who have best assimilated his influence are Thomas Mann, Henry Green, and Samuel Beckett. A recognition of this fact might, indeed, lead us to assert that Sterne was two hundred years ahead of his time.

Who among his earlier admirers either in America or elsewhere could appreciate, we might ask, how skillfully he constructed a fictional archetechtonic with a new concept of time, how deftly he developed a fresh comic approach to the idea of human isolation in a world where everybody is victimized by the limitations of language and by his own peculiar "association of ideas," and how keenly he achieved a new fictional awareness of the life process itself. Of such a sophisticated comprehension, few of his early admirers and imitators in America, even the most intelligent of them, seemed capable.

But Sterne, like any sensible writer, was willing to settle for far less. "I am very proud sir," Sterne wrote to Dr Eustace, "to have had a man like you on my side from the beginning; but it is not in the power of any one to taste humor, however he may wish it—'tis the gift of God—and besides, a true feeler always brings half the entertainment along with him" (*Letters*, p. 411). The appeal of his humor was demonstrably not lost on the kind of American readers that Sterne would have been most pleased to acknowledge—readers who, to compound the compliment regarded him as a sort of prophet of men of good will. If other kinds of "feelers" turned out to be more extravagant than "true," the novelist himself was only partially to blame. Indeed, both classes of readers took different "handles" of his work from those taken by twentieth-century readers. But who will say that these handles are not also valid?

NOTES

1. "Literary Tastes in Virginia before Poe," *William and Mary Quarterly*, XIX (1939), 55–68. See also Van Wyck Brooks, *The World of Washington Irving* (New York, 1944), p. 31.

2. *The Head and Heart of Jefferson* (Garden City, New York, 1954), pp. 246–247.

3. *The Papers of Benjamin Franklin*, ed. Leonard W. Larrabee (New Haven and London, 1966), X, 274n and 277.

4. *Ibid*, p. 212.

5. *The Philosophy of Thomas Jefferson* (New York, 1943), p. 30.

6. *The Papers of Thomas Jefferson*, ed. Julian P. Boyd, I (Princeton, 1950), 77.

7. *Ibid*, XII (1955), 15.

8. Dumas Malone, *Jefferson and the Rights of Man* (Boston, 1951), p. 67.

9. *The Papers of Thomas Jefferson*, VI (1952), 196–197.

10. Richard Beale Davis, *Intellectual Life in Jefferson's Virginia*, 1790–1830 (Chapel Hill, 1964), p. 405.

11. See my own "The Eustace–Sterne Correspondence: A Note on Sterne's Reputation in America," *English Language Notes*, V (1968), 175–183.

12. Davis, p. 294.

13. *Memoirs of the Life of William Wirt*, ed. John P. Kennedy (Philadelphia, 1849), I, 57.

14. [William Wirt], *The Letters of a British Spy* (Richmond, 1803).

15. Brooks, p. 35.

16. James A. Parton, *The Life and Times of Aaron Burr* (Boston, 1890), II, 321–322.

17. S. H. Monk, "Laurence Sterne at Princeton," *Princeton University Library Chronicle*, X (1949), 137–139.

18. R. H. Pearce, "Sterne and Sensibility in American Diaries," *Modern Language Notes*, LIX (1944), 403–407.

19. D. W. Tompkins, *A Columbia College Student in the Eighteenth Century* (New York, 1940), p. 16.

20. See L. N. Richardson, *A History of Early American Magazines* (New York, 1931), 260–261 and 261n.

21. Wirt, p. 118.

22. See the checklist of American editions of Sterne in the appendix.

23. See Charles Evans, *American Bibliography* and Roger P. Bristol, *Index of Printers Publishers and Booksellers Indicated by Charles Evans*; also J. C. T. Oates, *Shandyism and Sentiment*, 1760–1800 (Cambridge, 1968), *passim*.

24. Tremaine McDowell, "Sensibility in the Eighteenth-Century American Novel," *Studies in Philology*, XXIV (1927), 383–402.

25. (Durham, N. C., 1940), pp. 74–79.

26. Brown, pp. 90–91.

27. See my own, "Sterne and the Eighteenth-Century Stage," *Papers in Language and Literature*, IV (1968), 144–157; G. C. D. Odell, *Annals of the New York Stage*, I (New York, 1927), 275–277; *The Fathers*, edited with an introduction by Thomas J. McKee (New York, 1887).

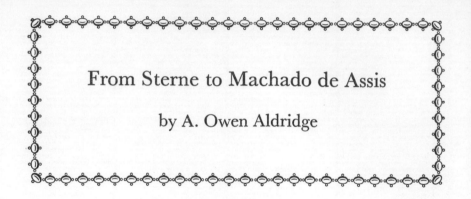

From Sterne to Machado de Assis

by A. Owen Aldridge

Machado de Assis is generally considered to be the greatest Brazilian novelist of all times, and the case could well be argued that he was the first author in the entire western hemisphere to experiment with the structure of the novel in a significant manner. Since Machado was well acquainted with his eighteenth- and nineteenth-century forerunners in English, French, Spanish, and Portuguese literatures, it is not surprising that he should reveal some knowledge of Sterne. Indeed Machado indicated that his most important novel, *Memórias Pósthumas de Brás Cubas*, owed much to the double influence of Sterne and Stendhal. The only previous attempt to draw these novelists together was that of a nineteenth-century editor of Xavier de Maistre, a French disciple of Sterne. In a note to a comparison of the humor of Sterne with the fantasy of de Maistre, this editor remarked, "if we had dreamed of comparing Xavier de Maistre to the most celebrated French humorist of the same period, H. Beyle (Stendhal), it would be merely a comparison by contrast, for we do not know a mind more paradoxical, more sceptical, more coldly ironical, more incapable of naive emotion than that of Stendhal."[1]

Machado in the preface to his *Memórias* places Sterne and Stendhal side by side in much more direct fashion:

> When we learn from Stendhal that he wrote one of his books for only a hundred readers, we are both astonished and disturbed. The world will be neither astonished nor, probably, disturbed if the present book has not one hundred readers like Stendhal's, nor fifty, nor twenty, nor even ten. Ten? Maybe five. It is, in truth, a diffuse work, in which I, Brás Cubas, if indeed I have adopted the

Professor of Comparative Literature, University of Illinois, Editor of *Comparative Literature Studies*

free form of a Sterne or of a Xavier de Maistre, have possibly
added a certain peevish pessimism of my own.[2]

In later editions, Machado added a reference to the Portuguese
novelist Almeida Garrett and commented, "All of these writers went
on tours. Xavier de Maistre toured his own chamber, Garrett his own
country, Sterne foreign lands. Of Brás Cubas one could say that he
made a tour of life."[3]

The works to which Machado referred and which in addition to
Sterne's he considered his models were *Voyage autour de ma chambre*,
1794, by de Maistre and *Viagens na minha terra*, by Garrett. In so far as
technique is concerned, Machado borrowed considerably more from
Sterne than Diderot did in his *Jacques le fataliste*, a relationship which
has been widely explored in scholarship.[4]

According to Sainte-Beuve, two passages in particular of de Maistre's
Voyage are reminiscent of Sterne, one in which the protagonist sheds a
tear of repentance because he had unjustly rebuked his manservant
(Chap. XIX), and the other in which he feels remorse for callous
treatment of a poor farmhand (Chap. XXVIII). The narrator is
instructed in philosophy and humanity by his servant and his dog.[5]
Another French critic observed one of the techniques which de
Maistre adopted from Sterne: that of leading up to a profound
philosophical contemplation or sublime sentiment, but turning it off
by a "boutade humoristique."[6]

Like Sterne, de Maistre illustrates the literary doctrine of "digressive method" by applying a zig-zag organization. "I do not like," he
proclaims, "the people who are masters of their steps and their ideas
... My mind is completely open to all kinds of ideas, tastes and sentiments. It absorbs avidly everything which is presented to it."[7] The
only direct reference to Sterne in de Maistre's *Voyage* concerns Uncle
Toby's predilection for military affairs, or "le démon de la guerre."
Ending one chapter on this note, de Maistre comments in the next
chapter on the difficulty he encounters in switching to another subject.
"I am unable to descend entirely from the point to which I had
climbed a moment ago: moreover it is the *dada* of Uncle Toby" (p. 51).
The *dada* or *idée fixe* of Uncle Toby is, as we have said, "le démon de la
guerre." The style of de Maistre is somewhere between that of
Montaigne which it follows and that of Lamb, which it precedes. The
Voyage is really a discursive essay approaching the method of stream of

consciousness. Indeed it strangely foreshadows the technique of Proust: the narrator has an extraordinary proclivity for "meditating in the sweet warmth" of his bed (p. 29). The division of the novel into short chapter segments is the major stylistic resemblance to Sterne, but these brief chapters incorporate other Shandyesque techniques. One of them, following the description of a romantic encounter on a bluff, contains nothing but a series of dots with the word "bluff" in the middle. The subsequent chapter consists of a single sentence, covering only two lines of type. Chapter XXXIII is almost as brief.

Another chapter suddenly takes up a theme which had been dropped two chapters previously (p. 39). In the middle of the entire work appears a dedicatory chapter, having no relation to the chapters immediately preceding or following and introducing a new character (p. 48).

Most important of the techniques borrowed from Sterne is that of intermittent direct address to the reader, in alternating cajoling and scolding terms. Sterne may not have invented this technique, but there is no question that it is associated with him and that he had more influence than any other eighteenth-century writer upon its later adoption. With Sterne, addressing the reader is a permanent attitude of mind, not an occasional one as it is in Fielding. The most famous single line of address to a reader in any literature is that of Baudelaire: "Hypocrite lecteur!—mon semblable—mon frère!" De Maistre is much more conciliatory, calling on his "reasonable reader" to "grasp firmly, if you can, the logic that I am going to explain to you" (p. 7). By the middle of the nineteenth century, appeals to the "dear reader" had made the technique of direct address banal, but in 1794 it was still rare enough to be associated with Sterne.

The intermediary between de Maistre and Machado was the Portuguese romanticist Almeida Garrett, who gave his work an epigraph from his French model as well as a similar title, *Viagens na minha terra*. Certain passages, however, indicate the direct influence of Sterne. Garrett drew more from Sterne's emotional attitude of sentimentalism, however, than from his artistic technique or defiance of tradition. "I am," he wrote, "like my friend Yorick, the highly intelligent clown of the king of Denmark, who several years later was resurrected in Sterne with such elegant pains."[8] After this introduction, Garrett presented a close translation of the following quotation from *A Sentimental Journey* (pp. 128–129):

Having been in love with one princess or another almost all my life, . . . I hope I shall go on so, till I die, being firmly persuaded, that if ever I do a mean action, it must be in some interval betwixt one passion and another: whilst this interregnum lasts, I always perceive my heart locked up—I can scarce find in it to give Misery a sixpence; and therefore I always get out of it as fast as I can, and the moment I am rekindled, I am all generosity and good will again. [9]

Garrett's subsequent remarks on this passage indicate his sincere dedication to the philosophy it incorporates. "Yorick is right—he is much closer to the truth than his august friend, the king of Denmark. However little one generalizes the principle, it remains indisputable, unexceptional forever and everywhere. The human heart is like the human stomach—it cannot be empty, it constantly needs food." This is sentimentalism, but not quite the sentimentalism of Sterne. As we know, his objects of compassion are unorthodox, a fly, a dead ass, a caged bird, or a chambermaid.

Nor did Garrett imitate Sterne in his most flagrant eccentricities of style. From the point of view of technique, he follows Sterne merely in digressions and addresses to the reader. As we see from the following passage, however, he was aware of Sterne's other stylistic innovations, which he considered appropriate for the English novel.

There is a great lacuna in our story—but first of all what does the imagination fill it with?
Oh! I detest the imagination.
Where the chronicle was silent and tradition did not speak, I used to love a page entirely devoted to periods, or all white—or all black—as in the venerable history of our special and respectable friend, Tristram Shandy, in which a single line of invention gives a chronicle.
This is good for novels and romances, insignificant books which everyone, nevertheless, reads, even those who oppose them. And indeed it seems to me that you read them [benevolent reader] although you are always saying that you do not (Chap. XLI).

Garrett's own novel begins as a conventional travelogue, but develops into the recital of a three-cornered tragic love story. His primary concern is to tell a story, not to play tricks on the reader.

When we come to Machado de Assis, the first exponent of the experimental novel in the western hemisphere, we see that he knew his French and Portuguese precursors and that he gave them appropriate complimentary recognition in his prologue "To the Reader."[10] But for the fountainhead of his inspiration he went directly to Sterne. There is nothing in the body of *Memórias Pósthumas* referring to Garrett. And the only notable resemblance to de Maistre is a reference to the duality of human nature, *l'ange et la bête* (Chap. 98). This certainly suggests de Maistre's metaphysical system *de l'âme et de la bête* based upon a division of the human personality into these elements. Machado, however, specifically attributes his duality to Pascal, whom he elsewhere characterizes as one of his "intellectual grandfathers" (Chap. 142).

As Machado describes his own style, the resemblance to Sterne becomes apparent. His chapters are uniformly short, and in one of them he pauses to remind himself not to prolong its length (Chap. 22). "For long chapters are better suited to ponderous readers," he explains. "We are not an *in-folio* public, we are an *in*-12 public, preferring little text, large margins, elegant type, gilt-edged pages and illustrations." Elsewhere he remarks that he and the reader are in a sense opposed to each other (Chap. 71). "You [the reader] want to live fast, to get to the end, and the book ambles along slowly; you like straight, solid narrative and a smooth style, but this book and my style are like a pair of drunks: they stagger to the right and to the left, they start and they stop...."

Following the example of Sterne, Machado has one chapter (136) composed of but a single sentence. In its entirety it reads: "And, if I am not greatly mistaken, I have just written an utterly unnecessary chapter." An earlier chapter (125) contains nothing but an epitaph of twenty words. Also in the manner of Sterne, Machado includes two chapters filled with punctuation marks, but virtually no words (55 and 139).

Chapter 130 has as its title "To Insert in Chapter 129," and its last sentence reads, "This chapter is to be inserted between the first two sentences of Chapter 129." The attention of the reader is constantly directed to the artificial construction of the book. In recalling past events, Machado refers to chapter numbers as well as to the events themselves. In Chapter 61, for example, he remarks, "the yellow, morbid flower of Chapter 25 began to open within me." Two chapters later in reintroducing a minor character, he inserts in parentheses the identifying phrase, "the future college graduate of Chapter 6."

Both Sterne and Machado deal unrealistically with time, but in opposite perspectives. Sterne has Tristram Shandy, speaking in the first person, narrate events which took place before his birth as well as the physical details surrounding his own coming into the world. Machado has Brás Cubas open the novel by narrating his own death. As he says, the radical difference between his book and the Pentateuch is that Moses placed his death at the end.

Sterne is famous for his delicate approach to indecorous subjects— his ability to arouse erotic or scatological ideas in his readers without directly verbalizing them himself. One example is the passage in *Tristram Shandy* suggesting the baleful consequences of a slip of the forceps (III, 17); another is Corporal Trim's story of having his knee massaged by an attractive nurse, the story which reappears in Diderot's *Jacques le fataliste* (VIII, 22). Brás Cubas uses the same technique of indirection and suggestion to reveal the pregnancy of his mistress (Chap. 86). He notices signs of weariness and tells us, "I persisted, and she told me that—A subtle fluid ran through my whole body." At the end of the paragraph we are told, "There is a mystery here; let us give the reader time to solve it."

One of the themes in *Tristram Shandy* which Sterne treats in a suggestive manner is that of noses (III, 35 to IV, 1). Machado has a chapter on "The Tip of the Nose" (49), which considers noses in the literal sense, but nevertheless reminds us of Sterne's ascribing philosophical significance to various portions of the anatomy. Sterne cites Grangousier's explanation that one man's nose is larger than another's because it pleases God to have it so, and Machado cites Pangloss's explanation that noses were created to support spectacles. Machado also has a chapter on "Eyes and Ears" (65) and one on "Legs" (66). The latter treats the legs as having a will or personality separate from that of their owner.

We have already referred to Uncle Toby's hobby-horse as one of the primary themes of *Tristram Shandy*. According to Sterne, a hobby-horse is an intellectual obsession, which a man persists in expounding no matter how it may contradict the realities of life or even his own fundamental personality. A man and his hobby-horse, Sterne suggests in a chapter devoted to this subject, react upon each other much in the way that the soul and the body do (I, 24). Uncle Toby's obsession is with everything military, and Sterne, therefore, proposes to "draw my uncle *Toby*'s character from his HOBBY-HORSE" (I, 23, p. 77). Machado has a chapter on "The Fixed Idea," in which he contrasts fixed ideas with supple, flexible ones (4). The former "make both supermen and madmen." As examples of fixed ideas in the chapter of the same name, Machado cites one contemporary scholar who tried to reverse the judgment of history concerning the Roman Claudius, and another scholar who had tried to idealize the character of Lucrezia Borgia. Parallel to Uncle Toby and his obsession with militarism, Machado depicts an eccentric bachelor Quincas Borba, who has devised a philosophical system, Humanitism, the form taken by his Hobby-Horse (Chap. 91). Humanitism is a system which, like the books of Machado's scholars, upsets conventional notions. Everything which is commonly considered evil is actually good, for example, envy and war. According to Quincas Borba, therefore, Pangloss was not such a great fool as Voltaire made him out to be.

Brás Cubas, the narrator, has his own hobby-horse, which he reveals in Chapter 2. "One morning, as I was strolling through the grounds of my suburban home, an idea took hold of the trapeze that I used to carry about in my head. Once it had taken hold, it flexed its arms and legs and began to do the most daring acrobatic feats one can possibly imagine. . . . Suddenly it made a great leap, extended its arms and legs until it formed an X, and said, 'Decipher me or I devour thee'." The great idea is an "anti-melancholy plaster."

Machado refers to the reader in the first chapter of Brás Cubas and continues to address him throughout the work. Giving the device a novel turn, he considers the reader as a critic and combines the two personae in a missive to "My dear critic." Here he recognizes the difficulty implied in a sentence in an earlier chapter where he had characterized his literary style as "less spirited than in the early years." If he were already dead when beginning the book, he could not very well be any older in its midst. After noting that his style throughout each phase of the story of his life is designed to reflect the emotion or attitude corresponding to that stage in life, he concludes: "Good God, do I have to explain everything!" (Chap. 138). The treatment of the passage of time in this chapter also resembles that of Sterne. Tristram's father looks at his watch, remarks that no more than two hours and ten minutes have passed, but nevertheless comments, "I know not how it happens, brother *Toby*,——but to my imagination it seems almost an age" (III, 18, p. 188). Sterne reveals that he knew very well how it happens and that he was prepared to give a metaphysical discourse on the subject, but Uncle Toby cuts his brother off short by affirming, "'Tis owing, entirely ... to the succession of our ideas." Machado gives the corresponding explanation, but then rebukes the reader for desiring it. The subject of direct address to the reader is so important in Machado that a later critic has written an entire chapter on it.[11]

The universally recognized incongruity in Uncle Toby's character is that of total obsession with military maneuvers combined with a temperament of gentle kindness. Probably the most famous passage in *Tristram Shandy* is that in which Uncle Toby, whose greatest pleasure consists in discoursing on the science of military fortifications, refuses to take the life of a fly. "I'll not hurt thee, says my uncle *Toby* ... I'll not hurt a hair of thy head: ... ——go, poor devil, get thee gone, why should I hurt thee?——This world surely is wide enough to hold both thee and me" (II, 12, p. 113). Passages such as this served to bring the concept of sentimentalism into reproach. Yet the same intellectual dichotomy of extreme feeling in private concerns and disregard of feeling in public or professional concerns had existed since St Augustine. The latter reveals "a nagging incongruity ... between his private and public ethics, between the requirements of a charity so strong that in one sphere an evil man may not be slain and in the other an innocent man may be."[12]

In *Brás Cubas*, Machado first introduces a black butterfly, which flutters around a sixteen-year-old girl, who curses the creature in horror and fright. Brás Cubas does not kill the butterfly, but drives it away with a wave of his handerkerchief (Chap. 30). In the next chapter an even larger black butterfly appears to Brás Cubas as he is alone in his room. After fluttering around it alights on Brás Cubas' forehead, but he brushes it off. He chases it around the room and is annoyed by the derisive way in which it seems to move its wings. Finally, giving way to his nervousness, he grabs a towel and strikes the butterfly, which does not die immediately. In the words of Brás Cubas:

> I felt sorry for it; I took it in the palm of my hand and placed it on the window sill. It was too late; the poor creature expired within a few seconds. I became disturbed and a little annoyed. "Why in the devil couldn't it have been blue?" I said to myself.

The latter comment is based on two circumstances: first, that black butterflies are an omen of evil; second, that Machado was personally attracted to blue insects.[13]

When Brás Cubas compared the black butterfly to a blue one, he was temporarily reconciled to his misdeed, but soon after, in looking at the corpse, he experienced a certain sympathy. He then tried to put himself in the place of the butterfly and to imagine the emotions which the butterfly had felt on encountering him. The butterfly had said to himself: "This is probably the maker of butterflies."

In a later chapter, Brás Cubas, staring at the floor, notices a fly dragging an ant, which was biting the fly's leg, and exclaims "Poor fly! Poor ant!" (Chap. 103).

> With the delicacy so characteristic of a man of our century, I caught these two unhappy creatures in the palm of my hand. I considered the distance from my hand to the planet Saturn and asked myself what interest there could possibly be in this miserable and minute entomological episode. If you think that I was about to perform a barbarity, you are mistaken, for what I did was to ask Virgilia for a hairpin in order to separate the two insects; but the fly perceived my intention, opened its wings, and fled away. Poor fly! Poor ant! And God saw that it was good as the Scripture saith.

Like Sterne, Machado felt a sympathy for the suffering of the lower animals, but unlike Sterne, he questioned the world order which permitted suffering on all levels of being.

Machado adopted from Sterne another of his famous sentimental situations, but extended the sardonic interpretation of benevolence beyond the limits suggested in the English author. In *A Sentimental Journey*, a beggar asks two middle-aged ladies for an alms between them of twelve-sous, an unusual request since beggars do not usually specify an amount—and this one was twelve times greater than the usual alms. When both revealed their astonishment, the beggar remarked that "he knew not how to ask less of ladies of their rank." Both replied that they would give willingly if they had this much money. The beggar then asked the question, "What is it but your goodness and humanity which makes your bright eyes so sweet, ... and what was it which made the Marquis de Santerre and his brother say so much of you both as they just pass'd by?" (pp. 258–259). Each of the two ladies then impulsively pulled out a twelve-sous piece, and after discussing which should be the one to make the gift, each gave her own coin. The beggar's secret, Sterne explains in the subsequent chapter, was flattery.

A similar scene occurs in the course of *A Sentimental Journey* in the last of the chapters named Montriul. In response to the entreaties of a series of beggars, Sterne first of all feels an instinctive impulse of benevolence, which is succeeded by a practical or rational withdrawal. He conceals from the reader the actual amount of his gift to the last of the beggars, explaining "I am ashamed to say *how much*, now——and was ashamed to think, how little, then" (p. 134). One of Sterne's foremost modern critics has interpreted this clash between natural benevolence and natural selfishness as the key to all of Sterne's sentimental comedy.[14]

In Brás Cubas, several passages reflect on Sterne's theory of benevolence. First, Brás reports the remarks of the midwife who had brought him into the world. She "boasted that she had opened the doors to the world for a whole generation of noblemen. Quite possibly my father had heard her say this; I believe, however, that it was paternal sentiment that induced him to gratify her with two half dobras" (Chap. 10). The reader, though, cannot miss the suggestion of flattery.

However, Brás himself, who has penetrated Sterne's secret, learns to moderate his charitable impulses. He is saved by a muleteer from death or at the least a painful accident through a runaway donkey. At first he decides to give the kind muleteer three of the gold coins in his possession; then he wonders whether the reward is not excessive; whether two gold coins would not suffice; he takes out one coin, watches it shine in the sunlight, puts it back again, hesitates, and finally, places a silver coin in the muleteer's hand. When he perceives that the muleteer looks overjoyed, he decides he should have given some copper pennies instead of the silver. He muses that there had been no personal merit in the muleteer's act, that he had merely yielded to a natural impulse or to the habits of his trade, and that he had been placed in the road by providence. Brás actually felt remorse for his prodigality.

Machado's third observation on sentimental generosity concerns the arrangements made by Brás Cubas for regular visits with his mistress, a married lady. He acquired a house on a secluded street and placed it under the care of Dona Placida, a poor relative of his mistress. Dona Placida was "the ostensible, and in some respects the real, lady of the house" (Chap. 70). "It pained her to serve in that capacity," a capacity which Machado—like Sterne—fails to label more specifically. Since the calling of a Madame is not regarded as a savory one, Brás Cubas "was not unappreciative." He established a fund "for her as a bulwark against poverty in her old age." He adds: "Dona Placida thanked me with tears in her eyes and thereafter prayed for me every night before an image of the Virgin that she had in her room."

The benevolence of Brás Cubas was exaggerated, and the amount of the fund for Dona Placida was excessive. Machado's treatment is sardonic, first, because of the dubious relationships which brought the gift about, and, second, because the money which Brás Cubas uses he had originally found on the beach (Chap. 53). When finding it he had resolved to use it "for a good purpose, perhaps a dowry for some poor girl." The contrast between this projected use of the funds and the actual use to which they were put represents an ironical commentary on sentimentalism.

II

We have covered the obvious resemblances between Sterne and Machado, but perhaps a more important consideration is the nature of the humor of the two novelists. Fundamental differences are quite as apparent as are the resemblances. Sterne's work represents the comedy of sentiment; Machado's the comedy of ideas. A Brazilian critic concerned with the spirit of comedy in Machado has written that "Swift considerou o seu tempo incomparável como modêlo de amoralidade, hipocrasia e decadência. Não houve um humorista, verdadeiramente digno dêsse nome, que não olhasse para a sua época do mesmo modo."[15] This judgement is true of Machado, but certainly not of Sterne. One may argue whether Sterne was even a satirist; he was a parodist of literature and an amused observer of individual human behavior, but he completely lacked the social perspective of a real satirist. Above all, Sterne was a humorous rhetorician. He loved to play with words, rather than to excoriate the evils of society or even the incongruities of the cosmos, as did Swift or Voltaire.

It was probably because of Sterne's stylistic eccentricities that

H. G. Wells in a conversation with Sterne's Mexican translator, Alfonso Reyes, expressed surprise that Reyes had found it easier to translate Sterne than G. K. Chesterton. Reyes explained that "la lengua de Quevedo y Gracián . . . está muy bien preparada para todo juguete de conceptos."[16] Machado obviously took pleasure in word play, but he was also a satirist with a cosmic vision, and he was more concerned with ideas than with words. It was primarily form, or perhaps more accurately formlessness, that Machado derived from Sterne. His satirical method and matter have more in common with Voltaire.

We have given several illustrations of Sterne's sentimentalism and shown how Machado used the same ingredients without himself penetrating the bounds of sentimentalism. A further passage from Machado will show that his approach to sentimentalism is sardonic rather than sympathetic. In the chapter following that in which Brás Cubas assures himself that the married lady whom he has been pursuing will become his mistress, he finds a gold coin on the ground which he picks up and puts in his pocket (Chap. 51). The next day he suffers an attack of conscience over pocketing the coin and therefore sends it with a letter to the chief of police. Immediately he finds complete peace of mind and he tells himself "You did the right thing, Cubas; you behaved perfectly." He had atoned for corrupting another man's wife by refusing to keep a coin he found on the ground. Thus he formulated "a sublime law, the Law of the Equivalence of Windows, and established the principle that the way to compensate for a closed window is to open another window, so that the conscience may always have plenty of air." In the next chapter Brás Cubas finds on the beach a package of currency, representing a small fortune, and he deposits it in the bank to his own account.

Not only does Machado have a sardonic view of sentimentalism, but he intellectualizes his opinions in a manner foreign to Sterne. He specifically subscribes to the theory "that self-interest is the mainspring of human action," which he ascribes to Helvétius rather than to Hobbes or other English sources (Chap. 133). But he adds as a personal observation that vanity is one of the strongest forms of self-interest, so that "men are governed less by considerations of ultimate safety than by vanity, which is more intimate, more immediate." This comment has an axiomatic ring. Indeed the axiom as a literary form had a great appeal to Machado, as to most Brazilians of his generation, and he included a large number in *Memórias Pósthumas*, particularly in one parenthetical chapter containing nothing else but maxims (Chap. 119).

The final difference between Sterne and Machado is one that the latter himself pointed out in the Prologue to the Fourth Edition of *Memórias Pósthumas*. "That which makes my Brás Cubas a special author is that which he calls peevish pessimism. There exists in the spirit of this book, no matter how smiling it may seem, a bitter and disagreeable sentiment, which is far from appearing in its models."[17]

Indeed *Memórias Pósthumas* reflects Swift's principle in *Tale of A Tub* that "Insanity is a matter of degree" (Chap. 155). Citing a "famous Athenian madman," who imagined that every ship which entered the harbor of Piraeus was his personal property, Machado reflects the opinion of a psychiatrist that delusion makes a person "the happiest man in the world" (Chap. 154). One of Machado's best satirical strokes against the entire race is his question: "what would the sparrow hawks say of us if Buffon had been born a sparrow hawk?" (Chap. 6).

Some time ago, Max Lerner, in *The Nation* (21 October 1939), developed the theme that the genius of his age was the discovery of the irrational. "The intellectual revolution of the twentieth century is likely to prove the charting of the *terra incognita* of the irrational and the extraction of its implications for every area of human thought. . . . The rational, right-thinking man has as surely ceased to be considered the center of our intellectual system as the earth has ceased to be the center of our planetary system." One could certainly add that Sterne and Machado earlier recognized that much of human behavior is not logical.

There needs to be a distinction made between two ways of viewing the lack of logic in the universe. Thinkers such as Machado, Camus, and Sartre use a rational process to arrive at the conclusion that the universe does not absolutely conform to the system of order which these rational processes indicate to be the norm. Machado, unlike Camus and Sartre however, colored his view of cosmic irrationality by a profound pessimism. Other writers—called exponents of the absurd, such as Beckett and Ionescu—themselves completely abdicate the rational process by portraying the world in a non-rational manner. Sterne has as much in common with this second group as with the first.

In conclusion, to compare Sterne and Machado in a nutshell we could well adapt the comparison of Sterne and Stendhal quoted in our opening paragraph: "It would be merely a comparison by contrast, for we do not know a mind more paradoxical, more sceptical, more coldly ironical, more incapable of naive emotion than that of Machado."

NOTES

1. *Œuvres inédites de Xavier de Maistre* (Paris, 1877), I, 216.

2. This quotation is taken from the English translation of *Memórias* by William L. Grossman under the title of *Epitaph of a Small Winner* (New York, 1952). Other quotations from this novel are taken from this edition. All other quotations from Portuguese sources in this paper are my own translation.

3. *Obras escolhidas de Machado de Assis*, III (São Paulo, 1955). One may even extend the series of stay-at-home travelers into the twentieth century by referring to *Viaje alrededor de mi infancia* by Delfina Bunge de Galvez (Buenos Aires, 1938). The latter, however, is primarily a work of childhood recollections and religious meditation and is linked to Xavier de Maistre only by the similarity in titles. The literary genre devoted to a character who had once lived but is now free from human restrictions was developed as early as the second century A.D., by the Greek Lucian in his *Dialogues of the Dead*. In the eighteenth century, the genre was used by Tom Brown and Henry Fielding; the former in *Letters from the Dead to the Living* (London, 1702); the latter in *A Journey from this World to the Next* (London, 1783). Sandra M. Cypess has written a dissertation "The Dead Narrator in Modern Latin-American Prose Fiction: A Study in Point of View," (Department of Spanish, University of Illinois, 1968).

4. J. Robert Loy, *Diderot's Determined Fatalist* (New York, 1950), pp. 41–49. See also Alice Green Fredman, *Diderot and Sterne* (New York, 1955).

5. "Notice sur l'auteur," *Œuvres completes de Xavier de Maistre* (Paris, s. d.), p. x. The combination of philosophy and a dog represents a significant parallel to another of the novels of Machado de Assis, *Quincas Borba*, 1892, which has been translated with the title *Philosopher or Dog*.

6. *Œuvres inédites* (Paris, 1877), I, xlix.

7. *Œuvres complètes*, p. 9. Virtually every critic of Sterne considers his work a practical illustration of Locke's doctrine of the association of ideas. Kenneth MacLean, however, in "Imagination and Sympathy: Sterne and Adam Smith," (*Journal of the History of Ideas*, X [1949], 398–410) traces the doctrine of association to Adam Smith's *Theory of Moral Sentiments*, 1759. Arthur H. Cash, moreover, argues that Sterne's "digressive method" is based not on Locke's theory of association of ideas, but on Locke's empiricism. Although the psychology based on Locke's empiricism has never been given a special name, Professor Cash calls it "the psychology of the train of ideas." "The Lockean Psychology of *Tristram Shandy*," *E.L.H.*, XXII (1955), 125–135.

8. *Obras de Almeida Garrett* (Porto, 1963), I, 53.

9. *Ibid.*, I, 173.

10. I am deeply indebted to the splendid study of Eugênio Gomes, *Espelho contra espelho* (São Paulo, s.d.). The first section of this work is entitled "Machado de Assis, Influências Inglêsas," of which pages 43–57 concern Sterne. There is also some discussion of Sterne in the same author's *O Enigma de Capitu* (Rio de Janeiro, 1967), a study of *Don Casmurro*.

11. J. Mattoso Camara, Jr, "Machado de Assis e as Referências ao Leitor," *Ensaios Machadianos* (Rio de Janeiro, 1962), pp. 63–79.

12. Richard Shelly Hartigan, "Saint Augustine on War and Killing: The Problem of the Innocent," *Journal of the History of Ideas*, XXVII (1966), 204.

13. See his lyric poem "Amôsca azul," *Obras escolhidas de Machado de Assis*, IX (São Paulo, 1965), 229.

14. Arthur H. Cash, *Sterne's Comedy of Moral Sentiments* (Pittsburgh, 1966), *passim*.

15. Vianna Moog, *Heróis da decadência* (Rio de Janeiro, 1964), p. 18.

16. *Obras completas* (Mexico, 1956), IV, 295. I have not been able to locate the translation of Reyes. The printed catalog of the Library of Congress lists no translations of Sterne into either Spanish or Portuguese. That of the British Museum lists none in Portuguese and only the following in Spanish: *Viaje sentimental de Sterne a Paris, bajo el nombre de Yorick. Traducido libremente al castellano. Madrid 1821.* The following work is an imitation of Sterne's *Sentimental Journey* rather than a translation: *El viajador sensible. En castellano por D. Bernardo Maria de Calzada.* (no place) 1791. My colleague at the University of Illinois, Professor Luis Leal, has shown me his personal copy of the following edition of Sterne: *Viaje sentimental por Francia e Italia, con un estudio preliminar por D. Francisco-Luis Cardona Castro, licenciado en Filosofía y Letras. Editorial Bruguera, S.A.* (Barcelona, 1967). Since the title page does not say that the author of the introduction is the translator, it is possible that this translation is the one by Alfonso Reyes. The following passage from the introduction (p. 23) indicates that the Reyes translation has at least appeared somewhere in print: " '... *El viajero sentimental* produjo en Francia una larga descendencia, que llega a Xavier de Maistre y a Charles Nodier', dice Alfonso Reyes en su prólogo al *Viaje Sentimental* (págs. 7–8). Y nos han parecido curiosas estas apreciaciones de Reyes que nos indican la trascendencia de Sterne."

17. *Obras escolhidas*, III, 21.

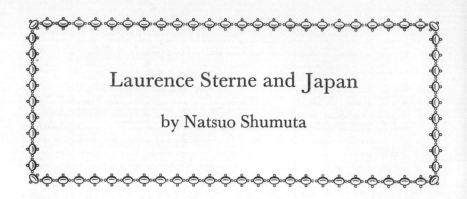

Laurence Sterne and Japan

by Natsuo Shumuta

It was a great honor and privilege to have been invited to address the Laurence Sterne Bicentenary Conference. As Professor Clifford was kind enough to mention in introducing me at the time, I am the first translator into Japanese of *Tristram Shandy*. The translation was published in June 1966, and I was awarded for the work a rather well-known literary prize in my country in early 1967. The publisher issued a limited de luxe edition (with some revisions on my part) in April 1968. Luckily enough, so far the translation has sold something between 20,000 and 25,000 copies, and another version, this time a handy three-volume paperback edition, has just come out. These facts, I believe, show that the work is enjoying some welcome among the Japanese reading public. So much by way of introduction.

In speaking about the relationship between Laurence Sterne and Japan, I must ask you, first of all, to remember that there was practically no affinity whatever between English literature in general and our nation. Japan was a remote and closed country to Westerners for a long time, and the import of foreign books was strictly prohibited except for those in Chinese or Dutch. Our modernization started in 1868 (by coincidence another sixty-eight) and this is a memorable date for the Japanese, as the year of Meiji Restoration, or the first year of Modern Japan. A new educational system was initiated a few years later, and naturally it was also after that that Japanese students began to be taught English in schools and colleges. Shakespeare began to be read, as did Wordsworth and other authors. We can count among our earliest translations of English literature *Julius Caesar* by Shakespeare and some of Disraeli's novels. In the eighteen-eighties and nineties, *The Vicar of Wakefield* and *Rasselas* were widely used as textbooks for

Professor Emeritus, Tokyo University; Professor of English Literature, Chuo University

English classes in various colleges and sometimes in schools; indeed, the first Japanese translation of *Rasselas* seems to have come out as early as 1886. (This work of Johnson's, by the way, has had quite a few different translations since then, the latest being my own, which was first published in 1948.) In 1894, the first life of Samuel Johnson written in Japanese by a Japanese, a slim volume, came out. These were not days when lives of various Western writers were in fashion in Japan, and I do not know how to account for this rather rare phenomenon, except by resorting to the Japanese author's personal interest in the eminent doctor.

The first Japanese who introduced the author Laurence Sterne and the book *Tristram Shandy* at any length to our reading public was Sôseki Natsumè (1867–1916), who was to become one of the representative Japanese novelists, and who is still very widely read. He was one of the earliest graduates of the English Literature course in the University of Tokyo (finishing as an undergraduate in 1893), and later, one of the two first Japanese lecturers in the same course (serving from 1903 to 1907), all the lectures having been given until then exclusively by either English or American scholars. He wrote his article "On *Tristram Shandy*" when he was still an unknown young scholar. It first appeared in a small magazine in 1897, but it is very easy to come by now, for it is included in several sets of his complete works, which are still very popular. But before going into some details of this article, since this scholar-novelist was not only the first introducer of *Tristram Shandy*, but retains some influence of this fantastic work in at least one of his well-known novels; in other words, as I esteem this writer as the most important character in the history, so to speak, of Laurence Sterne in Japan, I should like to speak a little more about the man himself.

Sôseki, his first name, was a *nom de plume*, while the second name was his real family name. It was a very common custom of long standing among our men of letters in those days to substitute only their given names by pen-names while retaining their family names. So in that case, Sôseki only followed an established custom, but this particular name which he adopted on his own choice has a rather peculiar nuance of meaning and gives a key to some extent to elucidating what kind of a man the writer was. In the summer of 1968, I visited Stratford-upon-Avon and enjoyed the performance of *As You Like It*. (You may take this as an instance of a pseudo-Shandian digression.)

When during the play the Duke sonorously delivered that famous passage at the beginning of the forest scenes:

And this our life exempt from public haunt,
Finds tongues in trees, books in the running brooks,
Sermons in stones, and good in everything,

I was suddenly reminded of a certain character in one of Aldous Huxley's earlier novels, who unfortunately misquotes this passage as "sermons in books, stones in the running brooks." It would be of course too natural to find sermons in books and stones in brooks for the passage to become so world-famous, and the character feels instantly that something is wrong with his own quotation, but he cannot tell what exactly is the matter. He is simply embarrassed. Now, at Stratford, this recollection in its turn reminded me of the name Sôseki. "Sôseki" literally means "to rinse (one's mouth) with a stone," and this phrase has its origin in a somewhat similar case of misquotation which is said to have happened in ancient China. The legend goes that a young Chinese scholar, yearning for a hermit's life and intending to express his wish to "pillow (his head) on a stone and rinse (his mouth) at a stream" to a friend of his, said instead that he wished to "rinse with a stone and pillow on a stream." Naturally the friend laughed at the absurdity of what the other said. The young would-be hermit was immediately aware of his own mistake, but he was a kind of die-hard, far from the frankness of Huxley's character, and was not willing to admit the error. He is reported to have instantly insisted: to pillow on a stream means to wash my ears, and to rinse my mouth with a stone is nothing else but to clean my teeth with a pebble. That is the end of the story, but cannot the fact that Sôseki picked up this legendary phrase as his own name from among thousands of possible candidates be taken to throw some light on his own cynical character?

Let us come back now to his article on *Tristram Shandy*. This is not very long, and besides was written mainly for general readers, most of whom had never so much as heard of such a novel. So we cannot expect anything very profound or subtle, but we can safely say that the article shows something of the writer's wit and also that his appreciation of the work is almost always to the point. I myself feel proud when I note that this predecessor of ours, within a dozen years of studies of English literature being first taken up in Japan, had already attained

Mr. Clough

The Bearer is the poor Woman who was presented at Stillington Visitation; and has left her Child to go & get these said Penances, wch I & Mr Mosely talked so much about. She is as poor as a Church Mouse & cannot absolutely raise a Shilling, to save her Life. so pray let her have the Penance — and as far as the Stamps, I will take care to discharge. If not above 3 or 4 Shillings — Wm L Sterne

Pray dispatch her, That she may not have a 2d Journey as she has a Child to leave ——

STERNE TAKES A KINDLY INTEREST IN JANE HARBOTLE, an unfortunate parishioner presented for the crime of fornication, after the birth of her third illegitimate child, at the Stillington visitation of 1753. Addressed to John Clough, Register of the Dean and Chapter. From the York Minster Library Collection. See No. 22, p. 287.

Thos. Bridges and Lawrence [*sic*] Sterne, as Mountebanks

this level of appreciation of this extraordinary work. He compares the amorphous structure of the novel to a holothurian or sea-cucumber, a grotesque sea animal sometimes eaten in Japan, of which "one cannot tell where its head or tail is." The reader of the work, according to the writer, never knows where he is being led, just as if he were a calf forcibly dragged about by a naughty cowboy with a rope pierced through its nostrils. After these introductory remarks, Sôseki goes on to quote some representative passages from the original work, sometimes giving his own partial translations and comments. Although I am afraid I have no time to go into detail, passages which seem to have been to Sôseki's liking include, for instance, the scene of Yorick's death (I, 12, p. 31), where the dying parson beseeches his friend Eugenius to see whether his head is bruised or not; the scene where Walter Shandy receives the report of his elder son's death (V, 3), especially a few pages beginning with "'Tis an inevitable chance—— the first statute in *Magnâ Chartâ*" and so on (p. 353); and the famous episode of Phutatorius and a roasted chestnut (IV, 27). The no less famous episode of Uncle Toby letting a fly go without killing it (II, 12, p. 113) is also duly mentioned, while that paragraph, for instance, where "love" is described with various adjectives alphabetically arranged (VIII, 13, p. 551) is flatly rejected as too artificial. "There might be some people who would find this interesting," he says, "I should do nothing but appreciate the writer's labor."

I cannot believe that this article by Sôseki got a warm response from those who read it at the time. The readers, if there were some, must have either simply neglected it, or been just dumbfounded. For that matter, it is ten to one in my opinion that the article itself would have been lost altogether now, were it not for the fact that the writer later became a nationally famous novelist.

Sôseki, a few years after he wrote this article, came over to England for study in 1900, and stayed for about two years in London. A story is told that, when he went to see Queen Victoria's funeral procession he found that, on account of the big crowd, he could see nothing of it, however hard he might endeavor to stretch his neck and back; some kind English gentleman picked him up and hoisted him on his shoulder in order to give him the honor of a glance over the thick rows. Anyway, on his return to Japan, Sôseki was given the post of lecturer in the University of Tokyo. In his lectures there, which have all been published since in book form, he dealt with many of the representative eighteenth-century English writers, e.g., Addison and Steele, Jonathan Swift, Alexander Pope, and Daniel Defoe. His lectures on Swift, for instance, still rank high among the writings in Japan on this author. As a matter of course, his original plan was to take up the other important writers of the time, e.g., Henry Fielding, Tobias Smollett and so on, one after another, giving each something like half a year, but it is to our great regret that Sôseki was deprived forever, because of his rather abrupt change of course (i.e., taking up the career of a professional novelist instead of that of a scholar), of a chance to treat in his lectures at any length such authors, especially our Laurence Sterne, with whom we find he had much in common.

Among his earlier fictions, there is a work entitled *The Present Author Is a Cat*, which was written in 1905–06 as a sort of serial while he was still giving lectures at the University, and in this one can detect the influence of *Tristram Shandy*. In this work, surrounding the central couple, a melancholy school teacher and his wife, there are a handful of main characters who keep coming and going throughout the story and play important parts in giving some unity or harmony to the whole. The construction of the story is rather loose, and various episodes are taken up seemingly quite haphazardly, but the general effect is extremely comical, showing such strange figures, for example, as a young physicist who insists on giving vent to his erudite knowledge in the form of a lecture on the dynamics of hanging oneself. Of course, there are many inventions on Sôseki's part for which we cannot find any counterpart in *Tristram*. For instance, the story is told from the point of view of a cat kept by the school teacher's family (hence the title), while, on the other hand, the complete lack in this work of "ticklish sexual innuendoes" must be taken as another instance of an important difference from *Tristram*.

I cannot think of any other Japanese work or writer conspicuously in the Sternian line. One of the disciples of Sôseki, Hyakken (or Hyakki-en, meaning Pandemonium) Uchida by name, is rather famous for developing stories in his own peculiar way. He himself calls this method of his "scattering his story," meaning flying freely from point to point, instead of keeping to a more or less straight line. Although this reminds one to some extent of the Shandian digressional way of progress, still, as this particular writer makes use of this method mainly when he writes essays, not novels, and as he was brought up more on German than English literature, it is slightly far-fetched to suppose he was very familiar with Sterne's works, and I am inclined to conclude that the seeming similarity between this writer's method and that which we find in *Tristram* is nothing but mere coincidence.

I will touch briefly now upon some of the more important works in my country concerning Laurence Sterne since Sôseki. An annotated edition of *A Sentimental Journey* by Y. Okakura, another pioneer in Japan in the study of English Literature, with an introduction and detailed notes in Japanese, was published in 1931, and this may more or less account for three different translations of the work into Japanese which came out almost simultaneously side by side with one another, soon after the end of the last war; two in 1947 and one in 1948. A short biography of Laurence Sterne was also published by the same Okakura in 1934, as part of a Japanese equivalent of the English Men of Letters series, consisting of just one hundred slim biographical volumes of as many representative British and American writers and poets. Another work worthy of note since the second World War is a book entitled *Literature of Laughter* (1955) by Professor S. Murakami, which deals with the main works of Smollett and Sterne.

Now, last of all, a few words about my own translation of *Tristram Shandy*. Since Sôseki wrote about the work, many years passed without anything worth mentioning being added to the studies of this phantasmagoric book. It is true that there was a highly esteemed friend of mine, a little older than myself, who published in a magazine a "tentative translation" of the first ten or twelve chapters, and it seems to have been his intention to continue this arduous work, but eventually he gave it up. Later, I was invited by a publisher to undertake the task, and I accepted the invitation in 1960. This was genuinely a case of fools rushing in where angels might well fear to tread. I remember vividly, when I told a well-known senior professor of the University of Minnesota specializing in eighteenth-century literature, the peculiar expression with which he looked at me as though full of pity at my recklessness or imprudence. The work took me the better part of two years and a half, from the late summer of 1963 to the winter of 1965–66. Every step of it was very hard work indeed for me, and very often I felt I was under the pressure of heavy drudgery. But at the same time, I almost always felt pleasure in going on with the labor slowly but very steadily, and I am very glad that finally I reached somehow or other the fool's goal.

I must admit I owe a great deal to Professor J. A. Work's admirable notes which became available with the publication of his edition by the Odyssey Press, although I must confess at the same time there are very rare occasions where I feel like disagreeing with him. (To quote just one example, his note to the passage where Sterne alludes to Italians boasting of the exactness in their designations of human characters from "a certain wind instrument" [I, 23, p. 76].)

Now, even with these reliable notes for my assistance, I had naturally many hard nuts to crack on my way. The first problem was the kind of style I should adopt. To reproduce exactly the same kind of style as the original in another language is almost out of the question, especially when the original is so unusual. But I wanted to convey in my translation as much of the original atmosphere or flavor as possible, even in the trying circumstances resulting from the wide differences of the two languages. At the same time, it was not my wish to impose too much effort on my readers by making the sentences too obscure. In other words, I wanted to have my style readable for ordinary readers, and acceptable without too much labor on their part. When I translated *Tom Jones* years ago, in some passages I deliberately used a pseudo-classical style, with some success I hope. In the case of *Tristram* too, I felt some temptation in the same direction. But I was afraid that if the translator indulged too much in that kind of hobby-horse, so to speak, especially in this particular work, it would possibly result in putting too much burden on the readers' digestive capacity. One of the significant differences, I felt, between such works as *Tom Jones* and this fantastic *Tristram* lay in this, necessitating the different attitudes in treating these two works. My conclusion in connection with the style to be taken up was to avoid pedantry or archaism as much as possible, and to make it as easy as possible, trying to keep the meaning at the same time as implicit and as suggestive as the cases required. I do not believe it is my job to judge whether my aim is sufficiently realized in my work or not.

As to my grapplings with individual hard passages or phrases, there are quite a few examples which I feel like mentioning. But this may be only of interest to me, I am afraid, and here it will suffice to give just a few instances at random. In Volume I, Chapter 8, there is a passage where "my Lord A, B, C, D, ... O, P, Q" appear in a group, and there the text speaks of all these Lords "all of a row" etc. (p. 14). In my first draft I took this as the same as "all *in* a row," and it was a little later that it occurred to me that they could not be "in a single row" and that the phrase meant they were all of the same rank (in other words, there was not much to choose among them). Well, this may be entirely self-evident to native speakers, but it is not rare for us foreigners to overlook or neglect the differences of such small particles, and I am glad that I was saved from a misrepresentation in this instance.

Only a few lines after that in the same chapter, the author complains that it is no use to try to "unhorse" these Lords, and the text runs: "'tis ten to one but that many of them would be worse mounted by one half before tomorrow morning" (p. 14). Well, this passage, if transplanted into my tongue word for word, would not make any sense at all. But I had to manage the passage somehow or other. After a few futile attempts, a Japanese word meaning a "steed" occurred to me, which has a homonym meaning "a woman in a dubious profession." My translation of the sentence above runs something like this: Even if these Lords were dismounted from their steeds this very night, most probably they would be on (the homonym) before tomorrow morning.

In the passage which I referred to earlier, where "love" is described alphabetically, we find as many as sixteen adjectives. Now it is not very difficult to find exactly the same number of equivalent words in Japanese, but if I try to put them in the order of the Japanese alphabet, and to have each word corresponding in meaning occupy the same position in the order, I do not think it is easily manageable nor do I believe it worth the labor. I just put up with having all the corresponding adjectives on the list, each beginning with one of the first sixteen letters in our alphabet, but in quite an arbitrary order compared with the original. That much of freedom, I hope, should be permitted a traitor who goes by the name of a translator.

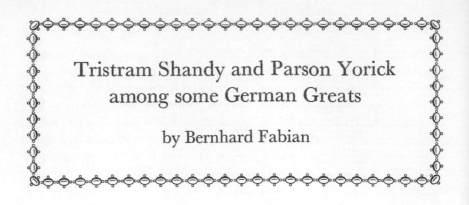

Tristram Shandy and Parson Yorick among some German Greats

by Bernhard Fabian

In the second half of the eighteenth century Germany witnessed an outburst of literary activity which raised its literature, within a few decades, from a provincial level to the contemporary European standard. Due to the lack of a rich and variegated native literary tradition the German *littérateurs*, both major and minor, had to turn to other literatures in search of more advanced and more sophisticated forms than those of the naive drama and the post-baroque fiction which dominated, together with second-rate didactic writings, the German literary scene prior to 1750. For well-known reasons this search centered on contemporary English literature, and apart from a widespread though even-tempered Anglomania a host of conscious or unconscious imitations of the English masters was the inevitable result. It is in the context of an intensely national literature rapidly developing under the strong impact of a foreign literature that the reception of *Tristram Shandy* and *A Sentimental Journey* must be seen.[1]

Despite the favorable climate of opinion (which even provoked novels with "as good as translated from the English" on the title-page) Sterne was at first not readily accessible to the German reader. *Tristram Shandy* not only had to wait for its first translation; it also proved a *pièce de résistance* in that it was too genuine an example of English humor and English eccentricity. Though "Laune" was frequently discussed at the time, "humor" has hardly ever passed for an outstanding trait of the German national character. Lichtenberg noted that the peculiarities of English social life afforded material to the humorous novelist for which there was no equivalent in Germany.[2] And in his *Essay on the Novel* Friedrich von Blanckenburg observed

Professor of English, University of Münster

that, while the English had more than one book of this kind (*Tristram Shandy* being the prime example), there would hardly ever be a German novel with a humorous character as hero.[3]

Other explanations notwithstanding, there is some logic in the fact that the eighteenth-century German reader discovered *Tristram Shandy* in the wake of the *Sentimental Journey*. Sterne's second book had a more spontaneous appeal to the emerging age of sentimentalism, and it presented fewer difficulties than the apparently chaotic *Tristram Shandy*. Also, it found at once its congenial translator in Johann Joachim Christoph Bode, who brought rich experience to his task and had the encouragement of Lessing and others. Bode produced a translation of the *Sentimental Journey* which became a minor classic and is still read today. His translation of *Tristram Shandy*, which followed the well-meant but hapless attempt of Johann Friedrich Zückert, a Berlin physician, appeared to convey the essence of Shandyism (or what passed for it) and finally established Sterne with the German reading public.[4] It is perhaps noteworthy that, while Bode was at work, Wieland recommended that a translator should simply leave out some parts of *Tristram Shandy* because of the crudity of the composition.[5] As late as 1829 Goethe, one of Sterne's most perceptive critics, remarked that Sterne "tended to formlessness," whereas Goldsmith was all formal perfection.[6]

II

It is to the credit of the leading German men of letters that none of them disparaged Sterne. The journals carried their usual amount of condescending disapprobation, but none of the major writers was of Johnson's opinion that "nothing odd will do long."[7] On the contrary, long before the cult of Sterne found its popular prophets, literati like Moses Mendelssohn, Herder, Wieland, and Lessing were among the first to recognize Sterne's qualities as an author.

One of the distinctive features appreciated in Sterne was "originality." As early as 1763, having just finished Volume IV of *Tristram Shandy*, Moses Mendelssohn told Lessing: "*Tristram Shandy* is a masterly original." Characteristically enough, Mendelssohn found the book difficult to read; it annoyed and irritated him. But he plodded through it, since the recommendation came from Lessing. Surprisingly he does not compare Sterne to Fielding or any other English novelist, but to

Voltaire. For him Sterne was "a greater painter than Voltaire" and Sterne's fable was superior to that of *Candide* because it was morally good. "I am no friend of the burlesque," Mendelssohn closed, "but I know few examples where the burlesque is so instructive, where the caricature is so true, and the manners, besides being so droll, are so noble."[8]

In the notes Immanuel Kant made for his book on philosophical anthropology there is another reference to Sterne's originality: "Klopstock is very easy to imitate, Milton difficult, because his images are original. Sterne."[9] Obviously Sterne was a case of "difficult imitation," and one would like to believe that Kant had a progression in mind from Klopstock to Milton to Sterne. Here Sterne makes his appearance in a totally unfamiliar environment, as he does—to quote a third example—in one of Lichtenberg's aphorisms: "There is no surer criterion of the greatness of an author as when passing remarks of his can be turned into books. Tacitus and Sterne are, each in his way, examples of this."[10]

Comparisons and confrontations like these are characteristic of the German reaction to Sterne. There is hardly any of the novelistic criticism which the student of Sterne's reputation in England is accustomed to. Practically no German critic was in a position to say, as did a reviewer in the *Monthly Review*, that Sterne was "a writer infinitely more ingenious and entertaining than any other of the present race of novellists."[11] At that time the classical German novel was in a very early phase of its development and there was, with the possible exception of Wieland's *Agathon*, no native production against which *Tristram Shandy* could have been measured. References to the work as a novel (in the technical sense) are scarce. When Herder, for instance, in 1769 listed *Tristram Shandy* together with other English novels, the catalogue is revealing only insofar as it mixes the trivial with the outstanding.[12] Herder later realized that the novel was a protean form of unusual scope and capable of the most divers treatment ("keine Gattung der Poesie ist von weiterem Umfange, als der Roman; unter allen ist er auch der *verschiedensten Bearbeitung* fähig").[13] But like the majority of the German readers, he had no adequate idea of its technicalities as an art form. Consequently topics like the parody in *Tristram Shandy* of the conventional novel are never touched upon.

That the German reader should have thought of Sterne primarily in terms of "originality" was due to the impact of Young. The *Conjectures*, as is well known, was one of the most influential English books in Germany between 1760 and 1790. Not only did it stimulate the growth of the German *Genielehre*, it was also responsible for the exuberant German *Geniekult* which was sharply, though ineffectively, satirized by such rationalists as Kant and Lichtenberg.[14] Contrary to the habitual separation of Young and Sterne in literary histories, the contemporary German reader had no difficulty in establishing a close relation between the two. Living in a literary environment in which imitation and originality were vital issues, he naturally regarded *Tristram Shandy* and the *Sentimental Journey* as "original compositions" in Young's sense. In his view, Sterne answered Young's call:

> Let not great Examples, or Authorities, browbeat thy Reason into too great a diffidence of thyself: Thyself so reverence as to prefer the native growth of thy own mind to the richest import from abroad; ... The man who thus reverences himself, will soon find the world's reverence to follow his own.[15]

In Germany a passage like this must have sounded like a prediction of Sterne by Young. One must consequently not be surprised at Wieland calling *Tristram Shandy* an extraordinary and superb work of nature— "ein so ausserordentliches und vortreffliches *Werk der Natur*."[16]

About 1770, when the early vogue of Sterne in Germany had reached its climax (illustrated, incidentally, by the fact that Herder addressed Hamann as Tobias Shandy and was in turn addressed by Hamann as Yorick)[17] Herder distinguished a Youngian and a Sternian era in the preceding decade of German literary history:

> If it can be said that hardly any other author knew and seized the sweet weaknesses of mankind so well as Sterne: so perhaps nobody among the moderns knew its strength, the dormant powers making for moral greatness, so well as Young. There was a time where everybody in Germany was swept away by strong Young, as now everybody is swept away by sweet Sterne; but the true human morality certainly lies between the two. However, I shall not try to find out closer to whom.[18]

Three things are obvious from this passage: first, the German reader (and Herder here stands for a number of *littérateurs*) made his own selections and his own comparisons, which were dictated by the immediate literary needs of the hour; second, the interest in Sterne centered more on what he had to say about human nature, on his real (or supposed) insights, than on the mimetic form in which he presented them; and third, Sterne's two books belonged, together with Young's *Night Thoughts*, to the highest class of original literature: to what Herder on another occasion termed "books of humanity"—"Menschheitsschriften."[19]

On the other end of the scale, originality of the Sternian (or Shakespearian or Swiftian) variety became a standard term of abuse with those who, like Lichtenberg or Helfrich Peter Sturz, opposed the rising tide of sentimentalism in Germany and fought their satiric battle against the self-adulation of the self-appointed geniuses of the literary movement of *Storm and Stress*. Sturz heard Garrick denounce Sterne during his visit to England in 1768.[20] Lichtenberg drew a character sketch of "poor Yorick" as "a crawling parasite" and "a flatterer of the great" which marks the nadir of Sterne's reputation in Germany.[21] Elsewhere he added: "Foolishly affected eccentricity . . . becomes the criterion of originality; and the surest proof that one has a head is to stand on it several times a day. Even if this were a Sternian skill, so much would be certain that it was not one of the most difficult to acquire."[22]

III

For the student of German literature the lack of technical criticism of Sterne's works is more than adequately compensated for by the numerous counterfeits both of *Tristram Shandy* and the *Sentimental Journey*, which form part of the collective effort of the German *littérateurs* to found the modern German novel. Some of these have been studied in detail, but most of them, a "crop of trashy imitations,"[23] seem once and for all to have been relegated to the literary limbo. There can be no doubt that Sterne was a decisive factor in the rise of the eighteenth-century German novel. However, the majority of these endeavors painfully demonstrate that the progress towards the acknowledged masterpieces of a later period was slow and difficult.

The only interesting way through this territory is via the *Versuch über den Roman* which Friedrich von Blanckenburg, a military man and amateur in the field, published in 1774. As one of the major contributions to the eighteenth-century theory of the genre, this study proceeds on the assumption that the novel was ultimately destined to become for the modern world what the epic had been for the ancient. Less oracular than Goethe and less philosophical than Hegel, who made the same observation in the early nineteenth century,[24] Blanckenburg declared the individual human being to be the essential theme of the novel. Contrasting the epic and the novel he remarks: "As the epic celebrates public feats and events, that is, actions of the citizen (in a certain sense of the word): so the novel is concerned with the actions and sentiments of man."[25] Whether or not this juxtaposition of the epic and the novel was suggested by Fielding's prefaces, it is at once apparent that Blanckenburg goes far beyond Fielding's formal pattern. His argument incorporates, besides recent English aesthetics, Sterne's advanced concept of the novel.

Though Wieland's *Agathon* plays a prominent role in the *Essay*, Blanckenburg appears to be indebted primarily to Sterne for the two controlling ideas of his book: first, that the novel should delineate character; and second, that character should have priority over plot. Portrayal of character means a representation of what Blanckenburg calls "the being of man" and "his inner state and condition" ("das Seyn des Menschen, sein innrer Zustand"; p. 18). One of the prime requirements is that the novelist should concentrate on such sentiments and actions as provide agreeable entertainments to the reader.

Blanckenburg rejects the "complete" and "perfect" character (concurring with Shaftesbury that it is "the greatest monster, and of all poetic fictions not only the least engaging but the least moral and improving").[26] Instead, the novelist should present a truly virtuous character. Significantly enough the concept of virtue is illustrated from the *Sentimental Journey*.[27] A quotation from "The Conquest" defines true virtue as tried virtue, as those felt movements which, as Yorick says, "rise out of [my situation], and which belong to me as a man" (pp. 237–238). Blanckenburg attached no importance to Yorick's particular situation, but he regarded his reflections and sentiments as universally significant. They revealed the nature of man. They disclosed moral life not as a state but as a process. Sterne, it would seem, suggested a possible alternative to the "perfect" character by providing an outstanding example of change and movement, of progress and growth in a "real" character. Blanckenburg concluded that a novelist should not make the character appear as he is (as Richardson did with Grandison) but show how and why he came to be.[28]

Blanckenburg's concept of the novel is the familiar one of the German *Entwicklungsroman* or *Bildungsroman*. As his quotation from the

Sentimental Journey suggests, this type of novel must be dissociated from *Tristram Shandy*. The static characters and the essentially changeless world of *Tristram Shandy* are in direct opposition to the idea of development and transformation which is at the core of the *Entwicklungsroman*. The Sternian background to the *Entwicklungsroman* is almost exclusively constituted by the *Sentimental Journey*. Blanckenburg's very definition of the province of the novel—"the actions and sentiments of man"—betrays something of the pervasive influence of the *Sentimental Journey* in Germany.

The contribution of *Tristram Shandy* to Blanckenburg's concept of character is perhaps even more important. Despite his thesis that the novel should be entertaining, Blanckenburg is far from appreciating *Tristram Shandy* merely for its entertaining qualities. The "humor' (German *Laune*) of the Shandys leads him to an analysis of its psychological components. After reviewing some contemporary theories of humor, primarily that of Lord Kames, Blanckenburg identifies *Sonderbarkeit* as "the main ingredient of humor." The German word conveys the ideas of oddity, peculiarity, eccentricity, and even originality. *Sonderbarkeit*, Blanckenburg maintains, not only makes a character likeable: it constitutes that irreducible element in a character which makes him a singular human being worthy of regard and respect.[29]

The appraisal of the humorous character implies the discovery of a new and refined concept of the individual. Sterne not only taught, as Blanckenburg expressly notes, the "whole value and the nature of the ridiculous" (in the positive sense of the word) and such distinctions as the humor of the head and the humor of the heart.[30] He also drew attention to humor as a basic principle of individuation. He pointed the way towards a more adequate appreciation of the individual and hence of the possibilities of the fictional character. What Blanckenburg learned from Sterne is perhaps best illustrated by a passage he quotes from the dedication of *Tristram Shandy*: ". . . being firmly persuaded that every time a man smiles,——but much more so, when he laughs, that it adds something to this Fragment of Life" (p. 3). He significantly adds: "Voltaire says almost the same."[31]

Blanckenburg's progress under Sterne's guidance finds its logical end in a quotation from the *Sentimental Journey*: "I think I can see the precise and distinguishing marks of national characters more in these nonsensical *minutiae*, than in the most important matters of state"

(p. 160).[32] What Sterne said about nations Blanckenburg applied to individuals, recognizing in the *minutiae* the true marks of distinction in which the individual manifested himself. This may not be penetrating criticism of Sterne. But it was a precious insight at a time when the German novelist was beginning to explore the German character both in its national and individual aspects. Sterne marked the transition from the fictional type to the fictional individual. And Blanckenburg became the herald of the modern "Sternian" novel in Germany.[33]

As an inevitable corollary to this concept of character, Blanckenburg insisted on the subordination of plot. Theoretically the genre permitted two types of narration: either the representation of a complete course of events or the representation of a complete character. In Blanckenburg's scheme the historical novel and—significantly enough —Richardson's *Clarissa* are examples of the first type, which he rejects on account of their lack of veracity and psychological plausibility.[34] The most successful works of the second type are those of Wieland and Sterne. Both these authors write what Blanckenburg calls "inner history," reducing the number and importance of external events.[35] Their characters are—the phrase occurs in another context— "rounded" and "living," because they make their plots depend upon character.[36] The type of novel, then, for which Sterne and Wieland could serve as models was one in which the character was the true image of an individual living and acting in a world of his own creation.

IV

In the history of Sterne's reception in Germany Friedrich von Blanckenburg's *Essay on the Novel* is not an isolated episode. In retrospect Blanckenburg's reception of Sterne appears to be the very epitome of the German reception of Sterne. Though Blanckenburg wrote a treatise on the theory of the novel (which presented his contemporaries with a revolutionary view of a literary genre of increasing importance) he did not look upon Sterne primarily as a novelist. In the first place Sterne was a philosopher, if not a sage.

The major English novelists were greatly admired in Germany, and some of them were indeed considered as *moralistes*. Herder, for instance, listed Richardson's novels (though not Fielding's) among his "books of humanity."[37] None, however, was so unanimously and so highly praised for his wisdom as Sterne. Wieland set the tone when he confided to one of his correspondents:

> I admit . . . that Sterne is almost the only author in the world whom I regard with a kind of awful admiration. I shall study his book as long as I live, and I shall not have studied it enough. I know no other book in which so much genuine Socratic wisdom, such a profound knowledge of man, such a fine feeling of goodness and beauty, such a host of new and fine moral observations, so much sound judgment is combined with so much wit and genius.[38]

Why was Sterne so extolled? The answer is at once simple and intricate. When Sterne appeared on the literary scene Germany was about to enter a new phase of her intellectual history, a period which led up to her Golden Age. The seventeen-sixties and the seventeen-seventies were an interim period of change and re-adjustment. They were a period of rapid intellectual advances during which Germany, within a short span of time, moved from a post-baroque era to the pre-Romantic age. The new ideas imported from England and France became immediately current, and the primitivism and irrationalism of the day were widely accepted as the new norms of life and thought. As everywhere else, the pendulum seemed to swing from sense to sensibility, from the head to the heart.

In a period of fermentation like this, the message of the *Sentimental Journey* and, perhaps to a lesser extent, of *Tristram Shandy* was bound to have radical effects. To the large number of German writers and thinkers who were groping for a new concept of human nature Sterne appeared to hold the ideas of the future. It is more than lexical curiosity that Lessing suggested a new German word—*empfindsam*—for the translation of "sentimental." As his letter to Bode (written in the summer of 1768) reveals, Lessing was under the impression that "sentimental" had been coined by Sterne and that Sterne's concept was so new as to require a new word. *Empfindsam*, he thought, would gradually be filled with meaning. In other words, it was a word of the future.[39]

What Sterne's sentimentalism, his intuitive understanding of man, and (in Blanckenburg's phrase) his "knowledge of the human heart"[40] meant in contemporary Germany was conveniently summarized by

Goethe. In 1827, he published a short retrospective essay designed to draw attention to "a man who originally initiated the great period of the purer knowledge of man, of noble toleration and tender love in the second half of the last century."[41] In Goethe's view Sterne made a unique contribution to the study of human nature and conduct by adding the concept of peculiarity to the concepts of truth and error. He thereby modified a narrow (one might add: rationalistic) view of man, so that hitherto unnoticed phenomena came to view and were appreciated. Sterne recognized in the peculiarities the constituent elements of the individual. In short, he brought out "the human in man" (*das Menschliche im Menschen*).

The interesting aspect of this essay is not so much its similarity to Blanckenburg's earlier pronouncements on Sterne as the unrestricted validity which is assigned to Sterne's discovery of the individual. Blanckenburg had abstracted from Sterne a general pattern. Goethe deduced from Sterne a universal rule, namely, that man is actuated and kept living and moving by his peculiarities *qua* ruling passions. The relevance which Goethe claims for this proposition suggests that he credits Sterne with the formulation of the fundamental law by which human nature is organized and governed. From novelist, Sterne had turned philosopher or rather, in the more precise terminology of the period, philosophical anthropologist.

The dissociation of the philosophical message from the mimetic medium appears to be a distinctive feature of the German reception of Sterne. It can be accounted for by the fact that, while *Tristram Shandy* and the *Sentimental Journey* were post-classical literary events in England, they were pre-classical ones in Germany. In the English perspective *Tristram Shandy* appears as an attempt to parody, and thereby to destroy, neo-classical norms and forms. Likewise, in their very concreteness Sterne's characters would seem to be conceived as opposites to the early eighteenth-century "man in the abstract." In the German context such associations disappeared. Instead, "original" qualities (in the contemporary German sense of the word) came into prominence. The peculiar German background to Sterne is perhaps suggested by three dates: Goethe encountered Pope in 1766; Herder studied Percy's *Reliques* in 1771; Lessing proposed his translation for the word "sentimental" in 1768.[42] That is to say, otherwise distinct and separate literary phenomena could, and indeed did, associate for the German reader by virtue of their simultaneous presence.

The most significant association formed under these premises was that between Sterne and the rapidly growing classicistic tendencies in German literature. These tendencies made, as classicistic tendencies usually do, for a world picture in which the constant, the general, and the universal were stressed to the exclusion of the particular and the incidental. No matter how singular a literary figure Sterne was, in Germany he became a classicist, and his highly personal views were converted by the creators of German classicism into "original" quasi-philosophical pronouncements on man in general.

The shelter, so to speak, under which this transformation took place was provided by Pope. That "the proper study of Mankind is Man" was a favorite maxim with German classicists, reiterated by Lessing, by Karl Philipp Moritz (in the introduction to a journal of empirical psychology), and among others, by Goethe,[43] who furnished the Germans with a standard translation of the phrase and made it a central tenet of his *Elective Affinities*, the most representative of the classical novels. Pope's Newtonian anthropology was submerged, and Sterne's philosophy of man was substituted for it. The *ruling passion*—a phenomenon which fascinated Goethe[44]—survived. Man could remain the proper study of mankind, but *man* was "man in particular," if the phrase may be used, reconstructed as "man in the abstract."

This process would seem to constitute one of the most permanent of Sterne's contributions to German thought and letters. It is a process that has not been studied in detail because of the elusiveness of the evidence. Blanckenburg is a case in point, and so is Goethe.[45] I should like to give two other examples. They come from an author who was one of the most perceptive readers of English literature, though to my knowledge he has never been mentioned in connection with Sterne: Immanuel Kant.

A successful course of lectures which Kant repeatedly delivered in Königsberg was one on philosophical anthropology. Abounding in ingenious observation and witty remarks, the book makes fascinating reading. The pertinent passage appears in a section called the characterization of the sexes. Kant distinguishes masculine and feminine virtues and says: "Weibliche Tugend oder Untugend ist von der männlichen nicht sowohl der Art als der Triebfeder nach sehr unterschieden.—Sie soll *geduldig*, Er muß *duldend* sein. Sie ist *empfindlich*, er *empfindsam*."[46] The word-play is not easily rendered into English: "She ought to be patient, he must be enduring. She is sensitive, he is

ELIZA DRAPER. Painted by Richard Cosway. See No. 116, p. 309.

BUST OF STERNE. By Joseph Nollekens. See No. 118, p. 310.

sentimental." *Empfindsam*, it will be recalled, is the very word which Lessing suggested for Sterne's "sentimental."

The second passage occurs in Kant's lectures on pedagogics. His point is that in the education of children a middle course should be taken between complete freedom and complete restriction. Children ought to have their rights, but so should the adults. He concludes: "Toby in Tristram Shandy, letting a fly which had long tormented him out of the window, addresses it: 'Go poor devil. . . . This world is wide enough to hold both thee and me.' And this everybody should make his maxim. We must not molest each other; the world is wide enough for all of us."[47] Tristram's education an epitome of man's education— Uncle Toby a teacher of mankind. Would Sterne, despite his hint to parents and governors, have expected to reappear in a classic German treatise on education?

NOTES

1. The present paper is not a history, however concise, of the reception of Sterne in eighteenth-century Germany. It is no more than an outline sketch of some aspects of the relation of Sterne to German classicism. In any case it should be supplemented by such studies as Harvey Waterman Thayer, *Laurence Sterne in Germany: A Contribution to the Study of the Literary Relations of England and Germany in the Eighteenth Century*, Columbia University Germanic Studies, II, i (New York, 1905); Gertrude Joyce Hallamore, *Das Bild Laurence Sternes in Deutschland von der Aufklärung bis zur Romantik*, Germanische Studien, 172 (Berlin, 1936); Lawrence Marsden Price, *English Literature in Germany*, University of California Publications in Modern Philology, XXXVII (Berkeley and Los Angeles, 1953); Peter Michelsen, *Laurence Sterne und der deutsche Roman des achtzehnten Jahrhunderts*, Palaestra: Untersuchungen aus der deutschen und englischen Philologie und Literaturgeschichte, 232 (Göttingen, 1962).

2. "Über den deutschen Roman," *Vermischte Schriften*, ed. G.Ch. Lichtenberg und Chr.W. Lichtenberg (Göttingen, 1844), II, 215–221.

3. *Versuch über den Roman* (1774), ed. Eberhard Lämmert (Stuttgart, 1965), p. 191.

4. Herder wrote in 1794: "Die *Bode*'schen Uebersetzungen der *empfindsamen Reisen*, des *Tristram-Shandy*, *Thomas Jones, Humphrey Klinkers*, des *Landpriesters von Wackefield*, des *Westindiers* sind in Aller Händen." "Briefe zur Beförderung der Humanität: Vierte Sammlung," *Sämtliche Werke*, ed. Bernhard Suphan (Berlin, 1881), XVII, 250.

5. *Teutscher Merkur*, II (1773), 230.

6. *Diary*, December 20, 1829; *Werke* (Sophien-Ausgabe), III. Abteilung (Weimar, 1901), XII, 169: "Landpriester von Wakefield, mit Erinnerung an die frühsten Eindrücke. Wirkungen von Sterne und Goldsmith. Der hohe ironische Humor beyder, jener sich zum Formlosen hinneigend, dieser in der strengsten Form sich frey bewegend. Nachher machte man den Deutschen glauben, das Formlose sey das Humoristische."

7. Boswell, *Life*, March 20, 1776.

8. [May, 1763]; Lessing, *Sämtliche Schriften*, ed. Karl Lachmann und Franz Muncker, XIX (Leipzig, 1904), 179f.: "*Tristram Shandy* ist ein meisterhaftes Original. Vor der Hand habe ich zwar nicht mehr als die beyden ersten Bändchen gelesen. Anfangs machte mich das Buch ungemein verdrießlich. Ich schwärmte von Digression zu Digression, ohne die rechte Laune des Verf. zu *saisiren*. Ich hielte ihn für einen Mann, wie unsern Liscov, an dem ich, wie Sie wissen, keinen sonderlichen Geschmack finde; und gleichwohl gefällt das Buch Lessingen! . . . Als mir Shandy noch nicht gefiel, legte ich ihn aus der Hand. . . . Ich habe unterdessen den dritten und vierten Band von *Tristram Shandy* gelesen. Er ist nicht nur ein größrer Maler als Voltaire, sondern seine Fabel hat das vorzügliche Verdienst vor dem *Candide* voraus, daß sie sittlich gut ist. Ich bin sonst kein Freund vom Burlesken, aber ich weiß auch wenige Beyspiele, wo das Burleske so unterrichtend gewesen wäre, wo die Karrikaturen so wahr, die Sitten nebst ihrem Possierlichen so edel—Doch Sie erlassen mir es eben so wohl gern, Ihnen meine Lektion aufzusagen."

9. "Reflexionen zur Anthropologie," no. 914; *Gesammelte Schriften* (Akademie-Ausgabe), XV (Berlin, 1913), 400: "Klopstok kan sehr gut nachgeahmet werden, aber Milton schweer, weil seine Bilder original sind. Sterne."

10. *Vermischte Schriften*, I, 302: "Es gibt kein sichereres Kriterion von einem großen Schriftsteller, als wenn sich aus seinen Anmerkungen *en passant* Bücher machen lassen. Tacitus und Sterne sind jeder in seiner Art Muster hiervon."

11. XXI (Appendix 1759), 571.

12. "Journal meiner Reise im Jahr 1769," *Sämmtliche Werke*, IV (Berlin, 1878), 367.

13. "Briefe zur Beförderung der Humanität: Achte Sammlung" (1796), *Sämmtliche Werke*, XVIII (Berlin, 1883), 109.

14. See, for instance, Kant on "Genieaffen;" *Anthropologie in pragmatischer Hinsicht*, §. 58.

15. *Conjectures on Original Composition* (1759; reproduced Scolar Press, Leeds, 1966), pp. 53–54.

16. *Der Teutsche Merkur*, II (1773), 229.

17. *Herders Briefe an Joh. Georg Hamann*, ed. Otto Hoffmann (Berlin, 1889), pp. 25, 27.

18. "Recensionen. Aus der Allgemeinen Deutschen Bibliothek, 1770–1774," *Sämmtliche Werke*, V (Berlin, 1891), 290f.: ". . . und wenn man sagen kann, daß fast kein Schriftsteller die Menschheit nach ihren süßen Schwächen so gut gekannt, und zu treffen gewußt habe, als *Sterne*: so kannte vielleicht niemand der Neuern so sehr ihre *Stärken*, ihre *schlafenden Kräfte, zum großen in der Moral*, als Young. Es war eine Zeit, da in Deutschland alles vom starken Young schwindelte, so wie jetzt alles vom süßen *Sterne* schwindelt, und die wahre menschliche Moral liegt doch gewiß in der Mitte von beiden; ich will freilich nicht untersuchen, welchem näher?"

19. "Journal meiner Reise im Jahr 1769," *Sämmtliche Werke*, IV (Berlin, 1878), 367: Bin ichs geworden ["der Erste Menschenkenner nach meinem Stande, in meiner Provinz"], so will ich diesen Pfad nicht verlassen, und mir selbst gleichsam ein Journal halten, der Menschenkänntniße, die ich täglich aus meinem Leben, und derer, die ich aus Schriften sammle. Ein solcher Plan wird mich beständig auf einer Art von Reise unter Menschen erhalten und der Falte zuvorkommen, in die mich meine einförmige Lage in einem abgelegnen Scytischen Winkel der Erde schlagen könnte! Dazu will ich eine beständige Lecture der Menschheitsschriften, in denen Deutschland jetzt seine Periode anfängt, und Frankreich, das ganz Convention und Blendwerk ist, die seinige verlebt hat, unterhalten. Dazu die *Spaldinge, Resewitze* und *Moses* lesen; dazu von einer andern Seite die *Mosers*, und *Wielands* und *Gerstenbergs* brauchen; dazu zu unsern *Leibnizen* die *Shaftesburis* und *Locke's*; zu unsern *Spaldings* die *Sterne's, Fosters*, und *Richardsons*; zu unsern *Mosers*, die *Browne* und *Montesquieus*; zu unsern *Homileten* jedes Datum einer Reisebeschreibung oder merkwürdigen Historie dazu thun. *Jahrbuch der Schriften für die Menscheit!* ein grosser Plan! ein wichtiges Werk!"

20. *Schriften* (Karlsruhe, 1784), I, 18–19.

21. *Vermischte Schriften*, I, 184–186.

22. *Vermischte Schriften*, ed. Ludwig Christian Lichtenberg und Friedrich Kries (Göttingen, 1801), II, 173: "Töricht affektierte Sonderbarkeit . . . wird das Kriterium von Originalität und das sicherste Zeichen, daß man einen Kopf habe, dieses, wenn man sich des Tages über ein paarmal darauf stellt. Wenn dieses auch eine Sternische Kunst wäre so ist wohl so viel gewiß, es ist keine der Schwersten." Quoted from Price, *English Literature in Germany*, p. 196.

23. Price, *English Literature in Germany*, p. 194.

24. Goethe: "Maximen und Reflexionen," *Werke*, I. Abteilung, XLII, ii, 140; Hegel: *Asthetik*, ed. Friedrich Bassenge (Frankfurt, n.d.), II, 452–453.

25. *Versuch*, p. 17: ". . . so wie das Heldengedicht *öffentliche Thaten* und *Begebenheiten*, das ist, *Handlungen des Bürgers* (in einem gewissen Sinn dieses Worts) besingt: so beschäftigt sich der Roman mit den *Handlungen und Empfindungen des Menschen*."

26. *Versuch*, p. 47. English text: "Miscellaneous Reflections," V, i, *Characteristics*, ed. John M. Robertson (London, 1900), II, 319f.

27. *Versuch*, pp. 48–49.

28. See *Versuch*, pp. 67–68.

29. *Versuch*, p. 192.

30. *Versuch*, pp. 201 and 193.

31. *Versuch*, p. 201.

32. *Versuch*, p. 210.

33. In addition to Michelsen's book the two major studies of Blanckenburg's significance are the "Nachwort" to Lämmert's edition and Kurt Wölfel, "Friedrich von Blanckenburg's *Versuch über den Roman*," *Deutsche Romantheorien: Beiträge zu einer historischen Poetik des Romans in Deutschland*, ed. Reinhold Grimm (Frankfurt-Bonn, 1968), pp. 29–60.

34. *Versuch*, pp. 254f. and 336ff.

35. *Versuch*, p. 392.

36. *Versuch*, pp. 208ff.

37. See note 19.

38. *Ausgewählte Briefe von C. M. Wieland an verschiedene Freunde in den Jahren 1751 bis 1810* (Zürich, 1815), II, 287f.: "Ich gestehe Ihnen, mein Freund, daß *Sterne* beynahe der einzige Autor in der Welt ist, den ich mit einer Art von ehrfurchtsvoller Bewunderung ansehe. Ich werde sein Buch *studiren*, so lang ich lebe, und es doch nicht genug studirt haben. Ich kenne keines, worin so viel ächte Socratische Weisheit, eine so tiefe Kenntniß des Menschen, ein so feines Gefühl des Schönen und Guten, eine so große Menge neuer und feiner moralischer Bemerkungen, so viel gesunde Beurtheilung, mit so viel Witz und Genie verbunden wäre."

39. *Sämtliche Schriften*, XVII (Leipzig, 1904), 256: "Es kömmt darauf an, Wort durch Wort zu übersetzen; nicht eines durch mehrere zu umschreiben. Bemerken Sie sodann, daß sentimental ein neues Wort ist. War es *Sternen* erlaubt, sich ein neues Wort zu bilden: so muß es eben darum auch seinem Uebersetzer erlaubt seyn. Die Engländer hatten gar kein Adjectivum von Sentiment: wir haben von *Empfindung* mehr als eines. *Empfindlich, empfindbar, empfindungsreich*: aber diese sagen alle etwas anders. Wagen Sie, *empfindsam!* Wenn eine *mühsame* Reise eine Reise heißt, bey der viel Mühe ist: so kann ja auch eine *empfindsame* Reise eine Reise heissen, bey der viel Empfindung war. Ich will nicht sagen, daß Sie die Analogie ganz auf Ihrer Seite haben dürften. Aber was die Leser vors erste bey dem Worte noch nicht denken, mögen sie sich nach und nach dabey zu denken gewöhnen."

40. *Versuch*, p. 527.

41. *Werke*, I. Abteilung, XLI, ii, 252–253: "Es begegnet uns gewöhnlich bei raschem Vorschreiten der literarischen sowohl als humanen Bildung, daß wir vergessen, wem wir die ersten Anregungen, die anfänglichen Einwirkungen schuldig geworden. Was da ist und vorgeht, glauben wir, müsse so sein und geschehen; aber gerade deßhalb gerathen wir auf Irrwege, weil wir diejenigen aus dem Auge verlieren, die uns auf den rechten Weg geleitet haben. In diesem Sinne mach' ich aufmerksam auf einen Mann, der die große Epoche reinerer Menschenkenntniß, edler Duldung, zarter Liebe in der zweiten Hälfte des vorigen Jahrhunderts zuerst angeregt und verbreitet hat. (An diesen Mann, dem ich so viel verdanke, werd' ich oft erinnert; auch fällt er mir ein, wenn von

Irrthümern und *Wahrheiten* die Rede ist, die unter den Menschen hin- und widerschwanken. Ein drittes Wort kann man im zarteren Sinne hinzufügen, nämlich *Eigenheiten*. Denn es gibt gewisse Phänomene der Menschheit, die man mit dieser Benennung am besten ausdrückt; sie sind irrthümlich nach außen, wahrhaft nach innen und, recht betrachtet, psychologisch höchst wichtig. Sie sind das, was das Individuum constituirt, das Allgemeine wird dadurch specificirt und in dem Allerwunderlichsten blickt immer noch etwas Verstand, Vernunft und Wohlwollen hindurch, das uns anzieht und fesselt.) Gar anmuthig hat in diesem Sinne Yorick-Sterne, das Menschliche im Menschen auf das zarteste entdeckend, diese Eigenheiten, in so fern sie sich thätig äußern, ruling passion genannt. Denn fürwahr sie sind es, die den Menschen nach einer gewissen Seite hintreiben, in einem folgerechten Gleise weiterschieben und, ohne daß es Nachdenken, Überzeugung, Vorsatz oder Willenskraft bedürfte, immerfort in Leben und Bewegung erhalten. Wie nahe die Gewohnheit hiemit verschwistert sei, fällt sogleich in die Augen: denn sie begünstigt ja die Bequemlichkeit, in welcher unsere Eigenheiten, ungestört hinzuschlendern belieben." See also II. Abteilung, XLII, 2, p. 66. The best collection of Goethe's remarks on Sterne is W. R. R. Pinger, "Laurence Sterne and Goethe," *University of California Publications in Modern Philology*, X (1920–1925), 1–65.

42. See Goethe's remarks about Johann Georg Schlosser in "Dichtung und Wahrheit"; *Werke*, I. Abteilung, XXVII, 83; Price, op. cit., p. 138.

43. "German Echoes of a Famous Popean Line," *Notes & Queries*, CCIII (1958), 18–20.

44. See, for instance, *Werke*, III. Abteilung, X, 144 (January 5, 1826): "Für mich Sterne's Briefe. Ruling Passion! Den Sinn dieser Worte überdacht und commentirt."

45. In "Maximen und Reflexionen" there is the following aphorism: "Die Sentimentalität der Engländer ist humoristisch und zart, der Franzosen populär und weinerlich, der Deutschen naiv und realistisch." *Werke*, I. Abteilung, XLII, ii, 160.

46. "Anthropologie in pragmatischer Hinsicht," *Gesammelte Schriften*, VII (Berlin, 1907), p. 307. In a set of notes taken by a student the passage is more extensive: "Was die Empfindung anbetrifft, so könnte wohl die Zartheit von der Zärtlichkeit unterschieden werden, so wie die Empfindsamkeit von der Empfindlichkeit. Von Frauenzimmern sagt man, sie sind empfindlich, zärtlich, d.h. sie werden in dem, was Leid und Freude betrifft, leicht affiziert. Dies muß man aber von einem Manne nicht sagen können. Doch muß er empfindsam und zart sein, damit er Feinheit genug besitzt, seiner Frau Unannehmlichkeiten zu ersparen. Dies ist eine Delikatesse, worin Großmut liegt. Jede Sehnsucht mit dem Bewußtsein der Ohnmacht bringt Seufzen und Tränen hervor." *Die philosophischen Hauptvorlesungen Immanuel Kants: Nach den neu aufgefundenen Kollegheften des Grafen Heinrich zu Dohna-Wundlacken*, ed. Arnold Kowalewski (1924; repr. Hildesheim, 1965), p. 344.

47. *Gesammelte Schriften*, IX (Berlin und Leipzig, 1923), 469: "*Toby* sagt im *Tristram Shandy* zu einer Fliege, die ihn lange beunruhigt hatte, indem er sie zum Fenster hinausläßt: 'Gehe, du böses Thier, die Welt ist groß genug für mich und dich!' Und dies könnte jeder zu seinem Wahlspruche machen. Wir dürfen uns nicht einander lästig werden; die Welt ist groß genug für uns Alle." Quotation supplied from *Tristram Shandy*, II, xii, p. 113.

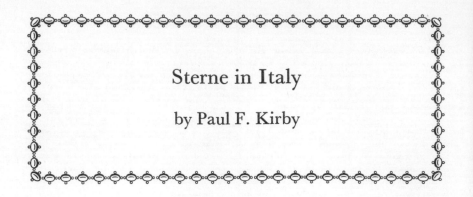

Sterne in Italy

by Paul F. Kirby

Sterne's personal tour in Italy—from late Autumn, 1765, to Spring, 1766—was exemplary. He travelled with the "GENTLE Spirit of sweetest humour" (IX, 24, p. 628). He never criticized. He did not complain of physical discomforts, though he felt them, as when the "Dromedary" of a horse fell and crushed him "flat as a Pankake" (*Letters*, p. 273). He was aware of being robbed. "My shirts! see what a deadly schism has happen'd amongst 'em——for the laps are in *Lombardy*, . . . a pistol tinder-box . . . filch'd from me at *Sienna*, and twice that I pay'd five Pauls for two hard eggs, once at *Raddicoffini*, and a second time at *Capua*" (p. 628). But he said, "We really expect too much." If charged "above par for your suppers and bed . . . who would embroil their philosophy for it? for heaven's and for your own sake, pay it——pay it with both hands open, rather than leave *Disappointment* sitting drooping upon the eye of your fair Hostess and her Damsels in the gate-way, at your departure——and besides, my dear Sir, you get a sisterly kiss of each of 'em worth a pound——at least I did——" (p. 629).

He was presented at court in Turin, received in the best society of Milan; dined with Sir Horace Mann in Florence; probably "trod the Vatican," and was presented to "all the Saints" (*Letters*, p. 266); at Naples was guest of princes; attended "punchinellos——festinos and masquerades" (p. 269). Everywhere his wit and affectionate understanding shed happiness. When he met the Nizzard priest, Gian Carlo Passeroni (1713–1803) at the Minister, Count Firmian's salon in Milan, he treated him kindly, and told him that he had taken the idea of *Tristram Shandy* from the facetious digressions of *Il Cicerone*.[1] Anyone who has attempted to read even short parts of the almost 3,000 pages of this doggerel epic will quickly appreciate that Sterne owed very little to its author. But he got something from it and was grateful.

Professor of English, University of Pisa

Afterwards Passeroni wrote:

> *E già mi disse un chiaro letterato*
> *Inglese, che dalla mia stampita*
> *Il disegno, il modello avea cavato*
> *Di scrivere in più tomi la sua vita;*
> *E pien di gratitudine, e d'amore*
> *Mi chiamava suo Duce, e Precettore.*[2]

Sterne's little tour of Italy was a triumph of good will and ended hopefully. From near Dijon he wrote Eugenius, "I must take up again the pen. . . . I shall live these ten years" (*Letters*, p. 277).

Now two centuries have passed. The essential Sterne is still alive in Italy, where he travelled so briefly and lived so happily. And yet, I must confess that I was attracted to this subject by what seemed to me unsatisfactory aspects of his posthumous survival there. Of course Sterne is a difficult writer, and is more difficult in a land where English is not the language. Even so I know several who enjoy him in the original, who understand him, admire him, are helped by him and love him; I believe there are several hundred such sprinkled up and down the peninsula. And there is a wide continuing diffusion of Foscolo's famous translation of *A Sentimental Journey*. There are five recent complete translations of *Tristram Shandy*. There is also a heavy weight of negative cultural dogma expressed in ritual phrases, such as: "all edifying motives, being lost sight of—analysis of feelings becomes an end in itself, and reflects the peculiar personality of the author, bizarre and sensual. . . . Not one to confer dignity on the cloth, a priest frivolous and flirtatious, his conjugal life was disturbed . . . especially [by] a young French woman, and at the end of his life, [by] Eliza Draper; he died deep in debt, in a rented room, and separated from his wife. *Tristram Shandy* for moral and literary reasons was attacked by Dr Johnson, Richardson, Horace Walpole, Goldsmith and others. . . . Broad stories, variability of feelings, tears, eccentricity, dead ass, starling in a cage, maid in a locanda, a green silk purse, a girl more important than Notre Dame."

These phrases—I have translated them literally—come from Mario Praz's widely known *Storia della Letteratura Inglese*, both the 1944 edition and the latest, the 1964 edition. Some of the comment is favorable. The impression remains, however, that Sterne is not Praz's cup of tea.

As Mario Praz has long been the leading Italian Professor of English literature, his influence is important. The only difference between these editions is that in the later some ideas of Carlo Levi are inserted. Levi's impression is that Sterne, with his minute observation of things, resembles Dutch genre painters (Levi is also famous as a painter in Italy). The Dutch school in the history of art and literature of the Occident has enormous significance because it leads to the breakdown of hierarchy of values of subjects, develops indifference to content, and leads to the notion, wide-spread in our time, that the highest accomplishment of the imagination is the producing of non-figurative art and non-narrative novels. This seems to me to over-simplify a complex tendency. Also it does not help us understand Sterne's work. It distracts our attention from it. One of Levi's ideas is striking: the digressions of Sterne are a kind of hide-and-seek with death prolonged *ad infinitum*. But I shall speak of Carlo Levi later.

In 1967 appeared a new complete translation, the fourth, of *Tristram Shandy*. The preface was written by a colleague at the University of Pisa and shows too clearly the influence of Praz. Referring to *A Sentimental Journey* he says Sterne "exhibits himself in a series of lachrymose scenes, very difficult for a modern reader to bear." Incomprehension does exist.

The central fact of Sterne's reputation in Italy, of course, is Foscolo's translation, *Viaggio Sentimentale*. There had been two previous translations, one at Venice, from the French, 1792, and another at Milan, 1812. Foscolo's first edition appeared at Pisa, 1813. There were editions in 1818 and 1825, and after Foscolo's death (1827) there were a succession of reprints, 1835, 1850 twice, 1855, 1856, 1874, 1878, 1883, 1884, 1912, 1914, 1916, 1922, 1926, 1932, 1942, 1944, 1952, 1957, 1959 (Rizzoli, Biblioteca Universale paperback). Since Foscolo's translation there have been no others—a monopoly which has given much more fame to *A Sentimental Journey* than to Sterne's other work and consequently emphasized the sentimental character of Sterne, but this is also because of the quality of the translation itself. Until 1922 *Tristram Shandy* remained untranslated into Italian, excepting selections. Though this first translation is excellent, four others have appeared: in 1958 with an introduction by Carlo Levi; in 1959, Rizzoli; in 1967, Unione Tipografica Torinese, Torino; in 1968, Istituto Geografico De Agostini, Novara. This is a reprint of the text published by the Club del Libro, 1968.[3]

Lettere di Yorick a Elisa e di Elisa a Yorick, with notes, appeared at Venice, 1792, adding to Sterne's reputation for romantic sentiment. Three parts of *Tristram Shandy* were translated and published by Carlo Bini, 1829, in *Indicatore Livornese*, "Death of Yorick," "Slawkenbergius's Tale," "Le Fever." These were reprinted in various editions of Bini's works. *Sermoni Sacri di Lorenzo Sterne* (ten sermons) were published at Milan, 1831. *Lettere di Yorick ad Eliza* were again published at Udine, 1836, privately for a wedding. At Milan, 1844, appeared two volumes, octavo, containing "The Monk," "The Ass," and "The Prisoner" from *A Sentimental Journey*, the first volume in English, the second in Italian.

Foscolo was an artist of such marked characteristics that, although he loved Sterne—this is the word—his Italian version is like a color filter, which passes the sentiment without Sterne's nuances of wit and humor. This phenomenon has been well studied by Rabizzani in his book, *Sterne in Italia, Riflessi nostrani dell'umorismo sentimentale* (Roma, 1920), a book cited in all the bibliographies, but I suspect not well known directly, because the edition was small, only 500 copies, and has long been out of print—and also because most scholars of eighteenth-century English literature have fewer occasions to exercise their Italian than they have to use French and German. Rabizzani died suddenly at Pistoia, victim of Spanish influenza during the world-epidemic in 1918, at the age of thirty-three. He had already published, in 1914, a very good sixty-page general monograph on Sterne (reprinted in 1940). He had a wide, discriminating knowledge of European literature, as anyone will see who reads his bibliographic introduction, pp. [3]–22, in which he summarizes Sterne's world-wide influence. He had also a very particular knowledge and appreciation of Sterne. He was moving towards the great tradition of critical literary history exemplified in Francesco de Sanctis' *Storia della Letteratura Italiana* (1870–1872). He comes swiftly to essential points, is lucid, well-balanced, witty, and writes with such agile grace that it is easy to see why he was attracted to Sterne. The first half of the book, devoted to Foscolo as translator, was complete and proof-read at Rabizzani's death. The second part, which was still in manuscript, is devoted to Sternian influence in nineteenth-century Italian literature. It is illuminating, but no doubt lacks some finishing touches. Rabizzani was a light put out too soon.

Foscolo was a dark, tragic, powerfully moving genius. In Italy he is ranked immediately after Dante and Petrarch for certain sonnets

which every Italian who has been to school can recite from memory—
for example:

> Nè più mai toccherò le sacre sponde
> ove il mio corpo fanciulletto giacque,
> Zacinto mia, che te specchi nell' onde
> del greco mar da cui vergine nacque
> Venere, e fea quell' isole feconde
> col suo primo sorriso, . . .[4]

Young Foscolo was attracted to Sterne by the scene of Maria of
Moulins. He was so impressed by it that he imitated it in the early 1798
version of his *Jacopo Ortis* written when he was twenty years old. Later,
ashamed of the imitation, he modified it. In the early version Lauretta
takes the place of Maria. "Has anyone seen the poor maid, Lauretta?
She is quite mad!" Jacopo Ortis is a fictitious young man, an alter-
Foscolo who resembles—perhaps too closely—Goethe's Werther. He
writes a diary of despair and fury to his dear friend Lorenzo. (Curious
coincidence: Lorenzo Sterne, Father Lorenzo.) His suicidal longing is
satisfied when he stabs himself in the heart with a dagger and is found
pale, blood-drenched, and dying. His last written request is that the
portrait of his Teresa (Eliza) be buried in his grave. Italian critics have
suggested that the discipline of translating Sterne—and re-translating
him—helped Foscolo outgrow the ungoverned gloomy frenzy of *Ortis*;
but Foscolo merely survived, became older and more restrained. His
character never changed much. *Ortis* is obviously a young man's book.
Anyone who reads it will be impressed by a poetic splendor, a glitter-
ing, magnificently passionate prose. Of course Ortis is an idealist,
sensitive to the injustices in the long past of Italy. He wanders about in
Napoleonic Italy, governed by Austrians, but it is not only the contemporary evils in Italy that stimulate his feelings. His is a more universal regret than that and reminds us of the visions of Rousseau. He
visits, for example, the little hill overlooking the battlefield of Monta-
perti, where on Saturday, 4 September 1260, the Sienese defeated the
Florentines. He stood under the cypresses at dawn and saw a vision of
the shadows of the Tuscans who had been slain going up and down the
steep roads of the hills—"with their bloody swords, glaring fiercely,
trembling with rage, scuffling together, tearing open their ancient
wounds——O! for whom that blood?" Nothing like this in Sterne.
Foscolo, when he attempted humor later, as in his *Gazzettino del Bel*

Mondo, achieved only a bitter, corrosive sarcasm or heavy irony something like Swift's, but less sustained.

Sterne wrote, 9 February 1768, to Dr Eustace of North Carolina Colony, "It is not in the power of any one to taste humor, however he may wish it—'tis the gift of God" (*Letters*, p. 411). But Foscolo *did* taste the humor of Sterne. Among his other troubles was that of being able to taste Sterne's humor without being able to create it in his translation. He worked conscientiously though not continuously, from about 1805 (aet 27) when he was an officer in Napoleon's army waiting to invade England, until 1813 (aet 35) when the first edition was published at Pisa. He understood that Sterne's way of writing called for an unusual Italian prose to translate it, and to prepare for this, he went through early Italian literature, making lists of curious words and phrases. The first thing that strikes a reader of Foscolo's translation— if he knows Sterne's writing—is that it does not seem to flow naturally. Some Italians, among them the late Professor Attilio Momigliano of the University of Firenze (1938), have praised the language and style-forming efforts of Foscolo in his translation.

It is almost a cliché in Italy: Foscolo's wonderful or Foscolo's superb translation. And of course it is not often that a poet of genius undertakes such a task. It is also true that Foscolo's translation has made Sterne's wonderful book into a wonderful Italian book—for those who read no English. But from the very first, it was seen that the diction was too affected, too round-about. While Foscolo was still working on his text, a friend named Pagnini, a Greek scholar, visited him; and Foscolo let him read two sheets, which he found generally unsatisfactory, even containing errors in the understanding of the original. The errors might be tolerated if the result were spirited and entertaining. But there is too much della Cruscan artificiality, too much forced brilliance, and it may be suspected, as Edoardo Gori pointed out in his introduction to Rabizzani's book, that Foscolo worked partly as a sporting rival, after trying unsuccessfully to render Sterne's spirit truly, and that he regarded himself as an artist in competition with Sterne. Foscolo knew well what he was doing and not doing. In a letter to Isabella Teotochi Albrizzi, 1810, he wrote:

Vado talvolta scrivendo ridicole bizzarie; così rido come ridevano Rabelais, Sterne e Cervantes; ma perchè io non ho una scintilla del loro amabile Genio, non aspiro alla loro palma, nè presumo di fare rider il pubblico alle spalle della stoltezza e della vanità; rido da me solo e quando considero le fantasie meschine che ho scritto, le lacero e rido da me. Quando poi me sento caldo e forte, sto dietro a lavori più seri che, o mi salveranno dall'oblio, o se non altro, mi frutteranno la compiacenza di avere spesa innocentemente e generosamente la vita.[5]

Nevertheless Foscolo's translation has had a continuing success in Italy, and is highly regarded even now by those who do not know Sterne in the original, or by those whose taste might not permit them to appreciate Sterne in the original. Foscolo's translation has been a matter of national honor for some critics. Let me illustrate. Rabizzani showed that Foscolo used the footnotes of Paulin Crassous' French translation (1801) in forming his own rather spirited footnotes. Rabizzani went so far as to use the word "plagiarized." A generation later, in 1942 Luigi Berti (later translator of Dylan Thomas) in an anti-British moment undertook to defend the national honor and Foscolo's translation in *Foscolo Traduttore de Sterne*. It is an interestingly offensive and polemic book. His adversary is Rabizzani. But on the first page he makes a pass at Sterne also, "Quel parroco erroneamente giudicato come 'man of God,' o come 'Christian citizen,' e che rispondeva al nome di Laurence Sterne, avido per tutti i casi di mantenersi all'altezza dei tempi," avid to keep up with the times!

According to Berti (p. 12) sentimentalism is an integral part of Sterne's philosophy, and Foscolo translated sentiment very well. This is true. Also Sterne's form and superhuman delicacy is rendered with such grace that his essence (p. 44) is preserved in the Italian. This is less sure. Then Berti comes to the footnotes, and tries to demonstrate that Rabizzani falsified by saying Foscolo plagiarized Crassous's footnotes. Rabizzani had used parallel texts of footnotes to show how much Foscolo had borrowed from the French translator. Berti used other footnotes to demonstrate Foscolo's originality. But this is a silly discussion, I think. In 1958 Gennaro Barbarisi reviewed the matter and stated what is quite evident, that the footnotes in Foscolo are partly derived from Crassous and partly original, e.g. "cicisbei: individui mirabilmente composti di qualità negative."[6] You see the bite of Foscolo's humor, if it is humor. The moral sarcasm sounds ill coming from a man of Foscolo's temperament.[7]

Claudio Varese wrote a more serious scholarly work on Foscolo's translation, *Linguaggio sterniano e Linguaggio foscoliano* (1947), which traces in Foscolo's own writings the growth of his awareness of Sterne's qualities as a man and artist, and follows his preparation for the translation. It shows too that Foscolo, much as he admired Sterne's spirit, always regarded his own nature as quite different.

Rabizzani in his title used a good word, *Riflessi*, "reflections" of Sterne's sentimental irony in Italy, surface reflections, a nice distinction. Now a glance at Italian authors to see these reflections.

There is a great deal of humor in Manzoni's *I Promessi Sposi*, and a steady vein of irony in what I would call a classic manner for want of a better word. For example in the opening sentences Manzoni says, "there was also a castle at the considerable town of Lecco, and it [Lecco] therefore had the honor of having a commandant and possessing a fixed garrison of Spanish soldiers who gave lessons in modesty to the girls of the town, and caressed now and then the shoulders of some husband or father, and who, at summer's end never failed to deploy into the vinyards to thin out the grapes and to lighten the labor of the contadini at grape-gathering time." This is very well, but it seems to have nothing to do with the humor of Sterne. The delicately turned calm, full-bodied picture-making writing of Manzoni is not like Sterne's delicate, picture-making but swift-flying, ever-changing, almost less-than-essential writing.

The other great Italian writer of the first half of the nineteenth century was Leopardi, whose prose *Zibaldone*, or miscellany, has a kind of ironic humor and psychological subtlety. Leopardi knew Sterne's work and admired it. He was a gallophobe and therefore enjoyed Sterne's observations on French manners, such as the French Captain's dancing down the street after asking the Countess de L***'s destination and family status, and also on the hyperbolic expressions such as *charmee, ravisee, extasie, desespoire*, "emerge it in the ocean," etc. Leopardi with a more Swiftian than Sternian irony was too sad, too pessimistic, too egocentric.

Carlo Bini (1806–1842) who translated selections from Sterne, was able to record his real imprisonment in his *Manoscritto di un Prigioniero*. The Granducal Government of Tuscany sent him to the Fortezza Stella at Portoferraio, Elba, for political reasons in 1833. Sterne's contemplation of a prisoner gives pleasure because it is a fictitious prisoner, and the emotions produced are fictitious. In Bini the emotions are real. There is no pleasure. He mentions Sterne and you feel that he is trying to imitate him. At the beginning of one chapter he writes, "Now where are we? Wouldn't it be something, if after all these digressions, I failed to remember what I was about?" And there are exclamations praising the comforts of religion. But these comforts do not appear to comfort. The substance of his memoir is bitterness against political injustice, bitterness against the rich who never get into prison, bitterness against empty boredom and dejection.

Also imprisoned for the same reason at the same time in the same prison but in another cell was Guerrazzi of Leghorn, once famous in Italy. The public library of Leghorn and a respectable street there still bear his name. In 1857 he published *L'Asino, Sogno*. Nothing to do with Sterne's ass. This ass dreams a Swiftian nightmare of history and civilization. It is a very long dream. Guerrazzi had a whiplike way with words and wrote with vigor and vitriol; he had none of the carefulness and humanity of Sterne. His best story—at least young Carducci was grateful enough for favors to call it that—is *Il buco nel muro* (1862). Foscolo prefaces his translation with a noble and gracious salute to "Yorick's readers and mine." Guerrazzi in a parallel salute wisely declares that his own "genius" is cruder than Foscolo's and much cruder than Sterne's. He lists different kinds of stories: *epica, oratoria, drammatica, pindarica, chiacchierina* or chattery, *bugiarda* or lying, *maligna*, just so we will have made these distinctions carefully before setting out; then he launches into what he may have imagined to be a Sternian-Shandyan chiacchierina tale, laid in Turin, where the characters speak a thick Leghorn brogue, because the author was a Leghorn man. Orazio (Horace), fat, bald, easy-going, a gentleman like Horace the poet and like Uncle Toby Shandy, comes home earlier than usual and happier, descends the stairs singing *Arabi nelle Gallie* (Lilliburlero), which renders unnecessary the ringing of the bell for the maid, Betta, who opens the door for him. He *descends* further to the bedroom, where Betta helps him out of his city clothes and periwig and in place of these dresses him in a *guarnacca* (dressing gown) and a white doublet, printed all over with apples and artichokes "and I don't know how many other vegetables and fruits, more than on the skirts of Pomona." After more of this he *descends* again, greets all his peasant families, visits Lilla the cat, which has just given birth to half a dozen kittens, and then according to old usage he visits Rebecca and Toby, bitch and dog of exemplary chastity, discretion, and many other cardinal virtues—though teleological virtues they were never known to have. Croce did not admire this tale, and we can't blame him much. It goes on with confusion, Passeroni-style digressions, delays, and minute meaningless descriptions. But of course a tale is a tale. This relates how Orazio's nephew, a very useless young man, most amiable and expensive, finally causes a bill to be sent to his uncle, which is just too much, and regretfully his uncle sends him away. Marcellino says that he has been thinking of going out to Australia to make his fortune; so now he will go, and he will not return until he has made a fortune of fourteen million lire. On the way to Australia from Turin is Milan, where Marcellino thinks it well to try the Bohemian life up fourteen flights (the lucky number) of stairs in an attic. One day he decides to hang a picture of the Virgin Mary on the wall, and driving the nail, knocks a hole in the plaster, through which he detects in the next attic one of the most beautiful young women in the world, wife to an unpleasant painter who is dying of the usual tuberculosis. When he dies, there is a young rival ready to replace him. But the Austrian police are searching for him. Marcellino generously helps him escape. The young lady, a rich heiress who had married against her father's will, now becomes useless Marcellino's wife. This is not a very good story, though it has a moral, but it is full of what the author intended to be imitations of Sterne. When, for example, Marcellino is telling his uncle of his knocking the hole in the wall and seeing the beautiful young woman, uncle Orazio asks him how he covered the hole so as not to be detected. "With a tegame," is the answer. "With a tegame!" "Yes. With a tegame." *Tegame* is literally a frying-pan. In the vulgar Tuscan jargon it also means *whore*. Perhaps there is something Sternian in this, but it is rather plebian.

Count Giovanni Ferri (1755–1830) lived long in England and was author of *Lo Spettatore Italiano* in which he imagined a tour—something like Sterne's, though the spirit was different. In his travels he visits the tomb of Sterne. He is with a certain Fanny, a very lovely and very sensitive young lady who would appreciate such a visit. At the tomb he exclaims, "O buono Sterne, non ho io avuto più care delizie, che le opere figlie del tuo ingegno e del tuo cuore. . . . Oh! io potessi un giorno meritar un qualche nome fra i buoni tuoi imitatori!"

Lorenzo Borsini wrote *Viaggio Sentimentale al Campo Santo Colerico*, 1837, a grim tale in which a stranger arrives contrary to the strict laws at the burial of a very young girl, victim of the cholera at Naples.

Only the cemetery workers are permitted to be present. The visitor is arrested and discovered to be a woman, the girl's mother. Maupassant has a similar story, *L'Horrible*.

A curiosity, which might have interested Sterne, is *Il Viaggio Sentimentale di Sterne Continuato*, 1874, Florence, by James Pincherle, who had lived in India. He supposes that as Eliza was a native of India, Sterne may have learned some Indian words from her. In one chapter appears a list of a hundred Indian words with translation. There are also gypsies, and in another chapter a fragment of *Othello* is translated in gypsy language.

The most unabashed and complete imitation of Sterne-Foscolo, a sort of Italian parallel to Mackenzie's *The Man of Feeling*, is Ugo Tarchetti's hundred-page story, *L'Innamorato della Montagna*, Milano, 1888. Tarchetti's true name was Iginio; but he always used Ugo because it had been Foscolo's name. The author sets out on a journey from Eboli (where Christ stopped according to Carlo Levi's famous title) to make a January crossing of the impenetrable mountains to Potenza. The best part of this story is the description of this little-known desolation. The coach is old. All coaches in the South of Italy are old. Everything is old, including the horse, Baruk. The author says his motive for such a trip is something he will not tell us, and that we may not be interested anyway. Nor can he explain why he enjoys the horrid precipices and sadness of the scene. The coachman is calm, talks cheerfully, has a tender look which reminds Tarchetti of Yorick and La Fleur; and so he determines to give him a half-ducat on arrival at Potenza. He reflects at length on the happiness of the poor in Lucania: beggars who live on four cents worth of snails a day, others "more naked than the palm of your hand," who pass carrying three zucchini under one arm, two under the other, and one in hand (Sterne's precision)—a total of six zucchini for two cents. They say "Buongiorno, Eccellenza" and are so blessedly happy you wish you were in their rags. This leads to a digression against the tyranny of assiduous work, of living for appearances, and on the pleasure of giving alms. The thought is interrupted by the settling of a swarm of birds on the backs of a herd of buffalo where they will peck fleas. The author is moved at the thought of birds that pick horse-droppings from the road. The coachman tells of the horse Baruk, now twenty-five years old, and full of wonderful memories. Anyone not moved by memories and all their beauty must be a clod; but Baruk, the horse, has a sensitive face. As a colt he had grazed in the fields of nearby Persano (then a royal horse farm), and he had a noble pedigree. It is a pity that something befell him during his first love affair, and he has a weak kidney, in fact he needs to ****. Here the coachman cannot say the word. In order to do what he has to do, Baruk must be taken out of his harness and allowed to tread softly on the green grass so that his kidney may relax. While this is done, the author descends to tread on the green grass also and moralizes on life. He looks up into the sky, where he sees a bit of new moon through cirrus clouds, and calls out "Dio Mio!—If I deny Thee, where shall I find a reason for life?" Five pages of pseudo-religious rhapsody, broken into by a loud exclamation from the coach. Baruk has succeeded. "Sta fruendo!"

Back in the coach, Tarchetti feels new faith; but coach travel is most uncomfortable. They leave the plain, enter the mountains, driving through snow, rain, hail, wind. They had hoped to reach Picerno, an ancient rock town, but do not, and are snowed up in a miserable inn with North-wind howling. There is a fine description of the kitchen, imitative of Ippolito Nievo's famous description of the great kitchen of his family's Castle of Fratta. The narrative is blocked by artificial reflections. Night comes on. The traveler goes to bed. Later the door of his room opens, and someone approaches his bed—a fierce-looking man whom he identifies by a ray of light as an old mortal enemy. During the night of waking with his enemy in bed with him, he hears through the roaring wind a strange music. Dissertation on music. Simple music is best, and this is simple. Finally he can stand the searching strangeness of it no longer. He leaps from bed, rubs snow in his face, rushes downstairs, where some sleepy persons tell the tale of the mad lover of the mountain who plays the spinet night and day and gazes through the open window at the mountain. Here Tarchetti longs for the power to prove the superiority of a risible universe. At sun-up he finds the lover of the mountain, a handsome man in his forties, playing his spinet. He, Giovanni, had grown up with a little girl called Fiordilisa. They had played together in mountain fields. He was seven years older. Their fathers were executed as conspirators, a common death then. The child sweethearts were separated. Time brought them together again, when she was a lovely maiden. They were to be married. One day picking flowers for him, she reached too far out over an abyss and fell. The flowers flew from her apron and fluttered down upon her poor torn body. Giovanni is living the rest of his life in the presence of his memory and of love. The author shakes hands with his enemy as the coach departs. There is something in this story. It would have been better if Tarchetti had thought less about Sterne.

By the last quarter of the nineteenth century the direct echoes of Sterne seem to have died away. There is nothing Sternian in Carducci, D'Annunzio, Pascoli, Fogazzaro, Pirandello, Papini, nor in the bitter humorist, Panzini; nor in the more recent Federico De Roberto, Brancati or Giuseppe Tomasi di Lampedusa to mention the most important. Generally there is not much that is Sternian, because there is so little humor. Recently, 23 July 1968, Giovanni Guareschi, author of *Don Camillo*, died. He was a humorist, and he believed like Sterne, that laughter goes a long way towards resolving misunderstandings and tensions—even political ones. But anyone familiar with Guareschi will not be reminded of Sterne.

Another very remarkable author of these times is Carlo Levi, acclaimed in the early post-war period for *Christ Stopped at Eboli*. The critics found it a difficult book to classify—as though good books can or should be classified. Levi knows English, and—as we have seen—knows Sterne. *Cristo si è fermato a Eboli* has some superficial resemblances to *A Sentimental Journey*. There is no plot. One scene follows another as one bead follows another in a string, the beads being selected. But this is because Levi himself saw experience in this way. There is no Sternian quality of humor or sentiment. Levi's milieu and his people are very different from Sterne's. There is human understanding, sympathy, beautiful prose, always natural, flexible, so transparent that it disappears and leaves only the sense of experience, which is one of the effects of the best Sterne, but this is not because of Sterne. It is caused by the intensity of Levi's own experience and his own talents.

In 1950 Carlo Levi's *L'Orologio* was published. On page nineteen we find these serious words. "C'è un senso terribile nel rapporto, col tempo, delle cose nascenti." On the next page the author tells of preparing to go to bed in Rome in the attic of an old palace, where he had found a place suitable for a studio, quiet and sufficiently clean, a refuge from the ugly facts of post-war Italy, an island in time. He undressed rapidly, his mind wandering in memories. He laid his watch on the small table by his bed and heard its ticking. "And I thought that watch-time was the exact opposite of that true time which was within and all around me." Later he dropped his watch, and the search for the proper artisan to repair it took him around the city in a most unsentimental and squalid journey in which the interest is in the men and women he saw and talked with, and in their problems, which were bound up with the inexorable passing of time. Levi's introduction to a translation of *Tristram Shandy* (1958) explains that he took the idea of his *L'Orologio* from the clock which is so closely related to the creation of Tristram. I have already mentioned Levi's belief that Sterne in his digressions was essentially trying to escape from clock-time, to seize a kind of time outside time, and thus avoid death, or defeat it. It seems to me there is something too symbolic, too serious and tragic in this way of looking at Sterne's problem. Sterne himself did not regard death with such horror. He may have hoped and believed that his art would give him a kind of life beyond death. He certainly wished to perpetuate his rare, undefinable wit and faith and to preserve from oblivion the things and persons he loved, just as any artist does. The watch in Levi's book is somehow different from Mr Shandy's clock.

* * *

A word on Sterne scholars and critics in Italy. Back in 1918 Rabizzani said there had been a lack of detailed Italian studies in English literature because there had been only a limited number of scholars devoting their energies to such studies, and those few had worked mostly on Shakespeare, Milton, Byron and other romantic poets. This is still true. Even so, if one looks back over two centuries, he will see that there has been a considerable number of Sterne comments. During the nineteenth century critical writings on Sterne were produced by Ferrigni, Zanella, Nencioni, Lo Forte Randi, Bellezza, and Massarani. I have glanced through these without finding anything of much penetration. But Luigi Carrer in *Prose* said that the art of Sterne in *A Sentimental Journey* resembled somewhat that of the brief pieces in the *Greek Anthology*. There is some truth in the suggestion. Then Carrer said, "It seems the author above all things abhors satiety, and as soon as he touches the limits of perfection in one kind of writing, he turns to the opposite kind, passing from supreme simplicity and strong feelings to affectation and shrewdness." Sterne is "concise: illumines in flashes, lets the heart and fantasy of his readers do the rest."[8]

Two general appreciative essays on Sterne were written by Carlo Segrè early in this century. Segrè knew English well and had a true appreciation of Sterne's art. He wrote after Cross's first edition of *The Life and Times* ... (1909), to which he refers; but the critical part is derived from his own sensitivity. In one essay he refers to the fatality that the skull of Sterne, who fancied himself as Yorick, should itself have become perhaps an object of admiration. He suggests in the words of Dante, that Sterne's bones may be

Or le bagna la pioggia e move il vento, [9]

as were those of King Manfred after the Battle of Benevento (1260).

Several recent studies are concerned with Sterne's relation to Foscolo: Attilio Momigliano, *Foscolo and Sterne* (Bari, 1938); Berti's (1942) and Varese's (1947) studies, both mentioned above; Corbellini, "La Versione Foscoliana del Viaggio di Sterne," *Ulisse* IX, 1955; Pino Fasano, "L'Amicizia Foscolo-Sterne," *English Miscellany*, Roma, 1963.

A very good introduction to Sterne may be seen in the Rizzoli paperback edition of Foscolo's translation, 1958, by someone who calls himself Gigi Cavalli. If there is a defect, it is in the over-praise of Foscolo; but Cavalli was presenting an edition of Foscolo.

In 1924 appeared an abridged version of the English text of *A Sentimental Journey* (Firenze). The introduction by G. S. Gargàno seems to me to be the best critical comment on Sterne in Italian. Gargàno was able to enter into Sterne's mind and interpret it. He quotes Sterne's letter to Lord Shelburne about tearing himself to pieces with his sentiments, and his exclamation to Sir George McCartney "The duce take all sentiments! I wish there was not one in the world!" (*Letters*, p. 405). Gargàno observes that Sterne's intellect "was stronger than his emotions, and even when he suffered most from his sensitivity, he was always able to master his feelings. . . . In subtle melancholy and delicacy, he has no rivals and the humor with which he expresses these emotions differentiates him from all his contemporaries. I have said humor, but perhaps *persiflage* is better— the quick understanding of weaknesses and ingenuousness, the feeling for the ridiculous or pathetic, the versatility, which includes a human solidarity, full of charity and indulgence, which sometimes seems Epicurean. But the indecency of Sterne (if such) is intellectual rather than sensual. The reader is led on by the attraction of Sterne's singular personality." Of the style he says, "A distillation word for word, phrase for phrase, with infinite attention to artistic beauty and melody . . . a difficult style in its freedom—in its interruptions, and suspensions, and varied language, now aristocratically literary—now simple and fluent, in which not infrequently neologisms appear." He concludes that Sterne deserves a wiser and subtler interpreter than Foscolo. Gargàno is well remembered in Italy for other contributions.[10] It is a pity that his comments on Sterne appear to have gone unheeded.

In 1968 I published in Italy for the first time the complete English text of *A Sentimental Journey*, with a general introduction, notes and bibliography. Nothing remarkable in this, except the objections by editors of the publisher, Mursia of Milan, to printing an integral text, for fear of corrupting the youth of Italy with Sterne's famous indecency. It was a battle which I am happy to say was won by Sterne, whose text was finally read through by those responsible and approved.

A well-known Italian professor of English was telling me recently that the Italians have a different sense of humor from the English and that—as if this were evidence—there has never been an Italian author like Sterne. But of course there is no English author like Sterne.

NOTES

1. The meeting of Sterne and Passeroni is reported in Rabizzani, who had it from the critic and biographer, Giulio Carcano: vide "Giancarlo Passeroni" in *Rivista Europea*, Milano, 1845, reprinted in Carcano's *Memorie di grandi*, Milano, 1869, 2 vols, I, 202ff. Sterne may have seen the first two volumes of *Il Cicerone*, printed in octavo at Venice, Remondini, 1756.

2. *Il Cicerone*, Pt. III, Canto 177, strophe 122, Vol. V, p. 475 of the complete edition, Bassano, 1775. 6 Vols. "Il chiaro Stern" [*sic*] is mentioned by name in Pt. II, Canto 2, strophe 37 in Vol. III, p. 40.

3. This information regarding translations of Sterne into Italian comes from Rabizzani supplemented by the card index files of the Biblioteca Nazionale Centrale, Florence, where copies of all books printed in Italy are deposited.

4. The sonnet, "Zacinto," lines to his birthplace (1778), the isle of Zante, near "petrosa Itaca" di Ulisse, the clear-seen stony Ithaca of Ulysses.

5. Quoted by Pino Fasano in "L' 'Amicizia' Foscolo-Sterne . . . ," *English Miscellany*, XIV (1963), 115–169. Foscolo says: "sometimes I write ridiculous things; and so I laugh as Rabelais, Sterne and Cervantes laughed: but because I have not one spark of their amiable genius, I do not aspire to their palm; . . . I laugh alone, and when I consider what miserable fantasies I have written, I tear them up and laugh at myself. But when I feel myself hot and strong, I work at serious things, which will either save me from oblivion, or if nothing more, will give me the satisfaction of having spent my life innocently and generously."

6. Barbarisi, "Le postille di Didimo Chierico al Viaggio Sentimentale" in *Giornale Storico della Letteratura Italiana*. Vol. CXXXV, fasc. 1⁰, 1958, Torino. (Comments on the peculiar unpleasant polemic tone of Berti.)

7. Another of Foscolo's sharp footnotes observes "alcune delle nostre gentildonne non aspirano alla celebrità dell'infamia," a slur at Marchesina F***. Emilio Sioli Legnani was provoked to defend the lady in "L'avventura milanese di Sterne con la Marchesina de F*** fu 'fabbricata di pianta,'" *English Miscellany*, VI (1955), 247–257.

8. Firenze, 1855, 2 vols., II, 394.

9. *Purgatorio*, Canto III, 130. "Where rain wets them and wind moves."

10. G. S. Gargàno, *Scapigliatura Italiana a Londra sotto Elisabetta I, e Giacomo I*, Firenze, 1923. (An account of some Italians Shakespeare could have known, and from whom he could have taken ideas about Italy.)

FIVE

Style and Composition

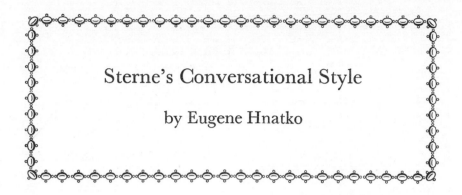

Sterne's Conversational Style

by Eugene Hnatko

Among the recurring epithets used by critics during the past two hundred years to describe the particular magic of Sterne's style, along with "whimsical" one of the most easily accepted is "conversational," appropriate, as James Work points out in his edition of *Tristram Shandy*, to a "life and opinions," rather than a "life and adventures" ("Introduction," p. xvii). Most modern critics and scholars speak of his loosening of the narrative and they defend his "heterodoxy" in syntax and pointing: "The punctuation is oral rather than syntactical; Sterne was a talker, not a grammarian," says Prof. Work in a note explaining his text (p. lxxv). Most of the statements, like Work's, assume a dichotomy between "talking" and "grammar," or at least that a recognizable distinction exists between conventional written prose and conversation, that the distinction is obvious to all, and that Sterne's unconventional qualities are partly explained by his ability to talk well and to embody his talk on the printed page. Virginia Woolf, for instance, says his punctuation is "that of speech, not writing, and brings the sounds and associations of the speaking voice in with it" (*The Common Reader*, series 2, London, 1932, p. 79). They take rather literally Tristram's own doctrine that "writing, when properly managed, (as you may be sure I think mine is) is but a different name for conversation" (II, 11, p. 108).

That Sterne was a fair talker is clear from several contemporary references, from the éclat with which he was received in London and on the continent after the publication of *Tristram Shandy*. Yet, as often has been stated, a great number of men of letters in the eighteenth century were notable as exceptional for conversational powers. Atticus, Pope tells us, was "born to write, converse, and live with

Associate Professor of English, Cortland College of the State University of New York ease." Boswell has recorded the pronouncements of one of the greatest talkers, and Burke was respected by Dr Johnson himself. Indeed, one might characterize the entire eighteenth century, from Dryden onward, as an age of conversation, when good talk was respected and sought after, and its influence seen in a number of ways in the written prose of the period.

Furthermore, from the evidence of the sermons themselves and from references in *Tristram Shandy*, Sterne was not dull in the pulpit: "*For we* trust *we have a good Conscience.*——Trust! trust we have a good conscience! Surely if there is any thing in this life which a man may depend upon, and to the knowledge of which he is capable of arriving upon the most indisputable evidence, it must be this very thing,—— whether he has a good conscience or no" (II, 17, p. 125).

However, when we compare the written prose of such talkers as Dr Johnson and Burke with that of Sterne, we note a vast difference immediately. It might be objected that Johnson and Burke did not attempt to affect talk in their prose—when Johnson in conversation amended "It has not wit enough to keep it sweet" to "It has not vitality enough to preserve it from putrefaction," one might conclude he was being the very opposite of conversational; i.e., he was converting his talk into what might be more fitting and appropriate to his stately prose. But even such conversational writers as Addison, and Boswell at his raciest, in his journals detailing his little victories and amusing embarrassments, do not allow us that omnipresent sense of the speaker which exists in Sterne. The reader from the very beginning of *Tristram Shandy* sees, or at least feels, the Sterne of the Reynolds portrait, or the Nollekens bust, or better yet the death caricature— talking, smiling, smirking, gesticulating with bony, indecent finger, so that the listener is spellbound under the deluge, capable only of smiling at the irrepressible, delightfully outrageous, seemingly random and undirected fountain of charming pseudo-confession and intimate revelation.

To assess that which constitutes the truly conversational in written prose and the special quality of Sterne's, one must consider the varying relationships between speaking and writing, a problem made more complicated in examining the prose of a former era because of the inevitable change in all language and the absence of sound recording prior to the twentieth century. However, certain aspects of language one can assume to have a continuity—the very fact that readers of

Tristram Shandy have agreed for two hundred years that it is conversational leads us to assume it from the continuity of response—and so some generalizations are possible. It is probably true, for instance, that written language is always read with some degree of testing upon the voice mechanism, no matter how suppressed, how silent, rapid and cursory. Even in an age of block reading in which is stressed the apprehending of whole lines or even whole paragraphs, there is always an intermediary between the word on the page and the mental comprehension of it, and it is the manner and degree in which that intermediary, the voice mechanism, is brought into play that constitutes much of what we recognize as the degree of "conversationality" in written language. Indeed, much of the change in English prose style over the centuries is probably due in part to the development of speed and intensity in the reading capacity of the literate public.

However, simply an attention to the sound of language does not insure "conversationality." Certainly that prose which is carefully ordered for balance and antithesis marked by alliteration, assonance and consonance—as found in Euphuism for instance—is aimed for effect upon the voice mechanism, and even more upon the ear. Instead of being conversational, it is incantatory, attempting an aesthetic effect akin to much poetry. The qualities of the conversational style more likely are those we assume broadly to characterize spontaneous talk as different from writing, oratory, or incantation: a less complicated or elaborate syntax and often indeed an abrogation of it; a heavier reliance on the fortuitous than on the foreseen in ordering, including more likely a greater trailing afterthought modification rather than anticipatory structures; among most speakers a tendency to less precision in word choice, probably a *copia* rather than a laconicism and conciseness; and finally a reliance upon a non-verbal context for part of the meaning, including formulaic phrases, gestures, insinuatives, and nuances of juncture, stress and pitch.

When we try to pin down Sterne's "eddying and flickering" style, to fix the "smoke curl" (from John Cowper Powys' introduction to *A Sentimental Journey*, London, 1950, p. 26), the lively and seemingly unpredictable turns and twists of his prose for the purposes of analysis and to draw dull statistics from them, we are perhaps somewhat surprised to find that few of the qualities we expect of everyday conversation are frequent or obtrusive in *Tristram Shandy* or *A Sentimental Journey*. Of course, one does find a number of sentences in

Tristram Shandy and even more in *A Sentimental Journey* which certainly could be called simple in both the grammatical and popular uses of that word—"A silence of some moments followed" (*Sentimental Journey*, p. 97). "Pray, what was your father saying?" (*Tristram Shandy*, p. 5). And, as might be expected, the quoted dialogue is fairly often simple. But these are hardly what we mean when we call Sterne conversational. More likely we find him so in the very sentences which, on the contrary, are long, complex, and intricate in order, usually thought to be the antithesis of free and easy talk:

> Therefore, my dear friend and companion, if you should think me somewhat sparing of my narrative on my first setting out,——bear with me,——and let me go on, and tell my story my own way:——or if I should seem now and then to trifle upon the road,—or should sometimes put on a fool's cap with a bell to it, for a moment or two as we pass along,——don't fly off.——but rather courteously give me credit for a little more wisdom than appears upon my outside;——and as we jogg on, either laugh with me, or at me, or in short, do any thing,——only keep your temper (I, 6, p. 11).

Or an example from Vol. VII:

> That be you in never so kindly a propensity to sleep——tho' you are passing perhaps through the finest country——upon the best roads,——and in the easiest carriage for doing it in the world ——nay was you sure you could sleep fifty miles straight forwards, without once opening your eyes——nay what is more, was you as demonstratively satisfied as you can be of any truth in *Euclid*, that you should upon all accounts be full as well asleep as awake——nay perhaps better——Yet the incessant returns of paying for the horses at every stage,——with the necessity thereupon of putting your hand into your pocket, and counting out from thence, three livres fifteen sous (sous by sous) puts an end to so much of the project, that you cannot execute above six miles of it (or supposing it is a post and a half, that is but nine)——were it to save your soul from destruction (VII, 16, 496).

Analyzing these sentences grammatically, though most would agree that they read in such a way as to be conversational, we find that they have few of those qualities associated with talk and much of what we think of as carefully and deliberately composed prose. They are long and complex and they make use of anticipatory hypotaxis to a great degree. Indeed, the second shows suspension and balance rather than trailing afterthought modification; if the parenthetical inclusions were slightly regularized or removed, we might expect that structure from Dr Johnson. What then brings about the effect or semblance of conversation is a number of the other qualities. One notes, for instance, that the sentences quoted, though grammatically complex and rather rigid, do not seem to be so because a great deal of complexity and rigidity of structure is concealed in the typographical presentation: the great number of punctuation marks—especially the dashes—all give the impression of the lesser coherence and greater inconclusiveness of recorded spontaneous talk. (In reading verbatim transcripts one is struck by the number of uncompleted sentence structures of even quite literate speakers.) Though one cannot, of course, be sure of the exact relationship of marks of punctuation to actual pronunciation in an earlier period—there is some question about just what juncture or junctures the comma signalled in Sterne's time since it often appears where we would omit it—the modern reading of *Tristram Shandy* probably takes full cognizance of a pause and juncture for the comma and especially the dash, thereby breaking up the long and somewhat formal development of the syntax into smaller units more suggestive of the greater simplicity of conversation.

The dashes, as Virginia Woolf observes, are usually not syntactically necessary; Saintsbury notes that were they and the asterisks removed, *Tristram Shandy* would be reduced by a quarter. When they occur in conjunction with the necessary commas, colons, and semi-colons, they have no exact spoken equivalents. They add to the conversational effect only by suggesting the almost limitless possibilities of pause, pitch, and stress in the speaking voice. Though linguistic scientists tell us that there are but four junctures and four phonemes each of pitch and stress, it is likely the allophones are indefinitely numerous, allowing for the wide variety of nuances possible in any given utterance. But the conventions of writing and printing allow for no precision in recording the variations. In effect, each reader attributes inflexions to dashes according to his own speech and his understanding of the purport of the words. The dash, then, used for purposes other than syntax, becomes fairly ambiguous as a signal of speech and ultimately more meaningful in terms of idea than of sound. The dash in Sterne often is an indicator of a mental leap required of the reader, forcing him to supply some material not explicit in the statement itself: "Is not all flesh grass?——'Tis clay,——'tis dirt.——They all looked directly at the scullion,——the scullion had just been scouring a fish-kettle.——It was not fair" (V, 9, p. 364). The dashes serve many purposes—they may be "heartbeats," they may be "breathless pauses," but they have no precise spoken equivalents.

In essence, Sterne's prose shows the clever adaptation and manipulation of typography to substitute for all the aids in conversational communication lacking to the writer. The dashes and other typographical marks are not really identical with, not really precisely indicative of the indefinite array of facial grimaces, shrugs, hand signals, nuances of pause, pitch, and stress involved in talk, but they are elements of an art akin to symbolic representation. The illusion of a recognizable, personal, idiosyncratic and inimitable speaking presence is created from the normally fixed and arbitrary marks which a printer could supply; Sterne is a master voice painter in the medium of typography.

The last of the qualities we expect of conversation, the reliance upon a non-verbal context for speech, consisting of and indicated by gesture, insinuatives, and attendant nuances of voice inflexion, is approximated or suggested wittily and brilliantly by a number of devices without violating the requirements of more formal written prose. Whereas a number of persons in conversation have as their context the physical presences of the others with their physical responses and usually an understood history or continuity of discourse into which the spoken words fit, the prose writer has to depend upon the tradition of his genre for context. With a heavy sense of that limitation, he may well begin by calling upon the allegiance of his readers to the genre with a "Once upon a time. . . ," or he might embark upon a description to set up a fictional illusion, or he might begin with a universal truth "that a single man in possession of a good fortune must be in want of a wife." To begin instead with a somewhat indecent wish that one's parents "had minded what they were about when they begot me," to anticipate objection gathering on the reader-listener's face ("Believe me, good folks, this is not so inconsiderable a thing as many of you may think it."), even to provide a question for the reader—"Pray, what was your father saying?"—and to give an order referring to an object ostensibly present ("Shut the door"), is to fabricate an intimate conversational situation, a talking context, where none of course exists (I, 1–4, pp. 4–8). The reader is swept up into the stream of events before he can gather his wits to object to the illusion. And again, instead of an explanatory introduction about the date of and reasons for travel, the reader comes upon "——They order, said I, this matter better in France——You have been in France? said my gentleman, turning quick upon me with the most civil triumph in the world" (*Sentimental Journey*, p. 65). What the French order better and who the gentleman was are matters the reader feels he just missed upon stumbling into a dialogue, but before he can question the solidity of the illusion, he again is hurried into that rapid channel crossing. In *Tristram Shandy*, the illusion is sustained by including the reader with the others, the madam and sir with whom Tristram has already established a relationship.

Those elements of conversation which can be directly carried over are the insinuatives, formulaic phrases and interjections which give the impression of *copia*: "As it were," "Great God!" "Believe me," "Let me tell you," "No—" and the occasional aposiopesis: "As for the clergy——No——If I say a word against them, I'll be shot" (III, 20, p. 199). Of all the elements which give the impression of talk, they are probably not the most important, and they do not destroy the normal syntax or violate the "rules" of grammar. They merely conceal the order.

From what has been suggested above, it is probable that Sterne's style might better be called "conversationalistic" rather than simply conversational. If Addison lightened the heaviness of the prose of the seventeenth century by including the fortuitous and thus incorporated an aspect of conversation, Sterne created the illusion of the speaking presence as perhaps no other writer has. Yet it is an illusion. It is no wonder that adaptations of *Tristram Shandy* and *A Sentimental Journal* for stage and radio presentation have not been remarkably successful: what at first seems like good material for a script or scenario is really a craftsmanship in printed language and like all written art it does not necessarily carry over well into another medium. In this connection one is reminded of the fate of some of the poetry of E. E. Cummings, seemingly so inviting to oral presentation. Yet what seems to be a positioning of words on the page for sound—"the little lame balloon-man whistles far and wee"—upon being read aloud fails to be effective. In both instances, we are confronted with an art which creates the illusion of the speaking voice through printing conventions. On reading Sterne, we are sure that we can hear, that we can duplicate with our voices, and that we are confronted with an engaging conversationalist. But when we read aloud, we are likely to realize we have been the willing victims of a master artist in prose style.

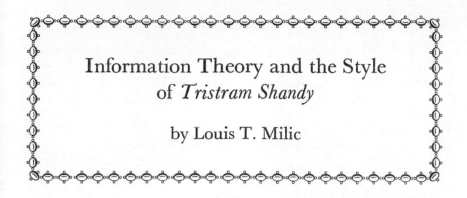

Information Theory and the Style of *Tristram Shandy*

by Louis T. Milic

The style of Laurence Sterne has been characterized in many ways, but most consistently as conversational.[1] That this term is only weakly descriptive and is based on an erroneous notion of the relation between speech and writing has recently been noticed.[2] Though the earlier commentators on Sterne's style had agreed to describe it as conversational, they did not really pay attention to its technical details, but the mass of critics have given a reluctant acknowledgment to what have been called the "external signs of originality,"[3] the typographical oddities with which Sterne larded his work. Curious paradox, this— that Sterne's style should be praised for its "colloquial" (i.e. oral) character when so much of what is remarkable in the book is exclusively visual.

Another problem which has pre-occupied Sterne's critics is whether *Tristram Shandy* is complete; whether, that is, Sterne merely left off where he did or intended to leave off where he did.[4] It is incontestable that Sterne did not know, when he began, how many volumes he would write and that he ultimately decided not to write a tenth volume. Whether this decision came to him while he was writing Volume IX or earlier or later is not very important, for it seems to be a conclusion that he could not help reaching. The evidence for this suggestion is to be found in the style of the work itself, if *style* can be interpreted to include the various typographical devices that Sterne used, as well as several other eccentricities that Sterne indulged himself in. In brief, my argument is that Sterne had exhausted the possibilities of the style of *Tristram Shandy* by the time he finished the ninth volume (and perhaps before) and that he had to look to a new manner to recapture his readers' interest. The details of this argument involve some ancient principles of rhetoric brought up

Professor, and Chairman, of English, The Cleveland State University to date by what is known among electrical engineers as Information Theory.

Originality is often defined as doing the unexpected. Sterne went to great lengths to accomplish this in *Tristram Shandy* and so announced:

> What these perplexities of my uncle *Toby* were,——'tis impossible for you to guess;——if you could,——I should blush; not as a relation,——not as a man,——nor even as a woman,——but I should blush as an author; inasmuch as I set no small store by myself upon this very account, that my reader has never yet been able to guess at any thing. And in this, Sir, I am of so nice and singular a humour, that if I thought you was able to form the least judgment or probable conjecture to yourself, of what was to come in the next page,——I would tear it out of my book (II, 1, p. 80).

Such a manifesto of originality or intention to be unpredictable has certain limitations, as Sterne discovered along the way. These limitations have their ultimate source in the nature of human perception but can be expressed in terms of several concepts of Information Theory, which seems to govern the nature of all messages, whether in code or language, regardless of the method of transmission.[5] These concepts are *information, redundancy,* and *noise* and to them must be joined the rhetorical concept of *emphasis.*

Information in this context is not to be interpreted in its normal sense of knowledge or news. The information content of a message is measured by the unpredictability of its successive units. The information, in this sense, of any stereotyped greeting is very low because the first unit or two give away (help to predict) the remainder, which becomes unnecessary or redundant. Thus, any well-known quotation need not be given in full to be recognizable. At the other pole of information content are such messages as telephone numbers. Telephone numbers are not predictable. Consequently, every unit bears maximal information. The unpredictability of numbers gives their units high information content. The predictability of much natural language, on the other hand, gives it a relatively low amount of information.

Because messages are subject to the vagaries of communication channels, which involve encoding, transmission and decoding, their formal characteristics are frequently altered by what is called *noise.* Noise is simply an interference with the communication process which causes the symbols of the message sent to differ from those of the message received. Noise includes typographical errors, mispronunciation, speech impediments, static on a radio, the crackle of a long-playing record, the sound of running water during a conversation and the like. In a sense, noise increases the information content of a message in an undesirable way, by making it unintelligible or misleading. To combat noise, codes (including natural languages) have a property called *redundancy*. Again, this term is not congruent with the usual meaning. The redundancy of a message is achieved by lowering the information content (the unpredictability). The higher the redundancy, the lower the information, therefore the higher the predictability and imperviousness to noise. The simplest way of increasing the redundancy of a message is to repeat it or spell out important words. Natural language is naturally redundant, however, and does not require such obvious safeguards in the usual communication situation.

The redundancy of language may be appreciated if it is recalled that information is unpredictability, which is inevitably derived from the freedom of choice of the sender in selecting constituent units of the message. Words selected at random from a dictionary would almost certainly not constitute an acceptable message in any language. No language allows such freedom of choice. The choice of one lexical unit constrains the choice of what follows. Such constraints as semantic compatibility, word order, morphology and syntax result in a much more limited set of messages in a language than the total number of random combinations. Because these constraints limit freedom of choice, they increase predictability and therefore redundancy.

Any speaker of English knows that a definite article is usually followed by an adjective or a noun, that a noun is a subject, an object or a complement, that certain verbs require human agents, etc. This intuitive knowledge in the native speaker permits him to reconstitute those parts of messages which have been affected by noise. What the redundancy of English really does, at the price of lower efficiency in the form of lower information content, is to safeguard the integrity and intelligibility of messages. Any communication which reduces redundancy by dispensing with any of the systems of contraint in the language increases the risk of ambiguity or unintelligibility of messages. Headlines sacrifice function words and are therefore often ambiguous. Poets, in the search for unusual collocations, ignore lexical compatibility and their poems are often obscure.[6] The speech of the mentally-disturbed, in whom the constraints have ceased to function effectively, is incoherent. Redundancy, therefore, is a valuable property of language when the communication of data is the primary object. Such is clearly not the case with writers of what is called "literature," to whom the achieving of novel effects, the heightening of the reader's attention, may be paramount. To achieve these goals such writers frequently tamper with the normal information structure of the language in the search for what the rhetoricians call *emphasis*.

In a sense, emphasis takes place whenever an expectation held by the reader is deceived or disappointed—whenever the readers' prediction is unfulfilled. It will be realized that this is the same as saying, whenever the information content is increased. Normally the reader of a passage of prose in English expects the standard word order (subject-verb-object) to prevail. If the writer inverts this order by placing the object first, he has achieved emphasis by means of the rhetorical device of inversion. Similarly, if the writer arranges two clauses in such a way as to stress the contrast in their meanings by means of a similarity of sentence structure, he achieves emphasis. Whatever is unexpected in a given context is emphatic.[7] For example, since writers do not usually say things twice, the simple repetition of a word or phrase is emphatic. Macbeth's "Tomorrow and tomorrow and tomorrow" is emphatic because of the repetition and because the polysyndetic *and* implies the conclusion of a series. Repetition in this context is not redundant but rather the reverse. Because it is unexpected, it is emphatic, it carries information, though it offers no new data. But a reservation should be noted here: to be emphatic it must be unexpected *in the context*.

If Macbeth went on with polysyndetic triads of identical units, we should not react to the second as we had to the first, and the third would not surprise us at all. By that time what had been unexpected at first would have become part of the norm and would cease to be able to produce emphasis. This is the significant point in the application of Information Theory to rhetoric: unpredictability fluctuates during the reading of a text as the author trains or conditions the reader to expect one or another deviation from the standard norm. At first every deviation from our expectation is emphatic, but after a time each such deviation becomes part of our expectation and so ceases to be emphatic. This poses a pretty problem for the writer. How is he to achieve emphatic effects if by so doing he loses the chance to use them later? He has two options: he can use them sparingly, to maintain their unfamiliarity, or he can exhaust one and devise new ones as long as necessary or as long as his inventiveness is equal to the task. It is plain to me that Sterne relied on the second of these proceedings. From this stems the unusual nature of the style of *Tristram Shandy*.

In the strictest sense, the style of an author consists of his vocabulary and his individual repertory of syntactical resources. But in a looser sense it is often taken to include also any use of rhetorical devices and even some aspects of narrative method. I shall use the term loosely here, as synonymous with what Mark Twain called the "author's way of setting forth a matter."[8] The style of Sterne in *Tristram Shandy* is understood to consist of a good deal more than is properly meant by the term. The purpose of this redefinition is to allow the fullest possible demonstration of the view that information-theoretic aspects of the linguistic code propelled Sterne into the originality, whimsy and oddity of the style of *Tristram Shandy*. The implication of this hypothesis is that much of what constitutes the style of the book, in the sense outlined, is not essential but accidental, though it may well have become characteristic of it for its readers.

Perhaps the obvious surface characteristic of *Tristram Shandy* for most readers is its diction. A modern edition of the book is chock-full of footnotes explaining the multifarious and sometimes obscure proper names, the foreign terms, the plays on words, the learned allusions, the familiar, dialectal and even slangy language of the eighteenth century and the extensive passages in Latin and French. Other, properly stylistic, features are the deviations from normal syntax which have been noticed: the many apostrophes, insertions, anacolutha which have been by many critics considered evidence of a "conversational style." The series of names reminiscent of Rabelais and Swift; that part of the typography concerned with punctuation and particularly the dash must be included in the "conversational" syntax. Next, there are the other typographical embellishments: the asterisks, page of music, index fingers, the black, marbled and blank pages, the schematic pictures of the plot, the entire paragraphs of dashes and asterisks, the occasional arrangement of items in tabular form (e.g., pp. 439–440), the capricious location and perverse numbering of chapters. On the narrative level, there are the various interpolations: the marriage contract, the opinions of the doctors of the Sorbonne, Slawkenbergius's Tale, the Excommunication of Bishop Ernulphus and other approximations on a larger scale to the parenthesis on the syntactic level. The use of lewd and vulgar material might also be included in any list of Sterne's stylistic devices in this book. Finally, there is the matter of the orders of language, the distinction, that is, between the discussion of the subject matter which is the ostensible purpose of the narrative and the discussion of the discussion that Sterne conducts with the reader. Sterne's handling of this array of resources is what is at issue. To what extent is Sterne compelled to rely on the items in this list in order to maintain the attention of his reader? To what extent is he successful in achieving emphasis by availing himself of this large store of devices?

James Work, in the introduction to his edition of *Tristram Shandy*, dismisses what he calls "the Shandean clowning in style and typography—the Rabelaisian catalogues of nouns and adjectives, and the excessive use of stars and dashes—which seemed so amusing to Sterne's earliest readers" (p. lxviii). To Work, the best and most characteristic aspect of the book is the comedy of character which involves the main actors in the work. Perhaps, Sterne thought so himself and yet he allowed himself to devote a great deal of the bulk of his book to the substance of his style. More recent critics than Work have found more modern matter for admiration in Sterne's novel than a revelation of "the eternal incongruities of human nature," as Work approvingly cites Traill as saying. These range from his apprehension of the absurd to his understanding of the relativity of time. Without arguing the merits of this question, I should like to suggest that Sterne must have set considerable store by these devices. He desired originality, as he himself admitted, and he sought to achieve it, at least in some part, by these means, which had not been used in fiction before, certainly not in such a configuration. Sterne wanted his reader to be in for a surprise.

What did the reader who picked up the two volumes of *Tristram Shandy* in January of 1760 expect to find in them, assuming that he did not know who Sterne was and that he was reasonably familiar with the writing of his time? What, in other words, was the literary context which had created the norm that shaped the expectations of Sterne's reader? If he had been reading novels for a decade, he would have just finished *Rasselas*, having previously read *Grandison*, two by Smollett (*Ferdinand Count Fathom* and *Peregrine Pickle*) and Fielding's last effort in the genre, *Amelia*. But if he had begun two decades earlier, he would have had nearly a complete knowledge of the history of the English novel in the eighteenth century: *Pamela* and *Clarissa*, *Shamela*, *Joseph Andrews* and *Tom Jones*, and *Roderick Random*. A really assiduous reader would perhaps also have known *David Simple*, *Peter Wilkins* and *John Buncle*. From these works, he would have come to take for granted the autobiographical narrative mode or at least the chronological treatment of the hero or heroine's development. He would be unruffled by the occurrence of an interpolated narrative and, if he had read *John Buncle*, not really surprised by finding odd bits of learned but extraneous matter in the mouths of the characters.

Thus, the reader beginning *Tristram Shandy* accepts as a normal convention that he is addressed by the narrator, who is also the hero. The fact that the speaker is discussing the details of his own conception is original, though not simply because it is bawdy. Rather, because it is bawdy in a way very different from the earthy bawdiness of a Fielding or a Smollett. The reader may perhaps go past the apostrophe to the "good folks" (p. 4), who are being invited to consider how the animal spirits have affected Tristram's future. But his attention will be caught by the really daring vulgarity of the interchange between Tristram's parents at the end of the first chapter, which is accented by the intervention of the reader, with whom the narrator engages in a colloquy which carries over into the second chapter. These procedures in themselves are sufficient to take the reader beyond any fictional context he may be familar with. Alone, they would be quite enough to create the unpredictability needed to produce heightened attention. But Sterne adds to them a discussion of the homunculus, inserts the names of Puffendorff and "Tully" and punctuates with a generous portion of dashes. All these things together guarantee that the reader of the first two chapters (at least) of *Tristram Shandy* will feel that he is dealing with something new and original, something he has not seen before. How long this feeling can be maintained as the reader proceeds through the book is of course a central question about the rhetorical nature of the work.

Sterne's dashes on the first page are an original kind of punctuation for whose immediate effect the reader may be moved to find an explanation. By the twentieth page, however, he is accustomed to it as a device, and by the time he puts down the second volume, he has incorporated this into his norm, so that no successive volumes of

Tristram Shandy can reach him with the same impact and even so that no other work punctuated with dashes can thereafter claim originality. The point to be stressed is that any device ceases to be emphatic when it becomes part of the norm, when it ceases, that is, to carry extra information. That Sterne was aware of this is suggested by an examination of some very simple data: the publication schedule of the successive installments of *Tristram Shandy*, shown below in tabular form:

Volume	Publication Date	Pages
I		180
II	1759 (Dec)	182
III		200
IV	1761 (Jan)	216
V		158
VI	1761 (Dec)	160
VII		162
VIII	1765 (Jan)	160
IX	1767 (Jan)	148

It may be observed from even a cursory glance at this table that the first three pairs of volumes appeared at intervals of about a year, followed three years later by the fourth installment and two years after that by the lone last volume. There was, so to speak, a lag in the speed of production, which is approximately matched by the decreased size of the last five volumes. The apparent increase in the second installment is largely due to the presence of dozens of pages of pleonastic Latin originals, actual or factitious, in each of the books. What is shown by the table is a steady decrease in volume and an increase in interval between installments. It took Sterne three years to produce Volumes Seven and Eight and two more to produce the slighter Volume Nine. What this implies is that the mine of invention was exhausting itself.

The movement in the narrative itself, from Tristram to the Grand Tour to Uncle Toby with all the detours provided by intercalated material, shows a necessity to prevent the reader from becoming habituated to the context. It was Sterne's constant effort to maintain originality, to insist on heightened attention, an effort he made on the stylistic as well as on the narrative level.

Among the larger typographical devices is the assignment of entire pages to a single use. The first volume contains the two memorial black pages, not to mention the words and music of "Lilliburlero." Sterne must have been satisfied with the effect, for he used the device again in the next installment, (Volume III), but this time in the form of marbled pages. The third variation on this device occurs in Volume VI: two blank pages. Sterne's inventiveness was not equal to another leap, for he merely repeats the device in the last volume.

The same pattern may be discovered in the use of asterisks. These occur in two forms, items and strings. Itemized asterisks correspond in number to a specific word or words, date or name that Sterne is transparently concealing. Strings are lines of asterisks, not divided into words but merely strung into lines suggestive of some deleted and obscure vulgarity. These go as high as fifty or sixty at a time. Instances of itemized asterisks go from a peak of six in the first installment to a low of one in the last. The use of strings begins in Volume III, with a single instance, rises to a peak of twelve in the third installment, drops to one in the next and rises again to five in the last.[9] These two uses of asterisks illustrate the two alternative paths which the information pattern may take. The itemized asterisks reflect the diminishing effectiveness of a device with use and the tendency of the writer to abandon it. The strings reveal the peak of use which shows the need for a deviation from the developing norm. The final peak is merely an attempt to re-use an established device, as with the blank pages.

The same patterning could perhaps be found in the use of Sterne's other devices and features of style. The demonstration has been illustrated with the crudest and most obvious features because they offer no sort of ambiguity in categorization. If the principles which have been applied here have any validity, the same patterns would be found operative in other features, even the subtlest. The structure of *Tristram Shandy*, both on the narrative level and the stylistic level (as defined earlier), is inevitably determined by the nature of information. Once Sterne had decided that originality was to be the predominant characteristic of his book, he was committed to a pattern required to maintain information at a high level, i.e., a constant shift in direction and a constant accumulation of stylistic devices to neutralize the contextualizing effect. Ultimately, as has been seen, the effort became too great, there were no more devices and the enterprise had to stop. That Sterne turned his attention next to a different kind of book is hardly surprising. He had exhausted the possibilities of the style of *Tristram Shandy*.

NOTES

1. See, for instance, the remarks by Ian Watt in the Introduction to his edition of *Tristram Shandy* (Boston, 1965), pp. xxvi–xxvii.

2. The matter is soundly treated by Eugene Hnatko in another paper in the present volume. A discussion of the concept "conversational style" may be found in my "Observations on Conversational Style," in *Studies in Eighteenth-Century Writers*, ed. John Middendorf (New York, forthcoming). For the relation between speech and writing, see Randolph Quirk, "Colloquial English and Communication," *Studies in Communication* (London, 1955), pp. 169–182.

3. Henri Fluchère, *Laurence Sterne: From Tristram to Yorick*, trans. and abr. by Barbara Bray (London, 1965), p. 422. Fluchère is particularly taken with Sterne's use of the dash, to which three pages are devoted in the cited edition of his book.

4. See, for example, Alan Dugald McKillop, "Laurence Sterne" in *Laurence Sterne*, ed. John Traugott (Englewood Cliffs, N.J., 1968), pp. 58–61, and Watt, op. cit., pp. xxxiii–xxxiv.

5. The primary statement of these principles may be found in Claude E. Shannon and Warren Weaver, *The Mathematical Theory of Communication* (Urbana, Ill., 1949). For a simpler statement, see also the "Introductory Essay" in my *Stylists on Style* (New York, 1969), pp. 3–8.

6. E.g., such expressions as Hart Crane's "seven oceans answer from their dream," Dylan Thomas's "a grief ago," and E. E. Cummings's "anyone lived in a pretty how town" and "he danced his did."

7. Emphasis, it must be noted, derives from unexpectedness in a *certain context*. Obscenity is only emphatic in a proper context. Formality is only emphatic in an informal context. Clarity is only emphatic in a context of obscurity. "Context" here means not only the mere immediate verbal environment but the entire set of influences governing the expectations of the reader.

8. "Cooper's Prose Style," *Letters from the Earth* (New York, 1962), p. 140.

9. In tabular form:

Volume	Itemized	Strings
I–II	6	0
III–IV	5	1
V–VI	4	12
VII–VIII	4	1
IX	1	5

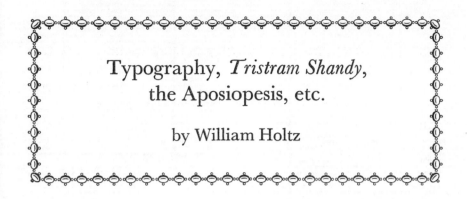

Typography, *Tristram Shandy*, the Aposiopesis, etc.

by William Holtz

Words fail us always, in some measure. "Human speech," Flaubert once said, "is like a cracked kettle on which we hammer out tunes to make bears dance, when what we long for is the compassion of the stars." More recently, modern semanticists remind us of the same failure when they point out that no statement is ever complete—that because the communal signs of a language represent abstractions from personal, concrete experiences, any statement by means of these signs is merely an approximation of its referent, and should be understood to imply, beyond its closing period, an infinite *et cetera*.[1] Small wonder, then, the student's complaint that he knows what he wants to say, but can't find the words to say it.

And if language must fail us so, how much more inadequate becomes the written word than the spoken, separated by another level of abstraction from what it represents: absent is the speaker and the potent, expressive supplements of tone and gesture. Or almost—for one of the mysteries of the writer's craft is his ability to evoke, by marks on paper, a sense of what the singer and the actor have at ready command. The poem and the novel, at their best, are no less compelling than the song and the drama, despite the intervention of the printed page and the reduction of an utterance to graphic signs. But whether the signs are aural, graphic, or gestural, what we bring to them is as important as what brought them forth: we are involved with the writer in a transaction in which the shared signs of language bridge the gulf between two minds. Two private systems interact, and the more skillful each participant, the less left to the trailing *et cetera*.

Perhaps no writer saw this so clearly, and so early, as did Laurence Sterne. His great, freakish novel *Tristram Shandy* derives much of its comedy from the failure of its characters to make themselves

Associate Professor of English, University of Missouri

understood; and its mock-author, the bumbling Tristram, reveals in his ineptitude and in his desperate stratagems Sterne's own perception of the long chances of communicating effectively by the written word. "'Tis one of the silliest things," Tristram complains, "to darken your hypothesis by placing a number of tall, opake words . . . betwixt your own and your reader's conception,——when in all likelihood, if you had looked about, you might have seen something standing, or hanging up, which would have cleared the point at once" (III, 20, p. 200). But between the writer's and the reader's conceptions there is nothing either can seize upon—merely the opaque words and the page on which their graphic equivalents must appear. This brings us to the problem of Sterne's typographical—or perhaps supra-typographical—devices.

For what are we to make of a book in which we encounter a page totally black? Or another ornamented with an intricate marbled pattern? Or—as Corporal Trim concludes his remarks on marriage with a free-floating subordinate clause ("Whilst a man is free," cried the Corporal, giving a flourish with his stick)—a bizarre line offered as an independent predication? These,[2] along with the dashes, asterisks, blank spaces, and pointing hands, bemused many readers in Sterne's day; and they continue to do so in our own. But Sterne's apparent whimsy often cloaks significant art; and these devices must be seen as a not wholly facetious response to the fundamental problem of communicating the substance of a conception. Indeed, they grow out of a thoroughly conventional eighteenth-century aesthetic premise; and, adapted to their particular contexts, they are not only artistically functional but also comic in a sense that questions one of the basic assumptions of prose fiction.

A key to understanding these devices as a part of a continuing tradition appears in Joseph Addison's *Spectator* No. 58, which he begins with the maxim from Horace, *Ut pictura poesis erit*. Thus Addison grounds his discussion in the generally accepted neoclassical pictorial theory of literature—that poetry was to a large extent a verbal equivalent of painting, an attempt to rival the painter in imitating the visible surface of life. Under consideration are those "Poems in Picture," in which it is "impossible for a Man to succeed . . . who is not a kind of Painter," that is, poems literally "shaped" into a figure of their subject. Some of these, he observes, citing minor Greek poems cast variously as an egg, a shepherd's pipe, or an axe, are nearly as ancient as the *Iliad*; others reflect a revival of this mode in "the last Age," notably George Herbert's "Easter Wings" and "Altar." Addison assigns these poems, however, a rank inferior to the more conventional works, which produce "pleasant Pictures and agreeable Visions in the Fancy" rather than imitative figures on the page (No. 62). But despite Addison's disdainful estimate, these poems in figure fall within the pictorialist tradition of western literature[3] and reflect, just as does the descriptive poetry that the German theorist Lessing deplored, the writer's attempt to give a concrete edge to his verbal signs. Lessing, a more penetrating critic than Addison, saw clearly that words could not literally be pictorial; and he appears to have been groping toward a more adequate poetic when he came to mention those "touches" which bring the "subject so vividly before us that we are more conscious of the subject than of [the] words," and when he observed that

> poetry must try to raise its arbitrary signs to natural signs. . . . The means by which this is accomplished are the tone of words, the position of words, measure, figures and tropes, similes, etc. All these make arbitrary signs more like natural signs.[4]

In our own time, the most discerning comment has been made by Austin Warren, who suggests that these emblematic devices "proceed from a principle analogous to onomatopoeia," that is, "the expressive adjustment of structure, phonetic or typographical, to theme."[5] The key word here, of course, is "expressive," as opposed to the largely imitative concept of art lying behind Addison's remarks, and to a certain extent behind Lessing's as well—although it seems clear that Lessing was attempting to offer some comprehensive account of the poet's ability to freight the abstract signs of language with a heavy increment, not necessarily imitative nor wholly visual, of the conception that gave them birth. Once the idea of expressive manipulation is extended to the appearance of the figures on the page, we can see its operation in a wide range of instances, from the emblematic poems just mentioned through such devices as paragraph and stanza divisions, sight rhymes and puns based on spelling, down to the careful patterns of E. E. Cummings' verse and the peculiar intensity of Faulkner's long passages in italics. Against such a background, real significance can be seen in the typographical oddities of *Tristram Shandy*.

Sterne (who was, incidentally, an amateur painter) suggests the relationship with the earlier tradition when he presents us with the marbled page, the "motly emblem of my work." Most of Sterne's visual wit is not deliberately emblematic, however; rather it derives simply from his manipulating a situation in which he must approach another person (his reader) by means of a page on which marks are made—marks which need not be words, but can be graphic symbols with both formal and expressive values to reinforce or interpret the verbal communication. Their effect, generally, can be said to be ambiguous and ironic, for they reach the reader's sensibilities in ways denied to conventional printed language, yet at the same time they call his attention to the comic limitations of the visual system of communication he is committed to. An obvious instance is the black page commemorating Yorick's death. Surprising, certainly, and comic; but the color has its full suggestive value, and the page serves as a grotesque punctuation mark, a monstrous period marking a biological as well as a syntactical full stop. It is strangely appropriate to the mingled humor and pathos of the death scene and also effective in halting the page-flipping reader for a moment's contemplation of (1) Yorick's grave and inscription, Alas, poor YORICK! , and (2) the general problem of getting such things on paper. Similarly, the wriggly lines which diagram Tristram's narrative represent a central problem in *Tristram Shandy*—that of forging an undeviating narrative line. But the word "line" itself here is a submerged metaphor for a very complex conception, which in Tristram's diagrams erupts into a page of graphic wit that reveals the very root-processes of language.

Others of Sterne's typographical devices are no less effective in demonstrating to the reader the part he himself plays in communicating by means of black marks on white paper. The asterisk, for example, becomes a cue for bawdy speculation: normally a conventional symbol for a polite or politic elision, in *Tristram Shandy* it occurs in clusters which Tristram calls the "stars . . . I hang up in some of the darkest passages" (VI, 33, p. 462), inviting the reader to translate his imprecision into impropriety. Consider Corporal Trim's account of the young woman who cared for his wounded knee:

> and yet, continued the corporal (making one of the strangest reflections upon it in the world)———.
> ———"*It was not love*"———for during the three weeks she was

almost constantly with me, fomenting my knee with her hand, night and day——I can honestly say, an' please your honour—— that * * * * * * * * * * * * * * * * * once.

> That was very odd, *Trim*, quoth my uncle *Toby*——.
> I think so too—said Mrs. *Wadman*.
> It never did, said the corporal (VIII, 20, p.572).

The meaning is as clear as the reader chooses to make it.

The Shandian dash, so suggestive of disorder yet used with such care, is the trademark of Sterne's style: critics have often admired but never wholly explained this extremely personal, flexible supplement to the normal marks of punctuation. Herbert Read perceives that it allows a rhythm in Sterne's periods that a full stop would destroy; Henri Fluchère finds that Sterne uses it to indicate duration; Wilbur Cross mentions the difficulty of doing it justice in editing the manuscripts, for its value seems to vary with its length. T. C. Livingstone describes it somewhat more fully:

> The celebrated Shandean dash, which . . . determines the appearance of the pages of *Tristram Shandy* and the associated *Sentimental Journey*, conveys in a typographical gesture the changes of tone, the confidences, the implicatory silences, the veerings of the narrative, the doubling of meaning, which characterise Sterne's methods as a writer. [6]

In the word "gesture" we seem to come closest to understanding the visual and kinaesthetic effect of Sterne's dash, and of some of his other devices. For despite the paucity of plot and action, *Tristram Shandy* is essentially dramatic: it consists almost entirely of monologue and dialogue; Tristram alternately presents scenes from his family history and steps before the curtains to engage his readers in a one-sided colloquy. In either case the language is vividly conversational and fully implies the dramatic situation. Sterne's dash seems to function as the graphic expression of the nuances of gesture inherent in language at its best; [7] stitching through and through the pages of talk, it constantly suggests something else, and that is the *presence* of the talker—the implicit substructure of tone, accent, rhythm, gesture, and expression, all highly personal and charged with dramatic power. Its effect is more easily felt than defined, but without it Sterne's style not only *looks* different but actually becomes pallid and limp. Compare Sterne's version with a more conventionally punctuated revision:

For as soon as my father had done insulting his HOBBY-HORSE,——he turned his head, without the least emotion, from Dr. *Slop*, to whom he was addressing his discourse, and look'd up into my father's face with a countenance spread over with so much good nature;——so placid;——so fraternal;——so inexpressibly tender towards him;——it penetrated my father to his heart: He rose up hastily from his chair, and seizing hold of both my uncle *Toby*'s hands as he spoke: ——Brother *Toby*, said he,——I beg thy pardon;——forgive, I pray thee, this rash humour which my mother gave me.——My dear, dear brother, answer'd my uncle *Toby*, rising up by my father's help, say no more about it;——you are heartily welcome, had it been ten times as much, brother. (II, 12, p. 115)

For as soon as my father had done insulting his HOBBY-HORSE, he turned his head, without the least emotion, from Dr. *Slop*, to whom he was addressing his discourse, and look'd up into my father's face, with a countenance spread over with so much good nature, so placid, so fraternal, so inexpressibly tender towards him, it penetrated my father to his heart: He rose up hastily from his chair, and seizing hold of both my uncle *Toby*'s hands as he spoke: "Brother *Toby*," said he, "I beg thy pardon; forgive, I pray thee, this rash humour which my mother gave me." "My dear, dear brother," answer'd my uncle *Toby*, rising up by my father's help, "say no more about it; you are heartily welcome, had it been ten times as much, brother."

Occasionally, the impulse toward gesture surges beyond the bounds of punctuation, and Tristram's gesticulating hand appears upon the page (p. 114); and Trim's rhapsodic flourish with his stick—his effort to "make clear the point at once"—is laden with such meaning that, as Tristram says, "A thousand of my father's most subtle syllogisms could not have said more for celibacy" (p. 604). The effect of Sterne's fusion of syntax and squiggle is to force us to agree.

Sterne's typographical devices, then, are not without point in their individual contexts and not without precedent in the literature that Sterne knew. In a broader perspective, their relevance would seem to be as parts of one of the grand comic themes in *Tristram Shandy*: the general inadequacy of man's abilities to his conceptions, the disparity between his aspirations and his accomplishments—whether he aims to make love, to write a book, or simply to communicate a thought. What I would suggest is that Sterne's typographical devices contribute to this effect by revealing the essential inadequacy of printed language. In an essay that casts light back over the whole history of comedy,[8] Henri Bergson has argued that the essence of comedy is "something mechanical encrusted upon the living," an imposition of unchanging form on the flux of reality. Ideally, language, like any other human behavior, would be perfectly expressive of the impulse that generates it, a wholly transparent medium. Bergson describes it thus:

> An idea is something that grows, buds, blossoms and ripens from the beginning to the end of a speech. It never halts, never repeats itself. It must be changing every moment, for to cease to change would be to cease to live.

But one of the necessary inadequacies of written language is that it must be fixed in time and extended in space: it is, inevitably, a static symbolization of a fluid movement, depending upon the arbitrarily arranged signs of alphabet, spelling, and punctuation, as well as the inter-relationships reflected by grammatical structure. Conventionally the static nature of printed language is virtually ignored, and at their best these graphic signs and static structures can evoke an equivalent of the flow of thought and feeling that produced them: the language, the style, approaches transparency.

Sterne's typographic devices, however, despite their expressive and kinaesthetic power, emphatically call attention to the mechanical imposition of static form on the movement of human awareness; like tiny mines, they explode in the reader's face just as he turns the corner of a conception. "Alas, poor YORICK!" is one graphic spatialization of the transient moment of feeling engendered by the little drama just played out; the black page is another, differing only in the antecedent concepts that give it meaning and transposing one static symbol into another less conventional. Similarly in the passages in which asterisks replace words: the reader, accustomed to words, which are an assumed equivalent of an underlying movement of thought, encounters a row of essentially similar but apparently meaningless symbols; but under the momentum of a developing idea and the rhythm of a developing structure he makes an adequate substitution of words for asterisks. And in the process he is forced to acknowledge the essential interchangeability of one mechanical device for another. Or we might consider Sterne's dash. In its various lengths it is a subtle aid to the rhythm of his periods, but when it extends for two or three lines of a printed page, it emphasizes the necessarily static nature of punctuation in printed discourse. Finally, the expressive flourish of Trim's stick and the antic curves of Tristram's narrative graphs fall within the same comic principle: each is a reduction to a graphic, static symbol of a free movement of human activity.

Ideally, in printed fiction, the words would rise like smoke from the page and disappear during each reading; the speeches and actions would recede into past time, as in drama or in life itself. The conventions of the novel demand, in fact, that we assume this to be so. But at odds with this demand is the physical nature of the novel itself, a relatively permanent thing operating through an intricate array of visual symbols in a fixed spatial series. The reader in his chamber normally ignores the mechanical necessities of printed language and draws from it an illusion of living reality. Sterne, writing in a day when the relatively private, subjective experience of the novel had begun to supplant the more objective, public experience of the theater, was sharply aware of the gulf between him and his audience; and in a work that burlesqued all of the conventions of the novel, he found humor in constantly pricking the bubble of illusion—not only by the persistent, awkward intrusion of Tristram into a story we would gladly attend to if he would let us (for Sterne was a consummately skillful writer, a master of those "touches" by which words evoke reality), but also by the intrusion of his typography, which lays bare the apparent absurdity that symbols on paper can represent experience in life. [9]

Thus, at the level of typography, Sterne forces the reader to keep the illusion at arm's length, conscious of the contrivance that supports it. And at a more general level, it is just such a relationship between author and reader that characterizes all comedy, as Maynard Mack has suggested in a brief essay[10] which essentially supplements rather than contradicts Bergson. Whereas in the tragic mode the reader is drawn into the illusion and participates with deep empathy in the fictional experience, in the comic mode the reader shares the author's perspective, detached from the work and in complicity with its fabricator:

> The comic artist subordinates the presentation of life as experience, where the relationship between ourselves and the characters experiencing it is the primary one, to the presentation of life as spectacle, where the primary relationship is between himself and us as onlookers.

In many obvious ways this comment is germane to *Tristram Shandy*. Always between us and the fictive world stands Sterne the showman, a painter before he took up the pen, who conducts his writing like a dramatic performance wherein he can paste up drawings and emblems as accessories to his narrative. But the success of this spectacle requires not only our collusion but our active participation, as our author enjoins us to draw from our deep stores of *et cetera* the substance to flesh out his conceptions.

Which is to say, finally, that Sterne was an accomplished rhetorician, playing artfully upon his reader's responses.[11] Early in *Tristram Shandy* (II, 6, p. 100), as Walter and Toby discuss Mrs Shandy's reluctance to allow Dr Slop to assist at Tristram's birth, Toby suggests that she "does not care to let a man come so near her ****." Tristram points out that, from the printed page, we cannot tell whether Toby had completed his sentence or not: if not, then it stands as "one of the neatest examples" of that rhetorical figure called the *Aposiopesis*. This, if we bother to inquire, we find to be the suppression by a speaker or writer of what he had seemed to be about to say. Here, two points only need be made: first, that this device depends heavily upon the *reader's* contribution for its effect; and second, that it is a device that can be said to operate, both small and large, throughout *Tristram Shandy*—from the suppression of single words to the suppression of entire scenes. In a letter Sterne described his method as "leaving off as soon as possible whenever a point of humour or Wit was started, for fear of saying too much" (*Letters*, p. 79). In *Tristram Shandy*, he puts the same matter somewhat differently: "Writing," Tristram asserts, "is but a different name for conversation"; and in this dialogue "the truest respect which [an author] can pay to the reader's understanding, is to halve this matter amicably, and leave him something to imagine" (II, 11, pp. 108–109). Sterne's art lies in keeping up his half superbly well—but he controls the conversation, and leads us to discover in our dialogue with him what a queer thing the novel is.

Thus Sterne's typographical devices, tripping us up as we read, reveal—as we regain our balance—the intricate dance we are engaged in with our author. If *Tristram Shandy* becomes, through its narrator's foreground prominence, an account of the problems of telling a story, one of its minor themes is the problem of getting it down on paper. We might conclude by noting Sterne's most deliberate attempt to entice us to join him in the venture of communication. Tristram is about to describe the widow Wadman, then gives it up and leaves a page blank for the reader to draw/describe her himself:

To conceive this right,——call for pen and ink——here's paper ready to your hand.——Sit down, Sir, paint her to your own mind——as like your mistress as you can——as unlike your wife as your conscience will let you——'tis all one to me——please but your own fancy in it (VI, 38, p. 470).

One wonders how many readers have accepted this invitation to collaborate. This writer's casual examination of several well-worn library copies suggests that the temptation of such authorized doodling is not to be resisted.

NOTES

1. See, for instance, the comment by Korzybski on the flyleaf of the journal, *ETC*.

2. Black page: I, 12, pp. 33–34; marbled page: III, 36, pp. 227–228; Trim's flourish: IX, 4, p. 604.

3. Comprehensively described in Jean H. Hagstrum's *The Sister Arts* (Chicago, 1958).

4. The first quotation is from *Laocoon* (1766), trans. Ellen Frothingham (Boston, 1910), p. 88. The second is from a letter quoted by René Wellek, *A History of Modern Criticism, 1750–1950* (4 vols.; New Haven, 1955), I, 164–165.

5. *Rage For Order* (Chicago, 1948), p. 31. See also René Wellek and Austin Warren, *Theory of Literature* (2nd ed. rev.; New York, 1956), pp. 130–131. I am indebted to J. M. Stedmond, "Style and *Tristram Shandy*," *Modern Language Quarterly*, XX (1959), 250 n. 18.

6. Herbert Read, Introduction to Scholartis Press ed. of *A Sentimental Journey* (London, 1929), pp. xliii–xliv; Henri Fluchère, *Laurence Sterne* (Paris, 1961), p. 625; Wilbur Cross, *The Life and Times of Laurence Sterne* (New Haven, 1929), p. 557; T. C. Livingstone, Introduction to Collins ed. of *Tristram Shandy* (London, 1955), p. 12. See also "The Dashing Sterne," *Times Literary Supplement*, March 3, 1951, p. 132.

7. This is the premise of R. P. Blackmur's *Language As Gesture* (New York, 1952). "When the language of words most succeeds it *becomes* gesture in its words" (p. 3).

8. *Laughter*, trans. Cloudesley Brereton and Fred Rothwell (New York, 1917), pp. 37, 31–32.

9. Bergson deals with the comedy of language but not with typography: my remarks are an extension of his theory. But see his remarks on clothing: every fashion, he contends, is potentially comic; but custom prevents our making an imaginative dissociation of the living body and the rigid garment. "A sudden dissolution of continuity," such as a person in period costume, reveals as comic in fact what is comic by right. Sterne's typographical devices seem to force just such a "dissolution of continuity," compelling the reader to "contrast the inert rigidity of the covering with the living suppleness of the object covered" (pp. 38–39). See also Ian Watt's remarks on typography in his study of Samuel Richardson: *The Rise of the Novel* (Berkeley and Los Angeles, 1962), pp. 196–198.

10. Introduction to the Rinehart ed. of *Joseph Andrews* (New York, 1948). The quotation is from p. xv.

11. Amply demonstrated by John Traugott, *Tristram Shandy's World* (Berkeley and Los Angeles, 1954). For a more general study of the fiction writer's manipulation of the reader, see Wayne Booth, *The Rhetoric of Fiction* (Chicago, 1961).

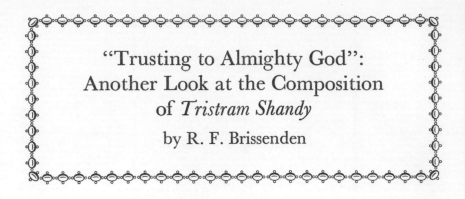

"Trusting to Almighty God": Another Look at the Composition of *Tristram Shandy*

by R. F. Brissenden

"Never trust the artist. Trust the tale." Surely there is no work of fiction to which D. H. Lawrence's remark[1] can be applied more aptly than *Tristram Shandy*. Sterne is the most deliberately deceptive of narrative artists, especially when, wearing the mask of Tristram, he appears to be talking about himself. One of the most misleading statements in the whole novel is his—or Tristram's—observation: "That of all the several ways of beginning a book which are now in practice throughout the known world, I am confident my own way of doing it is the best——I'm sure it is the most religious——for I begin with writing the first sentence——and trusting to Almighty God for the second" (III, 2, p. 540).

Nobody today takes this assertion at its face value. Owing primarily to the brilliant detective work of two scholars, we now know that behind the apparently spontaneous and erratic mannerisms of the narrator there lies a relatively firmly constructed tale. I refer, of course, to Theodore Baird's article, "The Time-scheme of *Tristram Shandy* and a Source,"[2] and Wayne C. Booth's "Did Sterne complete *Tristram Shandy*?"[3] Mr Baird demonstrates that, with a few unimportant exceptions, almost all the major events in the novel can be given a fairly precise date; while Mr Booth argues very convincingly that *Tristram Shandy* ends where it does not merely because Sterne had become tired of it, but because the writing of the last volume "represented the completion of a plan, however rough, which was present in his mind from the beginning."[4] This plan was to tell the story of Uncle Toby's amours with the Widow Wadman and to substitute them for the life and opinions of the ostensible hero, Tristram, thereby deliberately contradicting the promise given on the title page.

Reader in English, Australian National University

It is scarcely necessary for me to say that these two articles are amongst the most useful that have ever been produced on Sterne; and I certainly have no wish to quarrel with the argument that *Tristram Shandy*, considered as a whole, is to a large degree a planned and ordered work of art. But although Sterne may have had, practically from the beginning, a fairly clear idea of the basic framework of his story, *Tristram Shandy* remains in detail and in origins a rather more spontaneous and haphazard production than these two scholars, Mr Booth in particular, would have us believe. There is a sense in which Sterne did trust to Almighty God for his second sentence; and this is especially obvious, paradoxically enough, in what was probably the most heavily revised section of the novel, Volume I.

Mr Booth maintains that before Sterne sat down to write a word of *Tristram Shandy* he knew how it was going to end:

> only by planning whatever was to follow Uncle Toby's amours *before writing the first instalment* could he write a book [i.e. volume] which belonged as well with the continuing material as the entire present book [Volume I] belongs with the present conclusion.[5]

A close reading of Volume I, however, suggests that this may not have been so. It suggests, indeed, that the inspiration for Uncle Toby's story came to Sterne in the course of composition. Moreover, the stage at which this occurred can, I believe, be established fairly precisely.

So far as Mr Booth's main argument is concerned, the point I wish to make is of minor importance—I intend not so much to disagree with him as to add a corrective footnote to what he has said. But so far as *Tristram Shandy* itself is concerned it may be of some significance. If what I am putting forward can be substantiated it suggests that, like *Pamela* and (*pace* Martin Battestin[6]) *Joseph Andrews*, *Tristram Shandy* is in origin what we might call an *accidental* novel. When Sterne began Volume I, he did not, I think, intend primarily to write a work of realistic fiction. By the time he had reached the end of the first volume, however, he had realized that this in fact was what he was doing—he had discovered, as Richardson and Fielding had before him, that he had brought into being a set of living characters involved in a credible human situation. And it is because, and only because, this miracle of literary creation took place that *Tristram Shandy* became a great novel and not simply a learned joke.

There is abundant evidence to show that Sterne's primary intentions when he began *Tristram Shandy* were to produce a work in the tradition of *The Memoirs of Martinus Scriblerus* and *A Tale of a Tub*, with enough local coloring to ensure that it would have a similar *succès de scandale* in York to that which had attended the publication of *A Political Romance* (*The History of a good Warm Watchcoat*) in the previous year. Indeed it is possible, as Margaret R. B. Shaw has suggested, that Sterne began to write *Tristram Shandy* in 1758, before or concurrently with his production of the almost embarrassingly successful attack on Dr Topham.[7] At any rate, there seems little doubt that the first volumes of the novel were aimed at a local audience—and the easy intimacy of tone with which the style is pervaded may well reflect the fact that Sterne had a particular circle of friends and acquaintances in his mind's eye when he began to write. We know that the manuscript was read by several people before the book was actually printed, and the whole thing probably began as a private and in places very elaborate joke. One of the main satiric targets in the first two volumes and in Volume III, for instance, is Dr John Burton; and as Arthur H. Cash has recently demonstrated,[8] Sterne's attack on Burton's obstetrical theories was worked out in great detail. It is possible that Walter Shandy's obsession with medical science and the whole episode of Tristram's birth were seen in the first instance by Sterne mainly as devices for attacking a foolish pedant who was well known to the citizens of York, although the role these things play in the total structure of the book as we now know it has a much wider significance.

In the letter which he sent to Robert Dodsley with the manuscript of the first volume of *Tristram Shandy*, Sterne gives a clear statement of the sort of book he intended originally to write—and provides, incidentally, a hint of the atmosphere in which it was conceived.

> The Plan, as you will perceive, is a most extensive one,——taking in, not only, the Weak part of the Sciences, in wch the true point of Ridicule lies——but every Thing else, which I find Laugh-at-able in my way——
> ... Some of our best Judges here w^d have had me, to have sent into the World——cum Notis Variorum——there is great Room for it——but I thought it better to send it naked into the world

——if You purchase the MS——We shall confer of this hereafter—— (pp. 74—75).

In another letter to an unknown correspondent in which he defends
his book against the criticisms that had been made of it, he owns that
he "proposed laying the world under contribution when I set pen to
paper," but goes on to say that he also had "other views": "——the
first of which was, the hopes of doing the world good by ridiculing
what I thought deserving of it——or of disservice to sound learning
..." (pp. 89–90). A hint of the bias the first two volumes must have had
before they were rewritten (and Sterne told one correspondent that he
"Burn'd More wit than [he] . . . published" [p. 77]) is contained in
the postscript to another letter to Dodsley: "All locality is taken out of
the book——the satire general; notes are added where wanted, and
the whole made more saleable" (p. 81).

These letters indicate that, to begin with at any rate, *Tristram
Shandy* was intended to be a satire against pedantry in that tradition of
learned wit which has been outlined for us by Douglas Jefferson.[9]
Both Walter and Tristram himself were obviously intended as Scriblerian humors; both are scavengers in the scrap-heap of learning and
Tristram, partly as a result of his father's fads, and partly as a result of
his inherited Shandy nature, is as strange and whimsical a creature as
Walter, and as much the sport of fortune. It seems very likely that, at
this point in the writing of *Tristram Shandy*, the hero himself was intended to play a much greater part in the action of the novel than he
actually does. He promises, for instance, to give the reader "The
delectable narrative" of his "travels through *Denmark* with Mr.
Noddy's eldest son, whom, in the year 1741, I accompanied as governor . . . thro' most parts of *Europe*" (I, 11, p. 24). The promise, of
course, is completely forgotten (and quite rightly) when Tristram
comes to describe his travels in France in Volumes VII and VIII: he
does not attempt to disguise that this is his first trip abroad, any more
than he worries about the discrepancy caused by Eugenius's being the
bosom friend of both Yorick and Tristram. There is also a promise—
never to be fulfilled—of "a map, now in the hands of the engraver,
which, with many other pieces and developments to this work, will be
added to the end of the twentieth volume" (I, 13, pp. 35–36). More
important still is Tristram's claim that "in due time" he will lay before the reader not only how "I was doom'd, by marriage articles, to

have my nose squeez'd . . . flat to my face," but also, "what a train of vexatious disappointments, in one stage or other of my life, have pursued me from the mere loss, or rather, compression, of this one single member" (I, 15, p. 41). The "vexatious disappointments" would have provided a fitting illustration of the theme of trivial frustration and human limitation which runs through the whole novel, but they are never described.

These unkept promises are obviously part of some scheme of Scriblerian satire; and it is significant that there appear to be more sallies at particular sorts of pedantry and false learning in the first three volumes of *Tristram Shandy* than in any of the later books. The law, medical and military science, philosophy, aesthetic theory, and religious bigotry are all guyed. Walter advances his hypotheses concerning names, noses and the balance of population, and Uncle Toby is set firmly in the saddle of his military hobby-horse. It is patent that the presiding geniuses in this section of the novel are Rabelais, Burton and Swift.[10]

We must also number Cervantes, Scarron and Marivaux as amongst the immediate ancestors of *Tristram Shandy*. But it seems to me that it was not simply, or even primarily, as *novelists* that they influenced Sterne. What he derived from them mainly was a generally satirical and anti-romantic attitude to life. It is true that he also learnt from Cervantes and Scarron something about presenting set character sketches (Yorick, for instance, is a set-piece in the Cervantic manner); and he inherited the device of the comic narrator. But he learnt nothing from them, as Fielding did, about the business of conducting a long narrative, or constructing a complex plot (*Tristram Shandy* may have a plot, but it is not a complex one). He learnt nothing of this because this was not the sort of thing in which he was mainly interested. It is probable that at the outset Sterne was not intending to write a novel of any kind—sentimental, anti-romance, mock-epic or picaresque. He merely intended to *use the devices of the novel*, as he used anything else that came to his hand, for his general satiric and humorous purpose. *Tristram Shandy* became a novel simply because the Shandys and the Shandy world began to live. To begin with, Shandeism, rather than the Shandys themselves, was probably the most important thing with Sterne. The characters were there primarily to illustrate a theory (or set of theories). This, of course, they do—but they also begin to live in their own right. And that is why *Tristram Shandy* is, amongst other things, a novel.

They do not begin to live in this way immediately, however, and there are, in the first twenty chapters of Volume I, several inconsistencies in style and characterization which, I would suggest, indicate with reasonable clarity that Sterne, at this stage, was not quite sure what kind of book he was writing. Consider, for instance, the treatment accorded Parson Yorick. Almost anything is permissible in Tristram Shandy's autobiography, but the space allotted to Yorick (even if we allow for this symbolic importance) seems somewhat disproportionate. The account of the country clergyman's life and death takes up almost a quarter of Volume I[11]; and the tone of the whole section (Chapters 10 to 12) is markedly different from the tone of the surrounding chapters. In some ways, particularly in details such as the description of Yorick's silver-studded saddle, it is very reminiscent of *A Political Romance*; and the style in general is more formal, more even and more restrained than it is elsewhere in Volume I; it seems as if Sterne is at last trying to tell a straight story. At the same time, his presentation of Yorick gives him an opportunity to make a straightforward and sustained statement of belief: Yorick's hatred of gravity and affectation, his admiration of sincerity, spontaneity and good-humor are described in a direct and uncompromising way. His portrait is sketched in humorously, but the humor is of the grave, realistic, Cervantic sort. Yorick is put forward as a poor man's Quixote, and there are several parallels between Cervantes' account of the knight of La Mancha, and Sterne's description of the country clergyman (who is, of course, an idealized version of himself). But if the initial description of Yorick is realistic, the conclusion of his story is sheer fantasy. Eugenius prophesies that unless Yorick is more mindful of the opinion of the world he will suffer for it:

> REVENGE from some baneful corner shall level a tale of dishonour at thee, which no innocence of heart or integrity of conduct shall set right.——The fortunes of thy house shall totter,. . .——thy character, which led the way to them, shall bleed on every side of it,——thy wit forgotten,——thy learning trampled on. To wind up the last scene of thy tragedy, CRUELTY and COWARDICE, twin ruffians, hired and set on by MALICE in the dark, shall strike together at all thy infirmities and mistakes (I, 12, p.29).

The attack takes place "just as *Eugenius* had foreboded."

> *Yorick*, however, fought it out with all imaginable gallantry for some time; till, over-power'd by numbers, and worn out at length by the calamities of the war . . . ——he threw down the sword; and though he kept up his spirits in appearance to the last,——he died, nevertheless, as was generally thought, quite broken hearted (I. 12, p. 30).

Now this is not only fantastic but also obscure. And moreover it has nothing whatever to do with the Shandy family. It obviously has reference to Sterne's own contemporary situation in Yorkshire, and probably describes in a veiled but extravagant manner the rumpus raised over the publication of *A Political Romance*. People in York would no doubt have got the point of the episode, but to everyone else it must have been completely puzzling. And it is all conducted in a high allegorical vein that is completely out of harmony with the way in which Sterne deals with his other characters. The only emotions of any consequence involved in the wry (and quite unsentimental) account of Yorick's death are the feeling of friendship for Eugenius and a certain amused self-pity. In its own way it is a neat enough piece of writing. But this is not the point: the point is that one cannot imagine Sterne, at a later stage in the novel, treating Walter or Uncle Toby in such a fanciful manner. The whole Yorick episode—black page and all—demonstrates more clearly than anything else that Sterne was not yet certain just how important characters were going to be in his work: he could still do much as he wished with them. He had not yet set them talking with each other—and at this stage Walter Shandy is nothing but a Scriblerian humor, and his brother Toby a mere foil. It must have been from this section that the more obvious bits of local satire were removed—and indeed the death of Yorick (apart from its place in the general quixotic and sentimental pattern[12]) has little meaning out of its local context.

There are some other inconsistencies, trifling enough in themselves, which are perhaps even more interesting. The story of the unfortunate Tristram begins—as one should scarcely need to mention—with that untimely and unfortunate interruption which "scattered and dispersed the animal spirits, whose business it was to have escorted and gone hand-in-hand with the HOMUNCULUS, and conducted him safe to the place destined for his reception" (I, 2, p. 5). In the third chapter of Volume I, Tristram tells how he learnt of this mishap:

To my uncle Mr. *Toby Shandy* do I stand indebted for the preceding anecdote, to whom my father, who was an excellent
natural philosopher, and much given to close reasoning upon the
smallest matters, had oft, and heavily, complain'd of the injury;
but once more particularly, as my uncle *Toby* well remember'd,
upon his observing a most unaccountable obliquity, (as he call'd
it) in my manner of setting up my top, and justifying the principles upon which I had done it,——the old gentleman shook his
head, and in a tone more expressive by half of sorrow than
reproach,——he said his heart all along foreboded, and he saw it
verified in this, and from a thousand other observations he had
made upon me, That I should neither think nor act like any other
man's child:——*But alas!* continued he, shaking his head a
second time, and wiping away a tear which was trickling down
his cheeks, *My Tristram's misfortunes began nine months before ever
he came into the world.*
——My mother, who was sitting by, look'd up,——but she
knew no more than her backside what my father meant,——but
my uncle, Mr. *Toby Shandy*, who had been often informed of the
affair,——understood him very well (I, 3, pp. 6–7).

There are several things worth noting about this scene and about
Tristram's description of it. To begin with, Tristram himself is in it—
and the occasions when he actually appears in a scene with the other
Shandys can be numbered on the fingers of one hand. More unusual
than this, however, is the behavior of Walter: a tear trickles down his
cheek; and he is described as having "oft and *heavily* complained of the
injury"—there is nothing here of that "little subacid humour" which
distinguishes his character so delightfully in the rest of the novel. Nor
does he exhibit that heroic fortitude with which, elsewhere, he en-
dures such disasters as the misnaming of Tristram, the crushing of his
nose, and the death of Bobby. Tristram in fact specifically informs us
later on that although many authorities hold "that it is an irresistable
and natural passion to weep for the loss of our friends or children. . . .
My father managed his affliction otherwise; and indeed differently
from most men either ancient or modern; for he neither wept it
away . . . nor did he curse it, or damn it, or excommunicate it, or
rhyme it, or lillabullero it" (V, 3, p. 351). Tears do come to Walter's
eyes on at least two other occasions, but they are in the one case tears

of delight at his own wit (V, 3, p. 353), and in the other tears of generous sympathy with his brother (II, 4, p. 92). Clearly the lachrymose "old gentleman" depicted in Chapter 3 of Volume I has little in common with the fully developed character of Walter Shandy as Sterne was finally to imagine him.

The differences between the Toby Shandy of this episode and what we might call the "real" Uncle Toby are even more surprising and significant—especially if we bear in mind that this is the scene in which he is first presented to the reader. First of all there is no hint of his military background. Throughout the rest of the novel he is called either "my Uncle Toby" or "Captain Shandy"—but here for the first, and so far as I know the only, time he is called "Mr. *Toby Shandy*." Moreover, we are told that he understands his brother "very well." Not only does he understand him very well, but it is in a matter which ill accords with his modesty. One wonders how a man of Toby's temper, a man who, even after his encounter with the Widow Wadman, still did not know the right end of the woman from the wrong, was able to bring himself to retail this particular story to his nephew. But at this point in the composition of *Tristram Shandy* the brilliant notion of Uncle Toby's modesty, and the equally brilliant notion of the inability of the two brothers to communicate, had not, I think, occurred to Sterne. We are told, for instance, in the next chapter, that Uncle Toby was fully cognizant of the strange regularity with which his brother carried out his conjugal duties:

> My father, . . . had made it a rule for many years of his life,——
> on the first *Sunday night* of every month throughout the whole
> year . . . to wind up a large house-clock which we had standing
> upon the back-stairs head . . . he had likewise gradually brought
> some other little family concernments to the same period, in
> order, as he would often say to my uncle *Toby*, to get them all out
> of the way at one time, and be no more plagued and pester'd with
> them the rest of the month (I, 4, p. 8).

It is true that in the later sections of the novel Uncle Toby occasionally displays a certain degree of sexual awareness—he acknowledges Dr Slop's crude attempts to pun on "curtins and hornworks" (II, 12, p. 111), for instance, and he is alive to the dangers which may attend the presentation of the hip rather than the head during the delivery of his infant nephew (IV, 10, p. 280). But his easy familiarity with the details of Tristram's conception does seem radically out of character. Nor is this the only discordant note: it is Toby we are told (in Chapter 15) who, exhibiting a quite improbable familiarity with the ways of women, and a quite unusually nasty suspiciousness, was responsible for the insertion of that saving clause in the marriage articles which stated:

> That in case my mother hereafter should, at any time, put my father to the trouble and expense of a *London* journey upon false cries and tokens;——that for every such instance she should forfeit all the right and title which the covenant gave her to the next turn (I, 15, p. 40).

It is because of this saving clause that Tristram has to be born in the country, and all his troubles fall upon him.

It is not until Chapter 21 that we learn that Toby was a man of "a most extream and unparallel'd modesty of nature."[13] Significantly enough it is in the same chapter—in fact, on the next page—that we learn he had been in the army. The two are, of course, connected, for it was at the siege of Namur that, as Sterne here informs us, he was inflicted with his modesty by "a blow from a stone, broke off by a ball from the parapet of a horn-work . . . which struck full upon my uncle *Toby's* groin" (p. 67). And it is at this point that Walter and Toby are displayed to us for the first time in conversation together: only now do we learn that the two brothers, though animated by a great affection for each other are, because of their "contrariety of humours" subject to "many a fraternal squabble" (p. 68). In fact it is with Chapter 21 that the novel proper may fairly be said to begin. This chapter opens with Uncle Toby and his brother listening in the parlor of Shandy Hall to the commotion upstairs attendant on the imminent arrival of Tristram himself: it opens, that is to say, on the prelude to the life of the hero, that prelude which is, in itself, one of the great comic scenes in English literature. In this same scene that note of sentiment which is distinctive to Sterne is sounded clearly for the first time. There have been hints of it earlier in the story of Yorick, but these are insignificant in comparison with the effect which Uncle Toby has on the story. The perpetually recurring disagreements and reconciliations between the two brothers are a constant and unforgettable demonstration of the necessity and the possibility of the sentimental virtues of sympathy and tolerance; while in the character of Toby himself, comic, pathetic and admirable, Sterne seems suddenly and accidentally to have discovered a poetically compelling symbol of that theme of impotent and distressed virtue which everything he wrote seems in some way to reflect.

Tristram Shandy is a most humane book, and its humanity is imaged paradoxically in the tragi-comic figure of Uncle Toby and rendered dramatically in the responses and reactions of the other characters—including and especially Tristram—to him. It is my contention that Sterne probably discovered Uncle Toby—the *real* Uncle Toby—by chance, "by writing the first sentence——and trusting to Almighty God for the second." In so doing he also discovered his own genius and transformed himself from an obscurely learned Yorkshire wit into a great and uniquely delightful novelist.

NOTES

1. *Studies in Classic American Literature* (New York, 1964), p. 2.

2. *PMLA*, LI (1936), 803–820.

3. *MP*, XLVIII (1951), 172–183.

4. Op. cit., 183.

5. Op. cit., 181.

6. In *The Moral Basis of Fielding's Art* (Middletown, Conn., 1959) Mr Battestin has, of course, most effectively disposed of the notion that *Joseph Andrews* "began simply as another parody of *Pamela* and somehow got gloriously out of hand" (p. 3). But although I can agree that Fielding composed his first novel according to a well-formulated plan, it still seems to me that something spontaneous and unplanned occurs with the appearance of Parson Adams: *Joseph Andrews* acquires a human dimension which up till this point it lacked—it takes on the character of a piece of realistic fiction.

7. *Laurence Sterne: The Making of a Humorist, 1713–1762* (London, 1957) pp. 163–165.

8. "The Birth of Tristram Shandy: Sterne and Dr. Burton," in *Studies in the Eighteenth Century*, ed. R. F. Brissenden (Canberra, 1968), pp. 133–154.

9. "*Tristram Shandy* and the Tradition of Learned Wit," *Essays in Criticism*, I (1951), 225–248.

10. Rabelais and Swift are mentioned more than once in Sterne's letters written at this time.

11. It is interesting to note that Mr Booth, firmly in the grip of his hypotheses, completely fails to acknowledge the existence of the Yorick episode: "the only sizable body of material in the first part not dependent on Tristram's story," he asserts, "is the account of Uncle Toby's Hobby-Horse" (op. cit., 180).

12. See John M. Stedmond, *The Comic Art of Laurence Sterne* (Toronto, 1967), pp. 9–10.

13. I, 21, p. 66. Mr Booth remarks that "the first volume has not been long under way before we are introduced to Uncle Toby's campaigns. . . . But even before his Hobby-Horse, which *is* his campaigning, is presented to us, we are given a passage on his modesty" (op. cit., 177). In fact Toby's modesty and his military background are introduced practically simultaneously, and not until we are almost four-fifths of the way through Volume I.

SIX

In Memory

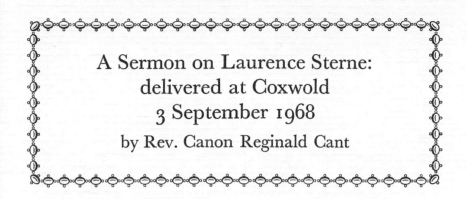

A Sermon on Laurence Sterne:
delivered at Coxwold
3 September 1968
by Rev. Canon Reginald Cant

1. The parson who becomes in his own lifetime a famous writer is less common now than he used to be. I can think of two or three priests in England today who are poets of repute; I harbor the perhaps exaggerated suspicion that most detective stories are written by clergymen of the Church of England—under pseudonyms. But the number of men of importance in literature who are also ordained dwindles. In the *Concise Bibliography of English Literature*, 1958 edition, there are in the section 1500–1660 at least a dozen clerics; in 1660–1800, if I have counted correctly, the number is down to 8; 1800–1900, it is 6; 1900–1950—with the dubious exception of Frederick Rolfe—none.

One may speculate on the reasons. In days gone by there were fewer ways of achieving an education or of earning a livelihood, and until Sir Robert Peel and Bishop Blomfield undertook the "Second Reformation" of the Church of England the medieval notion prevailed that ecclesiastical revenues existed to support ecclesiastical persons rather than, in the first place, to get ecclesiastical work done. Before the two movements which transformed the clerical ideal—the Evangelical and the Tractarian—it was not so commonly taken for granted among the clergy as it was until yesterday (but it will be interesting to see the outcome of today's restiveness among the clergy at their professionalization)—it was not so commonly assumed then as it has been this last century and a half that a John Donne, a Dean Swift, a Sydney Smith could be no model for the seminarist, and that the clerical profession demanded the unremitting pursuit of souls, and that their ordination vows to draw all their cares and studies one way relegated the cultivation of letters by clergymen to the status of a hobby.

Perhaps a literary cleric can flourish only within an assured and

Chancellor, York Minster

stable framework of social and ecclesiastical life, when the Church, however much disliked or attacked—as it was in the eighteenth century—is yet taken for granted as part of the context within which men live their lives. The great divide in English society over the place of institutional religion within it comes not at the Reformation but much later, at the time when large numbers of people ceased to take it for granted that—willingly or unwillingly—they should go to church. Laurence Sterne lived in almost the last age when the assumption that this was the natural thing for Englishmen to do could reasonably be made.

2. By the accepted standards of the day Sterne was a competent and satisfactory parish priest. It was only late in life, when health began to fail—and fame grew, it must be admitted—that he did not reside in his parish for lengthy periods; and he always observed the correct procedure for obtaining leave of absence and in providing for the pastoral care of the parish. I like to think of him, in his earlier years at Sutton and Stillington, identifying himself, as country parish priests had done since the middle ages, with the farming life of his people— "pruning, digging, trenching, weeding." I think of his Sunday catechizing in Lent; of those confirmation classes which lasted for three hours—three hours!—of the sacrament administered five times a year, which was quite as often as most people then thought necessary.

As a preacher he belonged to the ethical tradition of Tillotson. Consider the titles of his sermons—*Self-Knowledge, Forgiveness of Injuries, The Duty of Setting Bounds to Our Desires, Pride*. It was the generally accepted style of preaching. It was logical, sensible and coherent. It appealed to the intelligence and to the will. It allowed for the average carnally minded Englishman's limited aspirations towards sanctity, but it could encourage a godly, righteous and sober life. I recall the story of the North American college president who sampled all the churches around his campus to see which suited him best, until the day he went to the Episcopalian one and heard the congregation saying, "we have left undone those things that we ought to have done, and done those things that we ought not to have done. . . ." This, he said, is where I belong. But already in Sterne's day this ethical preaching was being challenged. The experience of another literary parson, a few years later, is instructive. George Crabbe's sermons were in the same tradition: but they failed to please—

"Heathens" they said "can tell us
right from wrong,
But to a Christian higher points belong."

While Sterne stood in the pulpit of York Minster persuading His Majesty's judges of assize of the temporal advantages of a rational piety, John Wesley was already preaching "to beget, preserve and increase the life of God in the souls of men."

This is not to suggest that Sterne's sermons—even if (as some darkly allege) they were sometimes borrowed—were other than sincere. Sometimes I wonder whether his tongue was in his cheek, and I think the answer is "No." It is simply that he could still, in his day, take so much for granted. It was in all seriousness that he preached in Paris to a congregation which included David Hume, Diderot and the Baron d'Holbach about King Hezekiah, recalling to them one of the least likely of all Old Testament miracles, the shadow on the dial returning ten degrees.

No less a judge of preaching than John Henry Newman praised the sermon "Search the Scriptures" in which Sterne contrasted "those laboured and polished periods, tinselled over with a gaudy embellishment of words which glitter but convey little or no light to the understanding with the true eloquence of scripture, with its simplicity and majesty." His own mind and style, he confessed, were affected by his daily reading of the Old and New Testament, books which were to his liking as well as necessary to his profession.

Even in his pastoral preaching—likely to be the most conservative element in a literary clergyman's output—Sterne was not merely saying what it was the custom to say in the way in which everyone else said it. You well know that in the choice of texts, in the opening sentences, in the turns of phrase, sometimes in the "feel" of his discourses there are gleams of those qualities which make his books of such interest today. A theologian might be inclined to enlarge on the connection between Sterne's sense of the absurd and the paradoxical element in the orthodox Christianity, or between Sterne's "sentiment" and "sincerity."

3. We might say, in Shandyian fashion, that today we have come not (as we had hoped) to bury Laurence but to praise him. I admire his kindness, for example, to that unsatisfactory curate who set fire to the rectory and ran away; his patience with not the easiest of wives; his

befriending of a Negro slave; his generosity with money; and perhaps most of all his dislike of that deadly virtue of discretion, "which encompasses the heart with adamant." Not for Sterne a mitre or a deanery. Even in the eighteenth century something more was asked of a candidate for such honors than that he should be the English Rabelais. A proper deference to the opinions and sensitiveness to the susceptibilities of one's seniors were then, as always, among the qualities which merited promotion. Sterne was not a smooth man.

And how—in Yorkshire phrase—did he make out as a Christian minister? It is the duty of a minister to serve, and it is possible to serve one's fellow men by making them laugh as well as by persuading them to believe. Sterne in fact did both. After all, Lord Bathurst said that his desire to live was rekindled by reading *Tristram Shandy*. And if Sterne jested with an aching heart—well, serving involves suffering. It was Sterne's fame as a writer which led him to the Parisian salon in which he encountered the unbelieving coquette, Madame de Vence. I think of a "new theologian" of our day in such company: how humble he would be in seeking wisdom from such a one! Not Sterne. In one half hour—she acknowledged it—he had "unperverted" her and had "said more for revealed religion than all their encyclopaedists had said against it."

We have very high authority indeed for thinking that there is more than one kind of ministry to human need, and that it is not always necessary to be solemn or self-conscious about it:

> John the Baptist is come eating no bread nor drinking wine, and ye say, he has a devil. The Son of Man is come eating and drinking, and ye say, Behold a gluttonous man and a winebibber, and a friend of publicans and sinners. *And wisdom is justified of all her children.*

APPENDIX
Of Books

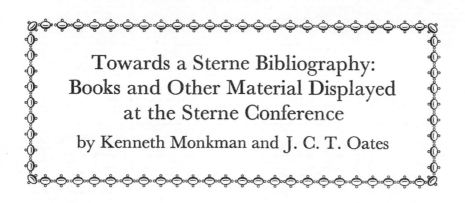

Towards a Sterne Bibliography:
Books and Other Material Displayed
at the Sterne Conference
by Kenneth Monkman and J. C. T. Oates

The exhibition of books and other materials at the York Minster Library during the Laurence Sterne Bicentenary Conference aimed to trace Sterne's life and achievement from the first stirrings of Shandyism before he was born to the latest of modern interpretations. For this catalog, however, we have had reluctantly to cut short the story at about the year 1800, and even the years before that have been pruned. What is left, we hope, is of permanent interest. Much of it has never been in print before. But here a word of warning is called for. Whatever else it is, this catalog is not a bibliography. Descriptions of books have been abridged, collations omitted, not all points or editions included. But as far as it goes, we have tried to make the information we do give accurate. Someday a worthy bibliography of Sterne will be compiled. This catalog, we like to think, will be a stimulus and a stepping-stone toward it.

Most of the exhibits, it will be seen, were drawn from the York Minster Library's own rich collection (YM) or from those of J. C. T. Oates (JCTO) or Kenneth Monkman (KM). Our grateful thanks for other loans and for help of various kinds are due to Mr G. P. Brown, of the Beverley Public Library; Mr A. B. Craven, of the Leeds Central Library; Mrs N. K. M. Gurney, of the Borthwick Institute of Historical Research; Capt Victor Malcolm Wombwell, of Newburgh Priory; and, not least of all, Mr C. B. L. Barr and the staff of York Minster Library.

Mr Monkman is Honorary Secretary of the Laurence Sterne Trust. Mr Oates is Fellow of Darwin College, Under-Librarian of the University Library, Cambridge

279

BEGINNINGS

It was impossible to show more than a few of the many books which influenced Sterne or foretold that kind of noticeable departure from the human norm which sober north-country folk were calling "shandy" long before he was born. The selection included early editions of the Authorized Version of the Bible, Burton's *Anatomy of Melancholy*, Phillips' transation of *Don Quixote*, Cotton's of Montaigne's *Essays*, Urquhart and Motteux's of Rabelais, Locke's *Essay Concerning Human Understanding*, Béroalde de Verville's *Moyen de Parvenir*, Bruscambille's *Pensées Facétieuses*, and the following small signpost:

RAY (John)

1 A COLLECTION OF ENGLISH WORDS NOT GENERALLY USED, in two Alphabetical Catalogues, the One of such as are proper to the Northern, the other to the Southern Counties. The Second Edition. London: printed for Christopher Wilkinson. 1691.

12mo. On page 62, among the north-country words, is the first recorded appearance in print of the word *Shandy*, meaning "wild." Nearly a hundred years later John Marshall amplified this to "a little crack-brained; somewhat crazy." (*The Rural Economy of Yorkshire*, 1788, ii, 351.)

[KM]

2 PHOTOGRAPH, taken July 1967, of the reputed birthplace of Laurence Sterne in Clonmel, Co Tipperary, Ireland.

Tradition in Clonmel points to this house, now an empty shell, in Mary Street, formerly Our Lady's Street, as the birthplace of Sterne in 1713. It lies only a short distance from St Mary's (Protestant) Church, where he was almost certainly christened; unfortunately the registers for the period have not survived. "My birth-day was ominous to my poor father, who was, the day after our arrival, with many other brave officers broke, and sent adrift into the wide world with a wife and two children——" (*Letters*, p. 1).

[KM]

3 INSTITUTIONS (COMMISSIONS) 1731-1742.

On 6 March 1736/7, soon after graduating from Jesus College, Cambridge, Sterne had been admitted to the Order of Deacons by the Bishop of Lincoln and licensed as Assistant Curate at St Ives, near Cambridge. The register of the Archbishops of York, displayed here, records his first connection with the Yorkshire church. Under the date of 18 February 1737/8 is recorded his license as Assistant Curate of Catton, in the East Riding. Under 24 August of the same year, his collation to the Vicarage of Sutton-on the-Forest, in the North Riding, his first living, which he retained until his death. Because Archbishop Lancelot Blackburn was so negligent of his duties, Sterne had to go elsewhere to be admitted to the priesthood. The Bishop of Lincoln ordained him on 20 August.

[Lent by the Borthwick Institute of Historical Research, York]

4 CHAPTER ACT BOOK OF THE DEAN AND CHAPTER OF YORK, 1737-47.

In 1741 Sterne's rich and influential uncle, the Rev. Dr Jaques Sterne, Precentor of York and Archdeacon of Cleveland, secured for him the prebendal stall of Givendale in York Minster. A year later Sterne exchanged the stall of Givendale for that of North Newbald. (Cf. item 13.) His installations are recorded here.

[YM]

ADVENTURE IN POLITICS

Important new light was thrown on Sterne's early activities as a political journalist by Professor L. P. Curtis in *The Politicks of Laurence Sterne*, 1929. Since then, a few further fragments of the paper-war fought by Sterne on behalf of the Whig candidate in the strongly-contested Yorkshire election of 1741 have been identified in Yorkshire libraries by Kenneth Monkman and are here made public (marked *) for the first time.

5 THE YORK GAZETTEER: No. 41. Tuesday, December 15. 1741. [York:] Published by John Jackson.

The earliest known surviving issue of the pro-Whig weekly

newspaper founded by Sterne and his uncle "partly . . . to correct the Weekly Poison of the [pro-Tory] York-Courant." Pages 3 and 4 carry two articles by Sterne, one written under John Jackson's name. The essay listed below, No. 6, is earlier than these.

[YM]

6 *[Begins:] A PARAGRAPH TAKEN FROM THE YORK-COURANT, June 9th 1741 [with an answer] From the YORK-GAZETTEER, June 16th 1741.

Broadside. Reprinted in part from a lost issue of the *York Gazetteer*, this is the earliest known surviving piece of Sterne's political journalism. In it he attacks John Garbut, a Tory coal-merchant with a criminal record. Later, at Garbut's instigation, Sterne's publisher and printer, John Jackson, was lured to a York alehouse and beaten-up; the story is told in an issue of the *Gazetteer* in the Monkman collection not listed here. Professor Arthur Cash has recently discovered evidence in the Public Record Office in London showing that Garbut was bound over at York assizes to keep the peace towards both Jackson and Sterne.

[Lent by Leeds Central Library]

7 THE YORK COURANT. Numb. 837 Tuesday, Oct. 27, 1741. [York:] Printed for Caesar Ward.

Sterne's essay "Query upon Query" appeared here. It was addressed to "J. S.", of questionable identity, Sterne's chief antagonist in the electoral paper-war. To keep this sharp personalized contest going, and doubtless to increase sales, the publisher and printer of the *Courant*, Caesar Ward, invited Sterne to carry the battle into his columns. This was Sterne's first salvo, slightly softened by Ward's editorial pen. (Cf. the following two items.)

(YM)

8 QUERY UPON QUERY; being an Answer to J. S's Letter Printed in the York-Courant October 20, relating to the present contested Election. York: 1741.

8vo (a half sheet). The only known copy of a pamphlet version of the essay (cf. the above item), possibly altered by Sterne's uncle, the Precentor, Dr Jaques Sterne.

[YM]

9 THE DAILY GAZETTEER. Numb. 1855. Wednesday, October 28. 1741. London: Printed for T. Cooper.

Another version of "Query upon Query" appeared here. (Cf. the above two items.) Sterne had sent a copy of his letter to the leading Whig paper in London. This version may be free of editorial tampering. Yet a further version appeared in the *Leeds Mercury*.

[KM]

10 *AN ANSWER TO J. S's LETTER, Address'd to a Freeholder of the County of York. November 3. 1741.

Broadside. The hitherto unrecorded first appearance of a further attack by Sterne on "J. S." It was reprinted in the *York Courant* of 10 November, a version published by L. P. Curtis in *The Politicks of Laurence Sterne*, 1929, pp. 63–69.

[Lent by Leeds Central Library]

11 *TO THE REV. MR. JAMES SCOTT AT LEEDS. York, Nov. 27. 1741.

Broadside. Hitherto unpublished. By now the contest with "J. S." had centered upon the question of his identity. At the risk of some dishonor if he were mistaken, Sterne here announced openly the name of his antagonist—The Rev. James Scott, Vicar of Bardsey, near Leeds. He later decided he had made a mistake. (Cf. the following item.)

[YM]

12 *THE YORK GAZETTEER. No. 46. Tuesday, January 19, 1742 [York:] Published by John Jackson.

The final election figures show victory for the Whig candidate, Cholmley Turner, over the Tory, George Fox, and Sterne celebrates the discomfiture of "J. S." with a twelve-line mock epitaph which makes punning reference to the Tory candidate's name:

An EPITAPH.
On the Death of J——k St—n—pe

Since poor J. S. is dead and gone,
Let this be writ upon his Stone.
Here lies J. S.
Devoid of Sense and eke of Strife,
Who in a Fox-Chase lost his Life,
That Tongue alas does now lie still,
That us'd the Strangest Things to tell;
So strange you'd swear 'twas all a Lye,
But for his KNOWN VERACITY.
——Whoo——Whup ye Jacks! ah weep full sore,
That he of Fox Chace says no more.

From this it is clear that Sterne now believed his opponent to have been John Stanhope, of Horsforth near Leeds, a well-known attorney who was to cross his path again during the protracted marriage negotiations of his friend, the Rev. John Blake, in 1758. The fact that Stanhope was a noted sportsman adds further point to Sterne's pun.

[Lent by Beverley Public Library and Art Gallery]

YEARS OF PROMISE

13 LEGAL DOCUMENT, dated 5 January 1741 [i.e. 1742], appointing the Reverends Charles Cowper and Robert Reynolds to act as proxies for Laurence Sterne in the ceremonies of 8 January when Sterne is to be inducted into the "real actual and corporal possession" of the Canonry and Prebend of North Newbald "and of all and singular the Rights Members and Appurtenances thereunto belonging."

This more profitable prebend was given to Sterne in reward for his journalistic services in the election. He later adapted the phraseology of this and other similar documents to describe the licensing of the old midwife in *Tristram Shandy*. The impression of Sterne's seal shows clearly the starling crest, as later used by Yorick in *A Sentimental Journey*.

[YM]

14 LETTERS TESTIMONIAL, dated 25 February 1743 [i.e. 1744].

Three of Sterne's friends and fellow clergy declare that for the past three years he has "led his Life Godly soberly and honestly" and has "applyed himself diligently to his Studies and never (that we know) written or taught any thing but what the Church of England approves of." The occasion was Sterne's presentation to the living of Stillington.

[YM]

15 THE YORK GAZETTEER. With News both Foreign and Domestic. Numb. 120. Tuesday, June 14. 1743 [York:] Printed by John Jackson.

On page four is a news item describing the first appearance of the new archbishop, Thomas Herring, in York Minster, when he "was sung up by the Choir . . . attended by the Chancellor, Advocates, Proctors and Officers of the Ecclesiastical Court in their Robes, and it being the Anniversary of his Majesty's happy Accession to the Throne, an excellent Sermon was preached by the Rev. Mr. Lawrence Stern [*sic*], . . . from Genesis iv Chap. Verse 7." This text, announced by Sterne in the assembled presence of "their Reverences and their Worships," possibly reflects the early stirrings of Shandyism. Revealed here for the first time, it alludes to the responsibilities of the new archbishop and the distinctly shady reputation of the late one, Lancelot Blackburne: "If thou doest well, shalt thou not be accepted? And if thou doest not well, sin lieth at the door."

[KM]

16 THE GENTLEMAN'S MAGAZINE: For July 1743. London: Printed by E. Cave, jun.

On page 376 is the first known printing of *The Unknown World. Verses occasioned by hearing a Pass-Bell. By the Rev. Mr. St—n.* The poem is undoubtedly by Sterne: the text of a manuscript version in his hand, now lost, was printed by Thomas Gill in *Vallis Eboracensis*, 1852.

[KM]

17 THE HYMNS ANTHEMS & TUNES with the Ode used at the Magdalen Chapel set for the Organ, Harpsichord, Voice, German-Flute or Guitar. London Printed for C. and S. Thompson N⁰ 75 Pauls Church-Yard. [*ca.* 1765.]

4to. Engraved throughout. Pages 26–27 contain a setting, so far unrecorded, of Sterne's poem *The Unknown World*. A variant edition containing the same setting was published, probably slightly earlier, by "Henry Thorowgood under the Royal Exchange."

[KM]

PREACHING AND PARISH AFFAIRS

18 THE CASE OF ELIJAH AND THE WIDOW OF ZEREPHATH, consider'd: A Charity-Sermon, Preach'd on Good-Friday, April 17, 1747. In the Parish Church of St. Michael-le-Belfrey. By Laurence Sterne, M.A. Prebendary of York. York: Printed for J. Hildyard. 1747.

8vo. Sterne's first published sermon. Advertised in the *York Journal*, 19 May 1747, as "Next Week will be publish'd...."

[YM]

19 THE ABUSES OF CONSCIENCE: set forth in a Sermon, preached in the Cathedral Church of St. Peter's, York, at the Summer Assizes, on Sunday, July 29, 1750. By Laurence Sterne, A.M. York: Printed by Caesar Ward. 1750.

8vo. The famous sermon later read aloud by Corporal Trim in *Tristram Shandy*. Advertised in the *York Courant*, 7 August 1750.

[YM]

20 MANUSCRIPT TITHE RECEIPTS, dated 30 November 1745, 21 October 1748, 18 May 1755, 15 November 1758, issued by Sterne to Stephen Croft, of Stillington Hall.

286

Four of a series of 20, 1745–67. "At Stillington, the family of the C[roft]s shewed us every kindness . . . an amiable family, who were ever cordial friends," wrote Sterne (*Letters*, p. 4). It was Stephen Croft who rescued the manuscript of *Tristram Shandy* at Stillington Hall when Sterne, annoyed because several of the company assembled to hear him read it fell asleep, threw it into the fire.

[KM]

21   ARCHBISHOP HERRING'S VISITATION RETURNS, 1743.

A folio volume. In preparation for his primary Visitation in 1743, the new Archbishop, Thomas Herring, sent a printed *questionnaire* to all 903 parishes in his diocese. 836 were completed and returned, including the one by Sterne shown here. His answers as vicar of Sutton-on-the-Forest reveal him to have been more diligent in parish affairs than most of the Yorkshire clergy of his day. (See *Letters*, pp. 21–23.)
[Lent by the Borthwick Institute of Historical Research, York]

22   AUTOGRAPH LETTER: Sterne to John Clough, Register of the Dean and Chapter of York, [Sutton, August 1753.]

Sterne takes a charitable interest in the case of an unfortunate parishioner, Jane Harbotle, presented by his churchwardens for the crime of fornication after the birth of her third illegitimate child. (See *Letters*, p. 47.)

[YM]

PARSON'S PLEASURE

"Books, painting, fiddling, and shooting were my amusements . . . at Sutton." (*Letters*, p. 4).

23   MANUSCRIPT: BORROWER'S REGISTER OF YORK MINSTER LIBRARY, 1741–54.

Narrow folio. Sterne made considerable use of the Minster Library, then housed in another building. The book here shown contains entries in his hand recording the volumes he borrowed, including music; the volumes themselves were to be seen elsewhere in this exhibition. This sidelight on Sterne's reading habits was first revealed by Elizabeth Brunskill in *Eighteenth Century Reading*, York Georgian Society Occasional Paper No. 6, 1950.

[YM]

24 CRAZY TALES. London: 1762.

4to. First Edition. Engraved frontispiece of "Crazy Castle." Sterne was a frequent visitor at Skelton Castle, in North Yorkshire, where his college friend, John Hall-Stevenson, played host to a set of wags who called themselves the Demoniacs. These broad tales, written under the nicknames of various members of the club, including Sterne, were probably all by Hall-Stevenson himself. In the old library at the castle, as well as in the company there, Sterne found many of the sources of Shandyism.

[KM]

25 PHOTOGRAPH: "Thos. Bridges and Lawrence Sterne, as Mountebanks."

The engraving, by C. J. Smith, appeared first in T. F. Dibdin's *Bibliographical . . . Tour of the Northern Counties of England*, 1838. It represents a painting, now lost, in which Sterne and his friend Thomas Bridges, for a joke, portrayed each other as mountebanks on a stage. They copied the design from a seventeenth-century broadside.

[KM]

A POLITICAL ROMANCE

In 1758 Dr. Francis Topham, a York lawyer who held many church appointments, wished to ensure that one of them would be handed on to his son. The Dean of York, Dr. John Fountayne, refused. Whereupon Dr. Topham started a ball rolling which led to *Tristram Shandy*. . . .

26 A LETTER ADDRESS'D TO THE REVEREND THE DEAN OF YORK; in which is given a full Detail of some very extraordinary Behaviour of his. York: 1758.

8vo. Dr Topham accuses the Dean of having gone back on his word.

[YM]

27 AN ANSWER TO A LETTER ADDRESS'D TO THE DEAN OF YORK, in the Name of Dr. Topham. York: Sold by Thomas Atkinson. 1758.

8vo. A sharp reply to Dr Topham's accusation, put together by the Dean with the help of Sterne and possibly others.

[YM]

28 A REPLY TO THE ANSWER TO A LETTER lately addressed to the Dean of York. York: 1759.

8vo. Dr Topham's rejoinder.

[YM]

29 A POLITICAL ROMANCE, addressed to — — Esq; of York. To which is subjoined a Key. York: 1759.

8vo. With this shilling pamphlet Sterne pricked the bubble of this silly dispute so comically, reducing it to a village wrangle over who should own an old watchcoat and a pair of cast-off breeches, that all copies had to be withdrawn to save the face of the Establishment. Only some half-dozen are known to have survived. A unique printer's copy with a first page, later cancelled, naming the allegorical village as "Cocksbull, near Canterbury," was discovered recently by Edward Simmen at Texas Christian University.

[YM]

30 A POLITICAL ROMANCE, addressed to — — Esq. of York. London: Printed by J. Murdoch. 1769.

12mo. Reprinted from an imperfect copy of the suppressed edition of 1759.

[JCTO]

31 THE BABY, A NEW SONG. To the tune of, A Cobler there was, and he liv'd, &c. [York: 1759.]

Ballad slip. A postscript to the Topham-Fountayne dispute. Authorship unknown, but it is possible that Sterne himself wrote it. He appears in it as *Slim*, the nickname he applied to himself in *A Political Romance*. The first two of the eight verses run:

> Of a Quarrel I sing, not a Mile from a Church,
> How a D[ea]n left a D[octo]r trepann'd in the Lurch;
> And an Adv[oca]te nick'd made a terrible Rant,
> That his Baby was *bobb'd* of a *lucrative Grant*.

> Enrag'd as they were, how they squabbled and wrote,
> Asserted, evaded, deny'd, and what not?
> And something let slip of a Tale of a Tub,
> Of *Whisler* and *Slim* having out-witted *Sc[ru]b*.

[YM]

THE TEXT OF TRISTRAM

A Political Romance was the key which unlocked Sterne's latent genius. The result was *Tristram Shandy*, published in five instalments over the years 1760–67. Although many later editions were shown in the York Minster Library exhibition, those listed below are confined to editions published during Sterne's lifetime and therefore of possible textual significance:

32 THE LIFE AND OPINIONS OF TRISTRAM SHANDY, Gentleman. Vol. I. [II.] [York:] 1760.

8vo. First edition. First advertised in the *London Chronicle*, 1 January 1760, though an advertisement may have appeared earlier in the *York Courant*, of which no issues survive for the final weeks of 1759. The book was undoubtedly printed in York, on the press of Ann Ward in Coney Street. Sterne's first intention had been to find a London publisher, but James Dodsley, to whom he offered the manuscript, turned it down.

Sterne thereupon had a small edition printed at his own expense (on borrowed money) and sent a parcel of the books to Dodsley to be sold on commission. The price of the two volumes "neatly bound" was five shillings. Final proof of the York printing, which has often been challenged, appears in "The Bibliography of the early editions of *Tristram Shandy*," a paper read before the Bibliographical Society in London by Kenneth Monkman on 19 March 1968, and printed in *The Library*, March 1970. The brief notes which follow are based on that paper.

[KM]

33   [—] Vol. I. [II.] The Second Edition. London: Printed for R. and J. Dodsley. 1760.

8vo. Advertised in the *London Chronicle*, 3 April 1760. Frontispiece to Volume I engraved by S. Ravenet after a drawing by Hogarth; it exists in two states. Sterne has added a Dedication to the Prime Minister, William Pitt; this also exists in two states. There is evidence that Dodsley, who had now bought the copyright of the two volumes for five times the sum he had refused to give before publication, employed different printers to speed up the appearance of a new and large edition of a book that had become the talk of London.

[KM]

34   [—] Vol. III. London, 1760.

8vo. This was the next volume to appear, in September 1970. It was not by Sterne but was an attempt to capitalize on the lively *Tristram* market by a young schoolmaster, John Carr, who may have known Sterne personally. Sterne published an advertisement protecting at the imposition and promising the early appearance of the genuine next instalment.

[KM]

35   [—] Vol. III. [IV.] London: Printed for R. and J. Dodsley. 1761.

8vo. Advertised in the *London Chronicle*, 29 January 1761. The genuine second instalment, bearing a further frontispiece engraved by "F. Ravanet" after Hogarth; this is conjugate with A 8 in volume iii but, because it depicts an incident in volume iv, it is sometimes found prefixed to that volume.

[KM]

36 [—] Vol. III. The Second Edition. London: Printed for R. and J. Dodsley. 1761.

8vo. The frontispiece has been re-engraved by J. Ryland.

[KM]

37 [—] Vol. IV. London: Printed for R. and J. Dodsley. 1761.

8vo. A concealed "second edition". The text has been almost completely reset, with some slight alterations, and the press-figures are different. This edition has the word "fancy" correctly spelled on page 73, line 3; the first edition has the misprint "facy."

[KM]

38 [—] Vol. V. [VI.] London: Printed for T. Becket and P. A. Dehondt. 1762.

8vo. First appearance of the third instalment. Advertised in the *London Chronicle*, 22 December 1761. Sterne had not merely changed publishers but had gone into the business himself, as he had done with the York volumes. He employed William Strahan to print 4000 copies. As a precaution against further piracies, Sterne signed every copy of volume v on the first page of the text.

[KM]

39 [—] The Second Edition. Vol. V. London: Printed for T. Becket and P. A. Dehondt. 1767.

8vo. An important edition. As well as adding a third Latin quotation to the title-page, Sterne has inserted two new sentences on page 146 which are not in the first edition. As a further measure of his interest he has signed page one, as with the first edition. For some reason there are three "editions" of this "second edition," each, as can be seen, an entirely different setting, but only one of them bearing Sterne's signature.

[KM]

40   [—] The Second Edition. Vol. VI. London: Printed for T. Becket and P. A. Dehondt. 1767.

8vo. Much less interesting than the second edition of its companion volume. It does not even have the new third quotation on the title-page.

[KM]

41   [—] Vol. VII. [VIII.] Printed for T. Becket and P. A. Dehondt. 1765.

8vo. First appearance of the fourth instalment. Advertised in the *London Chronicle*, 23 January 1765. Again, Strahan printed 4000 copies at Sterne's expense, and each copy of volume v is signed. A complete resetting of the two volumes, with a number of small errors corrected, also exists; it is in fact a true second edition, though not so named. It is not signed by Sterne.

[KM]

42   [—] Vol. IX. London: Printed for T. Durham, and T. Caslon. 1766.

8vo. Small circular engraving on title-page. Despite Sterne's precautions, this further spurious volume, by an unknown author, appeared in February 1766, nearly a year before the genuine version. It ran to a second edition. Several reviewers were taken in, and a German editor translated it as Sterne's.

[KM]

43   [—] Vol. IX. London: Printed for T. Becket and P. A. Dehondt. 1767.

8vo. The genuine fifth and final instalment. Advertised in the *London Chronicle*, 31 January 1767. The vogue for *Tristram* was fading, and possibly the spurious volume had blunted anticipation; Sterne reduced the printing order to 3500. He signed each copy.

[KM]

44   [—] Vol. I. [–IX.] London: Printed for D. Lynch. 1760 [–67.]

8vo. The original nine volumes bound in three, each with continuous pagination. The so-called "Lynch" edition, which has attracted more bibliographical attention than it deserves. Despite the dates on some of the title-pages, it can be shown to have appeared no earlier than 1767.

[KM]

45   [—] Volume the First. [Second.] The Third Edition. Dublin: Printed for D. Chamberlaine, and S. Smith. 1760.

12mo. Frontispiece to volume i. A piracy, published soon after the second edition in London, and probably described as "The Third Edition" for that reason. No earlier Dublin edition is known.

[KM]

46   [—] Vol. III. [IV.] Dublin: Printed for D. Chamberlaine, and S. Smith. 1761.

12mo. Frontispiece to volume iv. First Dublin edition of this instalment.

[KM]

47   [—] Vol. I. [–IV.] The Second Edition. Dublin: Printed by Henry Saunders. 1765.

12mo. Four volumes in one, with continuous pagination. Probably the first collected edition of the first two instalments.

[KM]

48   [—] Vol. V. [–VIII.] Dublin: Printed by Henry Saunders. 1765.

12mo. Four volumes in one, with continuous pagination. First Dublin edition of the third and fourth instalments. With item 47, which is uniform in format, the first attempt by any publisher anywhere at a collected edition of *Tristram*. It lacks, of course, the final volume, which did not appear until two years later (Cf. following item).

[KM]

49 [—] Vol. IX. Dublin: Printed for W. and W. Smith, J. Exshaw, H. Saunders, S. Watson, and W. Colles. 1767.

12mo. First Dublin edition of the final volume. In similar format to the two previous items; with them it comprises the earliest known collected edition of the complete text of *Tristram*: a tribute to Irish piratical initiative.

[KM]

TRISTRAM IN TRANSLATION

50 TRISTRAM SCHANDIS LEBEN UND MEYNUNGEN. Hamburg, 1774: Bey Bode.

8vo, 9 vols in 4. Frontispiece, vol. 1 (The Sermon), vol. 3 (The Christening).

[JCTO]

51 LA VIE ET LES OPINIONS DE TRISTRAM SHANDY. Traduites de L'Anglois de STERN, par M. FRÉNAIS. A Yorck, et se trouve à Paris, 1776: Chez Ruault.

12mo, 2 vols (= *Tristram Shandy*, vols 1–4). The first French translation. The remaining vols. did not appear in French until 1785.

[JCTO]

52 DAS LEBEN UND DIE MEYNUNGEN DES HERRN TRISTRAM SHANDY. Aus dem Englischen u^{c}bersetzt. Zweyte Auflage. Nach einer neuen U^{c}bersetzung auf Anrathen des Herrn Hofrath WIELAND herausgegeben. Berlin, 1774: Bey Gottlieb August Langen.

8vo, 2 vols (vol. 1, pagination continuous, = *Tristram Shandy*, vols 1, 2 & 3, 4; vol. 2=vols 5, 6 & 7, 8 & 9, three series of pagination; vol. 9 is the spurious vol., cf. no. 42). Frontispieces, vol. 1 (The Sermon), vol. 3 (The Christening).

[JCTO]

52 HET LEVEN EN DE GEVOELENS VAN TRISTRAM SHANDY. Te Amsterdam, 1776–9: By A. E. Munnikhuisen.

8vo, 5 vols, of which vols 1 (2 pts: 1776, 1777), 2 (2 pts: 1777, 1778), 3 (2 pts: 1778), and 4 (3 pts: 1779) contain *Tristram Shandy*; vol. 5 (2 pts: 1778) is subtitled *Bevattende de Sentimenteele Reis van den Heere Yorick*. All five vols also have engraved title-pages dated 1779 and naming the translator Bernardus Brunius. The first Dutch translations: cf. no. 63.

[JCTO]

A SENTIMENTAL JOURNEY

"My design in it was to teach us to love the world and our fellow creatures better than we do—" (*Letters*, p. 401).

54 A SENTIMENTAL JOURNEY THROUGH FRANCE AND ITALY. By Mr Yorick. Vol. I. [II.] London: Printed for T. Becket and P. A. De Hondt. 1768.

8vo, 2 vols. On imperial paper (135 copies so printed, according to note on the printer's copy in the British Museum); with the Advertisement leaf promising the completion of the work "early the next Winter." Bookplate of George Thornhill, subscriber for a copy on imperial paper.

[JCTO]

55 [—]
8vo, 2 vols. On ordinary paper (2500 copies so printed); original blue-grey paper wrappers, uncut, as issued. Published in late February 1768, some three weeks before Sterne's death. There are minor variant states of two leaves.

[KM]

56 [—] The Second Edition. 1768.
8vo, 2 vols. A number of minor corrections and alterations have been made to the text.

[KM]

57 [—] A New Edition. 1768.
8vo, 2 vols. In fact the third edition. With it was sometimes sold the spurious "Continuation." (Cf. no.)

[KM]

58   [—] The Fourth Edition. London: Printed for James Fleming. 1769.

12mo. Not the genuine fourth edition but a piracy. This copy carries copious manuscript notes by John Scott (1739–98), Earl of Clonmel, Chief Justice of the King's Bench in Ireland. Shrewd and often perceptive, they must be among the first informal comment on Sterne's text. (See "An annotated copy of Sterne's Sentimental Journey," by Kenneth Monkman, *Antiquarian Bookseller's Annual*, 1952.)

[KM]

59   A SENTIMENTAL JOURNEY THROUGH FRANCE AND ITALY. By Laurence Sterne. Illustrated by Notes; Memoirs of the Author; and a Translation of the French Phrases. London: Printed by J. Cundee. 1803.

8vo. Engraved portrait frontispiece and plates. Probably the first annotated edition. An interesting note on page 78 reads: "It has been said, that our author added a word to the French language, on going to see some friend who lived in a street which a carriage could not enter; he told him the street was not *carossable*. The word took, and has been ever since in constant use." It is still in use in France today.

[KM]

YORICK IN EUROPE

"The *Sentimental Journey* has done more for the creation of a tolerant European consciousness than all the peace treaties...."

(Sir Herbert Read)

60   YORICKS EMPFINDSAME REISE durch Frankreich und Italien. Aus dem Englischen uᵉbersetzt. Hamburg und Bremen, 1768: Bey Johann Hinrich Cramer.

8vo, 2 vols in 1. The first German translation. A translation of the *Continuation* was published ("zwote Auflage, 1770") as vols III and IV. The translator was J. C. Bode.

[JCTO]

61 VOYAGE SENTIMENTAL, par M. STERN, sous le nom d'YORICK. Traduit de l'Anglois par M. FRÉNAIS. Se vend à Amsterdam chez Marc-Michel Rey et à Paris chez Gauguery, 1769.

12mo, 2 vols in 1. The first French translation.

[JCTO]

62 YORICKS FØLSOMME REISE igiennem Frankerig og Italien. Af det Engelske oversat ved H. J. BIRCH. Kiobenhavn, 1775: Paa Gyldendals Forlag.

8vo. The first Danish translation.

[JCTO]

63 SENTIMENTEELE REIS, DOOR FRANKRYK, EN ITALIEN. GEDAAN DOOR DEN HEER YORICK. Te Amsteldam, 1778: by A. E. Munnikhuisen.

8vo, 2 vols. Portrait-engraving of "Laurens Sterne, A. M. &c."

[JCTO]

64 VIAGGIO SENTIMENTALE del Sig. STERNE sotto il nome di YORICK. Traduzione dal Francese. Venezia, 1792: Presso Antonio Zatta e Figli.

12mo. Frontispiece (Yorick feeling the grisette's pulse). The first Italian translation.

[JCTO]

65 KANSLOSAM RESA genom Italien, Schweiz och Frankrike. Oswersattning. Stockholm, 1797: i Kumblinska Tryckeriet.

8vo. Translated from a German translation (1794) of *A Sentimental Journey intended as a Sequel to Mr Sterne's, by Mr Shandy* (Southampton, 1793).

[JCTO]

66 VIAGGIO SENTIMENTALE di YORICK lungo la Francia e l'Italia. Traduzione di DIDIMO CHIERICO. Pisa, 1813: Co'caratteri di Didot (colophon: dai torchi di Gio. Rosini).

12mo. Portrait-engravings of "L. Sterne" and "Didymus Clericus." The first edition of Foscolo's translation.

[JCTO]

67 VIAGE SENTIMENTAL de STERNE á Paris, bajo el nombre de
YORICK. Traducido libremente al castellano. Madrid, 1821:
Imprenta de Villalpando, Impresor de Camara de S. M.

12mo. The first Spanish translation.

[JCTO]

YORICK IN THE PULPIT

"To preach, to shew the extent of our reading, or the
subtleties of our wit . . . 'tis not preaching the gospel——but
ourselves" (*T.S.*, p. 317).

68 THE SERMONS OF MR. YORICK. Vol. I. [II.] London: Printed for
R. AND J. Dodsley. [1760]

8vo, 2 vols. Engraved portrait frontispiece. The first collected
edition of Sterne's sermons. They had a mixed reception; some
people were shocked that they should appear under the jesting
name of "Yorick." Bookplate of Nathaniel Cholmley, friend of
Sterne and a subscriber to this edition.

[KM]

69 [—] Vol. III. [IV.] London: Printed for T. Becket and P. A. De
Hondt. 1766.

8vo, 2 vols. First edition of the second instalment of Sterne's
collected sermons. Bookplate of Nathaniel Cholmley.

[KM]

70 SERMONS BY THE LATE REV. MR. STERNE. Vol. V. [–VII.]
London: Printed for W. Strahan; T. Cadell, and T. Beckett and
Co. 1769.

8vo, 3 vols. First edition of the concluding instalment, published
after Sterne's death and generally held to be inferior to the
earlier volumes.

[KM]

71 THE SERMONS OF MR. YORICK. Vol. I. [II.] Dublin: Printed for
G. Faulkner, P. Wilson, H. Bradley, and W. Smith, Jun. 1760.

12mo, 2 vols. First Dublin edition.

[KM]

72 [—] Vol. III. [IV.] Dublin: Printed for W. Smith and Son,
A. Leathley, J. Hoey, sen. P. Wilson, J. Exshaw, H. Bradley,
E. Watts, H. Saunders, W. Sleater, J. Hoey, jun. J. Potts,
S. Watson, and J. Williams. 1766.

12mo, 2 vols. First Dublin edition of these volumes.

[KM]

73 SERMONS CHOISIS DE L. STERNE. Traduits de l'Anglais par Mr.
D.L.B. A Londres et se trouve à Paris. 1786.

8vo. Despite the imprint, a Paris-printed edition, purged of all
anti-Popery.

[KM]

SHANDYANA

"There is a shilling pamphlet wrote against Tristram.—
I wish they would write a hundred such." (*Letters*, p. 107).
Sterne's wish in 1760 came true well before the end of the
century. Below are a few samples:

74 TWO LYRICK EPISTLES: one to my Cousin SHANDY, On his
coming to TOWN; and the other to the Grown Gentlewomen,
the MISSES of ****. London: Printed for R. and J. Dodsley: and
sold by M. Cooper. 1760.

4to. By John Hall-Stevenson. Advertised *London Chronicle*
15–17 April 1760.

[JCTO]

75 EXPLANATORY REMARKS upon THE LIFE AND OPINIONS OF
TRISTRAM SHANDY; wherein, The Morals and Politics of this
Piece are clearly laid open, By JEREMIAH KUNASTROKIUS, M. D.
London: Printed for E. Cabe. 1760.

8vo. Advertised *Public Advertiser* 23 April 1760. *Explanatory
Remarks upon the third and fourth Volumes* followed in 1761.

[JCTO]

76 THE CLOCKMAKERS OUTCRY against the Author of THE LIFE
    AND OPINIONS OF TRISTRAM SHANDY. London: Printed for
    J. Burd. 1760.

    8vo. Advertised *Public Advertiser* 9 May 1760 (2nd ed., 14 May;
    4th ed., 20 June).

    [JCTO]

77 TRISTRAM SHANDY. [*ca.* 1760]

    Slip ballad. Woodcut head- and tail-piece. Five midly bawdy
    verses beginning: "Earey [*sic*] one summer's morning, / It was
    down by Portsmouth ferry O!"

    [KM]

78 YORICK's MEDITATIONS upon various Interesting and Important
    Subjects. London: Printed for R. Stevens. 1760.

    8vo. Advertised *Public Advertiser* 16 July 1760. Reprinted Dublin
    1760; German translation 1769.

    [JCTO]

79 TRISTRAM SHANDY. [*ca.* 1760]

    Broadside. Engraved words and music. Six very bawdy verses
    beginning: "Have you not read a Book call'd Tristram Shandy
    Maam / If not O look in to 't quickly I pray / His precepts are
    sweeter than Sugar Candy maam / twould do you good to taste
    his Curds and whey...."

    [KM]

80 A FUNERAL DISCOURSE, Occasioned by the much lamented
    Death of Mr. YORICK, Prebendary of Y—k and Author of the
    much admired LIFE AND OPINIONS OF TRISTRAM SHANDY.
    London: Printed for W. Nicoll. 1761.

    8vo. Advertised *London Chronicle* 27–29 October 1761. Another
    edition of 1761 has the imprint "Aretopolis."

    [JCTO]

81 THE LIFE AND OPINIONS OF BERTRAM MONTFICHET, Esq; written by Himself. London: Printed for C. G. Seyffert. [1761]

8vo, 2 vols. Frontispieces. Advertised *Public Advertiser* 12 March 1761.

[JCTO]

82 A LETTER from the Rev. GEORGE WHITFIELD, B. A. to the Rev. LAURENCE STERNE, M.A., the supposed Author of a Book, entitled, THE LIFE AN [*sic*] OPINIONS OF TRISTRAM SHANDY, Gentleman. London, 1761.

8vo. [JCTO]

83 THE LIFE AND AMOURS OF HAFEN SLAWKENBERGIUS; Author of the INSTITUTE OF NOSES. Compiled from Authentic Materials ... by the learned Mr HEYDEGGER, of Strasburg. London: Printed for W. Flexney. 1762.

8vo. Advertised *London Chronicle* 17–19 December 1761.

[JCTO]

84 THE LIFE, TRAVELS, AND ADVENTURES OF CHRISTOPHER WAGSTAFF, GENTLEMAN, Grandfather to TRISTRAM SHANDY. Originally published in the latter End of the last Century. London: Printed for J. Hinxman. 1762.

8vo, 2 vols. Advertised *London Chronicle* 11–13 & 15–18 May 1762. Based on John Dunton's *Voyage round the World* (1691). A second edition appeared in 1763.

[JCTO]

85 SENTIMENTS on the DEATH of the SENTIMENTAL YORICK. By one of Uncle TOBY's illegitimate Children. With Rules for Writing MODERN ELEGIES. Alas poor Yorick! London: Printed for Staples Steare. 1768.

4to. [JCTO]

86 YORICK'S SENTIMENTAL JOURNEY CONTINUED. To which is prefixed, some Account of the Life and Writings of Mr. Sterne. Vol. III [IV.] London: Printed for S. Bladon. 1769.

8vo, 2 vols. First edition. A coarse and inept attempt to continue the *Journey* left unfinished by Sterne's death. It was designed to be sold to unsuspecting customers together with the two volumes of the genuine *Journey*; hence Vol. III. [IV.] on the title-page.

[KM]

87 [—] By Eugenius. The Second Edition, Corrected, with Additions. Vol. III. [IV.] London: Printed for S. Bladon. 1769.

8vo, 2 vols. Eugenius was the name Sterne gave in *Tristram Shandy* to his friend John Hall-Stevenson; the "Continuation" is accordingly sometimes ascribed to him, but with no certainty.

[KM]

88 The Posthumous Works of a Late Celebrated Genius, Deceased. In Two Volumes. Vol. I. [II.] London: Printed by W. and J. Richardson. 1770.

8vo. 2 vols. First edition. There are two issues, with varying imprints. Written in imitation of Sterne's style by Richard Griffith, who later confessed to his authorship. Under the title of *The Koran* it was sometimes included in collected editions of Sterne's genuine works.

[KM]

89 Tristram Shandy, a Sentimental, Shandean Bagatelle, in two Acts. By the Author of Retaliation. London: Printed for S. Bladon. 1783.

8vo. Dedication signed by Leonard MacNally. Performed at Covent Garden 26 April 1783. Two editions were published in 1783.

[JCTO]

90 Nouveau Voyage en France, de Sterne. Suivi de l'Histoire de la Fevre, & d'un choix de Lettres familieres du même Auteur. Traduit de l'Anglois par M. D. L*****, Avocat-Général au Parlement de ***. A Geneve, 1784.

12mo. The *Nouveau Voyage* is extracted from *Tristram Shandy*, vol. 5.

[JCTO]

91 FRAGMENTS: IN THE MANNER OF STERNE. London: Printed for the Author and sold by Debrett and Murray & Highley. 1797.

8vo. Three engravings. By Isaac Brandon. A second edition was published in 1798; translated into French (1799) and German (1800).

[JCTO]

92 ILLUSTRATIONS OF STERNE: with other Essays and Verses. By JOHN FERRIAR, M. D. London (Manchester pr.): Printed for Cadell and Davies. 1798.

8vo. A second edition (2 vols) was published in 1812.

[JCTO]

93 THE FALLACY OF FRENCH FREEDOM, and Dangerous Tendency of STERNE's Writings. By D. WHYTE, M. D., late Surgeon to English Prisoners in France. London: Printed for J. Hatchard. 1799.

8vo.

[JCTO]

LETTERS

"These if all collected . . . would print and sell to good Acct——" (*Letters*, p. 407).

94 LETTERS FROM YORICK TO ELIZA. London: Printed for W. Johnston. 1773.

8vo. First edition. Probably issued privately. It contains the text of ten letters from Sterne to Eliza Draper. It was reprinted the same year in Philadelphia.

[KM]

95 [—] Printed for T. Evans. 1775.

8vo. The second London edition, though not so named.

[KM]

96 [—] (1) London: Printed for T. Evans. 1775. (2) London, 1775. (3) London: Printed for G. Kearsly and T. Evans. 1775. (4)–(6) A New Edition. London: Printed for G. Kearsly and T. Evans. 1775.

All 8vo. See *Transactions of the Cambridge Bibliographical Society*, II, p. 160 ff.

[JCTO]

97 Yoricks Briefe an Eliza. Hamburg, 1775: Bey C. E. Bohn.

8vo. The first German translation.

[JCTO]

98 Yoricks och Elizas Brefvexling. Öfversatt från Ängelskan. Stockholm, 1797: J. Dahl.

8vo. The first Swedish translation.

[JCTO]

99 Lettere di Yorick ad Eliza e di Elisa a Yorick dall' Inglese recate in volgare Italiano. Milano, 1815: Presso Ferdinando Baret.

8vo. Rabizzani, *Sterne in Italia*, records an edition (perhaps another translation) published at Venice, 1792.

[JCTO]

100 Letters from Eliza to Yorick. London: Printed for the Editor, and Entered in the Hall-Book of the Company of Stationers, the 15th of April, 1775.

8vo. Spurious letters. See *Transactions of the Cambridge Bibliographical Society*, II, p. 155 ff. (issue A with later title-page).

[JCTO]

101 Letters Supposed to have been Written by Yorick and Eliza. In Two Volumes. Vol. I. [II.] London, Printed for J. Bew. 1779.

8vo, 2 vols. Claims have been seriously made for Sterne's authorship, but William Combe is generally held to have written them.

[KM]

102 [—] Dublin: Printed for Messrs. Price, Sheppard, Wilkinson, &c. 1780.

12mo, 2 vols with continuous pagination and collation. First Dublin edition.

[KM]

103 LETTERS FROM ELIZA TO YORICK, Transmitted from a Gentleman in Bombay, and now first Published. London: Printed by D.N. Shury. 1801.

8vo. Another spurious version.

[KM]

104 SOME MEMORIALS OF LAURENCE STERNE. A Paper read at the Bath Royal Literary Institution. By Thomas Washbourne Gibbs, February 22nd, 1878. Bath: Printed at the "Chronicle" Office [1878].

8vo. The first appearance in print of passages from the *Journal to Eliza*, which Gibbs had rescued from an attic in Bath. The manuscript is now at the British Museum. Modern editions may be found in Curtis's *Letters* or in the Ian Jack edition of *A Sentimental Journey, The Journal to Eliza*, and *A Political Romance* (Oxford University Press), 1968.

[KM]

105 STERNE'S LETTERS TO HIS FRIENDS ON VARIOUS OCCASIONS. To which is added, His History of a Watch Coat, with Explanatory Notes. London, Printed for G. Kearsley and J. Johnson. 1775.

8vo. Advertised in the *London Chronicle*, 13 July 1775. Only three of the twelve letters are certainly by Sterne. Probably the others are by William Combe.

[KM]

106 LETTERS OF THE LATE REV. MR LAURENCE STERNE, To his most intimate Friends. With a Fragment in the manner of Rabelais. Published by his Daughter, Mrs. Medalle. In Three Volumes. Vol. 1 [–111.] London: Printed for T. Becket. 1775.

8vo, 3 vols. Engraved frontispiece portrait of Lydia Sterne de Medalle with the Nollekens bust of her father, after a painting by Benjamin West. Advertised in the *London Chronicle*, 26 October 1775.

[KM]

107 [—] A New Edition. 1775.

8vo, 3 vols. A reprint of the above item.

[KM]

108 [—] Dublin: Printed for T. Armitage. 1776.

12mo, 3 vols in 1, with continuous pagination and collation. First Dublin edition.

[KM]

109 ORIGINAL LETTERS OF THE LATE REVEREND MR LAURENCE STERNE: Never before Published. London: Printed at the Logographic Press. 1788.

8vo. More forgeries by William Combe, though several of the letters may embody genuine passages by Sterne.

[KM]

COLLECTIONS AND SELECTIONS

110 THE WORKS OF LAURENCE STERN [*sic*], A.M. Prebendary of York, and Vicar of Sutton on the Forest, and of Stillington, near York. [No imprint, but 1769.]

12mo, 5 vols. Engraved frontispiece portrait. Undoubtedly a piracy but the first attempt at a collected edition: it contains *Tristram Shandy*, *Sermons*, *A Sentimental Journey* with the *Continuation*, and *A Political Romance*.

[KM]

111 THE WORKS OF LAURENCE STERNE. In Ten Volumes Complete. With a Life of the Author, Written by Himself. Volume the First [–Tenth.] London: Printed for W. Strahan, J. Rivington

and Sons, J. Dodsley, G. Kearsley, T. Lowndes, G. Robinson, T. Cadell, J. Murray, T. Becket, R. Baldwin, and T. Evans. 1780.

8vo, 10 vols. Engraved frontispiece portrait and plates. Countless collected editions of Sterne's works were published from 1770 onwards, but this was the first quasi-serious attempt at a critical edition; its claims as such, however, have been overrated.

[KM]

112 THE BEAUTIES OF STERNE: including all his Pathetic Tales, and most Distinguished Observations on Life. Selected for the Heart of Sensibility. London: Printed for T. Davies, J. Ridley, W. Flexney, J. Sewel, and G. Kearsley. 1782.

12mo. The first such compilation. Many editions followed.

[KM]

113 THE BEAUTIES OF STERNE; including many of his Letters and Sermons, all the Pathetic Tales, Humorous Descriptions, and most Distinguished Observations on Life. The Twelfth Edition. Ornamented with several Plates, from Original Drawings. London: Printed for C. and G. Kearsley. 1793.

12mo. Not the twelfth edition as it describes itself, but the first edition of a new selection, broader in taste. Bookplate of John Croft, author of "Anecdotes of Sterne."

[KM]

"NOW IT IS COME"

114 "DEATH MASK" OF STERNE.

Plaster cast of the mask at Princeton University. Its claims to be a true death mask are strongly suspect; almost certainly it is an impression taken from the face of the Nollekens bust, with which the sculpted "open" eyes and stylized lock of hair, as well as the features, tally exactly.

[KM]

115   A CATALOGUE of a Curious and Valuable Collection of BOOKS
       Among which are included The Entire LIBRARY of the late
       Reverend and Learned LAURENCE STERNE, A. M. . . . Which
       will begin to be sold exceeding cheap . . . on Thursday, August
       23, 1768. . . . By J. TODD and H. SOTHERAN.

       8vo. A facsimile from a supposedly unique copy was published
       in 1930, with a preface by Charles Whibley. Scholars have too
       seldom noticed that this catalogue includes books belonging to
       others besides Sterne, a point upon which Kenneth Monkman
       comments elsewhere in this volume.

                                                          [JCTO]

PORTRAITS AND PRINTS

In this primarily bibliographically-minded catalogue,
descriptions are omitted of many engravings, caricatures,
and portraits in the exhibition. But the following ought to
be listed:

116   PORTRAIT OF ELIZA DRAPER, BY RICHARD COSWAY.

       Photograph of an oil painting. Private collection. The proven-
       ance is good but not certain. Cosway is known to have painted
       Mrs Draper in 1767.

117   STATUETTE OF STERNE, "THE WORK OF HIS BIOGRAPHER,
       PERCY FITZGERALD."

       Cast in lead alloy. Seated, full-length, 33 ins. high. Sterne's
       first biographer, besides being a phenomenally active writer,
       possessed an unorthodox knack of hitting off a likeness in
       sculpture: witness also his statues of Dr Johnson, outside the
       church of St Clement Danes, in the Strand, London, and of
       Boswell, at Lichfield. Fitzgerald presented this statue of Sterne
       to York Minster Library in 1906. The base bears a roundel
       showing Uncle Toby examining the eye of Widow Wadman.

                                                          [YM]

118 BUST OF STERNE, BY JOSEPH NOLLEKENS.

White marble. Life size. Sterne sat to Nollekens in Florence in
1766, and the resulting bust brought the sculptor into great
notice. "With this bust he continued to be pleased even to his
second childhood." (J. T. Smith, *Nollekens and his Times*, 1829.)
From the terracotta original several marble copies were made:
others are in the National Portrait Gallery, London; the
Huntington Library, California; and at Skelton Castle. Cheap
versions in plaster were advertised after Sterne's death by his
publisher, Becket, as "the greatest likeness that can possibly be
conceived, and will be an ornament to any library or apartment
whatever."

[KM]

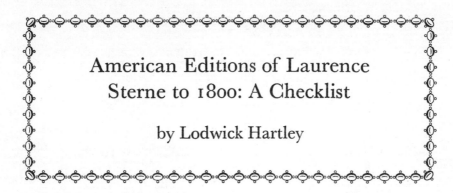

American Editions of Laurence Sterne to 1800: A Checklist

by Lodwick Hartley

1768   A sentimental journey. Boston, John Mein, 1768. 2 vols, 12mo. 1st American edition.

1770   A sentimental journey. Philadelphia, Printed for R. Bell. 2 vols in 1.

[Note that this edition is dated 1771 in Charles Evans's *American Bibliography*. The copy in the Lilly Library of the University of Indiana shows the above date. See also copy listed in *American Book Prices Current*, VIII (1902), 489.]

1773   Letters from Yorick to Eliza. London, Printed; Philadelphia, Reprinted for John Dunlap.

1774   The works. London, Printed; Philadelphia, Reprinted by James Humphreys, Jr. 6 vols, 12mo. 1st American edition.
The works. London, Printed; Philadelphia, Reprinted by James Humphreys, Jr. 5 vols, 12mo.

[*American Book Prices Current*, VIII (1902), 489, lists as dated in the same year a 5 vol. edition printed by Isaac Humphreys.]

1775   The sermons of Mr. Yorick. Philadelphia, Printed by James Humphreys, Jr.

1778   [The Koran. Philadelphia, Printed for Robert Bell. 2 vols.]

1778   Letters to his most intimate friends. Published by his daughter. Philadelphia, Printed for Robert Bell. 3 vols.

1789   The beauties of Sterne. ["The tenth edition."] Philadelphia, Printed for William Spotswood.

[The first edition was printed in London in 1782.]

Professor and Head of English, North Carolina State University

1790   The beauties. Philadelphia, T. Seddon.

1790   A sentimental journey. Philadelphia, T. Seddon.

1791   The beauties. Philadelphia, W. Woodhouse.

1791   A sentimental journey. Philadelphia, W. Woodhouse. 2 vols.

1792   A sentimental journey. Norwich, Bushnell and Hubbard.

1793   The beauties. ["The eleventh edition."] Boston, Printed by John W. Folsom.

1793   The beauties. Boston, Printed by John W. Folsom for Daniel Brewer of Taunton.

1793   A sentimental journey. Worcester, Isaiah Thomas. 2 vols.

1793   The whole story of the sorrows of Maria, of Moulines. Salem, John Dabney.

1795   A sentimental journey [including continuation attributed to John Hall-Stevenson]. New York, Printed for the Booksellers.

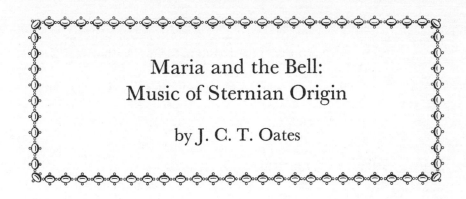

Maria and the Bell:
Music of Sternian Origin

by J. C. T. Oates

The bibliography of music publication at the end of the eighteenth century is obviously no fit subject for a bibliographer of the printed word. The list of songs which is printed below may well be incomplete, and the editions listed are simply those which I have either actually seen myself or merely encountered in books of reference.

Nos. 1, 3, 5, 10, and 13 were sung, with great skill and effect, at the after-dinner concert in the King's Manor, York, with which the proceedings of the Conference ended, by Miss Pauline Chadwick (soprano) and Mr David Ward (baritone) accompanied by Miss Clare Wright ('cello) and Mr Francis Monkman (harpsichord). Mr Monkman, who had organized the concert, gave an interlude of Scarlatti brilliantly and – as in *Tristram Shandy – con furia*.

Words by Laurence Sterne

1 Dialogue ("How imperfect the joys of the soul").
Sung by Mr Beard and Miss Fromantel.
   (*a*) Sheet-music edition, without imprint or date. (*b*) *In:* J. Baildon, *Collection of new songs sung at Ranelagh* [*c.* 1765]. (*c*) *In: The Laurel. A Collection of English Songs*, Book 2 (*New Musical Mag.*, no. 93) [*c.* 1785].

2 The Unknown World ("Hark, my gay friend, that solemn toll").
In: The Hymns, Anthems & Tunes with the Ode used at the Magdalen Chapel [etc.]. London, for C. and S. Thompson [*c.* 1765]. See Catalogue of the exhibition, no. 17.

Music by Thomas Billington

3 Maria's Evening Service to the Virgin ("At morn and eve to thee I pray").

Sheet-music editions: (*a*) London, for the Author [*c.* 1790]; (*b*) Dublin, J. & E. Lee [*c.* 1790].

4 Sterne's Soliloquy on hearing Maria sing her Evening Service to the Virgin.

Sheet-music edition: London, T. Skillern [*c.* 1795].

Music by William Carnaby

5 Yorick at the Grave of Maria ("Alas, sweet maid, thou art gone").

Sheet-music edition: London, R. Birchall [*c.* 1795].

Music by Haydn

6 Yorick's Fille de Chambre. Adapted to a favorite Minuet [from Symphony no. 53] composed by Sig^r Haydn.

Sheet-music edition: [London], Longman and Broderip [*c.* 1795].

Music by John Moulds

7 The Handkerchief, or Sterne's Pledge to Maria.
Written by S. Larken.

Sheet-music edition: [London], T. Jones & Co. [*c.* 1795].

8 La Fleur: a favourite Ballad from Sterne.

Sheet-music edition: London, W. Cope [1796?].

9 Sterne's Maria, *also entitled* Moulines Maria ("'Twas near a thicket's calm retreat").

Sheet-music editions: (*a*) London, J. A. & P. Thompson [*c.* 1785]; (*b*) [Dublin], E. Rhames [*c.* 1785]; (*c*) Dublin, J. Lee [*c.* 1790]; (*d*) Dublin, Hime, 1791.

See also: (1) *The Whole Story of the Sorrows of Maria* (Boston, Mass., 1793); (2) *The American Musical Miscellany* (Northampton, Mass., 1798); (3) *The American Mock-bird* (New York, 1801); (4) *The Temple of Harmony* (Baltimore, 1801); (5) *The Vocal Medley* (Alexandria, Va., 1801); (6) S. Larkin, *The Nightingale* (Portsmouth, N.H., 1804).

Incorporated in William Dunlap's unpublished opera Sterne's Maria, or The Vintage, produced in New York in 1799. Cf. Blanck, *BAL*, nos. 4985–7.